In *Seizures of the will in early modern English drama* Frank Whigham combines an analysis of English Renaissance plays with an enriched sense of their social surroundings. He traces the violent gestures of social self-construction that animate many such plays, and the ways in which drama interacts with the conflict-ridden discourses of social rank, gender, kinship, and service relationships. In Whigham's view, *The Spanish Tragedy* initiates the "matter of court," a complex and marauding discourse of gender warfare and master–servant manipulations; *Arden of Faversham* explores linked redefinitions of land, service, and marriage in county culture; *The Miseries of Enforced Marriage* and *A Yorkshire Tragedy* present a powerful critique of the traditional imperialism of kinship in northern England; and *The Duchess of Malfi* explores metaphors of erotic transgression.

Cambridge Studies in Renaissance Literature and Culture 11

Seizures of the will in early modern English drama

Cambridge Studies in Renaissance Literature and Culture

The last twenty years have seen a broad and vital reinterpretation of the nature of literary texts, a move away from formalism to a sense of literature as an aspect of social, economic, political, and cultural history. While the earliest New Historicist work was criticized for a narrow and anecdotal view of history, it also served as an important stimulus for post-structuralist, feminist, Marxist and psychoanalytical work, which in turn has increasingly informed and redirected it. Recent writing on the nature of representation, the historical construction of gender and of the concept of identity itself, on theater as a political and economic phenomenon and on the ideologies of art generally, reveals the breadth of the field. Cambridge Studies in Renaissance Literature and Culture is designed to offer historically oriented studies of Renaissance literature and theater which make use of the insights afforded by theoretical perspectives. The view of history envisioned is above all a view of our own history, a reading of the Renaissance for and from our own time.

Some recent titles

Voyages in print: English travel to America, 1576–1624
MARY C. FULLER, Massachusetts Institute of Technology

Subject and object in Renaissance culture
edited by MARGRETA DE GRAZIA, MAUREEN QUILLIGAN, PETER STALLYBRASS, University of Pennsylvania

Shakespeare and the theatre of wonder
T. G. BISHOP, Case Western Reserve University

Anxious masculinity in early modern England
MARK BREITENBERG

Seizures of the will in early modern English drama
FRANK WHIGHAM, University of Texas at Austin

A complete list of books in this series is given at the end of the volume

Seizures of the will in early modern English drama

Frank Whigham

University of Texas at Austin

CAMBRIDGE
UNIVERSITY PRESS

Published by the Press Syndicate of the University of Cambridge
The Pitt Building, Trumpington Street, Cambridge CB2 1RP
40 West 20th Street, New York, NY 10011–4211, USA
10 Stamford Road, Oakleigh, Melbourne 3166, Australia

First published 1996

Printed in Great Britain at the University Press, Cambridge

A catalogue record for this book is available from the British Library

Library of Congress cataloguing in publication data

Whigham, Frank
Seizures of the will in early modern English drama / Frank Whigham.
    p.   cm. – (Cambridge studies in Renaissance literature and culture: 11)
Includes bibliographical references and index.
ISBN 0-521-41877-1 (hardcover)
1. English drama – Early modern and Elizabethan, 1500–1600 – History
and criticism.   2. Literature and society – England – History – 16th century.
3. Literature and society – England – History – 17th century.
4. Assertiveness (Psychology) in literature.   5. Master and servant in literature.
6. Social classes in literature.   7. Sex role in literature.
8. Kinship in literature.   9. Will in literature.   10. Self in literature.
I. Title.   II. Series.
PR658.S46W38   1996
822'.309355–dc20   95-12759   CIP

ISBN 0 521 418771 hardback

This book is for K. A.

Contents

Acknowledgments   *page* x
Abbreviations   xi

Introduction   1

1   Forcing divorce in *The Spanish Tragedy*   22

2   Hunger and pain in *Arden of Faversham*   63

3   The ideology of prodigality in *The Miseries of Enforced*   121
    Marriage and *A Yorkshire Tragedy*

4   Sexual and social mobility in *The Duchess of Malfi*   188

Afterword   225

Notes   227
Works cited   279
Index   294

Acknowledgments

I am very fortunate in my friends, from whom I have gathered many teeming debts in the course of this book's gestation. Many colleagues across the country have read manuscript, contributed information, challenged my assumptions: Janet Adelman, David Bevington, Jackson I. Cope, Jonathan Crewe, Karen Cunningham, Stephen Greenblatt, J. R. Mulryne, Michael Murrin, Lena Cowen Orlin, Patricia Parker, Gail Kern Paster, David Riggs, Mary Beth Rose, and Valerie Wayne. My wonderful colleagues at the University of Texas have also aided in many ways: Evan Carton, John P. Farrell, James Garrison, Wayne Lesser, Eric Mallin, Leah Marcus, Susanne F. C. Paterson, Shannon Prosser, John Rumrich, Denise Sechelski, W. O. S. Sutherland, Hewitt Thayer, Warwick Wadlington, and Dolora Wojciehowski. And I owe thanks for release time to the University Research Institute of the University of Texas. I have been likewise fortunate in support from Cambridge University Press: I thank Stephen Orgel, Kevin Taylor, Josie Dixon, and Rosemary Morris, and also Rita Copeland and David Wallace. Finally, to speak of "families we choose," I delight in thanking those who, through thick and thin, in sickness and in health, have fertilized this book: Lance Bertelsen, Theodore Leinwand, Louis Adrian Montrose, Wayne A. Rebhorn, Dorothy Stephens, Richard Strier, W. B. Worthen, and especially Jo Anne Shea.

Abbreviations

Unless otherwise noted, citations from early modern English drama are taken from either *The Complete Works of Shakespeare*, ed. David Bevington, 4th edn. (New York: Harper, 1992) or *Drama of the English Renaissance*, ed. Russell A. Fraser and Norman Rabkin, 2 vols. (New York: Macmillan, 1976). Parenthetical references appear in the text.

Bibliographical references throughout the text and notes are abbreviated whenever possible. For full data see the list of Works Cited.

Other abbreviations:

EIC	*Essays in Criticism*
ELR	*English Literary Renaissance*
ES	*English Studies*
HLQ	*Huntington Library Quarterly*
JEGP	*Journal of English and Germanic Philology*
L&H	*Literature and History*
MLN	*Modern Language Notes*
MLR	*Modern Language Review*
N&Q	*Notes and Queries*
NLH	*New Literary History*
P&P	*Past and Present*
PQ	*Philological Quarterly*
RenD	*Renaissance Drama*
RES	*Review of English Studies*
SAQ	*South Atlantic Quarterly*
SEL	*Studies in English Literature, 1500–1900*
ShakS	*Shakespeare Studies*
ShS	*Shakespeare Survey*
SP	*Studies in Philology*
SQ	*Shakespeare Quarterly*

Statutes   *Statutes of the Realm, from Magna Carta to the End of the
              Reign of Queen Anne ... from original records and authentic
              manuscripts* (London, 1810–28)
Tilley   Morris P. Tilley, *A Dictionary of the Proverbs in England in
              the Sixteenth and Seventeenth Centuries* (Ann Arbor: Uni-
              versity of Michigan Press, 1950)
TSLL   *Texas Studies in Literature and Language*

Introduction

They that are glorious must needs be factious. ... Honour that is gained and broken upon another hath the quickest reflection; like diamond cut with facets.   Bacon *Essays*

Whether we fall by ambition, blood, or lust,
Like diamonds, we are cut with our own dust.   Webster *The White Devil*

The act of resentment is the touchstone of honour.
                                    Pitt-Rivers "Honour and Social Status"

In this study I investigate the recurrent fascination of early modern English drama with certain moments of self-construction or identification which I shall call "seizures of the will." I deploy this phrase as a programmatic pun, with multiple elements. I mean to point both to appropriation, the act of grasping, of taking, of violating, of seizing control, and to ecstasy, the thrill or spasm or fit of emotion, of transcendent feeling, that often accompanies the gesture in the plays of early modern England.[1] There is also a subject–object binary: one seizes something else, an external thing, another being, the self as made. I enter upon a construction of these elements because, I believe, historicist analysis must engage the conscious and concrete utility of the category of the *will* for early modern England. This venture is pursued in concert with a more general reappropriation of the category in contemporary social theory generally.

Much of great value has been done in literary studies in recent years to foreground external determinations of individual life in early modern England, but the men and women who lived out their complex lives then used the notion of personal will quite energetically to construe those lives. In endlessly debated matters of religion (free will and predestination), social order (obedience and rebellion, social mobility and subversion, crime and punishment), gender ideology (women's willfulness, the sexual will), and family structure (parental authority, infidelities), the category of individual will played a central role. Whether imputed

1

polemically, as recalcitrance or perversion, or used to mark the moralized givens of structure and commitment, the notion of will was accorded enormous explanatory force in the early modern world.

In recent work in early modern studies this term has been subject to much deconstruction. Postwar criticism of English Renaissance literature frequently consisted in blaming willful early modern victims in the name of an "order and disorder" hermeneutic. Such a stance, as Raymond Williams has taught us, generated an authoritative or authoritarian Tradition by selection, for needs specific to the analysts' own historical situation.[2] More recently, in reaction, many have turned to various categories of large external determination as a way of rescuing early modern oppositionalities from a condescending and obsolescent humanist moralism still at work at four centuries' remove. (This too, of course, is a practice specific to the conflicts of our own time.) Now that this work is in place it seems desirable to reconsider early modern willing subjects. Those subjects' sense, itself historical, of their own autonomy demands attention. I have been guided in such attention by what has come to be called "practice theory," a kind of analysis exemplified by such writers as Pierre Bourdieu and Anthony Giddens. Giddens sees himself as heir to a multi-voiced stream of European social theory whose schools of thought,

> with notable exceptions, such as structuralism and 'post-structuralism' – emphasize the active, reflexive character of human conduct. That is to say, they are unified in their rejection of the tendency of the orthodox consensus to see human behaviour as the result of forces that actors neither control nor comprehend. In addition (and this does include both structuralism and 'post-structuralism'), they accord a fundamental role to language and to cognitive faculties in the explication of social life. Language use is embedded in the concrete activities of day-to-day life and is in some sense partly constitutive of those activities.[3]

Regarding such active reflexivity in the conduct of language use and social life, many different kinds of difficult questions can be raised. Much new-historical analysis has been conducted significantly under the sign of poststructuralist thinking, which also problematizes our capacity to achieve "real" historical knowledge (however that might be construed), knowledge of the intentions of others, or of the self. That is to say, much of the productive energy of new-historical demystification sits uneasily with poststructuralist questions of epistemological impasse. Setting aside most of these large questions, I propose to enter the conversation at a relatively concrete level, on the following basis:

> The main concern of social theory is the same as that of the social sciences in general: the illumination of concrete processes of social life. To hold that

philosophical debates can contribute to this concern is not to suppose that such debates need to be resolved conclusively before worthwhile social research can be initiated. On the contrary, the prosecution of social research can in principle cast light on philosophical controversies just as much as the reverse. In particular, I think it wrong to slant social theory too unequivocally towards abstract and highly generalized questions of epistemology, as if any significant developments in social science had to await a clear-cut solution to these.[4]

To see the subject as complexly constructed is not to evacuate it, but to fill it, it seems to me. I propose to watch for the filling of the subject, both *naturata* and *naturans*, as it were: the dialectic of mutual determination between patterns of social construction and the appropriation and reconstruction of those patterns by individual actors, be they play-wrights, stage-players, staged characters, or social actors.

In the following pages I will argue, as I did in *Ambition and Privilege: The Social Tropes of Elizabethan Courtesy Theory*, that the struggle to gain or constitute or achieve personal identity was a central concern of early modern England. But my earlier book was on the whole a story of subjection, of what I called, following Kenneth Burke, the performer–audience dialectic. Any attempt to control the courtly audience's inter-pretive legitimation of the status of the proffered self, I argued, was doomed conceptually to bow to that audience's capacity to withhold such legitimation; the ambitious would-be courtier must forever, as it were, submit, subject, the self for approval. Since the courtier seeks to claim a specifically ontological position, as a born (that is, non-made) courtier, his actions may always themselves count (or be counted against him) as demonstrating his need for social transformation. Action here is self-defeating by definition. He who strives to prove himself static, absolute, given, must fail.

In the drama things are somewhat different. The struggle for culturally coded identity certainly remains a central matter, and on stage much emphasis still falls, in epilogues for instance, on submission to audience approval. But I suggest that there is originary force in the conceptually cognate status of identity as made on stage and its upsurge as made on the world's stage. Giddens has recently argued that the project of self-construction of identity – institutional, social, personal – is itself a central formative moment of late modernity at large. "The self is not a passive entity, determined by external influences; in forging their self-identities, no matter how local their specific contexts of action, individuals con-tribute to and directly promote social influences that are global in their consequences and implications."[5] I think we can observe a conscious inception of this social project in early modernity, on the early modern English stage.

Located in a London that itself presents, for most English men and women born in traditional rural society, a many-layered spectacle of social variety and change, the dramatic world on stage and the institution of the theater itself epitomize what Giddens calls "disembedding mechanisms": "mechanisms which prise social relations free from the hold of specific locales, recombining them across wide time–space distances.... [such mechanisms] radicalise and globalise pre-established institutional traits of modernity; and they act to transform the content and nature of day-to-day social life" (2).[6] Indeed, to some degree this radicalizing power derives precisely from the freedom of the professional actors from full dominance by a censoring State, from the access to a deniability that comes with speaking words *as* dramatic characters.

Enabled by such inordinate freedom, early modern dramatic characters also often attempt to escape or deny the enclosure of the performer–audience dialectic, in a struggle for identity. As fantasy vehicles for audience skepticism and wish-fulfillment, they consciously embrace achievement, not ascription, as their mode and goal. They attempt to seize access to personal power, not derivative hierarchical permissions. These characters, performing the work of "disembedding," thus function not only to release (or, under the sign of loss, to disorient or disenchant or maroon), but also, to adapt Göran Therbörn, to qualify.

> The formation of humans by every ideology, conservative or revolutionary, oppressive or emancipatory, according to whatever criteria, involves a process simultaneously of subjection and of qualification. The amorphous libido and manifold potentialities of human infants are subjected to a particular order that allows or favours certain drives and capabilities and prohibits or disfavours others. At the same time, through the same process, new members become qualified to take up and perform (a particular part of) the repertoire of roles given in the society into which they are born, including the role of possible agents of social change. The ambiguity of the words "qualify" and "qualification" should also be noted. Although qualified by ideological interpellations, subjects also become qualified to "qualify" these in return, in the sense of specifying them and modifying their range of application.[7]

This is to say, I think, that the early modern theater functioned not only to reinforce dominant ideological frames, but to release the emergent in both subversive and constitutive forms. The spectacle of social roles performed on stage equipped auditors to edit and improvise social roles off stage – roles of all kinds, dominant and subjected alike. And frequently the apparent stance or vector of such edits was less important than the exhibition of improvisation, seen equally in Prince Hal and Iago.

In this book I will examine a certain characteristic strategy of qualification. The acts of seizure examined below aim less, as the courtier did, to do something *before* others, striving to please an audience, than to do something *to* another, to write oneself man or woman upon the slate of another, to strive to become "the deed's creature." This is not to be captured by it, as Middleton and Rowley's Beatrice was by her suborned murder of her fiancé, but to achieve it, to attempt to secure self-creation. Francis Bacon says that "they that are glorious must needs be factious. ... Honour that is gained and broken upon another hath the quickest reflection; like diamond cut with facets."[8] Such actions are, all too often, not earning but taking, not persuasion but assault. In short, seizure. *Ecce signum.*

So the orbit of "seizure" embraces not only the actor but the Burkean scene into which he transforms his antagonist, the ripe taking but also being taken, Iago gazing raptly on the loaded bed, and epileptic Othello foaming.[9] And negations of many kinds, both Lear's potlatch dowries and his banishing divestitures of self and other loved ones, find ready places in the term's embrace.[10] An ultimate density can be glimpsed in Marlowe's Faustus, whose final goal or conquest involves more than just selling his soul. For another term that works like seizure is his fetish of ravishment. "Sweet Analytics, 'tis thou has ravished me!" he cries.[11] His own dominations, both achieved and desired, he experiences as ravishing, as one may seem to do when, "aroused" "by" another, he archly says "you look ravishing tonight."[12] (The notion of rapture, sharing a root with *rape* and *raptor*, conveys something of the same density of subject–object doubling.) The dream of conquest is sometimes experienced as, given voice as, the desire for loss, of self, autonomy, control. Perhaps this is finally aimed at something like Freud's "oceanic feeling," at a fantasy of original union, of the subsuming and filling return to enclosure or loss of boundaries signaled by Marlowe's favorite transcendental orality, "sweet."[13] Subject and object are to be annihilated.

Normally, however, seizure comes into view in binary interpersonal transactions which aim to transform individuals, and to mark them as who they are. Most of these collisions entail interdependent cathexes of conservative socialized authority and licentious seizure: each investment arouses its opposite and ups the ante, creating a feeling of hyperbolic investment, tending to produce a shift from linkages and alternatives to oppositions, to the seizures that form the plays' reservoirs of energy. The origins and surplus magnitude of these varied acts of conflict often participate in a complex relation between power and love, implicit in W. H. Auden's brilliant analysis of practical joking.

Auden speaks of the *lack* that fuels the practical joker, "a feeling of self-insufficiency, of a self lacking in authentic feelings and desires of its own."[14] This lack is often found in the insecure early modern aristocrat, aghast at risk from below at the hands of his structural inferiors. He often degradingly objectified his inferiors in order to gut them of the secure identity they possessed (frequently self-determined by just such acts of resistance and rebellion and imitation), both to deprive them and to appropriate that security for himself. While we no longer speak so readily of "authentic" feelings, Auden's hypothesis can help unpack the operations of destabilized interpellations, supplies of self or identity from without. These no longer feel doxic, as Bourdieu would say; no longer given, secured, as natural and self-evident.[15] Instead they have become commodities that must be consciously earned, demonstrated – in a word, seized. The insecure joker's mentality came *from* somewhere: Auden's pattern need not be simply individual and psychological (that is, ontological), nor the result of victimization by, as it were, another joker, another "individual." It can also describe a mental space of transindividual origin, typical of the collective early modern "crisis of the aristocracy," the uneven but widespread loss of confidence in the ruling account of social relations and identities.[16] This shift eventually helped to problematize *everyone's* senses, collective and individual, of social and personal identity and its constituent origins and grounds of being. This problematic was experienced differently from different social placements, but was, however differently, still experienced as loss, of a kind richly assimilable to Auden's analysis. Very generally speaking, I suggest, willful gestures of seizure derive from this felt experience of absence or evacuation.

Such actions tend to be read under the sign of a courtly will to power, seen as both origin and end of analysis, and as the inevitable tenor of the scenes of Elizabethan and Jacobean social tragedy. I wish to work somewhat past the opacity of this will to power by deriving acts of seizure from Auden's originary absence, and entertaining a dialectic of power and love. Auden's Lack seems to have the inverse shape of an absent or deficient loving Other, an absent presence taking many forms on the stage, whether social, personal, erotic, or parental. Address to this Other was a common early modern reply to the widespread feeling of insecure identity, as endless clamorous references attest, to loving gods and princes and parents and children and lovers and followers, present or absent. Such referents are in fact the normal sources for the provision of identity. But to achieve such ratification or substantiation, to secure such identity, one must cede power to this Other.

I suggest that the recurrent dramatic engagement with the issue of control rests on this correlative foundation of insecurity. The embrace of a relationality capable of funding one's ontology seems for many characters in Renaissance plays to have meant a voicing or revealing or acknowledgment of need, experienced as intolerable self-subjecting disabling vulnerability. Such characters seem not to have been able to tolerate anything to be experienced as love, which requires the endurance, indeed perpetuation, of vulnerability. Instead they often strove to seize such funding, by dominating another's will. Jean-Paul Sartre's fascinating exploration of sadism and masochism is useful for exploring such actions.[17] These positions entail either total dominance of or total submission to the other's will: wishing to be the absolute horizon of the other's freedom to choose (to arouse the response, "I can't help loving you") or equating the reality of love with the other's unbounded possession of that freedom (the other's love must rest on free choosing). Early modern drama in the line of Kyd often seems to deal obsessively with this dialectic: not with Sartre's ultimate conclusion, that these positions are irreducibly immiscible and thus that love is impossible, but with complex states of prior struggle.

These struggles foreground mobile states of seizure – possession, imposition, loss – of control. All versions seem extremely threatening. Frequently the openness, the vulnerability, the trust, the "love" that I have proposed as the ground to Auden's figural lacuna, is itself originally felt as loss. Think of Webster's Duke of Brachiano, "fallen" (as we say) for Vittoria: he broaches his predicament to her brother with the words, "Quite lost, Flamineo" (*The White Devil* 1.2.3). Such desire is subjection: opening the self to (and like) a woman is somehow equated to or threatens or produces loss of the masculine self where Brachiano lodges his essence. (Flamineo's comforting response trivializes the threat: "I must not have your lordship thus unwisely amorous" [1.2.38].) Many other male characters are unable to bear even this experience, and choose instead a manipulative isolation, as reserving, securing, and substantiating. For Iago the openly honest are absurd knaves, to be whipped; only those trimmed in forms and visages have some soul. Richard III, oxymoronic lover mocked from birth, is himself alone. Webster's Duke Ferdinand scorns all connections as hard as he can, but cannot completely repress the drive to relation. Kyd's Lorenzo is the original model: of his closest agents he decides, "I'll trust myself, myself shall be my friend, / For die they shall, slaves are ordained to no other end" (3.2.118–19). Trusting others entails vulnerability, so the trusted must be destroyed. Some few others try moving from one position to the other. Hamlet's paralyzing obsession with avoiding even epistemological subjection is relinquished at sea, when he comes to submit to a provident Other in the open and receiving spirit of readiness. Bastard Edmund ends his life of retributory string-pulling violations with the plaintive, aggrandizing cry, as his lovers murder each other for him, "Yet Edmund was beloved."

Of so many of these oscillations of desire we might say what Middleton and Rowley's Alsemero says to Beatrice, of DeFlores: "There's scarce a thing but is both loved and loathed" (*The Changeling* 1.1.126). Hunger for the welcoming embrace of positive relationality is intolerable to fill; trust cannot be given, however deeply desired. Those who can't stand love can settle for control. So many of these characters can only stand to take, to seize control and attempt to extract or extort or force the ratification, the acknowledgment of identity, that so often gets called "love." They reject the self-opening submissiveness of the courtier, but their strategies of domination are equally doomed to failure. Like Hegel's Master, they attempt to guarantee such authentication by enslaving it. However,

> the master was actually dependent on the slave for his status as master; both in the general society and in the eyes of the slave, the master was recognized as such only because he controlled slaves. What is worse, the master could not achieve the recognition he originally fought for in this relationship because he was recognized only by a slave, by someone he regards as sub-human ... He needed an autonomous person to recognize his desire as human, but instead of free recognition, he received only the servile, dependent recognition of the slave (13).[18]

Such attempts at self-substantiation in early modern English tragedy vary enormously in details, but a great many of them are, I believe, to be recovered and construed by means of a hungry anger at the self-defeating contradiction within this cultural strategy, of domination felt as an alternative to the loving embrace of an Other.

Such seizures come in many forms, which can help construe the preoccupying material of the analyses to follow. They tend to be marked by subjecting instrumentalizations; they are structured by relation to boundaries, usually though not always through transgression; they trigger major spikes of emotion, for actor, victim, and audience; and they overlap and interact elaborately.

Most of these categories of thrilling seizure of identity are familiar from Shakespeare as well as from the plays examined below. We can begin with gestures of *transgressive sexuality*, invasive or coercive: Claudius' incest, Othello's marriage, the Duchess of Malfi's forcible wooing of her steward husband, Don Andrea's gloating "in secret I possest a worthy dame" (1.1.10).[19] Closely related, though not always coded sexually, are achievements of *promotion, election, acknowledgment*: Black Will's ecstatic dispensation of hospitality with the stolen half ox;

Arden of Faversham's self-hugging ownership of monastic lands; Lorenzo's disdainful "I'll trust myself, myself shall be my friend" (3.2.118), Clare Harcop's hard-wrought betrothal. Another category, what might generally be called *abjections*, personal and structural, is similarly varied: bullying, tortures, subjections to witting or unwitting agency, judgments, the specular dominations of voyeurism.[20] Here we find innumerable specimens: Hieronymo's originary inset play; the mocking staged marriage of Alice and Mosby (with Arden cast as unwitting priest); Lorenzo's stooping friendship with Balthazar, and their repellent specular voyeurism in the arbor scene; Hamlet's stratagems with mousetrap and signet-ring; Iago's smooth managements of Roderigo; Bosola and Ferdinand's masque of madmen; and the Scarborrow Butler's enjoyable rescue of the disinherited younger Scarborrows from beggary and whoredom by means of outlawry and trick marriage.

Harsher forms follow. *Humiliations* are often risible, such as the joking death of Pedringano or Black Will's repeated failures to kill Arden; they are also often agonized, as in Horatio's grotesque practical-joke hanging, Scarborrow's enforced marriage, and the Husband's inflamed gambler's poverty in *A Yorkshire Tragedy*. Often more essentializing, of both actor and victim, are the many *betrayals of relation*, of trust: acts of repudiation or disbonding, experiences of divestiture, banishment, abandonment. Lear's self-stripping is perhaps the most famous, but the plays to follow offer many variations: the several betrayals by and of Pedringano; the accounting of the vagrancy of Black Will and Shakebag as an experience of expulsion, loss of place; Scarborrow's enforced betrayal of his betrothal, and his resultant systemic curse on his family, whom he blames for the enforced marriage; Ferdinand's masterly "neglect" of Bosola; Antonio's flight from his family for safety; and the wide range of adulteries, incestuous gestures, and exogamous sexualities throughout the drama.

Physical violation often results (if not itself constituting the humiliation or betrayal). Occasionally we find muted forms, of military conquest or physical supremacy in a crisis of honor, as with Horatio's conquest of Balthazar, the *Yorkshire Tragedy* Gentleman's thorough beating of the Husband, or even Scarborrow's threatened pissing in his Guardian's path and drawing on his uncle. Women often suffer physical outrage: Bel-imperia's gagging and imprisonment, the Duchess's torments by madmen. The complex symbolic act of suicide sometimes follows, as for Bel-imperia and Isabella and Clare. Even Hieronymo's vicious biting out of his tongue belongs here somewhere. The most directly criminal forms, purer and more frightening violations, occur more frequently: ultimately in the strong form of murders, often by relations, of children (Horatio, the *Yorkshire Tragedy* children), siblings (Michael's elder brother, Ferdinand's Duchess), masters or husbands and other superiors (Castile, Arden, Ferdinand), friends and allies (perhaps Don Andrea, certainly Serberine, Antonio, Bosola). The result so often is *revenge*: Bel-imperia's, Hieronymo's, Arden's, Alice's, Mosby's, Scarborrow's, the Husband's, Bosola's.

As this baroque catalogue suggests, *Seizures of the will* looks beyond interrogations and transgressions of the boundaries of social rank. In what follows I will seek to unpack the plays in light of the continuous mutual interactions of four separable ranges of structured and structuring practice, each of which was currently subjected to radical challenge and put to contradictory uses in early modern England. In addition to questions of *social rank* (which remain central), I address intersecting systemic challenges or transformations or deployments of *gender*, *kinship*, and *service relations*.

The ideological struggle over models of social rank in early modern England is now a familiar matter. The land dispersion attendant upon the dissolution of the monasteries, interacting with a variety of other factors, generated an increasingly disturbing sense that status previously constructed as absolute and God-given could in fact be acquired by various kinds of human effort. Conservative control mechanisms such as injunctive courtesy theory proved unreliable strategies, being often appropriated for the counter-movement of increasing change.[21] Linear, "ladder" conceptions of rank competed with the older, clearer (and often nostalgically fictional) essentialist binary structures of aristocratic and subject ranks. Variety began to be typical. Keith Wrightson suggests that

> local patterns of social relations would emerge from a particular accommodation between the forces of social *identification* – as kinsmen, friends, neighbours, patron and client, co-religionists, fellow countrymen – and the forces of social *differentiation* – as landlord and tenant, master and man, governor and governed, rich and poor. Both dimensions of social relations would be constantly present as everyday realities. The particular balance between them, however, would vary.[22]

The complex of self-defining vertical and horizontal allegiances (to superiors, inferiors, factional and status allies) had become ever more fluid and confused, varying greatly by context and over time, a ready general field for drift, evasion, opportunity, betrayal, uncertainty, rebellion. And new dramatic instantiations of this turmoil arose: gallants, upstarts, actors, well-dressed students.[23]

Second, the same sort of tectonic shift began to disrupt that most "naturally" grounded of ascriptions, gender. The binary of ascribed and achieved began to disturb the collective sense of proper limits, of the proper shape of the hierarchy of male and female (and related complementary sets such as parent and child). Competing accounts of women's origin, basic nature, proper roles became actively contestatory.[24] Complexly related metaphorics of mind and body, nurture and nature, increasingly distressed the roles of sexuality.[25] The binary's binary quality itself came into question upon the rise into view of various versions of cross-dressing and the homoerotic.[26] And the figure of the Virgin Queen on the throne amplified the problematic for public view.[27] The intense relationality of this field gave rise to a dense scrollwork of mixed, conflicting, and shifting loyalties and rivalries: men generally horizontal (addressed to each other, within and across class); "proper" women principally vertical (primarily to father, "love," husband, son – each with its own structures of taming, resentment, and rebellion, staged in time and positioned by affinal and agnatic relation). Even the queen and king who give their names to Elizabethan and Jacobean drama contributed to (and were shaped and reshaped, as mannish and womanish, by) this fluidity. An unusually varied array of distinct dramatic incarnations of this flux arose: "effeminate" princes and minions; boy actors; cross-dressed women; youthful homophilia; adult homoerotics; cross-generational fascinations with precocious pages and catamites; "unchaste" (that is, sexually active) and self-determining wild women, widows, witches, and Amazons; and tamed men, happy and otherwise – cuckolds, wittols, petrarchan and servant lovers.

Perhaps as a logical extension of the conceptual unrest regarding gender, sexuality, and social rank, a concomitant and varied disturbance of the categories of kinship, the third structural practice, began to preoccupy England and its stage. It has of late been generally said that in early modern England kinship was a comparatively weak structuring agent, whose influence was largely restricted to the elite and to the small nuclear family. Medieval and peasant extended family ties seem largely a nostalgic fiction: the "small and simple domestic group" was normative. Kin linkage and density were low, networks were loose, kin recognition was "narrow and shallow."[28] But David Cressy has recently disputed such a summary view, as overlooking important links and practices relating what Bourdieu would call "practical kin."[29] Their complex utility is often bleached out of the documentary record (of such sources as wills), but was for most early modern Englishmen and women, Cressy argues, a significant "store of wealth, like a reserve account to be drawn upon as need arose" (69). Such a store of symbolic capital was *a fortiori* crucial to elite families, so numerous in the drama, and so instrumental to much of the culture's collective view of itself. When kinship tensions arose, as they did quite variously, they were conspicuous.

One growing disturbance reflected increased social mobility. A. R.

Wagner, Garter King of Arms and historian of his own office, testifies to
the period disturbance within the official technology of heraldry:

> The making of false pedigrees is an immemorial vice, practised in antiquity,
> the Middle Ages, and modern times alike, but the age of Elizabeth I has a
> specially bad name for such activities. The rise of so many new families to
> wealth and station in a society where the prestige of ancient blood was great
> combined with a growing but as yet ill educated zeal for the study of English
> antiquities to produce a market for deplorable concoctions as well as for
> genuine research.[30]

Religious disturbances provided another motor. Following the Reformation and the partly resultant matrimonial adventures of Henry VIII,
much uncertainty had arisen regarding marital legitimacies.[31] Turbulence
continued under Elizabeth. Her sister's widower, Philip II, secretly
offered marriage, which she refused in part because "if she approved the
marriage of one man with two sisters, then she sanctioned the union of a
woman to two brothers. And 'if that were a good Marriage, then she
must be illegitimate.' "[32] This sense of change spread well beyond the
royal family. Of Henry's act legalizing his marriage to Catherine
Howard, Thomas Fuller judged as follows:

> The greatest good the land got by this match was a general leave to marry
> cousins-german, formerly prohibited by the canon and hereafter permitted by
> common law; a door of liberty left open by God in Scripture, shut by the Pope
> for his private profit, opened again by the king, first for his own admittance
> (this Catherine being cousin-german to Anne Boleyn, his former wife) and
> then for the service of such subjects as would follow him upon the like
> occasion.[33]

At the same time, the opposed outcry was heard. According to Strype,

> incestuous and unnatural Contracts and Mariages ... were now very rife, to
> the great Scandal of the Nation ... That unnatural Filthiness was too much
> known and blazed there abroad, in that great liberty of Mariage, which was
> then used. A thing that made good Men lament, and the Adversaries laugh.[34]

Queen Elizabeth's archbishop, Matthew Parker, attempted to still the
confusions by rewriting the rules governing incest when chartering the
Church of England. However, evidence suggests that this solution was
not immediately or generally effective.[35] The endless concern with
transgressive marriage in the drama perhaps suggests less simple rebellion
against a dominant mode than a widespread sense of cultural negotiation: perhaps the dominance was becoming approximate, even residual.

Furthermore, men became increasingly aware of, and uneasy about,
their genealogical dependence on women for identity. This is at least one
central account of the early modern enchantment, so seemingly inane to
the modern eye, with cuckoldry jokes. The basis of kinship can at one

pole seem reliably natural because bodily – producing tropes such as "flesh of my flesh" or "the villainous hanging of a nether lip," and iconic images of mother and child. At the other pole, however, it becomes intolerably textualized: "She said thou wast my daughter." Henry VIII provides only the most conspicuous example of a man driven to paroxysms of baroque suspicion, calculation, self-indulgence, guilt, and murder while attempting to synthesize endogamic and exogamic desires for sexual gratification and dynastic self-identity.

Finally, later Elizabethan years saw an increasing uproar over the Court of Wards' interventions in the marital decisions of the aristocracy – for the Crown, essentially a financial practice. When an aristocrat died before his heir reached maturity, the Crown became guardian to the heir, and retained veto powers over his marriage. These rights were often sold to the highest bidder, who often mulcted the heir and his family for any access to self-determinations erotic and familial. Dynastic kinship practices were thus disrupted by those both above and below the aristocracy (though also by many of those within it, buying and selling each other's heirs).[36]

Much to the discomfort of conservative moral guardians, under Henry's once-bastard daughter the stage reproduced the public fascination with innumerable portrayals of kinship instability: depictions of incest, enforced marriage, cross-generational sex, adultery, cuckoldry, whoredom, bastardy, disinheriting, banishments, fostering, foundlings, recoveries, recognitions, forgiveness, and forgetting. Indeed, like the heraldry that derived status *ab ovo* from William the Conqueror or Aeneas, the "facts" of kinship might be rejected wholesale. Proto-pornographic fantasies of the Family of Love beckoned to erotic as well as political leveling. And for Wilkins's gallants *all* genealogy is fraudulent; male friendship is the only reality.

The fourth structuration is that of service relations, disrupted by the shift from role to job, famously highlighted in *The Communist Manifesto* as the historical movement from feudalism to capitalism.[37] It involves many permutations of master–servant (or master–apprentice, or employer–employee) relations. The pure form of feudal service, nostalgically constructed even in early modern England, was generally imagined to be bonded, non-oppositional, closely resembling our modern notions of love, but obtaining here between social unequals happily unequal. Its metaphoric home is the family. Mutually open comprehension and motivation was often stipulated. A newer form, of bourgeois master and apprentice, seems to combine (or predict) contractual cash-nexus relations with role-modeling and transitional familiality. Mutual comprehension is more often restricted to the scene of what is more and more marked off as labor, rather than seen as unbounded service.

The problematic case, common on the stage, presents the second form as the first: comprehension is withheld, by one or the other side, and goodlordship and loyal service are experienced as naive, even degrading. Either "I follow him to serve my turn upon him" (*Othello* 1.1.51) or "Die they shall; slaves are ordained to no other end" (*The Spanish Tragedy* 3.2.119). The stage is flooded with hostile, blaming, envious and mobile servants, and with exploiting and evacuating puppet-masters. Moreover, agency is deeply problematized.[38] Sometimes the figures discover or take on differential attributes even as we (and they) watch. The vertical loyalties to master and family and business may shade toward the friendship of sidekicks, as with Bassanio and Gratiano or Brachiano and Flamineo, or they may undergo an internal distantiation, and be recognized as or made partial, through various reservations of self-commitment. Horizontal loyalties, of common livery or faction, also arise: servant romances occur, containing both bondings and the parities of rival suitors. Finally, complex multiplicities of vertical and horizontal bondings and frictions can result. Rioting apprentices may have achieved both rebellious and cathartic release and a recuperative group-construction by attacking "appropriate" women. Brothels can be seen as similarly gendered institutions, differently degraded, and so perhaps are targets for the apprentices' displacement of anger at masters' oppressions; yet to pillory such women is to seize the position of bourgeois moral condescension, of potential class unity with the masters.

The plays foreground many such seizures of the will. I take it as essential to locate both characters and the tensions their authors generate for and with them within a context continuously defined in terms of rank, gender, kinship, and service relations. These registers intersect in a variety of ways; now one, now another will loom forward as especially threatening or threatened. But generally they all remain visibly active. We must watch for how, say, adultery or betrothal is shaped by status, how kinship expectations are shaped by occupational locus, how murder is determined by gender, how, finally, all transgressions take place in a context of multiple boundaries and definitions, visible but shifting. Within these disruptions we can observe the several and only partially cognate presumptions and stipulations of structure in motion, seeking new points of balance, tipping toward and away from our own senses of the natural, often equally unanalyzed.

Most often, perhaps, the plays have been seen to present such motions as disastrous. However, failures of fit among different structurations produced opportunities for individuals as often as incoherences for some social totality. Indeed, sometimes the notion of transgression itself seems almost melodramatic: structural confusions deftly appropriated can relieve as well as disrupt. In many willful subordinations and improvisations and negotiations we can detect hope, empowerment, even mutual aid. The rich sense of what Theodore Leinwand has called "negotiation" is as present in these plays as are domination and subjection.[39] Respecting and parsing such multiple relations was a central aim of the early modern stage; reading those efforts is the central project of this book.

The obligation to such awareness is the more important, if the more complex, in that these discursive fields often stand in for or use one another, in complex ways. For instance, conflict or shift in gender and status can certainly resemble (and thus voice or explore or occlude) one another by analogy. Kenneth Burke insists on the bidirectionality of analogy: "the relations between classes are like the ways of courtship, rape, seduction, jilting, prostitution, promiscuity"; yet "psychoanalysis too often conceals ... the nature of social relations behind the terms for sexual relations."[40] Sometimes the relation is intensive and overdetermining (and the analysis counter-reductive), as when Lisa Jardine suggests of Gertrude that "rampant sexuality is the dramatic representation of independent choice on women's part."[41] That is, as we will see with Bel-imperia, intense sexual desire can certainly be itself, literal, yet also function as a synecdoche for more extended, less bodily, political tensions.

Such a discursive conjunction can sometimes function as a relatively full transcoding, as a vehicle for conflicts and shifts within and among other categories. As Maurice Godelier observes, "Sex-related differences between bodies are continually summoned as testimony to social relations and phenomena that have nothing to do with sexuality. Not only as testimony to, but also testimony for – in other words, as legitimation."[42] Plays about powerful or sexually uncontrolled women may sometimes address interdicted matters of class or kinship authority. Equally, to speak with, and of, such doublings, to metaphorize, can sometimes displace attention from the real lives thus made sheer vehicles. As with the metaphoricity of gender, so with that of status groups, kinship, and master-servant relations. Each may voice or mask or challenge or oppress others. When young Henry V exhorts his happy band of brothers to "dishonour not [their] mothers," and promises to "gentle [their] condition," it is hard to disentangle the swirl of tenor and vehicle in the formats of earned and alluring identity – of status, gender, kinship, and service – in his motivational rhetoric. Caryl Churchill's "early/modern" witchcraft play *Vinegar Tom* offers a clue. Henry V's audiences, on and

off stage, might say what her generic Man says, in response to the
sectarian seventeenth-century churches' agonistic reassurances and dam-
nations: "I believe it all in turn and all at once."[43] Early modern auditors
will often have experienced such a whirl as incoherent, whether threateningly or fascinatingly so, but I will operate on the presumption that they
were as capable as we are of complex interpretation, especially of their
own world. Late modern readers like ourselves can be similarly threatened or fascinated by such complexity, and be as ready to use, miss,
rewrite, or be changed by it. Our sense of what elements are in play, and
how to construe them, of the "real" tenor of a text, is, like theirs, a
product of overdetermined interpretive stance. My own aim here is, with
Burke, generally to multiply rather than reduce – to resist the summons
to a universal master-code, in favor of a thick address to the thickness of
these texts.[44]

However, Churchill's Man's desiring despairing spinning head and
the calm analyst's parsing, like my own frequent recourse (by turns and
all at once) to technical and colloquial registers, embody two kinds of
thickness. I take this discontinuity as an occasion to ground my pursuit
of these various social phenomena, often described in so technical or
social-scientific a way, in the field of expressly literary dramatic fictions.[45] I have situated my analyses of plays in a complex array of
structures that interlock and conflict in a variety of ways. Most of these
come to life in vocabularies that are anachronistic to early modern
England and esoteric to many modern readers. The theoretical and
critical bases for such discursively complex inquiries are themselves
thick with second-order technical reference (as this sentence is). Furthermore, much work that explores the structural bases of status, gender,
kinship, and service practices is extremely dense, thick with tables,
stemmae, marshalled data, statistical and distributive generalizations
and specifications. Building on this mass, I have suggested seven kinds
of seizure, four grids (each in multiple and contested formulations), and
a great range of pairs (ascribed and achieved, subjection and qualification, embedding and disenchantment, appropriations and fits, role and
job, and more).

I find this framing extremely useful, indeed essential. With Bourdieu, I
believe that " 'interpersonal' relations are never, except in appearance,
individual-to-individual relationships, and that the truth of the interaction
is never entirely contained in the interaction."[46] However, it is also
important that the authors of these plays did not deal thus abstractly
with their literary and social materials. The texts of courtesy literature,
with its ideological account of social structures and relations produced
consciously for management of those structures and relations, are self-

consciously theoretical. Plays are not, though conscious and sophisticated they obviously were. It is fruitful here to recall Bourdieu's caveats against theoreticist or calendrical illusions.

> It is significant that "culture" is sometimes described as a *map*; it is the analogy which occurs to an outsider who has to find his way around in a foreign landscape and who compensates for his lack of practical mastery, the prerogative of the native, by the use of a model of all possible routes. The gulf between this potential, abstract space, devoid of landmarks or any privileged centre – like genealogies, in which the ego is as unreal as the starting-point in a Cartesian space – and the practical space of journeys actually made, or rather of journeys actually being made, can be seen from the difficulty we have in recognizing familiar routes on a map or town-plan until we are able to bring together the axes of the field of potentialities and the "system of axes linked unalterably to our bodies, and carried about with us wherever we go", as Poincaré puts it, which structures practical space into right and left, up and down, in front and behind.[47]

I believe that plays provide a unique avenue of access to such lived journeys through the space of social life, that they capture a highly informative version of what our modern maps of social technology abstract, in the various Cartesianisms of the social sciences (already richly if embryonically present in analytic discourses of such writers as Elyot, Calvin, or Bodin). These disciplines have much to teach us, and I have made liberal use of them in the pages that follow. But the mimetic or depictive textuality of plays seems to me an even more important, and prior, production of knowledge. I believe it exfoliates and interrogates what Giddens calls "practical consciousness."

> The reflexive capacities of the human actor are characteristically involved in a continuous manner with the flow of day-to-day conduct in the contexts of social activity. But reflexivity operates only partly on a discursive level. What agents know about what they do, and why they do it – their knowledgeability *as* agents – is largely carried in practical consciousness. Practical consciousness consists of all the things which actors know tacitly about how to "go on" in the contexts of social life without being able to give them direct discursive expression.[48]

A great deal of what plays have to teach us about social tensions and structurations is carried not in abstracted theoreticist discursivity but precisely in the depicted unreflexive flow of the day-to-day conduct of social activity. Such activity, not only in the theater but in what Wrightson calls "the whole world of regular personal contact, at work, after church-services, in the streets, the field and the market place" continuously reaffirmed, negotiated, and rewrote the terms of the early modern social world (*English Society* 63). Wrightson specifies the affirmations usefully:

What was vital in this daily social intercourse was the regularity of daily face-to-face contact both between comparative equals and between superiors and inferiors. Indeed, in the latter case, individual demeanour in direct personal interaction was of singular importance, for it could simultaneously reinforce consciousness of the bond of personal identification and the reality of social differentiation upon which the whole structure of paternalism and deference rested.

Such interactions usually, perhaps, reiterated an "implicit recognition of the legitimacy of the prevailing social order ... and a tacit rejection of alternative definitions of the situation" (*English Society* 58). Clearly too, however, such daily intercourse could flee, deny, insult, or edit the structure, as the plays show, over and over: not only in the represented interactions on stage, but in the continuous interactive appropriations that constitute an auditor's multiple relations, face to face, to the social activity which is a stage-play.

The dramatists, that is, do not simply write about social activity, they write social activity. They write journeys made, which themselves not only constitute and rewrite maps, but may also be tried on, reused, played again, as scripts or scores or journals, for journeys outside the playhouse. Play-writing is of course a symbolic and abstracted activity, the playwrights themselves analysts of a kind. But the discourse they employ is one not of abstraction but of embodiment, perhaps reembodiment, not only physical (for I speak now of the written records, our mediate access to early modern performances) but linguistic. The words and actions of their created characters tend very much toward the locus of practical consciousness: sometimes groping (in soliloquy, author and character often in tandem) toward theoretical discursivity; much more often, exactly dramatizing the felt or disturbed or presumed – but known – provisional realities of capacity and limit in their social world, by acting with them, on them, instrumentally and effectively. And in turn the auditor's multiple and conflicted relations to such acting are not only determined by, but capacitate, social action outside the playhouse.[49]

This unabstracted quality is thus not a limitation of such texts, but, emphatically, a capacity. The nuanced fluctuations of greater and lesser self-awareness in actions witnessed on stage are themselves what Bourdieu sees as the primary modality of activation of structure, only present when embodied, acted with, and only secondarily present in theoreticist discourse, whether sixteenth-century or twentieth.[50] Neglect of such dividends is analytical impoverishment, as Giddens suggests.

What actors are able to say about the conditions of their action and that of others is foreshortened if researchers do not recognize the possible significance of a range of discursive phenomena to which, as social actors themselves, they would certainly pay close attention but which in social research are often simply discounted. These are aspects of discourse which in form are refractory to being rendered as statements of propositional belief or which, like humour or irony, derive their meaning not so much from the context of what is said as from the style, mode of expression or context of utterance. But to this we must add a second factor of greater importance: the need to acknowledge the significance of practical consciousness. Where what agents know about what they do is restricted to what they can say about it, in whatever discursive style, a very wide area of knowledgeability is simply occluded from view.[51]

The drama is a very thick palimpsest: of authors' words for actors to enliven, playing such "social actors" for a hungry and curious audience of such actors, fully but variously practically competent. That it operates by means of such stylistic modes is clear in literary studies; the practical capacitation of such modes also deserves a proper recognition as historical.

Several analytical imperatives flow from this placement of specifically dramatic literary discursivity. The first is a matter of rhetorical structure. Given the tools outlined above, it might seem reasonable to approach such a complexly stratified field by, say, exploring the seven transgressions in serial chapters, or treating transgressions of shifting status, gender, kinship, and service relations and models in a four-fold array of similarity and difference. Such approaches would neglect, however, the historical shape of the plays: these encounters and problems were presented and confronted by English authors and audiences in a generically determinate form. Analytical subdivision and reification seemed appropriate for an attempt to grasp the grammar of Elizabethan courtesy theory. Its texts were precisely not consumed and redeployed in a unified way, but by piecemeal "application."[52] Plays, however, were undergone in a narratively cohesive two hours' traffic, and each presented specifically embodied intersections on the terrain of structuration and identification. It is important to work with these intersections "play by play," as modern announcers have it, as they were constructed and ordered, to respect the narratives as particular historical specificities (one hopes, now as then), specifically shaping the experiences of stimulation, provocation, disturbance, fright, and relief that English audiences paid to see.

Another critical practice follows. Insofar as the shifting structurations in the plays were both taken for granted and newly contested, full both of the invisibly obvious and the unintelligibly shocking, we must also strive to apprehend their precise linguistic freighting. If we are no longer comfortable with claiming that "true meaning" resides "in the words themselves," I believe that historicity certainly does, which Giddens defines as "a definite sense of living in a social world constantly exposed to change, in which Marx's maxim [that human beings make history] is part of a general cultural awareness, not a theorem particular to specialist social thinkers."[53] We need to pay the closest attention to these texts' local and nuanced particularities, to those particularities' capacities to disturb and abrade and arouse both irrational, "natural," "stock" responses, and their more considered analytical equivalents. For unselfconscious usages (both banal and weird), inexplicable and impacted emotions, express turbulent vectors of emergent and residual cultural forms. As with Freud's emphasis on parapraxes, slips of the cultural tongue often reveal pressures and tensions unavailable to agents' discursive consciousness.

Finally, if literary texts can be related to practical consciousness, it is also the more important, I believe, to summon back to the foreground the personal complexes of emotional reaction and experiment and nourishment and capacitation to which the plays summon their auditors and readers. Louis Montrose has argued that the theater functioned as a very deep (and so very controversial) secular alternative to the authoritarian homiletic scene of the English Reformation church, that many city folk went to plays to get for themselves what the state had suppressed or appropriated from the cycle dramas' ritual life, as homogenizing ideology for the Virgin Queen.[54] If the early modern theater, like modern movies, provoked laughter and tears, not only disenchantment but avidity, then it seems to me that as best we can we must bring those reactions – undenied, untransformed, unsanitary, and full – to our critical venture.

It sometimes seems, as a colleague has put it to me, that the filthy secret of poststructuralist theory is that we like literature, are moved by it, respond incoherently, and with pleasures and desires indifferent and significantly inassimilable to currently institutionalized interpretive forms. It has seemed to me here that there is considerable critical payoff in returning such repressed factors to the forefront of reading and writing about these plays. There are, after all, enormous instructive energies lurking within the seemingly mathematical stratifications of, say, kinship diagrams, as any frontal inspection of the vocabularies of hostile and playful cursing reveals. (That's one reason why "native informants" so enjoy watching cerebral analysts write them down.)[55] The best modern example, perhaps, would juxtapose the different ultimates of the incest taboo and the arch-curse "motherfucker." But these effects are early modern too, as in Kent's delighted crescendo phrase for Goneril's upstart steward Oswald, the "son and heir of a mongrel bitch." Much of the discourse of social struggle and its passionate grapplings for orientation was expressed in registers less familiar to us than Kent's. Exhuming these unheard melodies requires much immersion in the banal and opaque, and much too in the way of ready imagination. If we are to catch early modern English men and women in the acts, we must allow our own reactions to be caught, to bloom and be felt and written past the preemptive withdrawal of the rationalist analyst. Such productive readiness of engagement and response is already powerfully felt in the contemporary analytic discourses of feminism and ethnic and gay studies. The sometimes more canonical and less contemporary subjects of early modern England respond with many of the same sizable rewards, exciting and chastening by turns.

Though I have taken many examples from Shakespeare in this introduction for familiarity and orientation, the chapters that follow deal only with plays by others.[56] The density of social awareness I address is no function of individual perspective or "genius," but a widespread, deeply self-aware, and constitutive investment of the institution of the theater. In search of the practical operations of this awareness I explore two sets of plays, arranged chiastically: two Italianate courtly plays (*The Spanish Tragedy* and *The Duchess of Malfi*) carefully distanced from English life, with sadistic guardian brothers, erotically aggressive sisters, ambitious and betrayed servants and lovers; and two (and a fraction) thickly English county plays (*Arden of Faversham*, *The Miseries of Enforced Marriage*, *A Yorkshire Tragedy*) based on contemporary "historical" tracts, energized by conservative and perhaps enforced marriages, systemic rebellions, comically ambitious servants, and cautionary didactic endings. The interlacings of structure and seizure, within and among these plays, are their subject, and mine. They allow, I believe, as rich and uncomfortable a view as we can get of the fitful process of social change in early modern England.

1   Forcing divorce in *The Spanish Tragedy*

Thomas Kyd's *Spanish Tragedy* provides an essential beginning for study-ing how fantasies of power and control and achieved security work within and against the social constraints of early modern English culture. This play thematizes such seizures, and its events are not just instantiations of these categories, but often their founding moments.[1] Kyd first troped and mapped what later became the obsessive landscape of Renaissance courtly tragedy. Such exemplary status has long been noted regarding Hieronymo's revenge, the originary gesture of Elizabethan revenge tragedy.[2] This aspect of *The Spanish Tragedy* has subsumed most inquiry into the play. However, my discussion will minimize questions about Hieronymo and revenge, focusing instead on the play's first movement, the complex events of Acts 1 and 2 that end with Horatio's murder. I hope to revalue what Philip Edwards, speaking for many readers, calls these "prolix early scenes" that seem "so laboured": "few readers fail to find the early scenes tedious," he feels, and many agree.[3] I don't. A close look at the complex events and conditions that authorize Hieronymo's revenge can be very useful in unpacking impacted nodes of social pain which Kyd discovered Elizabethans needed, and loved, to confront.

Over and over *The Spanish Tragedy* emphasizes adversarial presenta-tion. Lorenzo strives to control his sister Bel-imperia's erotic agency, and she, just as strongly, to invest it as and when she will. Noble Lorenzo and Balthazar struggle to dominate what they feel to be the poachings of ambitious gentlemen like Andrea and Horatio. Hopeful servants like Pedringano strive to make new places for themselves, to move from follower to friend, by secret services. The worthy state officer Hieronymo, Knight Marshal of Spain, must confront from inside and out the confusing dialectic of state power and authority, and eventually seek to confirm one by disrupting the other in his retributive inset play. The ultimate grounding of religious authority is itself split in the extruded Frame into asymmetrical and competing binaries that strive for hege-mony before the play's auditors. And these binaries are funded, in a variety of ways, by fears of, and desires for, the seizures of identity.

I

The first movement of *The Spanish Tragedy* opens with Don Andrea's stunning posthumous gloating about his secret sexual relationship with Bel-imperia, the childless king's niece. It closes by terminating a duplicate relation, with Don Horatio's murder, probably during intercourse with the same partner. Bel-imperia is the fateful *object* of desire for both men, but this formulation, like much else in both early and later modern thinking, can mask her agency as desiring *subject*. Each relationship proves a portmanteau of the categories of seizure, combining and recombining transgressive sexualities (extramarital relations, specular and ghostly voyeurisms); Bel-imperia's preferments of her base lovers, and Lorenzo's of Balthazar and Pedringano; Lorenzo's humiliations (received and imposed); everyone's experiences of betrayal, of nearly every bond; and the direct and vicarious physicalities of violation – by and of Bel-imperia, by and of her lovers, and by and of the murderers (nearly everyone in the play). But these actions share a common origin in Bel-imperia's desire, which enabled Don Andrea's founding declaration.

> When this eternal substance of my soul
> Did live imprisoned in my wanton flesh,
> Each in their function serving other's need,
> I was a courtier in the Spanish court.
> My name was Don Andrea, my descent,
> Though not ignoble, yet inferior far
> To gracious fortunes of my tender youth:
> For there in prime and pride of all my years,
> By duteous service and deserving love,
> In secret I possessed a worthy dame,
> Which hight sweet Bel-imperia by name.
> But in the harvest of my summer joys
> Death's winter nipped the blossoms of my bliss,
> Forcing divorce betwixt my love and me.   (1.1.1–14)

These lines, often parodied, unforgotten, present with amazing directness most of the issues we are concerned with: death, eroticism, status and its gaps, secrecy, and death again. The fundamental circuit of Elizabethan tragedy begins here, already retroactive, preconditioned, foreshortened. Don Andrea's report of his relation with Bel-imperia necessitates a particular view of the Horatio plot, which reenacts it so carefully, and needs close consideration in its setting of the issues.

Andrea is dead. So much is made, so strangely, to depend on this. The cryptic voice from the grave, speaking with simultaneous distance and immediacy, embodies the contraries of which Elizabethan tragedy is made: passion and judgment, seemings and ultimates, smugness and deprivation, gloating and rage. From the first line a beckoning of perspective comes: news from beyond the fleshly realm. Yet such transcendental fleshlessness is immediately embodied, one moment degradingly against its will ("imprisoned in my wanton flesh"), the next willingly, even naturally ("each in their function serving other's need"). The movement of the lines is echoic: each pure state is immediately contradicted, reevaluated, made to interpenetrate with its opposite.

The eroticism is very direct: the soul serves the needs of the wanton flesh, as that flesh (wantonly?) serves the soul's needs. In either direction the force of the flesh has a powerful legitimacy, even parity, quite at odds with a traditional Christian hierarchy of spirit over flesh.[4] And this legitimation is the more powerful in its transcendental origin: instead of a purging call from a ghostly father to transcend passion (as in "leave her to heaven") we have an unapologetic ratification of earthliness.[5] Andrea recalls his earthly sexual life with a matter-of-fact self-respect that soon rises into a very unghostly pleasure.

After embracing his body, Andrea speaks of his rank, making it equally central. Any Spanish courtier would exude punctilio, and the *sprezzatura* of "not ignoble" is very much elegant modesty. But Andrea specifies himself as self-transcended, as having gone beyond himself, by virtue of his fortune with Bel-imperia. He combines the modest claim to ascribed status and the deferent but gloating boast of achieved status, born of nerve and transgression. "In secret I possessed a worthy dame, / Which hight sweet Bel-imperia by name." The oxymoronic pressure of this crucial moment is intense. "A worthy dame which hight" brings chivalric force to the conquest, befitting a military hero and don. And Bel-imperia's resonant name itself belongs in a tapestry full of proud fairs.[6] But "in secret I possessed" moves us from fields of cloth of gold to the inner recesses of the court, from magnificent costume to the body. Really what has gone on here is illicit sexual action with the childless king's niece. And with this realization we reach the originary event of the play.

For, as Andrea's courteous modesty in fact accurately suggests, this social, political, sexual act must primarily be the royal *Bel-imperia's* act, a fortune far beyond the reach if not the dream of merely gentle Andrea.[7] He omits her initiative, as undercutting the self-regard of a courtly male of whatever rank. But he could not have acted without encouragement, given the lady's extreme dynastic status, her fiercely protective family, and the endlessly signaled gap separating her from her later lover Horatio, Andrea's peer and the king's cupbearer. And we (and we alone) see her give his double Horatio just such clandestine encouragement. On the other hand, as we see later, others are habitually disposed to impute responsibility for Bel-imperia's sexual activity to the men she consorts with. (Don Andrea's silence permutes such misogynist blindness. They can't stand the thought of her agency; he can't stand to mention it.) And Andrea certainly embraces his fate, as essentializing him; or rather, so Kyd constructs him. Andrea brought to the act all of his powers, in prime and pride, service and love. But for Andrea this is presented as fundamentally a piece of fortune, experienced relatively passively, to "possess" Bel-imperia. It was unforeseeable, a mystery of fate, but irresistible.

If Bel-imperia's adventure with Don Andrea is *hers*, then, rather than his, why begin with his report? Kyd has a dual agenda here, it seems to me. He begins with her sexual action because it embodies so many of the energies of social gesture he is concerned with. He begins with Don Andrea's report of it in order to situate the story as *told*, precisely not beginning with immersion, *in medias res*, but positioning the auditors as self-conscious recipients of choric report, not action. This invites us to judge, to interpret, to position ourselves. What is noteworthy above all else about this audience placement is that Kyd does not invite us to occupy a traditional politico-moral posture regarding this unmarried royal woman's heterodox sexual behavior. Such judgments are held *within* the fiction, by Lorenzo and Balthazar, with whom we must hesitate to identify our judgments. Like Lear's division of the kingdom, Bel-imperia's sexual freedom is placed by its author in detachment from the usual straightforward moralistic responses, calling up other more complex issues, visible only from outside the usual assumptions.[8]

This negation of moral judgment is quite remarkable, since such acts were high treason. The founding treason statute, 25 Edward III st. 5 c. 2, specified that if "a Man do violate the King's [Companion,] or the King's eldest Daughter unmarried, or the Wife the King's eldest Son and Heir" his act will be judged treasonous. The statute of 28 Henry VIII c. 24 (the Thomas Howard attainder) further detailed the crime, forbidding anyone to "espouse marry or take to his wife any of the King's children [being lawfully born or otherwise commonly reputed or taken for his children,] or any of the King's Sisters or Aunts of the part of the Father, [or any the lawful children] of the King's Brothern or Sisters [not being married,] or contract marriage with any of them, without the special license assent consent and agreement first thereunto had and obtained of the King's Highness in writing under his great seal, [*or defile or deflower any of them not being married*]" (my emphasis; brackets in original). Further, 33 Henry VIII c. 21 (the Catherine Howard attainder), par. x, specified that "if the Queen or Wife of the Prince move procure or stir any person by any Writing or Message word or tokens or otherwise for that purpose to use or to have carnal knowledge with them, or if any person do move procure or make means to the Queen or Wife of the Prince to use or have carnal knowledge of them or any of them," then all of them "and their aiders Counselors and abettors" shall be deemed high traitors.[9] Such fearfully precise language specifies the extra-dramatic realism in Kyd's presentation of early modern courtly sexuality.

Seen legally, such prohibitions should apply fairly clearly, if un-evenly, in the play. Kyd gives us a childless king whose heirs are his niece Bel-imperia and nephew Lorenzo. Lorenzo's heir-status is never mentioned,[10] whereas Bel-imperia's (to be married to Balthazar, to join Spain with Portugal) is a central focus. For the play's purposes she is, like Edward III's "King's eldest Daughter unmarried," the repository of the royal bloodline. Her men are thus treasonous: Andrea (for "violating" her), Pedringano (for aiding Andrea), and probably Horatio (if 2.4 contains consummation). Furthermore, if the Catherine Howard pro-vision extends from the prince's wife to his female heir (as Kyd's childless prince seems designed to require, and as the Edward III statute suggests) then Bel-imperia herself is also clearly guilty of high treason.[11] Horatio would then be guilty even if only moving rather than achieving carnal knowledge.

However, Kyd actively occludes the legal placement of the event as a *criminal* matter, of state.[12] The issue is not allowed to arise in those terms. Kyd activates the corrosive force of the issue, but his aims can be specified more clearly in relation to *petty treason* – seen as *ideological murder, of social authority*: murder of husband, master, mistress, or religious superior.[13] Bel-imperia's dissident sexual relations are certainly murderous, not literally of her superiors, but of their sustaining ideology. Kyd foregrounds her actions as *ideological treason* – not only against the statutes of the realm, but against the status, kinship, and gender norms that ground much of the statutes' cultural authority.[14] What is most remarkable is that he positions audience sympathies *with* erotic hetero-doxy, blocking from view only the most intolerable criminality, of direct statutory high treason. What remains, he embraces. Such occlusion and embrace are substantial indeed, and mark the text as very strongly dissident.

Unlike Kyd's silence about treason, Don Andrea's self-censored male silence regarding Bel-imperia's essential agency is the first of many clues to its centrality in Kyd's design. The don's express and uncensured pleasure further guides us, in at least three separable ways: as the voice of a sexually and socially mobile gentleman; as a detached supernatural voice from beyond the grave; and as the voice motivated, armed, legitimated, and accompanied from the outset by his supernatural sponsor Revenge, whose project we are gathered to witness. Such multiple energies clearly function in favor of Bel-imperia, and against the forces that oppose and oppress her. What are those forces? What is the binary of conflict here?

I believe that Bel-imperia's status-oriented sexual actions with Andrea and Horatio must be understood as symbolic gestures *across* the received ideology of marriage of the early modern English aristocracy (hyperbolic in the royal setting). Aristocratic marriage is one of the group's central strategic provisions for its social reproduction, of its position, its values, and its authority. Such family relations are not static structures but *practices*:

> kin relationships [are] something people *make*, and with which they *do* something ... they are the product of strategies (conscious and unconscious) oriented towards the satisfaction of material and symbolic interests and organized by reference to a determinate set of economic and social conditions.[15]

In *Family Life in the Seventeenth Century* Miriam Slater marks the especially central role of marriage practice in such analysis for early modern England.

> The study of matrimonial procedures and attitudes is especially significant in an arranged marriage society, as much for what it can reveal about the specific nature of those practices as for what it can tell us about the institutions and values of the wider society. ... [S]ince marriage is the acid test for revealing many of the attitudes and prejudices shared by members of a social class, an examination of their marriage choices and practices can provide an understanding of their value system. ... [T]he study of marriage can point up the way in which various social arrangements dovetail and reinforce each other.[16]

Refusals and intentional despoliations of such arrangements (such as Bel-imperia's) equally specify the shape and logic of heterodoxies that include but exceed the orbit of marriage *per se*.

Barbara J. Harris offers a convenient summary of the hard strategic logic of the early modern English aristocratic ideology of marriage:

> The explicit purpose of marriage among the upper classes was to advance the political and economic interest of the patrilineally defined family. Fathers (or those substituting for them after their death) exploited their right to select their children's marriage partners to enlarge the family's estates, raise its social status, and increase its political power. In making their choices, fathers routinely ignored their children's preferences and subordinated their personal happiness to the interests of the patrilineage. A powerful combination of material and ideological factors ensured that most daughters and sons would accept the marriages negotiated for them.... Although fathers negotiated matches for both their daughters and sons, the burden of the arranged marriage weighed far more heavily on women than men ... [E]lite marriages

always involved the exchange of women, but men were objects of exchange
only until they achieved adulthood. This difference accurately reflected the
fact that women remained social dependents throughout their lives.[17]

The fundamental strategic element was thus a use of women, by a
familiar and taken-for-granted masculist logic of exchange and replica-
tion, where women are the conduits or links or circulating bonds of
lineage and affiliation between generations and between like-minded and
like-positioned male-dominated families. The classic inaugurating theoreticist analyses of such thinking, now long familiar, are Lévi-Strauss's
Elementary Structures of Kinship and Gayle Rubin's finely synthetic and
critical essay "The Traffic in Women."[18] Women provide, indeed,
constitute (so the argument goes) the necessary machinery for transmit-
ting name and inheritance, both forth through time and forth into the
social world.

But since, in this misogynist discourse, women are not to be trusted
with such potency, they require careful guarding, both against poaching
from without and against what Thomas Middleton calls "wandering
thoughts" from within.[19] A woman's fullest achievement of legitimate
selfhood, by this logic, ought to be the full self-willed subordination or
gift of herself and her capacities, her agency, to this *telos* of familial
reiteration, seen as extending back and forward in time in a maximally
coercive way (in obligations to ancestors and descendants alike). Such
obligation contains (and is reciprocally constituted by) an allegiance to
her status group, the most potent ground in the differentiated society of
early modern England of the family's place in the larger social
surround.

This subjection of women's lives to masculist ideology, though crucially an instrumentalization, is also an enabling subjectification, an
equipment or empowerment, even if substantially a vicarious one, as
Göran Therbörn has taught us to recognize.[20] Indeed, such recognition is
essential if we are to comprehend the subjection's effectiveness. Marriage
was frequently rewarding for those who embraced and lived within it, at
length and also over and over, given whatever quotidian floor of tension.
Slater summarizes the institution's mechanisms for rewarding gentlewomen as follows:

> For the single woman, marriage afforded the only possibility for personal
> success and preferment. A good match offered financial security and assigned
> a certain status; it also expanded the woman's capacity to engage in reciprocal
> social arrangements of the sort which were necessary in a patronage society.
> At the same time, marriage improved her relationship with her family of
> origin, by relieving them of the responsibility of providing for her as well as by
> expanding their social resources through increased kinship connections ... In
> addition, the great desire to marry, on the part of both sexes, cannot be fully

explained only in terms of the many real advantages which marriage offered as opposed to the dismal prospect of remaining single, even if one adds that it was an important vehicle of upward mobility. In addition to all of these justifiably important considerations was the fact that the arranged marriage gave rise to family formations of a particular kind. The families which emerged from this practice fulfilled a variety of vital functions that included and went quite beyond those which they are expected to perform today. The family was a societal institution of vastly greater significance in a wider variety of endeavors than it is today, and at the same time there were fewer specialized institutions that either duplicated its functions or offered alternative possibilities to the individual. The arranged marriage offered *entrée* into new family formations which served not only as nurturing and socializing agencies but also as credit institutions, levers of political power, arbiters of educational and professional advancement and marriage brokers. Marriage heightened one's contact with a whole range of societal modes which were only partially experienced by those adults who were unmarried, and who therefore were limited to operating through their family of origin.[21]

We ignore at obvious conceptual risk the continuous cathexis of early modern women in the marital institution. As a royal heir Bel-imperia is in some ways freer than many gentlewomen, in others much more constrained, but her placement and agency generally differ only in degree from her aristocratic cohort. Her refusal of this gateway to social praxis is a powerful gesture indeed, given the suite of enabling functions rehearsed above.

However practical its effectiveness, however romantically it may be expressed, the ideology enjoins subjection. Women may become most themselves, be most truly and productively women, they are told, by giving themselves over to, submerging themselves in, a purpose larger than themselves, gaining by losing in a familiar logic of near-mystic self-denial and self-gift. The blunt way to put this is that women are for *use*. Women are *for* something, for reproducing the family and its values. Women are not agents, but conduits; conduits are not persons. What can from one angle be presented (and certainly experienced) as a substantiation or capacitation, a coalescence of individual and dynastic identity, can from another be felt as the exchange of the former for the latter. That is to say, as *loss*.

For the simplest thing to say about Bel-imperia is that her family's attempted management of her sexual life is precisely a *denial*, of her *will*. Such talk might seem anachronistic to a degree. Young gentlewomen were beginning to be ceded a limited right of veto in marital negotiations, and this was counted as an advance.[22] But to presume that this delimitation, because supposedly taken for granted at the level of family praxis, carried all drives before it, is to conflate sexuality with marriage, the private, personal, and occasional with the public, institutional, and

permanent. Such conflation was continually asserted. The structure is
sharply stated in *The Witch of Edmonton*, in the defeated suitor
Warbeck's salute to the winner: "Love her, Thorney. / 'Tis nobleness in
thee; in her but duty. / The match is fair and equal."[23] These are said to
be the fruits of love.

For many women, perhaps they were. These pressures were especially
strong in technically dynastic contexts, among the aristocracy. A noble
woman's ideal devotion to dynastic ends is seen as, supposedly felt as,
collective, self-abnegating, an abnegation proposed from without, summoned from within.[24] But it is precisely such ends that Bel-imperia
repudiates, as she inhabits her body for her own gratifications and
establishments – as if it were her own. The ideology of marriage functions
for her as denial, constriction, subjection. Its principal logical vector is
against what many subjected to such arrangements experienced as
"love." Kyd's analysis has much in common with Rubin's. Their explorations of marital ideology – and the sex/gender system it derives from
and sustains – focus above all not only on the norms but on their
oppressive force, and on the evasion and resistance they occasioned.
Harris's analysis of the premarital experiences and efforts of Mary
Tudor, Henry VIII's younger sister, "certainly casts doubt on the
assumption that most early Tudor elite women accepted the values
embodied in the dominant marriage system" (60).[25] What we have to
deal with here in Kyd, with a similar brother–sister power relation at the
heart of things, in the maximized international context of royal power
relations, is a depiction of restraint and fury, centered on the pressures
and limits of the will.[26]

This tension is systemic, but Bel-imperia is nonetheless the only major
female character in *Seizures of the Will* who is not married or aiming for
it. As we shall see, Alice in *Arden of Faversham*, Clare and Katherine in
The Miseries of Enforced Marriage, the Wife in *A Yorkshire Tragedy*, and
the Duchess of Malfi all complexly resist subjections to patriarchal
authority; yet all, I will argue, engage with marriage, however variously
understood, as the only thinkable substantiating pathway for women.
Bel-imperia's studied resistance to that ultimate investment may partially
derive from the enabling powers of her exceptionally high status (perhaps
no higher than the Duchess's, who most clearly seeks "companionate"
marriage), or possibly from uncomfortable family resemblances to her
brother, the progenitor of Renaissance drama's many isolate villains.
Wherever it comes from, it is the most determined and raging rejection
we will see, and as such constitutes the most radical ideological critique
to be considered here, of a social practice which, however oppressive,
was still vigorously seized by most women.

Such problematics of the will have important analogues in extra-erotic space, as Kyd's multiplied action makes clear; and like the erotic events their analogues prove fertile for later drama. This central term of *Hamlet* and so many cognate plays finds its origin here, but not only, or even first, in Hieronymo's struggle to "act": the struggle over boundaries between Bel-imperia and Lorenzo provides the setting and the trigger for Hieronymo's toils, and rewards interrogation quite as much. If Hieronymo's complex relations to the ambiguous transcendental authorities of the Frame foreshadow *Hamlet* and *King Lear*, so the willful relations of Kyd's young woman and her men to the pieties and *Realpolitik* of sexuality and rank and kinship seed *Othello*, *The Duchess of Malfi*, and *The Changeling*. *The Spanish Tragedy* problematizes all of these relations, among individuals and categories, quite profoundly; that is its founding contribution.

In fact, the principal actions of *The Spanish Tragedy* are all some form of *hypertrophy* of will. The various concerns with control of Castile, Lorenzo, and the King; the explicitly achieved status of Hieronymo the corregidor and eventual Knight Marshal and his son Horatio the commander of lanciers (both explicitly marked as products of what Lawrence Stone has called the "rapid escalators" of early modern social mobility);[27] the artfully tempted and carefully self-buttressed ambitious behavior of the servant Pedringano; the conspicuously passive "weak nature" of Balthazar;[28] and the compulsive risk-taking rebelliousness of Bel-imperia, from which nearly everything else flows: all of these seem transformations along one axis or another of a willed and arguably excessive (or at least non-traditional) departure from norms. That is, they become visible as such in a setting that centers the issue of control.

To reverse the terms along another axis, the notion of individual will might be said to produce the derivative concept of the marital ideology, the latter conceived as a social tool for policing or containing the former capacity. Such, at any rate, was the explicitly held precept of William Cecil, Lord Burghley, Master of the Court of Wards and Elizabethan England's principal aristocratic marriage-broker. "Marry thy daughters in time lest they marry themselves," he told his son Robert, his successor at the Court of Wards.[29] The daughters of the aristocracy seem here a locus of willful riskiness almost proverbial in strength. The results of delay can be even worse than inappropriate marriage, as Bel-imperia's actions soon show. The servant Ralph in *A Yorkshire Tragedy* voices a similar thought, in terms equally ambiguous regarding gendered and active and passive will. "Why, apples hanging longer on the tree than when they are ripe makes so many fallings: viz. mad wenches, because they are not gathered in time, are fain to drop of themselves, and then 'tis common, you know, for every man to take 'em up" (1.3–7).

At one level these passages merely insist that women were untrustworthy, that their wills are uncontrolled, insufficiently socialized, inherently fallen. It seems more specific to suggest that for many women the intensities of love are defined in terms of rebellion. Love involves both intense and individually personifying willing and the most traditionally guaranteed path to loss of social control, as two opposed clusters of proverbs make clear: "Love cannot be compelled (forced)" (Tilley L499) and "Love is lawless" (L508).[30] It is no wonder that dynastic marriage and eros were traditionally felt as polar. Indeed, dynastic marriage and perhaps even the preliminaries of courtship *per se* were felt precisely to be *disciplinary* at least in *The Spanish Tragedy*, as we will see.

Burghley's specific reference to *daughters* is also suggestive.[31] We are more familiar, perhaps, with the hypertrophied male will, in Tamburlaine, Faustus, and their cognates. And it is easy enough to read the aristocratic ideology of marriage as an externalization of male or masculist will. Such hypertrophy aims at producing an "appropriate" constriction and eventual atrophy of will in women, under the usual sign of "doing what you are meant to do," i.e., of finding rather than losing the self. But the structural result of this ideology seems to be, at least in Bel-imperia's case and others like hers, that the masculist hypertrophy generates not atrophy but a correspondent hypertrophy of opposite sign, here called not (as with heirs) "coming of age," but *rebellion*.[32]

Bel-imperia's rebellious potency is foregrounded in a kind of theoretical sidebar in which Lorenzo and Balthazar try to account for and defang her willfulness. The tools are quotations from Thomas Watson's then-famous sonnet-sequence *Hecatompathia*.[33] Bel-imperia has scorned Balthazar, and Lorenzo tries to reassure him with images of persistence rewarded.

> My lord, though Bel-imperia seem thus coy,
> Let reason hold you in your wonted joy.
> "In time the savage bull sustains the yoke,
> In time all haggard hawks will stoop to lure,
> In time small wedges cleave the hardest oak,
> In time the flint is pierced with softest shower" –
> And she in time will fall from her disdain,
> And rue the sufferance of your friendly pain.   (2.1.1–8)

Lorenzo uses Watson here to place Bel-imperia's "coyness" in perspective – the reassuring perspective of masculist sonnets, which repeatedly confront female resistance with coercive despair, that is, with self-renewing persistence, however immediate the experience of intermediate rejection may be.[34] Watson's lines seem to sum up not only the kneeling lover's satisfying private mantra of hope, but the confident (and jussive) expectation of masculist ideology generally: "this is merely usual and conventional," Lorenzo suggests; "don't be too upset."[35] (I will return to Lorenzo's dismissive impatience with labile emotion below, but here notice the repressed fury – in authoritarian words like "rue" and "fall" – at the very thought of having to sue at all, much less at length.)

The notion of coyness might well serve the reassuring view: it often signified an unadmitted intention to coax or allure, thus meaning, quite literally, to encourage rather than discourage. (Indeed, *OED* notes a medieval usage of *coy* [sb.2] as "encouragement of an animal by clapping of the hands or the like": thus here perhaps a remote echo eggs on the horses of desire.) *Coy* also had the force of *silent*, *shy*, *retiring*: an effect quite the opposite of arousal. And, alas for Balthazar, the word could signify something actively threatening, like a trap, as with a duck decoy. However, surely Lorenzo means to employ the first nest of meaning, suggesting that all is a matter of token resistance. This view means precisely *not to take Bel-imperia seriously*, as a person who has a mind of her own to know: i.e., to deny her conceptually just what parental familial will would deny her practically – independent personal autonomy. Such autonomy is for a woman traditionally denied (and thus eventually relocated) in sexual terms, which are taken as constitutive and (re)definitive.

Though they speak of eventual control, Watson's lines weigh recalcitrance and domination very interestingly, for Bel-imperia's coyness is repeatedly equated with power – indeed, powers that reflect subversively on masculist ideology. The frontal gesture of Watson's accounting involves a secretly mocking or conciliatory crediting of the woman's power to refuse, designed really to flatter her on the way to eventual male seizure. But behind such self-serving mockery or conciliation lies a felt need to rectify or domesticate an uncontrolled female power that is experienced with real fear. Kyd arranges for us to take the clichés literally, to hear the male fright Bel-imperia finds there, and seizes on. What will prove quite literally to be her "daunger"[36] suggests first the savagery of the bull, with its tones not only of general wildness but specifically male and sexual potency.[37] Perhaps too there is a glance at the rage of the baited bull, as in Spenser's frequent similes.[38] Haggardness reiterates the wildness, in the untamed autonomy of the raptor, and further specifies a female hawk (a usage cognate with hag, associating Bel-imperia with the threatening and overtly sexual trull).[39] If "stoop" would here first signify "obey" (returning upon command), Bel-imperia would also feel that submission to Balthazar would involve "stooping," condescending to an unworthy end; recall Browning's Duke, who chooses never to stoop. Furthermore, the principal sense of stoop in relation to hawks is to dive in attack, here echoing the scariest sense of coyness. The hardness of the uncloven oak and unpierced flint seems to combine recalcitrant female resistance to penetration (however gentle or minuscule, as with small wedges and soft showers) with a directly phallic quality of their own – more role-exchange.[40]

Watson's lines (which seem chosen by Lorenzo, though not by Kyd, for their conventionality) identify for Bel-imperia exactly the sphere where repudiation can seize the phallus, can matter, can strike home. Her sexual wanderings constitute a fully responsible violent recovery of self, a retranslation of "will" from the doubly limiting territory of gendered sexuality, coded either as fearful virginal passivity or as the slut's automatic desire, both closed to questions of significant intention and agency. Bel-imperia seizes upon the performative force of cross-class erotics as the exhibitive device of personal autonomy. I think we should see Bel-imperia's gender predicament as similar to Shylock's ethnic one. When Antonio calmly says to that financial functionary, "I am as like ... to spit on thee again"(1.3.128–29), he speaks his sense of Shylock's fundamental unreality as an independent human. (We will meet this attitude again in Lorenzo's self-consciously olympian relations to Horatio in 1.4 and to Pedringano and Serberine later.) In response to Antonio's self-constitutive dismissal Shylock gives free rein to murderousness, as an evidence of undeniable undismissable reality.[41] So too with Bel-imperia, first with a capitalized and focused promiscuity, then with a violence as theatricalized as Shylock's.

Given the poem's presentation of the corresponding male powers, Balthazar's reappropriation of Bel-imperia's phallus seems unlikely. Supposed domination is first equated with the *yoke*, the only one of all the tropes that figures mastery; but the mastery is attained over violent and doubly fertile animal force (the bull as stud and as the force driving the plow), so the power-relation remains concessive of female potency. The *lure* is wonderfully dissonant, itself a figure of coyness, even feminine; the wooer is thus feminized, unmanned, perhaps capable only of pleading? The *small wedge* is hilariously phallic, and the would-be piercing (again a tiny point?) *soft shower* meek and castrated. Here are no storms of passion such as begin *The Faerie Queene*, when "angry Ioue an hideous storm of raine / Did poure into his lemans lap so fast, / That euery wight to shroud it did constrain" (1.1.6).[42]

Watson's original affirms the lover's hopelessness even more intensely:

No yoake preuails, shee will not yeeld to might;
No lure will cause her stoop, she beares full gorge;
No wedge of woes make printe, she reakes no right;
No shewre of tears can moue, she thinkes I forge . . . .[43]

Watson's lady is impervious to mighty yokes,[44] and having eaten her fill (explicitly a carnivore here, and haggard) she ignores all lures. She will not accept the inscription of her identity that the lover's wedge-pen seeks to write upon her, recking nothing of models of rightness that might subject her, and indeed she thinks his forceless tears false, and will not be roused to sympathy.

Soft Balthazar quotes no further, however, and settles for agreeing that "she is wilder, and more hard withal, / Than beast, or bird, or tree, or stony wall" (2.1.9–10). Instead, he further meditates the binaries of will, parsing her "daunger." He denigrates his looks, his words, his letters, his presents, worrying each for a chink of explanation, and then turns to the play's concerns with power and will.

Yet might she love me for my valiancy;
Ay, but that's slandered by captivity.
Yet might she love me to content her sire;
Ay, but her reason masters his desire.
Yet might she love me as her brother's friend;
Ay, but her hopes aim at some other end.
Yet might she love me to uprear her state;
Ay, but perhaps she hopes some nobler mate.
Yet might she love me as her beauty's thrall;
Ay, but I fear she cannot love at all. (2.1.19–28)

Bel-imperia repudiates Balthazar's suit over and over, he feels, first because of Horatio's degrading triumph over him. Then she denies her family too: her own will (surely the referent of her "reason" – female reason being something of an oxymoron in this discourse) "masters" her father's, and she ignores her brother's wishes as Balthazar's sponsor, attending only to her own aims. Those may be "to uprear her state," he thinks, and fears a "nobler mate"; here he reads her rightly, but misses the rebellious vector. As normative criteria go, he would be an impressively elevating mate, bringing the crown of Portugal with him. But her deepest urges are to flout authority, to brandish her will, and we should probably hear rebellion, perhaps even erection, in "uprear." Compare Joseph Hall's usage in his satire on stage tragedy: the drunken actor sets "his soaring thought / On crowned kings that Fortune hath low brought: / Or some upreared high-aspiring swaine / As it might be the Turkish Tamberlaine."[45] Or recall Henry IV's statement that the rebels "capitulate against us, and are up" (*Henry IV, Part One* 3.2.120).

Balthazar comes closest to understanding when imagining that Bel-imperia might wish above all to continue her power over him, in denial: a perpetuation of the premarital scene of wooing, taking the lover's self-subjectings literally. But in concluding fearfully that "she cannot love at all," he confronts without really knowing it her repudiation of the entire received ideology of "love." It is no accident that Kyd makes this the line that drives Lorenzo to tooth-grinding dismissal, saying "My lord, for my sake leave these ecstasies" (2.1.29). For Balthazar's painful passions are deeply distasteful to both Lorenzo and Bel-imperia (siblings crucially here if not often elsewhere). Each objects to emotions that bring loss of control. Lorenzo's irrepressible contempt is rendered the more compulsive by what otherwise seems the utterly unreal character of Balthazar's desire, unmotivated except as homosocial device. Even to sham, or mime, the expected erotic pieties elicits his hissing. Lorenzo, as our first great English stage machiavel, inaugurates such impatient rationalities as a typifying trait; and it makes sense that Bel-imperia be seen as, one might say, mimetically male, seizing and deploying a masculine behavioral vocabulary that functions almost like a Burkean antinomy of definition.[46] Both Lorenzo and Bel-imperia declare their identities by scorning subjection (of or by Balthazar) to the socially structured intersubjective emotions of "love."

Yet for Bel-imperia, phallic erotic action is not only ideologically errant and repudiating but a positive means, to the inseparable gains of self-satisfaction and self-construction. Above all, it is renewable. In Don Andrea's vegetable mythography death's winter nips his summer harvest blossoms. But for Bel-imperia these joys are repeatable. Life goes on, a new crop is planted from the seed of the old, and forcing divorce is defeated once again (for a while, at least). As she puts her first words to Horatio, Don Andrea "living, was my garland's sweetest flower, / And in his death hath buried my delights" (1.4.4–5). From this buried garland's flower she will make Horatio rise.[47] For this iron-age Flora, the past is prologue.[48]

This fact of plot raises a highly important question: why does Kyd supply his play with such an active past, with Andrea and the Frame? One facet of the answer certainly has to do with Kyd's interrogation of transcendental categories of religion and external control – with, that is, the Hieronymo action.[49] Here I inquire as to the structure's relevance for the earlier half of the play, for the Bel-imperia action. Why is Bel-imperia given a previous lover? She might as easily have embraced heroic improper Horatio without his friendship with Andrea, without the revenge-linkage with Balthazar. But by giving Bel-imperia two similar lovers Kyd produces a very particular effect of *social pattern*. Had Bel-imperia had only one lover, we would be tempted to read that relation in sheerly personal terms, having supposedly to do with Horatio's individual romantic attributes, with the submissive theophanies of "love," and so forth. But when Bel-imperia moves to take Horatio, she seizes what now, in light of Andrea, counts as another specimen of a *type*, the type she likes. Bel-imperia's sexual choices are marked as trans-individual and categorical; they tell us especially about *her* drives, seen as anterior to any external blow from Cupid's arrow. The presence of *two* lovers – so alike, so successful, so potent on the field of battle, so ambitious, so precisely and self-consciously lower in rank, so aroused and indulged, and thus so requiring (and receiving) secrecy of access, and for all of these reasons, so shocking and infuriating to her family – compels awareness of the filter, the structured requirements of Bel-imperia's selectivity.[50]

This categorical quality of her desire leads us past (without dismissing) notions of erotic love (with its aura of opaquely transcendental hyper-individual intersubjectivities, of being "swept away") to notions of willed erotic rebellion. She wishes, I have suggested, to refuse the received categories for her desire, to refuse the obligatory self-abnegation expected of her, by taking what *she* wants.[51] Such desire is by no means without the force of erotic pleasure; I do not suggest that Bel-imperia is not aroused by these men. I believe she takes her fill of each. But the body's embrace functions dialectically, as simultaneous end and means, enjoyment and use. Indeed, the meaning (and thus the affect) of such embraces, perhaps all embraces, is always social, always learned; we acquire and inhabit the body inside culture and history. Bel-imperia certainly achieves, I believe, sexual pleasure in Andrea and Horatio. The question is, why here? Why do they turn her on? Why are *they* who (or perhaps what) she wants?

If Andrea and Horatio trigger Bel-imperia's intense eroticism, I think the discharge is perhaps as much a libidinally gratifying instrumental display, pugnaciously addressed to the condescending and voyeuristic third-party watchers, shown up for blind, as it is an expression of an intersubjective cathexis. The familial ideology she has refused to receive was supposed to subsume the erotic in the familial, to transform it into the procreative (from play to work, so to speak), and so, ultimately and literally, to bring it to an end. But Bel-imperia makes clear that she is not to be thus reduced to order, that the traditional language of "love" contains much surplus meaning, from which she can fashion her own unreduced, indeed excessive, identity.

II

Such oxymoronic emotions, hard and soft, are at the center of Bel-imperia's first scene with Horatio. Our view of her relation with him begins when she asks about the death of Andrea. She hears the tale, and interrupts only to wish Balthazar's death and to ask about Andrea's physical body – or "carcase," as she calls it (1.4.31). Horatio reports how he recovered Andrea's corpse: "[I] wound him in mine arms, / And welding him unto my private tent, / There laid him down, and dewed him with my tears, and sighed and sorrowed as became a friend" (34–37).

The tones here are rich and strange. *OED* tells us that *carcass* generally meant simply "dead body" and did not take on its usual modern tone of "contempt, ridicule, or indignity" (sb.3) until "later times" (specified under sb.1 as ca. 1750), but quotes examples with that harsher meaning from 1528, 1563–87 (Foxe), and 1586. It is not easy to avoid the feeling that something obscure becomes audible in Bel-imperia's use of the word. Still, it is probably impossible to recover sixteenth-century feelings about dead lovers' corpses. We cannot, I imagine, really understand how Thomas More's skull could be kept as a family heirloom for so many years.[52] But Bel-imperia's concern with Andrea's body is surely that of a lover, if no term seems less tender than *carcass*.

Tenderness is certainly Horatio's vein: his language here is also highly bodily, even erotic. (Or perhaps he is venting an incipient reaction to Bel-imperia.) When we hear that Horatio wears Andrea's scarf "in remembrance of [his] friend" (43), as a favor, and that it was originally given as such by Bel-imperia, "at his last depart" (47), the circulations of erotic energy become very powerful. For the favor is first of all a public sexual sign (a talismanic pocket version of a removed and thus meaningful garment like a girdle or sleeve or glove, related at some distance perhaps to marked stained wedding sheets): a sign of fruited possession, sponsorship, bonding, exchange.[53] (In *The First Part of Hieronymo* Bel-imperia gives it to Andrea with these words: "Lend me thy loving and thy warlike arm, / On which I knit this soft and silken charm / Tied with an amorous knot" [ix.15–17].)[54] This semiosis becomes the more powerful if we accept Ejner Jensen's suggestion that this is also the scarf that Hieronymo keeps, bloody, to memorialize Horatio's murder and his blood bond to revenge.[55] (The parent–child relation is equally bodily, not to say erotic.) When Bel-imperia says "now wear thou it both for him and me" (48), we have a triadic bond established between the three lovers; the upsurge of "love" between the two survivors only completes the circuit. (Note, however, Kyd's final obtrusion of the status variable, when a servant's duty finally calls Horatio and he reverts to heavy deference in leaving: "But now, if your good liking stand thereto, / I'll crave your pardon to go seek the prince, / For so the duke your father gave me charge" [55–57].)

Bel-imperia's discovery of her love for Horatio has caused some discomfort, being seen, as Mulryne has it, as "sudden, unmotivated, and even (ll. 66–8) unpleasantly mixed with calculation."[56]

> Yet what avails to wail Andrea's death,
> From whence Horatio proves my second love?
> Had he not loved Andrea as he did,
> He could not sit in Bel-imperia's thoughts.
> But how can love find harbour in my breast,
> Till I revenge the death of my beloved?
> Yes, second love shall further my revenge.
> I'll love Horatio, my Andrea's friend,
> The more to spite the prince that wrought his end.   (1.4.60–68)

In dramatic terms the suddenness cannot be denied: she begins this soliloquy with Horatio already identified as her second love, though we are not told about narrative time passed. To Lorenzo also, speaking later to Pedringano, "it is not long" (2.1.45; a direct anticipation of *Hamlet*, though without quite the emphasis on female dexterity). But what is the status of a concern with matters such as haste and calculation? Bel-imperia's calculation is unpleasant only if female agency is unseemly. Her timing is hasty, that is, inappropriately rapid, only if we aim to hold her to just those standards of female decorum she hates, and consciously rebels against. (It is not clear that such a defense would apply to Shakespeare's Gertrude.)

Instead, I would argue, Bel-imperia's change of heart – more an adjustment of will – seems fairly fully motivated. Balthazar has already begun to plead (see 70: "himself now pleads for favour at my hands"), if not yet on stage. Perhaps Bel-imperia's self-gift to Horatio is reactive, a rejection (thus a product) of the coercive imposition of Balthazar's candidacy, either on his own or, much more likely, through Lorenzo. (Lorenzo has probably seen Balthazar as an opportunity since before the battlefield conversation when Lorenzo spoke him fair. In *The First Part of Hieronymo* Lorenzo immediately exclaims, after having horned in upon the credit for taking Balthazar, "I'll choose my sister out her second love" [xi.148].)

Rejecting Balthazar would appeal to Bel-imperia in any event, but whether she should be thought disloyal to *Don Andrea* has seemed troublesome. Conceivably she delights in some half-overt way in a mercurial reinvestment, scorning vestigially dutiful female constancy.

But her soliloquy certainly confronts her own discomfort with her
(completed) transfer of affections. (Shakespeare gives us no comparable
glimpse of Gertrude's thoughts in her interregnum.) We watch Bel-
imperia's efforts to sort out and work out of the subjection of Don
Andrea's death.

One thing is clear: she feels both abandoned and abandoning. Her
irritation with Horatio (whom she does not give leave to go) must also
channel some of (and thus displace) the larger loss of Don Andrea
(which perhaps peeked angrily forth in "carcase"). Yet a modest and
instrumental self-reproach follows, for claiming even to herself to suffer
abandonment when she has already begun to exchange the passive role
for the active, and recover the initiative quashed in Castile and Lorenzo's
intervention in the Andrea affair.[57] As she seeks to find her feet in this
new situation, Horatio's loyalty to Andrea begins to stand in for her own
(so that Andrea is not betrayed), and to authorize her new regard for
him. She begins to wish for a way to relinquish, or complete (both "close
off" and "render permanent") her sense of continuing self-commitment
to Andrea. It is at this point that the crucial notion of *revenge* first enters
the play proper, as a *perfective* form of commitment (to use the word in
its grammatical sense). Revenging Andrea is a ritual device allowing
completion, allowing Bel-imperia the same oxymoronic bonding and
releasing funereal reverence Horatio has already tenderly paid his friend
(enabling his transit to Elysium).

Such a social-psychological processing of death and desire seems
clearly at work here, but the hypothesis does not exhaust the process
analytically. Along with adjustments of erotic economy, Kyd's particular
posing of Bel-imperia's transfer of investment also produces effects for
the politics of gender and kinship. First of all, it clearly restores to Bel-
imperia the conduit of gender-political action earlier afforded by
Andrea.[58] However, it does more than enable her to return to contesting
her brother's control. It also visibly inverts Bel-imperia's own gender-
inferiority to her *lovers*, making her structurally a user instead of a
victim. In the interests of testing for anachronistic sentimentalization,
this goal seems important for a complicating sense of Bel-imperia as her
brother's sister. She is certainly a woman at war with the masculist
gender-ideology Lorenzo represents, and invested in inferior men as
erotic ends, men he views as contaminating; but she is also, at the same
time, *like* Lorenzo: quite ready to avail herself of their privileges of rank
in terms of superior irresponsibility, to subjugate and use the men she
"loves."

A situation comparable to some degree appears in Mary Tudor's
relations with her future husband, the Duke of Suffolk, Charles

Brandon, chronicled so ably by Barbara J. Harris. Henry VIII had agreed that she should wed after her wish when her first husband Louis XII died, and detailed Suffolk to negotiate the return of sister and dowry to England after that sad event. (Her love-marriage would not be allowed without this dual restoration.) While waiting for Henry to act she also had to endure the unwanted attentions of the new French king Francis I. She was riven with fears that Francis would dishonor her while they all waited, that Henry would not really allow her her love-match, and even that Suffolk, Henry's best friend, had been detailed to deliver her to Flanders to wed Charles V. Eventually she forced the issue.

> Since her brother had already agreed to their marriage verbally, she insisted, "I will have the time after my desire"; and presented the hapless duke with an ultimatum, "I put [my lord of Suffolk] in choice [whether he would] accomplish the marriage within four days, or else that he should never have enjoyed me." ... Should her worst fears prove to be correct, Mary would reveal the clandestine union to Henry [who had explicitly forbidden that they marry in France]; if all went well, she and the duke would marry publicly at her brother's court without revealing their secret.[59]

Mary claimed her love for Suffolk throughout as a romantic personal choice, but that did not stop her from subjecting her beloved to great personal risk, through something like blackmail, in order to ensure both her escape from the hateful French court or another political marriage, and her seizure of her love-match with him. A similar logic underwrites the more familiar example of the Duchess of Malfi's dangerous wooing of her steward Antonio, at once loving and forcing (so far as the coercive presence of her maid Cariola as secret witness behind the arras goes). Bel-imperia, Mary Tudor, and the Duchess all seem ready to utilize the enforcements of their status superiority to dominate as well as enjoy the men they say they love.

A second result of Kyd's carefully shaped transfer of Bel-imperia's affections also rewrites the politics of gender and kinship. The two elements of male–male affection and female transfer of affection seem to work together here, by means of a transformation for Bel-imperia's oppositely gendered purposes, of the patriarchal structure of Sedgwick's homosocial triad. The previous affection of Andrea and Horatio for each other functions to make them fit vessels for her own investments of will, releasing and channeling useful energies, both political and emotional. And the transformation may offer some site for female subjectivity here, occluded in the homosocial model, for the focus falls here on woman's desire, not man's. The core of it seems to be the allowance of prohibited affect within a triad of two men and one woman. (That is, the transformation is not an inversion, not one with two women and one man – not about misrecognizing the homoerotic, which, in a mild form, is quite apparent, perhaps enabled by one partner being dead). In the homosocial model the male–male libidinal bond is forbidden out of respect for essentialist masculine constancy, but enabled by diversion through a woman. In Bel-imperia's transposed case, libidinal bonding to each of the two men (the serial transfer of investment) is negatively sanctioned out of respect for essentialist feminine constancy (to maintain the attitudinal singleness of focus – of virginity and married chastity – most productive of patriarchal instrumentality). However, for her the double investment (excessive? retrieved from faithlessness?) of the serial transfer is enabled by undisplaced male affection between her serial lovers. She seems to be able to move from one to the other because *they* love each other: she can love both men because they both love both (each loves both her and his brother-in-arms). If the homosocial triangle generally uses women to enable cross-class bonding with socially superior men, Kyd depicts an early modern redistribution of the Sedgwick triangle's energies which resupplies and liberates female subjectivity and desire (for socially inferior men), and enables Bel-imperia to appropriate, to seize, a gender-political superior position, the "masculine" one. (One thing doesn't change: female desire is still punished.)

Whatever construction we make of the cultural logic of Bel-imperia's action, her soliloquy enacts a growing clarity of direction: she gradually figures out how to recover the initiative. Horatio's only partly conscious eroticism (coupled with his extreme deference) seems to confirm the placement of the initiative with her, here and after. The specificity of this initiative is made quite clear later, in 2.1, when Lorenzo grills Pedringano as to whom Bel-imperia loves. "She sent him letters which myself perused," Pedringano says, "Full-fraught with lines and arguments of love, / Preferring him before Prince Balthazar" (2.1.84–86). This shows not only that Horatio is the man, but that Bel-imperia's rebellious act is fully self-conscious and intentional. Why else have Bel-imperia mention Balthazar at all in these letters? She makes explicit the repudiatory force of her choice of a man of lower rank, actively *arguing* for it, presumably having to address Horatio's fears and hesitations (perhaps reasonable enough). She marks her choice to her chosen love in explicitly compara-tive terms. She does this (has to do it? against resistance?) several times, and the letters are "full-fraught," dense with argument and insistence.

We must stress once again that Bel-imperia wants not just sex, but specifically illicit sex. For (to use the vocabulary she spits on) fornication, not improper marriage, is at issue here. Her motive is not that of the Duchess of Malfi, who wants to construct a companionate marriage and children, but a destructive repudiation of her family's dynastic ideology of control. Thus she chooses as her maximal immorality (the ideological kernel of her principled action) the act of fornication, which is precisely *unredeemable*. She *hates*, I think, others' use of her sexuality, and moves to construct it as sheerly and irrevocably its own reward, that is, *her* own reward, an end in itself, rather than as leading to anything for her "friends."[60] (This is, of course, itself a use.) Marriage, on the other hand, being by definition dynastic, future-oriented, aimed, she rejects, intentionally ruining her potential for it.

The sense of calculation in Bel-imperia's loving Horatio must not only be admitted, but seems to be Kyd's point. If "love" be the end-in-itself phenomenon of earlier criticism, then this scene of transferred affection may well be unpleasant. But Kyd was not exactly trying to please here. Rather, I think the element of calculation points squarely at the use of "love" as a means to a further end (and thus can hardly be held unmotivated). This end is presented as a spiteful revenge on Balthazar for killing Andrea, but such a statement just repeats the question; her love for Andrea himself was already a revenge, as I have said, a vengeance on the familial ideology of dynastic marriage. When she spies Balthazar entering, and says "here he comes that murdered my delight" (1.4.76), she names the delightful activity of defiantly illicit and self-defining love that Don Andrea offered her, and which she is on the way to replacing.[61] She has irredeemably disabled herself for canonical patriarchal purposes, delights in it, and rages at any proposition of undoing the disabling.[62]

However, it seems unwise to deny the presence of for-itself affection between Bel-imperia and Horatio. Beyond the sheerly erotic, some further feeling seems to derive from the (unusual) fact that Andrea is never jealous of Horatio; that is, he does not feel devalued by Horatio's relation with Bel-imperia, and remains well-disposed to them throughout. Nor does she feel otherwise; compare, for instance, her outcry in captivity: "Andrea, O Andrea, that thou sawest / Me for thy friend Horatio handled thus, / And him for me thus causeless murdered" (3.9.9–11). There is then perhaps some utility in considering Bel-imperia's trinary relation with Andrea and Horatio as some kind of ideologically anti-marital analogue of the Old Testament custom of erotic fraternal duty called the *levirate*. In this custom, a younger brother is obliged to marry the wife of his deceased elder brother in order that the line of his brother be maintained; the children of the pair were to be seen as those of the dead brother.[63] (This line of reasoning was used to deflect the imputation of incest in the trinary relation of Prince Arthur, Henry VIII, and Katherine of Aragon.[64] Far from supplanting his predecessor, usurping his place with a forbidden love-object (as would be the monstrous case if the elder brother were alive), the younger brother functions as his elder's lieutenant, fulfilling familial imperatives.[65] In our case here such teamwork or shared goals may also be discerned; the intervention of death does not interrupt loyal affection but activates a strategy for continuing and reaffirming the anti-familial values it propounds. We have no record of Prince Arthur's reaction to Henry's lieutenancy, but Andrea's consistent sponsorship and approval here make this analogy at least suggest an answer for what might otherwise seem an oddly generous response from a punctilious dead Spaniard.

After abusing Balthazar for a while, Bel-imperia walks out on his petrarchan wooing, and creates another incident. The stage direction reads, "She, in going in, lets fall her glove, which Horatio, coming out, takes up" (1.4.99 s.d.). Mulryne finds the action awkward, but may we not read that she stages this little unit of theater for Balthazar, dropping the glove for Horatio to spite his superior?[66] Given the chivalric link between Bel-imperia's handkerchief (now Horatio's), her glove (now also Horatio's), and the (contrasting?) use of gloves as gages for challenge, it seems right to see this dropped glove as Bel-imperia's aggressive appropriation of the (masculine) chivalric challenge. (Shakespeare's Aumerle calls his gage "the manual seal of death" [*Richard II* 4.1.26].) Bel-imperia gives the glove to Horatio "for his pains," thus marking the move as *only* symbolic (she rewards him with the glove for picking up her glove). Balthazar observes that "Signior Horatio stooped in happy time," and Horatio replies, "I reaped more grace than I deserved or hoped" (101–03). Noting Balthazar's annoyance, Lorenzo says, "My lord, be not dismayed for what is passed" (104). He speaks with studied aristocratic hauteur, as if Horatio were not present – that is, as if he were merely a servant. Just as above with Bel-imperia, Kyd shifts us abruptly from Horatio's special private intimacy with Bel-imperia to his obtrusively inferior status.

This effect of contestatory status disjunction is further emphasized when the banquet begins, for Horatio had come in to announce this to the other two young men ("Dinner is served"?). There, while Balthazar and Lorenzo sit (as "second guest" and in his accustomed place, respectively), the king "elevates" Horatio to serve as his cupbearer: "Wait thou upon our cup, / For well thou hast deserved to be honoured" (1.4.130–31). Next a Dumb Show follows, in which three English "knights" – actually, two earls and a duke – take three Iberian kings captive, seizing their crowns. The inset spectacle purveys not only "primitive" English-audience patriotism,[67] but also the very discomfort about discrepant rank and conquests from below that strains the surface of the Spanish action. Consider too that in the Fifth Addition Hieronymo describes Lorenzo as one who "might ha' come to wear the crown of Spain" [35]. And the audience-pleasures in the shepherd Tamburlaine's even more pyrotechnic seizures of crowns date from nearly this time too.

Tensions of rank get mixed with gender tensions once Pedringano identifies Horatio in 2.1, for Balthazar's meditation on his rival specifies Bel-imperia's ideological placement too. Balthazar is glad to know "the hinderer of [his] love" (112), glad to know "on whom to be revenged" (114). He has experienced Horatio's triumph over him in battle as enslaving (123), and now he reads Bel-imperia's affair with Horatio as Horatio's doing:

> Now in his mouth he carries pleasing words,
> Which pleasing words do harbour sweet conceits,
> Which sweet conceits are limed with sly deceits,
> Which sly deceits smooth Bel-imperia's ears,
> And through her ears dive down into her heart,
> And in her heart set him where I should stand.
> Thus hath he ta'en my body by his force,
> And now by sleight would captivate my soul.... (2.1.124–31)

Horatio's eloquence has "smooth[ed] Bel-imperia's ears," overcome her supposedly rightful instincts, and displaced Balthazar. This appropriation is felt, moreover, as a homosocial violation, as if Horatio has thus acted upon Balthazar: he takes "my body" and then in strict parallel "would captivate my soul." (How much more sheerly instrumental can Bel-imperia be felt to be? The acts of her body are written *by* Horatio on *Balthazar's* consciousness.)

Lorenzo replies, "Do you but follow me and gain your love: / Her favour must be won by his remove" (135–36). To get Bel-imperia one must (just?) remove Horatio. *Her* own determining relation to the issue, her female will, is never considered here. It is the primary constituent of her perspective (which encompasses her sense of herself and Horatio's sense of her), but it is essentially invisible to the other side except as an obstacle – and only intermittently in that way, since they cannot easily see anything but masculine will as potent.[68] (In this light we must not discount one typical positionality of "Horatio our Knight Marshal's son." Stone tells us that "for a young man of gentle birth, the fastest ways of moving up the social scale were the lotteries of marriage with an heiress, Court favour, and success at the law. The first of the three is usually neglected or ignored by social historians, but it was probably the commonest method of upward movement for gentlemen."[69] The noblemen's fearful suspicions of such ambition would not be utterly groundless, though the king's niece would certainly be well out of bounds for Horatio.)

Nonetheless, it is Bel-imperia's enabling will that is primary, though it gets Horatio's own fantasy racing, as the beginning of the next scene foregrounds. By 2.2 the affair is much advanced, Horatio quite explicitly erotic.

> Now, madam, since by favour of your love,
> Our hidden smoke is turned to open flame,
> And that with looks and words we feed our thoughts
> (Two chief contents, where more cannot be had) ...   (2.2.1–4)

His eroticism is reactive ("by favour of your love"), permitted, escalated, though not yet gratified. Yet Horatio is meditative, thinking on dangers and pleasures, on the wars, on Andrea and Balthazar, his predecessor and rival (presumably unaware that Balthazar and Lorenzo are watching at this very moment).[70] Bel-imperia turns his words of war to erotic sense, moving them along firmly toward sex:

> Speak thou fair words, I'll cross them with fair words;
> Send thou sweet looks, I'll meet them with sweet looks;
> Write loving lines, I'll answer loving lines;
> Give me a kiss, I'll countercheck thy kiss ...   (2.2.34–37)

Her turn of metaphor here and in 2.4 is perfectly traditional, yet I think we should take it more literally. Bel-imperia habitually speaks to Horatio of the erotic in such terms, choosing not the traditional hunter-and-chased/chaste mode,[71] but the (equally traditional) non-hierarchical language of binary-oppositional contest. Remember Kyd's choice of a sonnet-discourse that failed to contain the female energies it sought to organize. Can the choice of contestatory language too exhibit some kind of externalization of the deeper force of sexuality for her, of hostility toward the enclosures of traditional sexual pursuit, externalizing her own pugnacity, the means of which is "loving" Horatio? Surely for someone so given to self-definition (and wildness) by erotic means the choice of erotic vocabulary, however public or traditional, will be revealing.

In this speech Bel-imperia puts herself in a reactive role, but she does the putting, instructing Horatio, encouraging his initiative, controlling his actions by extracting a male initiative that he might well be afraid, like Webster's Antonio, to employ without a sign from her. She outlines a hierarchy of interaction (words, looks, lines, kisses): three are already done; next – take physical action. Horatio takes his instruction, replying, "But gracious madam, then appoint the field / Where trial of this war shall first be made" (39–40). Horatio is still accepting orders. (Even this reactive move begets Balthazar's outraged reaction: "Ambitious villain, how his boldness grows!" [41]. Again, Balthazar must occult any element of Bel-imperia's will in the matter.) Bel-imperia plans the assignation, in Hieronymo's garden, with the hand of an experienced dealer in secrecy: "The court is dangerous, that place is safe" (44).

Such confidence is highly ironic, given that Lorenzo and Balthazar overlook the scene and plan to destroy the lovers. The right vocabulary for this procedure is probably a dramatistic one, since really what the voyeurs do is to rewrite the lines of the lovers, to textualize and edit (and cut) the script of their life together. But the play abounds with scenes where unknown superior knowledge of others constitutes a domination that fits deeply with Auden's model of the controlling joker; the metaphoric vehicle varies widely, but the core of subjection remains constant. Indeed, the play begins on such a note: Andrea thinks he possessed Bel-imperia in secret, but the affair was known by just those whom they thought to deceive (a hint of the usual smugness can still be heard in Andrea's lines).[72]

Kyd interleaves here the brief 2.3, wherein the king asks Castile in public, before the ambassador, about Bel-imperia's possible resistance, putting on the line Castile's commitment to, and capacity to enforce, the ruling ideology of dynastic marriage. Ironically, Castile repeats some of Watson's uncomfortable terms, reassuring his brother as Lorenzo did Balthazar:

> Although she coy it as becomes her kind,
> And yet dissemble that she loves the prince,
> I doubt not, I, but she will stoop in time.
> And were she froward, which she will not be,
> Yet herein shall she follow my advice,
> Which is to love him or forgo my love. (2.3.3–8)

Once again we see the categorical judgment of her actions, with its disregard of individual identity and any capacity for atypical behavior. And her father insists that she is "dissembling," that is, that she is *pretending* not to love Balthazar; both the resistance and the love are taken as if conventional. But there is in Castile's repetitions a nagging tinge of insecurity. Perhaps the king hears it, for after the ambassador leaves, he feels the need to give his brother a final and more private reiteration of advice that perfectly (and jussively) embodies their ideal assumptions:

> Now, brother, you must take some little pains
> To win fair Bel-imperia from her will:
> Young virgins must be ruled by their friends.
> The prince is amiable, and loves her well,
> If she neglect him and forgo his love,
> She both will wrong her own estate and ours. (2.3.41–46)

The king privately acknowledges the publicly unmentionable: the possible independence of Bel-imperia's will (which Castile had to recast in public as coy "dissembling"), marking his own efforts to secure what's at stake – matters of estate – and daring confidentially to name, *in camera*, the force that requires control. "Whiles I do entertain the prince / With greatest pleasure that our court affords, / Endeavour you to win your daughter's thought: / If she give back, all this will come to naught" (49–50).[73]

In 2.4. comes the climax of this plot, for here Horatio is murdered and the lead shifts to Hieronymo. The scene opens in the bower, with various trembling variations on light and darkness, first the lovers' traditional welcoming of the night, in which "pleasures may be done" (2.4.3), replete with the usual bipolar ironies. Night, darkness, and evil are traditionally linked; but so are night, bedtime, and love, as in Spenser's *Epithalamion*: "Now welcome night, thou night so long expected ... Spread thy broad wing over my love and me, / that no man may us see, / And in thy sable mantle us enwrap, / From feare of perrill and foule horror free."[74] We also may hear insecurity within delight in Horatio's presumption that the enclosed bower is safe (5), in the irrational flutterings of Bel-imperia's "fainting heart" (7), in Horatio's immediate suspicion of Pedringano (8), in Bel-imperia's misplaced trust (9), and finally in the danger brought by Pedringano when he brings the match to light for Lorenzo.[75]

But very soon Bel-imperia turns her thoughts to love, and suggests they sit, "for pleasure asketh ease" (23). Then begins the famous couplet stichomythia, music for coupling (though the rhymes are self-enclosed, rather than interlaced between the lovers, as perhaps fits for these two).[76] Bel-imperia speaks again of wars, echoing her earlier language, and cues Horatio to begin physical contact: "If I be Venus, thou must needs be Mars, / And where Mars reigneth, there must needs be wars" (34–35). He takes her hand ("Then thus begin our wars"), and she instantly escalates, commanding him to test her strength: "Set forth thy foot to try the push of mine" (38). And so they progress along this challenge ladder, by combative looks, darted kisses, struggling embraces, to their final shared couplets.

> BEL-IMPERIA O let me go, for in my troubled eyes
> Now may'st thou read that life in passion dies.
> HORATIO O stay a while and I will die with thee,
> So shalt thou yield and yet have conquered me.   (46–49)

Perhaps the resistant "O let me go" is meant as a heating figure of the chase, perhaps as a "real" hesitation, Bel-imperia resisting even at the heart of giving herself. For we surely have all the ironies of *dying*, first among them the suggestion that this is the verge of literal intercourse, given "elms by vines are compassed till they *fall*" (45; my emphasis): twining and falling at once – to the ground? On the bench? Horizontal, anyway.

It is at just this moment of penetration that the trusted murderers burst into the garden. This horrific primal scene is subjected to the penetrating gaze of excluded have-not child (Lorenzo as jealous oedipal sibling), Balthazar as sponsored voyeur, and Pedringano the recreant servant-guardian. It prefigures Hamlet's witnessed boudoir scene with Gertrude, and Iago's "Would you, the supervisor, grossly gape on? / Behold her topped?" (3.3.392–93). Indeed, in a certain sense Bel-imperia herself is looking on all along at her spectacular gesture of defiance, from an internal distantiation. It thus makes sense that she would hear the murderers first, as the more watchful, the less engaged, playing a role addressed to an absent audience: "Who's there? Pedringano! We are betrayed!" (50).

When that audience suddenly forces an entry (in costume, disguised, as players) Bel-imperia's autonomous revels are ended. Specular rape becomes physical violation, forcing divorce. Lorenzo never addresses his sister, but hands her over like a prop to Balthazar for silencing and concealment. He reserves his words for Horatio, who is shocked to incomprehension, unmanned;[77] Lorenzo rewrites Horatio's part for him, explaining its new meaning with earnest patient sarcasm. "O sir, forbear, your valour is already tried" (52), he says. Such ironic quieting of Horatio's struggles, so olympian and bitter, is meant as the most total castration. The active violence is left to Lorenzo's thugs (invoked with the deferent "my masters"), who hang and stab Horatio in the arbor. Once again the harvest of summer joys is cut off. As Lorenzo puts it, while Horatio is stabbed, "These are the fruits of love" (2.4.55).[78]

Such harvest is ironic, of course, for Horatio, but more literal for Lorenzo and Balthazar. The latter seizes his desired Bel-imperia (for a time, anyway).[79] The former's specular triumph, proved on Horatio's mockingly elevated body, is much more conspicuous, seeming to bring to climax the energies of his endless self-withholding voyeurism (and to prefigure the much more explicit desires of his descendent, Webster's Ferdinand).[80] Kenneth Burke observes, writing of Krafft-Ebing, that "stories of lynchings make clear to us the hierarchic motive in fantasies and acts of sexual violence."[81] Though reversing the sexual and hierarchical terms (always dialectically entwined in Burke), this story of frontier justice likewise binds together sex, violence, and hierarchy, thrice over. First, it destroys the potent self-creative sexual seizure of will and autonomy that Lorenzo and Balthazar impute, only partly accurately, to

Horatio. And in castrating him, it likewise maims the truer referent, *Bel-imperia's* phallus. Recall Balthazar, upon learning of Horatio's "designs" on Bel-imperia: "Thus hath he ta'en my body by his force, / And now by sleight would captivate my soul (2.1.130–31). If Horatio conquered Balthazar's body in the field and his soul in Bel-imperia's body, the royals now conquer *her* soul – her willful desire, her phallus – in *Horatio's* body. Finally offending the eye, the member is cast out.[82] Finally, of course, when Horatio's strange fruit is finally plucked, Lorenzo's own sadistic pleasure springs, mandrake-like, from the arborial gibbet. Seizure achieves its full notable doubleness, both grasping and thrilling.

Perhaps we can also read the murder as an originary image of the machiavel as puppeteer, at once pulling the strings that control the lives of those who imagine they can become real people, and (like Fate) cutting them.[83] For this is, it seems to me, the inaugural Renaissance deployment of Auden's practical-joke notion, devised for Iago but so fitting for Lorenzo. The destruction of ambitious inferiors reaffirms the insecure superior's potency. Note too the layered emphasis in the fact that Lorenzo the puppet-master does his tricks effortlessly, with no hands, using agents who are thus themselves his puppets to hang up another one – and who both die puppets' deaths in their turn.[84] Nowhere is Auden's vocabulary so appropriate as in Lorenzo's crowing caption: "Although [Horatio's] life were still ambitious proud, / Yet is he at the highest now he is dead" (60–61).[85]

Horatio's new heights thus mockingly combine a remarkable density of reference: the ecstasy of erotic erection;[86] literal death substituting for its erotic metaphor; isolate erection displacing the transcendent companionate bonding with Bel-imperia; the hanged man's resultant fruitless ejaculation, the autonomous phallus evacuated; the degradation of death by hanging for a gentleman; physical elevation mockingly substituted for its social equivalent; and the final merest inert motion, of the dangling dead body, displacing the culmination of Horatio's multiple actions of achievement in love and war.[87]

And once again, in eerie echo, Bel-imperia participates. For when she is ignored and Horatio blamed as we have seen, she responds with infuriated passionate activity. "O save his life and let me die for him! / O save him, brother, save him, Balthazar: / I loved Horatio, but he loved not me" (56–58). She struggles still to play the man's part in the action, to seize the initiative, to take responsibility. In pleading that he be saved she emphasizes his passiveness, and finally denies him even to have willed his participation at all: "I loved Horatio, but he loved not me." *Her* will was active, not his.[88] Balthazar places her proposition perfectly in replying, "But Balthazar loves Bel-imperia," not a non-sequitur irrelevancy but a reminder that what counts is *his* will (male, if designated), not hers. When she screams for help, finally perhaps turning in desperation to "women's tools," reduced to an impotent order she has fought to deny, they silence her: they "stop her mouth," plugging the ideological leak, as befits one who has been neither chaste, silent, nor obedient, and bundle her away to concealing disciplinary enclosure. Perhaps, indeed, the stoppering is even more repulsive, if Balthazar "stops her mouth" with a kiss.

III

With Bel-imperia's sequestration Kyd largely fulfills his examination of sexual coercion in the dual context of rank and gender; the rest of the play is concerned with structurally similar subjections and controllings – of servants (Pedringano), of villains or victimizers (Bel-imperia and Hieronymo's retributive inset play), and of humans somewhat more generally (the extruded Frame). In each range rank and gender remain relevant, and the practical-joke maneuver is ramified. However, we need now to turn our attention to another zone: the differential modes of self-constructing status relations (of both alliance and conflict) between Lorenzo as aristocrat and Pedringano as ungentle servant. This is a very different (though complexly analogous) matter from the frictions explored within the ruling elite, between noble and gentle, Lorenzo and Horatio and Bel-imperia. Afterward I will attend more briefly to the doubly theatricalized subjugations of Hieronymo's control of Lorenzo, and the Framing control (Andrea's? Revenge's? Proserpine's?) of the entire matrix of actions.

When Lorenzo interrogates Pedringano in 2.1, forcing him actively to betray his mistress Bel-imperia and reveal Horatio's identity, he reminds his sister's servant how he protected him from their father's wrath:

> ... it is not long thou know'st,
> Since I did shield thee from my father's wrath,
> For thy conveyance in Andrea's love,
> For which thou wert adjudged to punishment.
> I stood betwixt thee and thy punishment;
> And since, thou know'st how I have favoured thee.   (2.1.45–50)

Lorenzo presents these events as imposing obligation, but Pedringano resists as best he can the threats and blandishments that follow. This resistance, Lorenzo's continuing suspicions about his loyalty to Bel-imperia, and the fact itself of what he possessed to betray, suggest an unusual cross-gender bond of service between Pedringano and Bel-imperia. The capacity for such bonding, however finite, may imply something about how hard it might be for Pedringano to so disconnect himself despite the incentives Lorenzo provides. The *locus classicus* for such master-servant bonding is found in *King Lear*, in the case of Kent, whose bond to Lear does not allow of cessation, even in the face of Lear's attempt to disown and banish him, the strongest moves the culture provided short of death (and even that does not dissuade Kent at play's end).[89] The relevant point of tangency between the plays grows from Kent's *irrevocable* relationality with Lear: without his master he is not himself, nearly nothing (as perhaps can be seen from his invisible namedness after the banishment, as Caius, a nearly literally useless name). Master and servant are inseparable, even unto death. Pedringano departs greatly from this model of self-defining bonding, giving himself over to betrayal, and following Lorenzo's example as best he can. What is interesting is how much it hurts him to do it.

The first time we meet Pedringano Lorenzo is bribing him with "lands and living joined with dignities" (2.1.53), a profoundly alluring cultural fantasy. Lorenzo offers freedom from servitude: lands confer rents, and the possessor could cease to be one who had to labor in the received, manual, base sense at all.[90] This had been the basic dream of every courtly aspirant since the dissolution of the monasteries in the 1530s, when the land market became so much more fluid, and many a "new" man achieved access to a hitherto limited landowning elite. Now, though this project was experienced as a kind of liberation, one would continue (indeed, become more enmeshed) in the network of the very bonds that the transfers of land and debt themselves afforded and imposed. But to any unlanded aspirant from below the line, acquiring what Lorenzo offers would have made life seem to open out into a whole new realm of opportunity and possibility. The potency of the fantasy is made clear by Pedringano's acceptance precisely in spite of conspicuous misgivings. (One set of these, in fact, can be seen in Lorenzo's presumption of their existence, as he shows in repeating his promises of reward, and comparing them to Bel-imperia's: "Thou know'st that I can more advance thy state / Than she" [2.1.103–4]. See also the similar structure of his threat at 2.1.70: "Thou diest for more esteeming her than me.") Lorenzo's threats are fearful, his lures intense. Pedringano is turned.

The results are immediate, and drastic. In 2.4 his services escalate from go-between and watch-dog to assassin. He begins 3.2 with explicit upstart cheek, sarcastically initiating Hieronymo's superior greeting "Now, Pedringano!": "Now, Hieronymo!" (53). Soon Pedringano and his master are planning the murder of Serberine, who did not, so far as we know, reveal the murder of Horatio. (As we see it, knowledge of the murder results from Bel-imperia's letter in red ink.) The details of these actions show Lorenzo carefully configuring Pedringano's self-concept as his lord's bonded intimate, in such a way as both to offer the immediate experience of social elevation (however generally secret: the lands and livings recede "for the duration") and to subject him further to the status of unconscious and unresistant tool.

Pedringano cannot see how Serberine could be guilty, given factors of time and alibi, but Lorenzo dismisses such details:

> Admit he have not, his condition's such,
> As fear or flattering words may make him false.
> I know his humour, and therewith repent
> That e'er I used him.... (3.2.74–77)

The resemblance to the way Lorenzo extracted Horatio's name from Pedringano himself in 2.1 could not be more evident, but Lorenzo manages the data so that Pedringano does not see the parallel, instead feeling himself allied by epistemological status with Lorenzo, seeing into Serberine's "condition" but right past himself.

> But Pedringano, to prevent the worst,
> And 'cause I know thee secret as my soul,
> Here, for thy further satisfaction, take thou this,
> *Gives him more gold*
> And hearken unto me. Thus it is devised:
> This night thou must [murder him] ...
> When things shall alter, as I hope they will,
> Then shalt thou mount for this: thou know'st my mind. (3.2.78–82, 92–93)

The pressures Lorenzo deploys here are such as later machiavels will find luscious cause for self-congratulation. He induces a crisis mentality in "to prevent the worst," and followed with a congratulation dense with allure and irony: "'cause I know thee secret as my soul." The layers in this phrase of "I know you [the familiar "thee"] deeply," "I trust you," and "I know and trust you as I would myself," or "as being like my inmost secret self" all draw Pedringano into Lorenzo's net of intimacy.[91] These meanings combine readily with Lorenzo's "I know [Serberine's] humour" (76), said despite, indeed in contempt of, any evidence. Such paraded penetration, deep knowledge, functions both as authorization, the magic source of unquestioned confidence in the expert, and as a sharing of secrets that effects a bonding superiority.

The final brick, after "I know him" and "I know you" is Lorenzo's stunning "Thou know'st my mind." Lorenzo occupies the classic power-posture of the voyeur, knowing without being known, yet he secures this position by the assurance of intimacy. How does this trope of fictional trust work? The puppeteer-voyeur, who in fact makes himself by making sure he sees and knows without being seen and known, *insists on the sense of being known*. His false self-revelations function as guarantees of intimacy and trust; he insists that he *is* known in order to stimulate the confidence and pliancy (the fruits of teamwork) that such knowledge is supposed to guarantee. He withholds the self and seizes power by lying about giving the self and thus embracing the vulnerability that comes with such self-gift. The vulnerability is presumed to confer power and status, to make the recipient into a (similar) superior. The tool is made a tool by offering him trust, giving him the illusory autonomy of secret knowledge and power over oneself; when the high-ranking Lorenzo condescends to (seem to) trust a man like Pedringano, he enables Pedringano to feel himself now (finally!) known for what he really is, a mate of princes. That is, he voices the inferior aspirant's strongest dream – of being known by men like Lorenzo as some kind of equal.[92] Thus Lorenzo forges bonds – and fetters.[93] (The analogy here with Belimperia's relations with her lovers is quite elaborate.)

When Pedringano departs to kill Serberine, Lorenzo arranges to have him caught in the act, and then pauses, having tied up these knots, musing with his bosom about how things must go. After having Lorenzo arrange the conditions of Pedringano's identity for him, Kyd turns him to configuring his own, for us. He thinks of himself as one of a collective category ("Thus must *we* work ... Thus must *we* practise" – 105,106; my emphasis) of "supervisors," as Iago called Othello [3.3.411], whose entitlement places them beyond judgment.

> As for myself, I know my secret fault;
> And so do they, but I have dealt for them.
> They that for coin their souls endangered,
> To save my life, for coin shall venture theirs:
> And better it's that base companions die,
> Than by their life to hazard our good haps.
> Nor shall they live, for me to fear their faith:
> I'll trust myself, myself shall be my friend,
> For die they shall, slaves are ordained to no other end.   (3.2.111–19)

He knows himself, and is known, since the employer of agents is necessarily vulnerable to them (though not so far as he leads them to believe); but he will soon become unknown again, pinching off blossoms of relation and standing alone in isolate power. And since he was able to buy them, they are thus shown to be merely purchasable, and thus disposable. If they can be bought, they are hardly people. They come not near his conscience. Servants, rightly used, are slaves, ordained for use.[94]

Thus enslaved, Pedringano faces his second suborned murder (of his friend, according to Balthazar at 3.4.28) both hungry and sweating with fear, unable to be as sure of himself as Lorenzo is; he spends fifteen lines in 3.3 in self-challenge and reassurance and denial, never mentioning his friend Serberine.

> Now, Pedringano, bid thy pistol hold,
> And hold on, Fortune! once more favour me;
> Give but success to mine attempting spirit,
> And let me shift for taking of mine aim!
> Here is the gold, this is the gold proposed:
> It is no dream that I adventure for,
> But Pedringano is possessed thereof.
> And he that would not strain his conscience
> For him that thus his liberal purse hath stretched,
> Unworthy such a favour may he fail,
> And wishing, want, when such as I prevail.
> As for the fear of apprehension,
> I know, if need should be, my noble lord
> Will stand between me and ensuing harms;
> Besides, this place is free from all suspect.   (3.3.1–15)

This self-address intones a non-internalized confidence, a self-encouragement that shows its own lack, rather than the admiring (or manic) mirror-distance of a Tamburlaine. Yet Pedringano has already at least partly internalized the sense of opportunity: is the "once more" a reference to the murder of Horatio, itself a piece of "good fortune" in placing Pedringano in Lorenzo's view and service? Or was his good fortune the time when Lorenzo saved him from punishment by Castile? In any case, he insists to himself that he is now an "attempting spirit": ambition establishes identity. Thus confident, he commands Fortune: "reward my spirit and leave the rest to me." (And is there a pun on "mine aim" and "my name" – self-substantiations both?) Yet doubt remains, for he must remind himself of the gold in his hand, the ocular proof: it is no dream, but material, real – and exactly as such, nearly magical, capable of dismissing, occulting, relieving him of the other, frightful reality of murdering Serberine. He must pile up reasons for doing this fearful thing, not only material ones but self-scorn too. Note too the strange relation between money and conscience, each as it were internalized from Lorenzo, and re-externalized in himself. Pedringano imagines himself a patron like Lorenzo (likewise part of a category: "such as I" [11]), and sternly invokes the criterion he has himself just decided to satisfy. The fantasized self-relocation upward seems to authorize him from above, future self approving the actions of present self in order to bring that future to pass. He honors himself (by potentially shaming himself) instrumentally in both positions.

Yet still he fears failure and capture: but if that happens, he "knows"
Lorenzo will protect him as (and since) he did so once before. Besides
(yet another self-reassurance), this place is free from all suspect, like
Hieronymo's bower – a similarly unwise confidence immediately con-
futed by the Watch's unseen arrival, straight from Lorenzo (another
bitter joke). Anticipating Macbeth, Pedringano screws his courage one
final notch, calls upon himself to "play the man" (29),[95] and shoots the
dag. When taken by the watch, he swears with fury by the sorrows of the
souls in hell that he'll fight: a raging and anguished reference to his own
feared fate, unknowingly completing a circuit to Andrea, Revenge, and
the layered inset planes of invisible puppeteers from Revenge to Lorenzo
to the Watch to Pedringano to Serberine and on to Bel-imperia and
Horatio themselves at the center of subjection.

Yet still, with something of the helplessness of childhood petulance, he
says he killed Serberine "because he walked abroad so late" (40).[96] This
reply, frightened and smug at once, shows us Pedringano struggling to be
Lorenzo, unmoved and untouchable, yet stripped to nothing but braying
in his moment of cruel exposure: "Hieronymo? carry me before whom
you will, / Whate'er he be I'll answer him and you. / And do your worst,
for I defy you all" (46–48). No audience ("anybody you like") can
frighten him, no one can see into him, understand him, and thus control
him, for he is guaranteed against the fruit of detection, public revelation,
by Lorenzo. The "carry me before" moment is a moment of terrible
exposure: it transforms the powerful secret interiority of intimacy with
Lorenzo into a latent nakedness, suddenly at risk. Hieronymo now
appears as the interrogator, who unwraps, lays naked, dominates like the
voyeur, visible but himself inscrutable, while probing, understanding,
controlling the patient tied down and etherized. Suddenly the drama is
one of agents and patients, and Pedringano keeps losing his grip as an
agent. He can maintain the effect of secrecy (invulnerability), he believes
and hopes, because no matter what is found out his secret knowledge will
save him, knowledge that Lorenzo will arrive from above the logic of the
capture and interrogation, *deus ex machina*, and lift him out of the net.
He answers to a higher court than this one, or so he hopes.

In 3.4 comes the news of Pedringano's arrest. (Note how even –
though this too becomes a convention – Lorenzo's *page* plays the
puppeteer, giving yet withholding the news of Pedringano's arrest,
jerking both Lorenzo and Balthazar on strings: "who murdered him?" –
"He that is apprehended for the fact" [23–24]). Lorenzo sets up the
silencing plot with the pardon-box, first setting Balthazar on to "exas-
perate and hasten his revenge" (3.4.31). We now learn that Serberine was

Balthazar's servant (21 – lent, or planted, by Lorenzo?), and that Balthazar knew him as one "that loved his lord so well" (27 – is this lord Lorenzo, or Balthazar?). To Balthazar Pedringano is "murderer of his friend" (28), the deed a "damned deed" (37). Lorenzo's plot contains plenty of detail allowing him to incense (that is, manipulate) his confederate Balthazar, who takes Pedringano's betrayal personally, as doubly immoral (betraying my servant and his own friend). Others' sincere emotions, heightened, are Lorenzo's tools.[97] Lorenzo distances himself once again, and quite self-consciously:

> ... thus experience bids the wise to deal ...
> Thus hopeful men, that mean to hold their own,
> Must look like fowlers to their dearest friends. ...
> 'Tis hard to trust unto a multitude,
> Or anyone, in mine opinion,
> When men themselves their secrets will reveal.   (39, 43–44, 47–49)

As above, he says "Let me alone" (3.2.88), seizing all power to himself, banishing vulnerability, even that of trusting his rank and faction ally Balthazar.[98]

Lorenzo replies to Pedringano's letter from prison with the ominously reassuring "Tell him I have his letters, know his mind" (3.4.57), and sets in motion the box-plot, telling himself, "This works like wax; yet once more try thy wits" (60). Such reflexive congratulation will become the trademark of the stage machiavel, and though there are predecessors for Lorenzo (such as Ambidexter in *Cambyses*) who use such self-address, he is much the most sophisticated and instructive specimen yet written. Indeed, insofar as such gloating is self-construction, it may be that the simile is drawn from the use of seal-rings, the unquestionable sign of identity, especially in view of the final line of the speech – "He shall not want while Don Lorenzo lives" (75) – supposedly putting his name and honor on the line. (Another false sharing of authenticity, this time with the page.)

Lorenzo sends money too, knowing how Pedringano's epistemology of self-trust works (see 3.3.6), bidding the page to convey it in secret and to bid Pedringano be secret, though "merry" and "boldly ... resolved" (64, 68). The emphasis on secrecy might be thought to convey to Pedringano a sense of weakness, since it implies that revelation might mar all; but I think it combines with the postured merriment and boldness to reinforce Pedringano's sense of sharing with Lorenzo the knowing practical joker's placement, above and beyond the sight of his captors.[99] Such secret intimate "empowerment" once again controls Pedringano, oxymoronically killing him just as Horatio fell in rising, at the end of enough rope.

When the page looks in the box and finds it empty, we have perhaps the purest practical joke in the play, leading as it does to a nearly literal pratfall. But the boy risks his life (see 3.4.73), and peeks, explaining that "we men's-kind in our minority are like women in their uncertainty: that they are most forbidden, they will soonest attempt" (3.5.3–5). The reflection on Bel-imperia is obvious, but in addition the idea foregrounds a by-product of the fetish of secrecy: the complementary fetish of penetration, discovery, smug knowledge. Indeed, here is perhaps another, equally rich, account of the schizoid insecure practical joker and all-knowing machiavel: secrecy deprives another of what might be called usual self-knowledge, to be the sole possessor of which confers a mantle of expertise or mastery. A practical joke may be seen as an arranged zero-sum game of knowledge, opening up a gap between equals. This pattern echoes the marxist account of capitalism's artificial satisfaction of artificial needs: Lorenzo's generation of artificial ignorance allows a grim reaping of manufactured artificial superiority.

Kyd manages one other effect here. When the boy peeks, he becomes a visible joker for us to watch. Auden believed that the joker must above all desire to reveal himself to his victim, but Lorenzo does not do so here.[100] Kyd delegates this role to the page, thus imposing on us the aesthetic "satisfaction" of watching Pedringano's final discomfiture unfold aesthetically before a surrogate perpetrator (the page himself scripts it for us in his soliloquy in 3.5), as the hit-man flouts, scorns, descants, and otherwise indecorously "jest[s] himself to death" (3.5.17). But Lorenzo himself never shows, and indeed, nor does the page: there is no textual sign that the box ever opens. *We* know, but the dead man, perhaps like Don Andrea, dies innocent of his betrayal, if of nothing else, with only one jolt of unconfident fear at l. 84, soon ignored. His ignorance allies us in our unseen knowing distance with Lorenzo in a formal state of what may be called "aesthesia." Indeed, perhaps we enjoy it more than Lorenzo does; after all, we watch it.[101]

Pedringano's life and death, then, begin a form in Renaissance drama: the examination from within of the experience of alliance between ambitious young men from the subject classes and noblemen such as Lorenzo – that is to say, of probably the predominant experience of social mobility toward the ruling elite. Like Bel-imperia in a central way, Pedringano dreams of a mimetic future in which he may occupy the site of Lorenzo's power and privilege. Instead he is occupied, discursively possessed, and then cast aside, not as dressed in borrowed robes, but as the robes themselves. Of course, he sought power and identity by employment, self-gift, commitment; Bel-imperia more deviously, by self-theft. Self-stealing, she is locked up. Being bought, he was sold out.[102]

IV

Hieronymo's seizure of control as revenger has been much handled in other analyses. I will only glance at it, to link it with other manipulations of will already examined. He rises into view upon Horatio's death, reacting to it and opting for secrecy and silence in 2.5; he grieves, questions the heavens, and distrusts Bel-imperia's red letter in 3.2; judges Pedringano in 3.6; beats at heaven's windows and then reads Pedringano's dead letter in 3.7; rages madly in 3.11, 3.12, and 3.13, meditating justice and revenge; and is officially and falsely reconciled to Lorenzo in 3.14.

In 3.13 he commences the final action, an artful and judicious seizure of control from Lorenzo (the puppeteer strung up), when he speaks of pursuing his revenge "not as the vulgar wits of men, ... As by a secret, yet a certain mean, / Which under kindship will be cloaked best" (21–24). Here begins for the drama the endlessly developed Elizabethan and Jacobean concern with the aestheticizing of revenge. Hieronymo will not be vulgar and blunt, but clever and artful, seizing Lorenzo's tools of secrecy and "kindship" and hoisting him up as he did Horatio, as Hamlet will Rosencrantz and Guildenstern. And indeed, his action here may be the seed of Hamlet's hated nightmare of dramatistic subjection by Claudius, of being known without knowing, being uncomprehendingly written and scripted – being the butt of an extended practical joke. In Hamlet's play, of course, the play within is a means of discovery, not revenge, final reckoning left to a dramatistic providence and others' plots. In *The Spanish Tragedy* the order is the opposite. Hieronymo leaves (or attributes) his discovery to a dramatistic providence (not "Bel-imperia drops a letter," but "A letter falleth," with the disembodied voice-over "Red ink"), and seizes his revenge by means of a cryptic script, the originary play-within-the play, itself an archaic ur-text he exhumes and uses for his modern purpose – as Hamlet and Shakespeare each did.[103]

The final act is introduced by a dumb show, meant for the Frame inhabitants alone, and further obscured in that no descriptive stage-directions are preserved for us. Revenge tells us it will aid in imagining "What 'tis to be subject to destiny" (3.15.28), and that it stars a Hymen, bloody and dressed in black, quenching nuptial torches.[104] Andrea says he "will sit to see the rest"; "Then argue not," replies testy Revenge, impatient at the other's expectation of understanding (39, 40). Andrea and Revenge are perhaps not the only avid spectators, however, for when Hieronymo finds that Bel-imperia is with him, he says, "Why then, I see that heaven applies our drift / And all the saints do sit

soliciting / For vengeance on those cursed murderers" (4.1.32–34).
Hieronymo is ready to entertain everyone, apparently, and happily
agrees to refurbish his old student play, which he happens to have to
hand, for the Spanish court, if they will play their parts.[105] Balthazar
bridles at the prospect of such indignity, but Hieronymo reminds them
that "Nero thought it no disparagement" (4.1.87), and they begin their
final theatricalized descent under the encouraging Roman sign of that
incestuous and artful precedent.

The actual production in all manner of ways enacts Hieronymo's
puppeteer purposes. He casts Balthazar as Soliman the Turk, outlandish
invader; Lorenzo as Erastus, the Knight of Rhodes (which means he
seeks to marry his own sister); now-silent Bel-imperia as "Perseda, chaste
and resolute" (140). (She is to dress like Flora or Diana, fecund or chaste
as you like, but surely mistress of death's winter come once again.) The
script is to be in four languages, a Babel that will fall when Hieronymo
rolls up the script, in the meantime "breed[ing] the more variety"
(4.1.174), as Bel-imperia's actions have done. And at the end Hieronymo
will, "with a strange and wondrous show ... That [he] will have there
behind a curtain," finally "make the matter known" (185–87), promising
to explain with a silent emblem what the final meaning is.

With only a pause for Isabella to kill both the arbor and herself,[106] as
prologue, as it were, the play begins, and moves through its expected
deaths without incident. Everyone's children are killed, Hieronymo
unveils dead Horatio, and cries, "Behold!" All lines are stopped, familial,
dramatic, and verbal; all that remains is for Hieronymo to bite out his
tongue, which he does with alacrity and great promise, if to no clear
practical purpose (since he has revealed all at length). Surely thus he bites
the thumb, sticks out the tongue, extends the finger. Symbolically, as
Jonas Barish has movingly argued, the act "betrays the final despair at the
uselessness of talk, the berserk resolve to have done with language
forever."[107] Like Tamburlaine, Hieronymo might be saying, "I have
said." Perhaps also he means both to reveal all, as Auden means the joker
to do for maximal spite, and yet also magically to leave his victim-audience
with the equally painful sense that there is an explanation they want but
can never have, that is forever beyond their reach.[108] (This severed
member surely provides the germ of Iago's final sadistic stroke: "what you
know, you know." And more distantly, perhaps, the stage audience's
experience of Hamlet's "the rest is silence"? Perhaps it even eventually
begets the unknown referent of Lear's "Look there! Look there!" Explanation is characteristically desired, offered, withheld, obscured, again and
again at such moments. Kyd seems to have prefigured Shakespeare in this
too, as in so many other characteristically Shakespearean matters.)[109]

Now Andrea alone is left to tell the tale, and play Shakespeare's Horatio. No flights of angels supervene, but instead the utterly unchristian voice from Hades, rejoicing with delight in enemies' deaths, rewarding friends. Andrea, like a child at a party, cries, "let me be judge" (4.5.30), and consigns all the dead royalty save Bel-imperia to various hellish ends, an almost miscellaneous effect closing with Pedringano's living death "Blaspheming gods and all their holy names" (44). For many strong readers, things now seem clear enough. Philip Edwards, very dark, rests in the clarity that it is "the infernal gods who are running things,"[110] and certainly there is great and satisfying caustic force, worthy of Marlowe, in the depiction of a world of people, even Spaniards, who believe they inhabit a Christian cosmos, and learn better. G. K. Hunter summarizes this view:

> ... the human beings who appear in Andrea's dream – the characters of the play, scheming, complaining, and hoping – are not to be taken by the audience as the independent and self-willed individuals they suppose themselves to be, but in fact only as the puppets of a predetermined and omnicompetent justice that they (the characters) cannot see and never really understand. But we (watching the whole stage) must never lose sight of this piece of knowledge.[111]

This seems right and finely said to me, especially as it chimes with Lorenzo's habits. However, it omits one compelling aspect of the play, conspicuous in the final supernatural scene. There the supposed end-all result seems, to my ear at least, to combine uneasily an air of final solutions with the sheerest dottiness. Don Andrea's apportionments seem less a revelation of justice than a furtherance of on-stage life by other means: not a final construction of a consoling ground of being, not even some kind of opiate vision, but a clowning nightmare. The general effect, it seems to me, is one of *extrusion*: the play proper eventually gives rise, as of a prior necessity, to an externalized transcendental embodiment of its own ruling passion, for frantic and willful yet uncontrolled and often inexplicable action. Over and over we have seen "data" held out for us as satisfying and determining of the lunges and shocks and batterings that mark the play, looking for all the world like explanations, and yet failing to explain. Shakespeare will work some of this territory in deciding not to have his Ghost reappear at the end of *Hamlet*, leaving us unmoored; Kyd gives us the ghost, all right, but no confidence. Of course, perhaps such weary doubt is an artifact of an analysis that ignores Hieronymo and seeks only to comprehend the almost Brownian motions that pose and repose the problem he tries to solve. It is a familiar view that the early materials get lost, perhaps well lost, in Hieronymo's later struggles. But the motions there are not really random: they are structured by and structure the multiple contradictory human social will as Kyd saw it at work. Even to name Bel-imperia and Lorenzo and Pedringano names the binary of puppeteer and paranoiac, exhibits Kyd's grasp of the interlocked fetishes of control and denial, rupture and seizure and gift – so typifying Kyd's "bitter times and privie broken passions."[112]

Arden of Faversham is a history play. It situates various local seizures – of land, of wife, of life, of self – in the aftermath of Henry VIII's seizure of the monasteries in the 1530s. These struggles have much to teach us about the cultural phenomenology of desire released and distributed by that founding act so paradoxically called the Dissolution. Its many catalytic effects – economic, social, ideological – precipitated a great deal of new social meaning. *Arden of Faversham* seems to me a direct dramatic study of the fruits of the Dissolution. The play's interrogations of hypertrophies of the will, so nourished by the newly unbound land market, involve three groups of characters, situated in unusually full social detail.

The principal group enacts a social struggle in the terrain of sexuality. Arden, leading grasping landowner of Faversham and direct beneficiary of the Dissolution (as the play's first lines make explicit), has married gentle Alice – possibly at her family's wish, to block her improper passion for Mosby, a rising servant. Chafing under this arrangement, Alice and Mosby continue or resume or begin their clandestine relations, decide to murder Arden, and eventually carry out their will.

For help with this project, the lovers turn to two different groups of subplot servants. In the first, Mosby's sister Susan is Alice's maid, sought in marriage by two rivals: Arden's loyal personal servant Michael and Clarke, a journeyman painter and technical expert. As family head, Mosby is the proprietor of his sister's sexuality, and offers to sell it to the most useful suitor. Meanwhile, the lovers also hire two funny and brutal thugs, Black Will and Shakebag, for the hands-on dirty work of the second subplot. For these vagrant men such work is an enormous opportunity; this fact makes visible its precondition of deprivation or placelessness, itself founded in turn on what we might call a concept of *home*.

The *Arden* author's profound exploration of such placelessness extends into various zones of negation many issues seen in the fluid ambitions of Andrea and Horatio and Pedringano. *Arden of Faversham* relocates the locus of need and ambition well down the social scale. This dilation exhibits the rippling effects of the changed land market on men and women whose relation to land and its status effects has been very different from Hieronymo and Horatio's, whose gentry is distant from most of the characters of this play both in its clarity and its urban courtly setting. Such status may have been achieved through legal and martial merit, but its effectivity is so unquestioned as to approach the ascribed or doxic – save in the extremely unusual situation of sexual relations with the blood royal. Only by such measures do they seem low or marginal. Pedringano is a transitional unendowed figure, enticeable (and enticed to court) by the fantasy of "lands and livings."

The comparable men and women of *Arden of Faversham* are a good deal more varied. The principals (Arden, Alice, and Mosby), much like those of *The Spanish Tragedy*, are currently gentle, though aspersions regarding this currency are continual, and Mosby is perhaps of particularly lower origin (if his enemy Arden is to be trusted on this point, which is unwise). Of the servants there is much more to be said. First of all, there are a great many of them, compared only to Pedringano and the shadowy Serberine. Their numbers keep them at the center of the play's concerns, and thicken their issues well beyond the privacies and instrumentalities of Pedringano.[1] Their relations to landed status are at best those of tenants, artisans, and domestic dependents, whose desires keep them at home, in market town or country, dreaming of farm, freehold, and decent middling marriage.

At the lowest reach of the play Black Will and Shakebag occupy the "free" (that is, abandoned or lost) state of active vagrancy, not only landless (which nearly everyone was) but homeless, immorally and illegally so, thus "shiftless," as our American southern idiom has it. The term gets used by "decent folk" to condemn the morally squalid or amoral condition of undisciplined propertylessness, but presents a somewhat different sense to the ear of those familiar with early modern English. There, the *OED* tells us, a *shift* suggests "an expedient" (sb. III.3), a "means of effecting an end" (sb. III.3b), a "stratagem" (sb. III.4). A man without "shifts," without capacities, is helpless, in shameful pain, at least potentially desperate. *OED* cites mild animals, the sheep and "the selie simple shiftlesse Bee," for this lack – though the bee has its sting for desperate measures, as do some poor men.[2] For such men ambition is driven not by desire but by need, not by pleasure but by pain. Furthermore, these lowest men barely have a place even in Faversham, and turn to the fluxing territories of London's urban underworld and the Netherlands battlefields, without ever, like Pedringano, getting anywhere near the court or the fields of Elysian opportunity that catapult Horatio into the king's eye. The author of *Arden of Faversham* deals with issues similar to Kyd's, but his *dramatis personae* and his county setting present these issues in a crucially different light.

Nonetheless, though the setting is township and sub-gentry rather than courtly and aristocratic, the will remains at the center. And though thrilling desire repeatedly demands attention, the play's events are as much about the mastery or control of the will as about its fruits, as much about conservation as transformation. The author lavishes much attention on the social tools for such management. Such capacities tend to interpenetrate, but I will stress at least two ranges. First, the *law*, as it specifies and controls *ownership* of land, ascriptive *authority relations* with wives and sisters, and contractual control of others' actions (at heart, the complex act of *hiring* another). Second, the technology of the *oath*: with its similarly transcendentalized foundation in religion, its self-constructing and self-alienating applications to bonding and obligation, its negations (curses), and its capacity for expressing *insistence*, making and taking stands.

Arden of Faversham thus presents a convergence of tensions: obsessive investments of the will in social conservation and transformation, stratified relations among three adjacent county social ranks (the gentry, their established servants, and their baser hired men), and new and shifting functions of laws and oaths. To explore this convergence I read the play in six movements: (1) Arden's inaugural reactions to the adultery, which necessitate an excursus on the play's complex relations with its sources. (2) Alice and Mosby's erotic struggles, exploring relations to marriage as both hated and desired. (3) The triangular love-contest among the servants (Susan, Michael, and Clarke the painter), orchestrated by Alice and Mosby as a means to killing Arden. (4) The professional self-fashioning of the murderers Black Will and Shakebag, whose origins in the early modern underclass significantly extend the bounds of the theater's social analysis. (5) More doubtful struggling between Alice and Mosby as the murder approaches, as its costs and difficulties come increasingly into view. (6) The final collective murder of Arden, where everyone's divergent desires come together for final exhibition and fruition.

I

The play opens with "lands and living joined with dignities," Pedringano's deepest wish (*The Spanish Tragedy* 2.1.53). Master Arden of Faversham has been deeded former Abbey lands by the hand of Edward Seymour, Duke of Somerset, Lord Protector of his nephew Edward VI and of England. Yet such achievement only appears a triumph, for Arden begins the play in grief: his friend (and Seymour's servant) Franklin reminds him of the award as a consolation, for marital infidelity:

Arden, cheer up thy spirits and droop no more.
My gracious Lord the Duke of Somerset
Hath freely given to thee and to thy heirs,
By letters patents from his majesty,
All the lands of the Abbey of Faversham.
Here are the deeds,
Sealed and subscribed with his name and the king's.
Read them, and leave this melancholy mood.   (i.1–8)[3]

Arden's social elevation is deflated by a sexual dejection. His wife Alice has (been) stolen away: "Love letters pass 'twixt Mosby and my wife, / And they have privy meetings in the town ... / Can any grief be half so great as this?" (15–16, 18). Such loss is certainly felt as a bitter violation of a personal bond, and this reaction (of personal anguish rather than the more typical – and more social – rage) would serve as evidence in the debate about the presence and absence of interpersonal familial emotion in early modern England.[4] But Arden also experiences his cuckoldry as a more specific public humiliation. For Mosby is of offensively lower rank: "Ay, but to dote on such a one as he / Is monstrous, Franklin, and intolerable" (i.22–23). He is

A botcher, and no better at the first,
Who, by base brokage getting some small stock,
Crept into service of a nobleman,
And by his servile flattery and fawning
Is now become the steward of his house,
And bravely jets it in his silken gown.   (i.25–30)[5]

Despite Mosby's elevation by a noble patron ("the Lord Clifford, he that loves not me" [i.32], as Arden describes him), he still feels base to Arden, and that baseness projects a painful insult. Such cuckoldry has made Arden "to be pointed at" (i.35) among the local gentry: "all the knights and gentlemen of Kent / Make common table-talk of her and thee," he tells Mosby (i.343–44). Both private and public pain, loss of love and of reputation, are active here.

   This then is the play's initial matrix, of interacting vectors of social mobility: Arden's social and acquisitive triumph in the highly politicized land market; Alice's sexual wandering; and Mosby's social and sexual invasions. Here in little is a triad of forces that still seemed in 1590 to express living tensions, tracing them to a historical origin in the clamorous times of Henry VIII. Or thus, it seems to me, we must account for the striking continuing life of this forty-year-old murder-story.[6] For

Arden, though presented as a grieving cuckold, is also a wealthy beneficiary of the Dissolution: the play is littered with names and patterns from this momentous historical event, perhaps the single most direct source of the whirlwind of social mobility that marked early modern England.[7] Such social change appeared in licit and illicit forms, much discussed and often interchanged: the point in this play seems to be as much the resemblances between Arden and Mosby as the differences. And such cross-class opportunities and collisions, quite variously weighted, were often played out along a sexual axis, at Henry's court as much as in Renaissance drama.[8]

These familiar patterns of conflict, over sexuality, status, honor, and money, were very complexly accelerated by the Dissolution. What makes *Arden* especially rich as an interrogation of those conflicts is its unusual detail. For a fine-grained sense of its selection and deployment of detail we can consult some striking gaps and variations among versions of the Arden story.[9] The main source was the narrative in Holinshed's *Chronicles*; this text itself apparently derived from a manuscript preserved among Stow's papers, which M. L. Wine believes the playwright may have known (xli). There are at least four points of suggestive discontinuity between the play and these source texts. Each involves issues of kinship, residence, and alliance patterns central to the play's concerns; each involves a streamlining of the matrix presented to a stage audience; and each helps focus attention on Mosby's hateful resemblance to Arden himself.

The first difference is a streamlining so active as to amount to concealment: the characters' specific links to one another were in fact much more entangled than the play admits. Mosby owes his advancement in the drama to an unhistorical Lord Clifford, rather than to his historical master Edward, Lord North. North was co-chancellor (with the notorious Sir Richard Rich, who betrayed Sir Thomas More) of the Court of Augmentations, instituted to handle the greatly increased land transactions resulting from the Dissolution. It was in the Court of Augmentations that North first employed Thomas Ardern, whose career he aided repeatedly. "In time Ardern married Sir Edward's stepdaughter, Alice Mirfyn, and was commissioned thereafter the King's Controller of the Customs of the Port of Faversham by his father-in-law" (Wine xxxvi). In the play there is no explicit connection made between Arden's fortunes as "new man" (so like Mosby's in the play), Alice's family, and Mosby's source of patronage, all of which zones of influence were in fact lodged in one man, Sir Edward North.

The eminent North family would certainly have been offended by actors making money naming names concerning Alice's petty treason.[10]

We are really thinking of her step-brothers, after all, who were well placed to cause trouble for the players in the 1590s. Roger, son of Edward and second Lord North, served with Leicester in the Low Countries, earning a battlefield promotion as Knight Banneret (and was a candidate to replace Leicester after his recall). He returned in 1588 to serve as Lord Lieutenant of Cambridgeshire to prepare for the Armada, and worked for Burghley on subsidies thereafter. Younger brother Thomas (the translator of Plutarch) was also a man of prominence: he commanded 300 men of Ely in 1588, was knighted in 1591, and served as Justice of the Peace in 1592 and 1597. Roger died in 1600; Thomas lived at least until 1601, when Elizabeth granted him a pension of 40 pounds.[11] Note also the eminent placement of Alice's North half-sisters, "Christian, wife of William Somerset, 3rd Earl of Worcester, and Mary, wife of Henry, 9th Lord Scrope of Bolton."[12]

Such prominent enemies could easily have encouraged the playwright to self-censorship: indeed, that the play exists at all is a little amazing. Holinshed himself suppresses the crucial fact that Alice was North's step-daughter (which can be found in the Stow text), though he retains Mosby's affiliation with North. If the playwright knew Stow, he elided both links, and goes further: his fictional Clifford is an active enemy to Arden – "he that loves not me" (i.32). Presumably the ultimate motive for the playwright's evasion, of whatever aspects of the "facts," is the Norths' dangerous noble shame. However, though the provocation is censored by renaming, its affect is recaptured and centered by the drama in the very pain with which Arden grinds his teeth.

For here is the second suppression of kinship data: Thomas Arden's response to the adultery was in fact much slower to the boil than the play suggests. Indeed, Holinshed reports that Arden played the wittol for some considerable time:

> ... although (as it was said) Arden perceiued right well their mutuall familiaritie to be much greater than their honestie, yet bicause he would not offend hir, and so loose the benefit which he hoped to gaine at some of hir freends hands in bearing with hir lewdnesse, which he might haue lost if he should haue fallen out with hir: he was contented to winke at hir filthie disorder, and both permitted, and also inuited Mosbie verie often to lodge in his house. And thus it continued a good space, before anie practise was begun by them against master Arden.[13]

Such behavior takes an even sharper form in the Stow manuscript.[14] There Arden

> was yet so greatly gyven to seek his advauntage, and caryd so litle how he came by it that in hope of atteynynge some benefits of the lord northe by

meanes of this mosby who could do muche wt hym, he winked at that
shamefull dysordor .... (Wine 149)

Holinshed links Arden to Alice's "friends"; Stow links him directly to
Mosby himself, who is cast as a principal family friend, indeed more
intimate than Arden, and potentially ready to intrigue on his behalf.
Holinshed emphasizes Alice's role, Stow Mosby's. In the former case
Arden passively indulges Alice's infidelity in exchange for other favors at
the hands of his superiors and former patrons. In the latter he trades for
her specifically with a fellow servant, a more embarrassing practice.[15]

Omitting these crass but interesting details from Holinshed and Stow
entitles Arden, at least logically, to the self-defining anger he voices to
Franklin about the adultery. Unlike the historical Arden, who found the
arrangement useful, the play's husband finds Alice's doting on Mosby
"intolerable." He claims he is ready to act honorably, aristocratically,
and take revenge – though, guided by Franklin, who counsels patience
(44ff.), he does not in fact do much. The readiness with which Arden is
repeatedly dissuaded from the act, as opposed to the posture, of
vengeance perhaps suggests the posture's *assumed* character, a would-be
aristocratic mantle of the *nemo me impune lacessit* stance ("no man
harms me with impunity") that reaffirms by negation Arden's actual
similarity to the mobile Mosby.

Indeed, the linkage of mobility and commodified sex runs deeper. Both
recent editors are ready to think Mosby explicitly a pimp, so reading the
"base brokage" that initially gets Mosby "some small stock" (i.26).
Martin White adduces Mosby's words to Clarke the painter: "You see
my sister's yet at my dispose" (i.604). This reading seems clearly wrong
so far as any notion of *literal* prostitution goes; Mosby simply exercises
the usual right of family head to control marriages. However, the
author's permutations stress the great complexity of this right's actual
practice. Mosby's strategy, playing off competitors for Susan's hand (as
we will see), aims at the criminal acquisition of a good marriage for
himself (with Alice, by murder). This certainly resembles Arden's wittolry
in Stow and Holinshed: each bestowed access to "his" woman's body for
personal gain. The Stow-Arden acquires the North family influence at
the price of his own husbandly honor; the play-Arden, unconcerned with
Norths, struggles to regain the honor Mosby and Alice have pilfered.
And this pilfering is abetted by Mosby's normative authority to dispose
his sister's marriage. Once again, the characters interpenetrate and
resemble one another across the gaps between textual boundaries: the
play-Arden's fury at Mosby conceals the very underlying resemblances
that the sources emphasize.

A third occlusion of source-texts concerns Arden's aged mother, "whose habit," Wine says, "of going abegging shamed even her rapacious son, who 'assayde all meanes posseble to kepe hir from it, whiche wowld not be'" (Stow MS; Wine xlii). This detail exhibits a mortification about origins intolerable even to the Stow-Arden, none too sensitive of his dignity. The play-Arden much prefers to occlude his own mobility by sneering at Mosby's.[16] After mentioning it once, he habitually averts his eyes from Mosby's elevation to the post of steward (a high if sometimes precarious one, as Shakespeare's Malvolio and Oswald and Webster's Antonio show). He insists relentlessly on the "botcher" view, saying nothing of his own advancement, similarly owed to high social contacts (though we get a minim when he obsequiously greets Lord Cheiny).

To some degree the whole play is party to this occlusion: opening with Arden's arrival in high place thanks to Somerset's grant, it largely takes for granted what he did to get there. However, Greene's embittered complaint to Alice reports Somerset's grant as a crooked land-grab, and describes Arden clearly as a grasping new man:

> Desire of wealth is endless in his mind,
> And he is greedy-gaping still for gain.
> Nor cares he though young gentlemen do beg,
> So he may scrape and hoard up in his pouch.   (i.474–77)

Greene feels Arden's goal as *wealth*, almost *money*; there is no reference to *status*, so precious to Arden himself. Indeed, he seems here almost a city (comedy) usurer, preying indifferently on gentility and its imperatives (e.g., not to have to beg). If his gentility were authentic, he would know better, but the language of hoarding confutes this option (which is why Greene uses it).

Alice responds, "Alas, poor gentleman, I pity you, / And woe is me that any man should want. / God knows, 'tis not my fault" (i.483–85). She credits Greene's story and status, dons the contrasting posture of "good lordship," concerned for the community (and for gentlemen), acknowledges Arden's responsibility, and speaks reluctantly of his equal hardness to her. Greene responds as one traditionalist gentle to another:

> Why, Mistress Arden, can the crabbed churl
> Use you unkindly? Respects he not your birth,
> Your honourable friends, nor what you brought?
> Why, all Kent knows your parentage and what you are.   (i.488–91)

His disrespect expressly denies Arden's ascriptive entitlement to gentle status, just the point of the Stow-Arden's panhandling mother. Such disrespect is mostly, however, left implicit, as a precondition for the action.[17]

If the playwright knew both Holinshed and Stow, then in each of these three cases he discards aspects of the historical Arden that would overtly silhouette him with the mobile profile Mosby exhibits. The play-Arden is now detached, as a landowner, from the great household that rewarded and elevated Mosby and himself alike; he is rewritten as (almost) honorably resenting the entanglements of sexual, social, and economic mobility; and he is deprived of the ascriptive lower origin denoted by his mother's degradingly importunate and determined begging. Such distancing, I propose, serves precisely to allow the play-Arden to enact this subtracted resemblance, by a pattern of *conspicuous denial*: insisting on *Mosby's* mobile rapacity, scorning *Mosby's* contaminated sexuality, delighting in *Mosby's* muddy amphibian origins below the poverty line.[18]

A fourth suggestive folding over on kinship matters differs from the others in having no firmly demonstrable period source at all. Wine reports a fascinating nineteenth-century oral tradition that Alice's marriage to Arden was perhaps an enforced or mantle marriage: that "Ardern was fifty-six years old when he settled in Faversham, his wife twenty-eight, 'and had had familiarities with *Mosbie* before she was married, which made her friends desirous of marrying her with *Arden*'" (Wine xxxvii).[19] To the existing frictions of kinship, gender-role, and rank this tale adds three rich additional ingredients, of generational strife, improper service relations, and enforced marriage. In terms of generational disparity, a distinctly older husband might well be thought more appropriate as a disciplinary agent for Alice; he would be a traditional target for infidelity, and would also figure more pathetically as a wounded and abandoned husband (a positioning made much of in the play). The shadowy presence of a May–January template behind the Alice–Arden marriage is a possibility that never quite comes into view in the text. It might perhaps be mimed by the obsessive insecurities Arden feels as the more materially substantial of the two rivals: January's superior age counts as a debit, and Arden's angry whining woundedness seems sometimes almost a feeling that he is betrayed *because of* his social fitness. Fear about age in any case appears throughout the drama in the period.

So far as service relations go, Mosby's exact status in the North household might shape Alice's impropriety in different ways. Clifford's steward would be far from negligible, and maybe even objectionable mainly on "personal" rather than categorical grounds. Olivia finds Malvolio unthinkable, but the Duchess of Malfi takes Antonio (though secretly, and it infuriates her brothers). These are, however, female heads of household, Alice "only" a step-daughter. Arden, after all, did historically begin as North's servant, and attained Alice. But if Mosby was not a servant with high public place (perhaps only an intimate of North), he might well be thought unsuitable on grounds of disparagement. Miriam Slater reports what might be such a case with Elizabeth Verney, unruly teen-aged sister of Sir Ralph. She

> "was a very forward young maid and very familiar with all sorts of people." Elizabeth was relatively unsupervised when she stayed at the family home at Claydon, and Lady Verney had been informed that she was "very great with [a servant of Uncle John Denton] and they have often found her sitting on his lap." Such behavior could do almost irreparable damage to a young lady's reputation, and Lady Verney was also concerned that "if she [Elizabeth] should be so silly as to cast herself away on him it would be a misfortune to all the family."

Such miscarriage was obviously far from unthinkable; the letter quoted concerns arrangements for protective relocation for Elizabeth, if not at other relations' then in a safe boarding school (well worth the "great charge," according to her Aunt Isham).[20]

An enforced-marriage substitution of Arden for Mosby would be very suggestive indeed. Most importantly, it would substantiate, even literalize, Alice's sense of (her) marriage as a mere form and a prison-house. It would ground Arden from the start in a position of absent rather than lost affection, since the infidelity would antedate, not follow, the marriage. The institutional gesture would itself be reactive, thus explicitly strategic, rather than inaugural and sacramental. It also offers interesting parallels with *The Spanish Tragedy*, reversing what the playgoer experiences as the temporal order of events. Mosby precedes Arden, rather than simply invading an established marriage. Something of the same, almost ontological, reversal is true in Kyd: instead of Horatio disrupting a fit relation between Bel-imperia and Balthazar, the latter must displace his predecessor Andrea, Horatio's double. Private desire precedes the public channel for it, and thus displaces the latter's conceptual status as the comfortable norm to which sexual errancy is mere exception. In each case the woman is identified from the outset as the site of this troubling energy, and is nonetheless taken seriously rather than simply judged as morally deficient. And the story sites the Norths at Lorenzo's endogamous displacement of inferior Horatio with superior Balthazar (though here as there the calculus of such hierarchical judgments is unstable). Like Balthazar, Arden becomes (as his play tends to cast him) a tool, patient more than agent.

If this tale were believed, or known, why not use it? It may be dubious history, but it provides a backdrop both orienting and provocative for the play's rather *in medias res* beginning. However, such material, like much else above, would offend the Norths: the dramatization of such disciplinary marriage would exhibit the disgraceful premarital behavior the marriage was supposed to conceal – and might well seem a craven solution. There are logical problems too. How could the scheming wittol of Holinshed seem in prospect an appropriate guardian of the North reputation? And how to square the threateningly contaminating Mosby of the oral tradition with the secure insider of Stow?

A coherent single answer is hard to find, but two things stand out. First, the Norths' frustrations with Mosby in the oral tradition are essentially those the play attributes to Arden: confronting a soiling sexual linkage between daughter/wife and an unfit servant;[21] struggling to respond in a measured way; and living to regret it. In such times any hypergamy is taken to stipulate the presence of ambition. This more impacted instance – like the modern notion of "marrying the boss's daughter" – holds in tension a trading on special intimacies and an unusually relentless ambition. What is striking is that Arden occupies *both* positions, as hypergamist and as offended guardian.[22] This is certainly a story of social relations of ownership and rebellion between members of different groups.

Second, however, the non-erotic management of sexual lives is also displaced *internally*, from the monitory third-party North family (and a cooperative Arden) *into the lovers themselves*, who often seem to behave structurally as well as psychologically, as it were, policing the very felonies they commit. (This balances the inoculation of erotic motive *into* the play-Arden, so unlike his cold Stow-Holinshed counterpart. Arden is made more erotic or romantic, Alice and Mosby less.) These erotic rebels sustain a mixed relation to the very battles they join, enacting contradictory subject-positions internally as well as externally. To inquire further along these lines will – no surprise – return to the presumption that sexuality is by no means an end in itself. The actions of the lovers are not simply erotic, but social and political and ideological. Or perhaps, better to say, we must ask once again about the *range* of the category of the erotic for Elizabethans.

However, there is still something of an intertextual overload. Behind the play (or beyond it, as explanatory revenant) stand several Ardens, several Alices, several Mosbys – and the Norths. The playwright's decision to cut (if that is indeed what it is) may have sought theatrical economy: perhaps he felt the crowd needed thinning. If so, it is not clear that it worked. Wine's suggestion that the play *guided* the nineteenth-century oral tradition presumes that in some fashion it could summon up such a notion.[23] Certainly a premarital relation such as Alice and Mosby have postmaritally could easily have raised the idea of enforced marriage in her family's minds. Equally, perhaps, it might have arisen in auditors' minds. The situation resembles the matter of Don Andrea's possible murder in *The Spanish Tragedy*: in each case the hypothetical prehistory provides an enabling interpretive or explanatory matrix, pulling various strands of the play closer together. It might, however, be a strictly *ex post facto* imposition of structure.

The ensemble of relations between the play, the Stow and Holinshed texts, and the tradition of enforced mantle marriage is hard to construe. Generally, I think, the shadow *personae* constitute a characterological discourse, of which the play's characters are particular utterances or assertions. Complaisant wittols, vengeful cuckolds, wandering women, scheming climbers, outraged repressive parents, bosom exploiters, all follow profusely in later texts, conveying not so much a culture's judgment as its angry and confused preoccupation. The search for a single vision here seems futile. Rather than work to discern the real or relevant or historical Arden, Alice, or Mosby, we need to be more ready to accept Falstaff's lead, I think, who seeks not to winnow, like Henry IV's counselors, but to multiply and proliferate interpretations and rogues in buckram, to grasp by dialectic rather than by elimination.

The dramatic Arden is initially placed, like many "real-world" cuckolds, across the apparent gap between thin-skinned punctilio and wittolry. He accedes to Franklin's advice for restraint, but his furies are unmistakable. Mosby may be favored by the great, he says,

> But through his favour let not him grow proud,
> For were he by the Lord Protector backed,
> He should not make me to be pointed at.
> I am by birth a gentleman of blood,
> And that injurious ribald that attempts
> To violate my dear wife's chastity –
> For dear I hold her love, as dear as heaven –
> Shall on the bed which he thinks to defile
> See his dissevered joints and sinews torn,
> Whilst on the planchers pants his weary body,
> Smeared in the channels of his lustful blood.   (i.33–43)

Arden gestures defiantly (and self-announcingly) against his own sub-ordination to Mosby, no matter what his alliance. Honor ("look at mine") respects no personal risk. Though Clifford, nay, even Somerset back Mosby, Arden will stand forth, a "gentleman of blood" (an explicit, if inconclusive, denial of Greene's aspersions). Such bluster struggles to repeat Franklin's material comfort, announcing the near-noble self, yet conceals a recession within the paraded fury; for these threats displace a present situation into the future. Mosby has *already* injured Arden's honor, but treating the injury as potential enables Arden to respond with words rather than deeds. His new status requires affirming the ascriptive sanctity of what has been (or rather, may be) injured: his achieved, now landed gentry. Alice's sexuality is a vessel for his honor, and its ("possible") injury a classic occasion for self-affirmation: *nemo me impune lacessit*, as Webster's Brachiano has it. Such assertions articulate Arden's claimed world-view.

Mosby's invasion is also a sacred defilement, that allows an imitative-form fantasy punishment on a rack-like bed and floor. The bed will apparently hold the criminal's severed limbs, which he will behold in agony from his own limbless trunk, the tortured panting spectator of his own judicial execution, lying on the floor at Arden's foot where he belongs. The scene seems to repeat the horrific social or judicial gesture with which the hangman disembowels his victim and raises his bowels before his living eyes, so that we the panting crowd may see him seeing them, all acknowledging together the privy vessel of his essential internal evil, torn out like an offending eye, offered to his view and ours, and cast away into the fire.[24] Arden's comparison is not simply, as it were, metaphorical: such bloody scenes were real, utterly semiotic tenor and utterly embodied vehicle alike. These tones, so frantic to the modern ear, were probably quite literal for Arden. They also reiterate once again his inescapable identification with his opposite, for they prefigure his own real bloody death, crushed on the floor of his counting-house, just as they echo by procrustean revenge the wound he sustained in his marriage-bed. The element of tortured self-witness surely reenacts Arden's own humiliated consciousness, once again marking the resemblance of the characters.

Similar effects animate Arden's verbal assault on Mosby at their first meeting. Arden and Franklin happen upon the lovers in privacy at Arden's house, and Mosby pretends, as a cover story, that he came to speak to Arden, about Greene's lands.

> Master Arden, being at London yesternight,
> The Abbey lands whereof you are now possessed
> Were offered me on some occasion
> By Greene, one of Sir Anthony Ager's men.
> I pray you, sir, tell me, are not the lands yours?
> Hath any other interest herein? (i.292–97)

This evasion, though fitting at one level, is counter-productive at another, for it identifies Mosby and Arden, as (here directly competitive) land-speculators. Arden's angry response repeats the endless link of land and status, and extends it to include sexual affiliation:

As for the lands, Mosby, they are mine
By letters patents from his majesty.
But I must have a mandate for my wife;
They say you seek to rob me of her love.
Villain, what makes thou in her company?
She's no companion for so base a groom.   (i.300–05)

Arden acts as if Mosby has no business even to think of land, or of Alice (similar categories, it seems). Inferior status, invoked and amplified, invalidates any right even to share Alice's company, much less desire her.[25] Arden rebuffs what he feels as invasiveness – legal, economic, sexual, and status – as if his entire enclosed suite of self-defining possessions was coextensively in need of protection from poaching.

Mosby responds with his habitual irresistible move in their dance, mirroring Arden's posture by threatening an aristocratic revenge "on the proudest of you both" (309). And once again Arden degrades such pretensions, here positioning himself as a physical as well as social superior: the stage direction tells us, "*Then Arden draws forth Mosby's sword*" (i.309 s.d.).

So, sirrah, you may not wear a sword.
The statute makes against artificers,
I warrant that I do. Now use your bodkin,
Your Spanish needle, and your pressing iron,
For this [sword] shall go with me. And mark my words,
You goodman botcher, 'tis to you I speak:
The next time that I take thee near my house,
Instead of legs I'll make thee crawl on stumps.   (310–17)

Two aspects of this speech call for attention. First, the linking of violence and legalism is striking. Arden seizes (given the legalism, perhaps "confiscates"?) the sword, and threatens to cut off Mosby's legs, once again making gestures that mix castration (the denial of Mosby's potency to revenge, perhaps denying it with his own sword) and social debasement (Mosby is literally to be brought to his knees, to crawl; indeed, crawling on his knees will be his only mode of walking).[26] At the same time, Arden feels the need to turn to the law, to legal certainty, for his power and superiority: the statute forbids Mosby's wearing the noble weapon, and Arden is empowered, "warranted" by it, not by his own unthought aristocratic citizenship.[27] (Nowhere is Arden's external achieved relation to his status more clear than in such resort to codified rather than intuitive traditionalist entitlements. Bourdieu makes much of the gap between the external social analyst's unknowing resort to accounts by rule and model and the native inhabitant's intuitive practical knowledge of what is done and not done, never theorized until the analyst requests the code. Arden gets his entitlement to degrade Mosby, like his entitlement to the Abbey lands, by express law, not by customary ontological possession. His claim is orthodox rather than doxic, as Bourdieu would put it.)[28]

Second, consider the sneering allusions to the tools of Mosby's trade: the bodkin, needle, and pressing iron. In the first place such jabs emphasize the relative degradation of one who performs manual labor, unlike Arden – dismissing the capacitation implicit in Mosby's query about land. But the jab goes deeper. The iron will of course figure in the murder, but the needle is also meaningful, first in terms of phallic competition. Arden attempts to take (back?) the phallus for himself, leaving Mosby only with a needle. And bodkin; and pressing iron. Mosby still seems better equipped, both generally and with weapons that will come into play in the actual murder. "Measure me not," Mosby replies (i.321). Moreover, the needle is the specific tool used to produce "Spanish work," the black silk embroidery so popular among the aristocracy at this time: the "Spanish needle" marks Mosby as a laborer, a servant, an employee, of gentlemen, not one who might consort with them as an equal, as Mosby's erotic venture implies. Arden allows him only his past, as "a velvet drudge, / A cheating steward, and base-minded peasant" (i.322–23): the elevated components of these pairs are false, the base true and irreducible. Mosby's insistence on the present – "Measure me what I am, not what I was" (321) – meets only stony misrecognition: to concede such change, even if it did not aid his enemy, would come far too close to acknowledging its relevance to his own case, and Arden will not do it.

So far, then, several issues have been arrayed. Henry's seizure of the monasteries unleashed a deluge of social flux deriving from the suddenly movable status of hitherto rock-solid land, once the uncirculating sign of the aristocracy, now increasingly a commodity. With the aid of legal linkages "new men" arose from various ranks, invading formerly ascriptive preserves and struggling to lock the gates immediately. Such patterns apply not only to land but to the sexual realm, in both erotic guise (Henry's religio-marital spasms, and male and female Seymours as much as the characters here) and procreative function (the machinery for reproduction and transmission of lineage, construing both Henry's and Arden's wives and daughters). The ascriptive status of both rank and sexuality has become beleaguered. The resulting siege mentality responds with increasingly pressured notions of honor and propriety: the iron yet manipulable structures of law and the passionately guarded sanctities of the self.

II

The performed erotic relations between Alice and Mosby (and those interspersed of the shadow triad of Susan, Alice's maid and Mosby's sister, and her two suitors Michael and Clarke) are centered, I will suggest, on a cultural sore or wound of ideological friction. These characters struggle to control an unruly centrifugal dialectic of conservative socialized authority and licentious seizure. Even to speak of a dialectic is to confer too much unity on the system: what the playwright is interested in is a continual state of frenzy, of overload, of constructive rupture and destructive bonding. In such an emotional and social plasma it is very difficult to distinguish anger from desire.

In such a matrix the bond linking Alice and Mosby comes to bear much weight, as a socially exploratory vehicle carrying an obscure cargo of cultural and ideological labor. The braided and tangled lines of force between these characters will finally not submit to a full unfolding, I believe; the Foucouldian knowledge they are trying to invent is not yet available to think with. In practice this means that the bond is sometimes just opaque, sometimes actively antithetical or combative. As with most profound departures, what is left behind is much more clearly visible and tangible than the undiscovered country of fantasy ahead. If Alice and Mosby, like Black Will and Shakebag, end by seeming "forlorn travelers," and begin in furious distrustful passion, they still mark the onset of a new erotics, drenched in anger but (or perhaps – and so) dreaming a new notion of marriage.

Though I will eventually argue that the lovers seek to reinvent or seize the category of marriage, Alice at least begins by lunging hungrily away from it:

> Sweet news is this. Oh, that some airy spirit
> Would, in the shape and likeness of a horse,
> Gallop with Arden 'cross the ocean
> And throw him from his back into the waves!
> Sweet Mosby is the man that hath my heart,
> And he usurps it, having nought but this –
> That I am tied to him by marriage.
> Love is a god, and marriage is but words,
> And therefore Mosby's title is the best.
> Tush! Whether it be or no, he shall be mine
> In spite of him, or Hymen, and of rites.   (i.94–104)[29]

The terms in which Alice construes her triad are very suggestive indeed. She certainly rebels against Arden's authority, and, as Catherine Belsey argues, "challenge[s] ... the institution of marriage, itself publicly in crisis in the period."[30] Yet Alice dreams of eros by means of a confused cloud of legal and material reifications that seek freedom from traditional bonds by reascribing just such possessive entitlements.[31] Mosby "hath" her heart, while Arden "usurps" it, having "nought" but the marriage-tie. Several patterns are at work here. Despite her rebellions, Alice begins with a culturally habitual submission to a masculist sense of female passivity, feeling herself as possessed, in two different senses, by her men. (She works her way partly out of this mode in time, and indeed, some might say that to be fought over in this way is precisely to be in effortless control. But this explains the matter away.) Much more important in the long run is the inversion of the possession and usurpation poles (between lover and husband), which presumably works here to deny the traditional force of marriage-vows, as she does in the next lines.[32] Arden has only mere words, which to Alice here seem empty quotidian formalities compared to the passions – though they *tie* (bonds now negative, like handcuffs); yet when she says therefore Mosby wins, she uses an even more legalist form of language: his *title* (repudiating the dessicating *tie*, yet escalating its technicality) is best. But perhaps she notices this proper and proprietary discourse in her own mouth, and dismisses it. She will have Mosby in spite of husband's rights and Hymen's rites.

Alice simultaneously (and confusingly? confusedly?) voices, uses, inverts, and repudiates the received social structures of relation when she scorns Arden's official legal status *and* Hymen's rites, a vocabulary expressly religious and transcendental. The only solidity to be found is in her own declaration, a defiant prophetic oath or self-commitment dismissing all other (that is, social, collective) determinations. This confusion seems not a matter of a choice between options but an attempt at ideological production, of a new mode of relational identity, insistent on founding official identity on preconditions of some new kind of personal choice. Lovers had long had errant desires, of course, often juxtaposed to officialized commitments to spouses. Chivalric adulteries like Lancelot and Guinevere's are an obvious example. Likewise, the new model of companionate marriage long associated with Puritan thought makes room for such a relation as an initial state.[33] But Alice reaches beyond both adultery and Puritan marriage (toward something like the then-nonexistent option of remarriage), repudiating and seizing the social in one and the same gesture. For Alice hates the discourse of oppressive marital propriety (much of which gets repeated in the so-called companionate context of the Puritan bond). At the same time, she also feels, wants to be, married to Mosby, with many of the public accoutrements of the fully social bond. (Such an agenda, however cloudily perceived, would activate a strong ideological significance for the suppressed or lost enforced-marriage prehistory.) Freedom and commitment, however oxymoronic, are both central to her venture.

The dissonant terminologies of adultery and (re)marriage are conflated in various ways throughout the play in the particular interactions between the lovers, most of which are structured around negations or frictions attendant upon this oxymoron of freedom and commitment. When old Adam the innkeeper comes to tell Alice of Mosby, he is reluctant even to name her lover, speaking first of "he whom you wot of" (109), speaking habitually in the adulterous go-between's surreptitious language of concealment. But then the message is not, it seems, of an assignation, but of Mosby's refusal to see her. And yet is this a mere tactical matter, of secrecy, or some deeper rejection? Alice and the audience are equally in doubt, a placement so frequently repeated as to constitute the lovers' usual relation, in substantial uncertainty.

When Mosby enters, his first word, unexplained and perhaps ontologically programmatic, is the dismissing vocative "Away" (i.179). She takes this as policy, and reassures him that he need not fear. "Where is your husband" (182), he replies, seeming to confirm the occasion as surreptitious, but when answered says, "There let him be; henceforward know me not" (184), rejecting in truth, not for show (though not really, as it turns out). Endlessly unable to rest in her new relation, fearful Alice takes the bait:

> Is this the end of all thy solemn oaths?
> Is this the fruit thy reconcilement buds?
> Have I for this given thee so many favours,
> Incurred my husband's hate, and – out, alas! –
> Made shipwreck of mine honour for thy sake?
> And dost thou say 'henceforward know me not'?
> Remember when I locked thee in my closet,
> What were thy words and mine? Did we not both
> Decree to murder Arden in the night?
> The heavens can witness, and the world can tell,
> Before I saw that falsehood look of thine,
> 'Fore I was tangled with thy 'ticing speech,
> Arden to me was dearer than my soul –
> And shall be still. Base peasant, get thee gone,
> And boast not of thy conquest over me,
> Gotten with witchcraft and mere sorcery.
> For what hast thou to countenance my love,
> Being descended of a noble house,
> And matched already with a gentleman
> Whose servant thou may'st be? And so farewell.   (i.185–204)

In this speech Alice raises to full visibility the central thematic of the oath. Perhaps ultimately the most important (and most typically patterned) aspect of this moment is its origin in negation or failure, but for our purposes it presents a first full look at this crucial human tool for the management of desire. It is clear that for Alice at this moment (or, she would say, up to this moment) the oath is a consciously willed and deeply personal, individual, extra-social binding, the root or core of the mere shadowed words of public speech and ritual. But all of this is very shifting: meanings drift in and out of each other, not only in terms of meta-social binary binding, but also toward the individualist exchange language of contract ("Have I for this given thee so many favours?"), and away from feudal bonds – and then back in again. Other territories of exchange and obligation will arise in due course; for now let us focus on those of "love."

Reproaching Mosby for his alienation of affection, Alice harks back to an originary moment of commitment: "Remember when I locked thee in my closet?" This coercive act partly prefigures the Duchess of Malfi's forcible wooing, and, doubling the privity of closet and body, implies as well the physical consummation of sexual intercourse (itself oathlike, as when marital). The scene she conjures up seems like a clandestine marriage *per verba de praesenti*: meant to be taken as completely binding, however private (indeed, here *because* private).[34] What is remarkable, however, is *how* they swore their love: "Did we not both / Decree to murder Arden in the night?" Arden's dead body (or, for that matter, Alice's opened one, with its magical exchange of fluids) is held out as a *signum* or proof of their love, a materialization of their oath, an embodied pledge of souls (and one that empowers them, as the use of "decree" suggests.) Of course, all sacrificial sanctifications work this way, from Greek hecatombs invoking divine witness to the more contemporary oath of fidelity implicit in the early modern rape victim's obligatory suicide. Thomas Nashe makes this logic explicit in *The Unfortunate Traveller*, when the raped Heraclide opts for this gesture: "The diuell, the belier of our frailtie, and common accuser of mankinde, cannot accuse mee, though he would, of vnconstrained submitting."[35] This suicide swears on her own dead body, as men sometimes will on their mothers' graves, or as in the pugnacious expression "over my dead body," still current. Arden's murder is not, then, merely instrumental or tactical or logistical; it is itself a gesture, a means of swearing, of self-constitution for the lovers' identity in love.

This makes the plot an embodiment of the ideological crime of petty treason, a category of act threatened and repeated several times in the play, though here most importantly. What makes this crime different from simple murder is its ideological freight. For the traitor, petty or otherwise, does not merely kill a human, but assaults what that human

stands for: the traitor betrays the king or his country; the married petty
traitor kills her husband; the servant his or her master or mistress; the
minor cleric his prelate. What is at stake here is obviously *hierarchy*,
"good order," established bonds, local human investments of the
systemic logic, to whom the murderer owes some kind of both personal
and transpersonal allegiance.[36] The lovers' sacrifice will not only inaugurate their new personal relationship, but strikes at the heart of the entire
system that upheld the old – and that the old upheld.[37] (Other motiva-
tions may be ascribed to Mosby, as we will see, but for the present let us
attend to Alice, whose speech this is.)

"The heavens can witness and the world can tell," Alice says, how
much she loved Arden before Mosby intervened with his "'ticing
speech." The phrase floats between the link of the murder-betrothal in
the preceding line, and her link with Arden in the following line. She
thus calls out their clandestine oath with the transcendental logic of
martyrs' address, before turning to scorn Mosby for his dereliction,
now felt as typical for such a base cur. And like Arden in his pain
Alice inflicts retributory pain by trying to strip Mosby of any self-
specific entitlement of worth for her interest in him. Like Henry VIII
"betrayed" by Anne Boleyn, she resorts to the charge of witchcraft. In
the sexual-treason trials Henry claimed that he was "seduced and
forced into his second marriage by means of sortileges and charms."
As in "ordinary" witchcraft cases, "witchcraft" is a practice of the
accuser: the use of a criminalizing term that absolves supposed victims
of any personal responsibility or agency for their engagement with the
accused. In these specifically erotic cases, the charge also strips from
the accused person any personal, non-magical entitlement to past
affections, now retroactively disavowed. The repudiator says, "It was
only 'witchcraft,' not your 'real' personality, parts, attributes, that led
me to love you."[38]

Alice also strikes Mosby with the language of rank. Indeed, she returns
in haughty summary to a direct measure of Mosby against Arden,
reminding her lover of his precise over-determined inferiority to his
alternate – recapturing old relational status from her husband as she
scorns the emergent status she had been seeking to forge with her lover.
Her ambivalence about the men here includes a concern with the
relational status she may derive from them: she wants both kinds of
status. What is so far not set clearly for us is whether she wants what the
social body has not yet figured out how to give, or whether her own
desires are internally contradictory. Does she want inner to match and
ratify outer, or does she want both established and rebellious subject-
positions, gentle wifery and masterless woman?

Mosby, it will now seem unsurprisingly, has all along held off out of *insecurity*: "To try thy constancy have I been strange," he says (i.209). At some level he has found it as hard to believe in this possibility as Alice did, as her fearful rage has just shown. Alice replies to Mosby's banal half-aware explanation ("love is jealous") with a reiteration of their precarious oxymoron:

So lists the sailor to the mermaid's song;
So looks the traveller to the basilisk.
I am content for to be reconciled,
And that I know will be mine overthrow.   (i.213–16)

Though she means them to refer to Mosby's insecure fantasy, the mermaid and basilisk prove more fitting as figures for Alice herself – or rather, for each lover to the other (reiterating the witchcraft explanation). Alice even seems in some way to know this, presuming as she returns to her errant commitment that it will be her overthrow. Each is a traveller, moving beyond the bounds of the familiar, going, like the Duchess of Malfi, into a wilderness. Each struggles to derive identity from this meta-social venture, but each finds it nearly impossible to feel whole with, and at the same time as, the other.

Mosby replies, "Thine overthrow? First let the world dissolve!" Such an apocalyptic declaration aims once again to assert by the main force of speech the new and transcendental mode of their love.[39] Alice accepts the spirit of the gesture, but demurs at the letter: "Nay, Mosby, let me still enjoy thy love, / And happen what will, I am resolute" (i.218–19). As we will see below in relation to the assassins, oaths frequently address the future negatively, as both lovers do here, usually as a self-coercion, sometimes as an indifference to eventual penalties. Resolute Alice, like Faustus and Macbeth, will jump the time to come. Wandering is all.[40]

And yet one shaped face of the future is paradoxically also very real to her, and central to my argument. For I believe her deepest fantasy is of some kind of marriage with Mosby, as her next lines begin to suggest: "My saving husband hoards up bags of gold / To make our children rich" (i.220–21). Holinshed mentions Arden's daughters twice, but they do not appear in the play unless here. I believe, however, with Martin White, that "Alice is enjoying the prospect of the children she and Mosby will have being made rich by the efforts of the unsuspecting Arden" (note to i.221).[41] This linkage between some kind of consummated and public relation and its profound socio-material results is as important to the lovers' feeling as the rebellion.[42]

Consider various allusions to the socially emplacing effect of this proto-marital union. When Arden and Franklin leave for London at the

end of scene i, Mosby reaches to Alice for what is clearly a major fantasy
come true: "I hope now Master Arden is from home, / You'll give me
leave to play your husband's part" (636–37). Alice, sharing in his
fantasy, replies, "Mosby, you know who's master of my heart; / He well
may be the master of the house" (638–39). The cross-tensions of variable
class and gender hierarchies are obtrusive here, as Mosby asks permission
to play (enact? imitate? frolic with?) the superior's part. At first, this
might seem to refer to the woman's part, a sexual wish; but Alice's reply
makes it clear that she knows he dreams first of enacting the householder.
Mosby conceives of his goal here in terms of substantiation, acquisition
or achievement of role.

Arden too thinks within this discourse: while he is in London he hates
the fact that "that base Mosby doth usurp my room" (iv.29), marking
the metaphoric range of places in the household and in Alice's body.
Mosby likewise later foresees trouble from Michael and the painter when
they will see him "sit in Arden's seat" (viii.31). After Arden's murder
Mosby reassures Alice by saying "I am thy husband" (xiv.271). And she
soon calls thus on Mosby, unable to deny this pleasure: "Master Mosby,
sit you in my husband's seat" (xiv.287).[43]

Such references to the substantial socio-material achievement of the
head of household's role are paralleled by other passages which treat the
lovers more specifically as if married. Alice has claimed that her bond to
Mosby supersedes her marriage-tie to Arden (i.101), and we have, I
believe, seen her dream of their children (i.221). But the most important
reference comes into view at the very beginning, when Arden laments to
Franklin, "Nay, on his finger did I spy the ring / Which at our marriage
day the priest put on" (i.17–18). Alice has passed on to Mosby the crucial
physical symbol of marriage – and of course of her married chastity.[44]
One may also detect some parallel with Bel-imperia's scarf, another
genital symbol transferred by a woman from one man to another. There,
of course, the symbolic function is private, the transfer unofficial. In
Alice's case the object is a public legal symbol, ritually positioned by
cultural authority, supposed inalienable.[45] (It also seems to operate in
some complex dialectic with its masculine equivalent, Mosby's sword,
(re)appropriated by Arden.)

This detail of the ring is the more interesting as it connects with
another most striking and at least partly unused source-element concerning Alice and Mosby's seizure of the means of kinship practice.
Holinshed tells us that "she had made a solemne promise to him, and he
againe to hir, to be in all points as man and wife togither, and therevpon
they both receiued the sacrament on a sundaie at London, openlie in a
church there" (Wine 153–54). In scene viii Mosby says of Alice, "she's

myself, / And holy church rites make us two but one" (37–38): such language probably contains the marriage model of "one flesh," (itself a peculiarly English and privatized way of thinking),[46] and very possibly refers to the source incident, though vaguely. (The tense is also obscure: such rites do make, would make, have made, them one?)

This utterly daring "marital" incident is extraordinarily suggestive. It is another oath, of course, affirming their mutual bond, but its illogic is very deep. The priest would think himself and his function utterly misused, in fact untapped. Such misuse cannot appropriate the holy force of the sacrament – save perhaps parodically (thus only temporarily, only by God's will, thus not at all), as witchcraft. But what is the gesture's phenomenology, its felt force for those who seize it? Witchcraft seems not at all what the lovers think they're up to. I believe it must be a kind of *seizure of the machinery of ascription*.[47] This is another quite conscious act like the Duchess of Malfi's, who names her act by denying it (to her brother): "Why might not I marry? / I have not gone about, in this, to create / Any new world, or custom" (3.2.110–12). In fact, what Alice and Mosby seek we would now call something like remarriage, an act of personal choice free from the controls of parents and "friends" – a freedom which divorce never allowed, and which was popularly hated in widows. They have driven themselves toward, insisted upon, some kind of claim to a legitimacy precisely denied by the system against which they are rebelling, and they attempt to seize the machinery of that system in order to constitute such legitimacy. They are not satisfied to rest outside of marriage; they must colonize it, make it theirs, be able to say "this is a *real* marriage," not like the sham with Arden, nor yet like Bel-imperia's eroticised denial of traditional dynastic marriage. This is to be a new sort of marriage, a "truer" marriage, a love-match higher than the socially ratified version that keeps them apart, which must be inserted, as a type or mode, into the system, in order to rectify and rationalize that system.

Of course, such a seizure contains numerous contradictions and incoherences; they are part of its active meaning, marking the lovers' partial inaugural grappling with received kinship practice. It is obviously significant, for instance, that they perform this act away from home, avoiding the banns, as it were – though even this locution cannot address Alice's existing marital status. The bann mechanism, normally functioning in regard to impediments (such as incest, pre-contract, and bigamy)[48] does not operate normally here: the couple return home, to live in their usual public environment, as unmarried, in Arden's company, whatever they have promised. There is no question of "actual"bigamy, for they do not make a separate life, and dual awareness is not limited to the "sharing" spouse, as would be usual. Alice and Mosby behave as (what for us would be) adulterers, but they somehow insist – privately – that they are married: a public institutionalized state which they appropriated in public, but elsewhere, not as a cover (like signing into a motel as married) but as a core, which they then bring "home" in concealment, pretending to be married away but to be unmarried at home. Yet even to perform this much of a groping gesture they appear to need to escape from the (non-urban? traditional?) zone of Arden's influence and the territory of the family (the orbit of the enforced marriage, Alice's friends, Lord Cheiny), to the future-fiction cityscape of flux and contractualities, where they can try to reinvent relationship. The act of flight means, presumably, that they seek somehow to tap the official power of legitimation, however furtively, as a bulwark against the sense or view or even knowledge (others' but surely also their own) that what they are doing is really precisely illegitimate. On the other hand, the ceremony would surely also have been experienced (making a virtue of necessity) as a private act of commitment, rather than as a public bounding within the larger social network. Yet to say "surely" at all here is to leap in the dark at their dense and maybe unavailable meaning, perhaps as they themselves did. Many effects seem possible.

If the enforced-marriage tradition is to be accepted, the lovers might well have perceived the public marriage to Arden as empty and unreal expressly because of its instrumental character as a move blocking Alice's path to Mosby. If so, then the first marriage was three-cornered, the second more truly binary: Arden as imposed context for interacting with Mosby, the second marriage an exclusion of the invading enclosure. This difference can be said to argue a more "meaningful" interpersonal and intersubjective binding, of course a more modern one too, more Protestant and bourgeois. (This is to set aside for the moment the possibilities, both voiced in the story, that both Arden and Mosby in fact sought out Alice for financial gain. More of this below.)

Furthermore, of course, this ceremony (think of it now as a wedding, as it were, rather than a marriage) might itself have been means rather than end. The context in Holinshed deals with Mosby's desire to pick a fight with Arden, rather than have him killed by agents in stealth. "For he said he could not find it in his heart to murther a gentleman in that sort as his wife wished: although she had made a solemne promise to him, and he againe to her ..." (Wine, edition 153). Perhaps taking the sacrament here does not address the bonding or marriage, but instead functions like the act of conspirators who take the sacrament as a self-committing spur, to the murder of a monarch, for instance.[49] On this reading, the wedding-like ceremony would constitute a dedication to the murder, rather than the reverse. Some kind of dialectic is probably inescapable.[50]

What, finally, of the dramatist's occlusion of this tale of London church-going? Obviously we cannot attribute the full ritual richness of this story to the play, though most of its elements (save the most interesting) arise at one point or another. Yet there seems *ipso facto* no reason to speak expressly of suppression. Perhaps we need only relinquish the specifically institutional seizure of ascription, while retaining the many other extra-social seizures the lovers attempt. Perhaps there is a presumption of nearly this knowledge in the introductory allusion to Mosby wearing Arden's wedding ring. It might even be that despite the tale's narrative relevance to this particular play, the church's vulnerability to seizure seemed too dangerous to stage at all, given the public stage's own institutional vulnerability to this oft-made charge.[51] Maybe staging a subversive wedding like this one was too much like staging a living monarch: both church and crown were, as it were, jealous gods hatefully intolerant of idolatry and imitability. Still, this "appropriation by miming" is too relevant to the subterranean foundations of the play to be dismissed entirely from any analysis of its role as a staging of social change.

For the moment we can leave the lovers, having located them in a context defined by the poles of restlessly mistrustful friction and sworn and trumpeted bonding. Such placement fits the insecure pugnacious invention that characterizes the gender politics we have been examining. Let us next turn to the more deferent mirror of the body-servant subplot.

III

Michael enters the play *reminding* Alice. This is typical of the subplot as of the main one: grave matters of crucial rewards are settled with strong talk, yet all seems always to require doing over again. Talk is never strong enough. Confidence is everyone's desire, yet it withers as soon as it is conjured up:

> MICHAEL I hope you'll think on me.
> ALICE Ay, but Michael, see you keep your oath,
> And be as secret as you are resolute.
> MICHAEL I'll see he shall not live above a week.
> ALICE On that condition, Michael, here is my hand:
> None shall have Mosby's sister but thyself. (i.143–48)

Such stichomythic oath-exchange of intensifications and reassurances and doubts is typical of the entire play, and is especially interesting in its

highly commodified format here. Michael expects forgetful neglect from
his mistress, as she does from him. He pumps up his claim ("not ...
above a week"), and she hers ("on that condition ... here is my hand").
The prize (or perhaps bribe) is Mosby's sister's hand in marriage. (The
denizens of the subplot are just as determined on such socially institutionalized goals as are their betters; perhaps more so, since direct erotic
affect seldom comes into view in this plot, unlike the other.)

Alice has given her word (and her hand) to Michael, yet he still worries
about his rival the painter, and plans to have a love-letter professionally
written that will put the other out of court.[52] Alice, annoyed at not being
thought sufficiently performative, says, "What needs all this? I say that
Susan's thine" (i.161). She has guaranteed Michael this wife (whom he
achieves without any direct address to her, the usual early modern resort
to her disposing "friends" being quite as usual). The negotiation is an
exercise of patronage, an exchange of services: for this guarantee Michael
contracts to make a highly thematized payment: "Why then, I say that I
will kill my master, / Or anything that you will have me do" (i.162–63).
Two elements are noteworthy here. I will notice one only briefly for the
moment: the second line presents in downscale size the limitless corrupt
obedience of the superserviceable servant, more familiar from such larger
scenes as those of Mephistopheles and Goneril's Oswald.[53] For the prize
of Susan there is (theoretically) no price Michael is unwilling to pay, and
she arouses the same commitment in Michael's rival, as we shall see.
(There will also be more to say in due course regarding the prices of such
obedience, and its more commercial equivalent in Black Will and
Shakebag's services.)

More important for the present is this subplot's version of petty
treason, discussed above regarding husband and wife. Like Alice,
Michael will commit petty treason (servant killing master), in order (like
Mosby) to marry upward. Susan would convey several benefits of
alliance, as we shall see in a moment, but marrying her would also mark
another developmental transition for Michael. Ann Kussmaul notes that
servant status was for most "a transitional occupation, specific to their
transitional status between childhood and adulthood."[54] Marital access
to Susan would provide an occasion for Michael to leave this transitional
servant status behind and establish full adult identity, an achievement he
also proposes to present to her, by another promise, as an enticement to
her personal acceptance of him. (Perhaps once again he doubts the
efficacy of the superior lovers' promises, seeking to enlist Susan's
influence with her brother, entering the circuit of influences at several
different points.)

But, mistress, tell her whether I live or die
I'll make her more worth than twenty painters can,
For I will rid my elder brother away,
And then the farm of Bolton is mine own.
Who would not venture upon house and land,
When he may have it for a right-down blow?   (i.170–75)

Here is another of this play's multiply self-constituting pleas. Susan is offered material enticement: if she marries him she'll get the farm whether he lives or dies. Compare Alice's related allusion to an uncertain future as a means of intensifying an oath, noted above: "Nay, Mosby, let me still enjoy thy love, / And happen what will, I am resolute" (i.218–19). This trope seems to say "no matter what," but there is more here, to do with a future feared even in the act of denial, a sign of doubt, sworn away, as if by so doing one could rise above the human weakness or limit of uncertainty. Michael seems both to offer the farm to Susan, for her hand, and to use her hand as motive and spur to his own seizure of the substantiated, as landed, identity – which his brother got effortlessly, by birth-order.

Such murder is not only fratricide, but heir-murder, a hierarchical crime somewhat like killing one's master. I have not found any express outlawing of sibling heir-killing as petty treason, but like the other specified crimes it assaults an embodiment of binding hierarchy, here primogeniture.[55] Once more ideological crime springs up in a niche of particular structural friction in the social system, jealous fury at elder brothers being as easy to comprehend (and as important to defend against) as fury against husbands and masters. Indeed, so familiar is the tension fueling this ambition that Michael imagines it a universal desire.[56] Who would not thus venture, when he may have house and land "for a right-down blow?" Killing a brother seems almost a stalwart piece of English yeomanry, especially given the prosaic yeoman prize of the elder brother's farm. Certainly the moral physicality of "right-down blow," deployed in a "venture," that is, a project with substantial inherent risk,[57] seems to buoy Michael's spirits. Recall a similar series of moments in the career of Pedringano, initially lured with "lands and livings," who murders not master or brother, but unsuspecting comrade, and who struggles manfully to achieve the vigor and clarity of purpose that Michael exhibits here.

The other suitor, Clarke the painter, also enters reminding, a bit later: we learn that Susan has been, on word of honor, promised to him too. Yet Clarke, like Michael, still doubts, despite the given word: "Then tell me, Master Mosby, shall I have her?" (i.259). Alice interjects, " 'Tis pity but he should; he'll use her well" (260: a new argument, nominally based on the good to Mosby's sister, unlike Alice's promise to Michael). Mosby gives the painter his hand, promising her yet again. Clarke replies, "Then, brother, to requite this courtesy, / You shall command my life, my skill, and all" (262–63). Does he read Mosby well enough (as perhaps Michael does Alice) to distrust him, and thus strive to bind him anew at every chance? Perhaps his efforts are based on something like the nineteenth-century logic of "condoning adultery." In such case, "if there was sexual intercourse between [husband and wife] after adultery by either was known to the other, the adultery was considered to have been condoned, and was no longer grounds for divorce, unless fresh acts of adultery were committed."[58] Is Clarke working away here at Mosby's unreliability, enforcing repetitions of the original oath as a way of erasing other intervening promises? Or is the logic perhaps one of accumulation, swearing over and over? Certainly Clarke also immediately affirms the new kinship relation, shifting from "sir" (248) and "Master Mosby" (259) to "brother," perhaps thus availing himself of the coercive entitlements of kinship. Coming from one whom he summoned with the words, "How, Clarke!" (246), Mosby (accurately) finds these words invasive and annexing, and brushes the painter back, as if he had gotten too close, saying, "Leave; I have talked sufficient" (i.265).

With Michael and the painter the *Arden* author once again triggers problematic relations between ascribed and achieved, here as the relation between kinship and contractuality. The male servants strive, like their unequal "betters" Alice and Mosby, to make a good, bettering, marriage. Susan, however erotically desirable in herself (an unspecified matter) would serve to link a husband politically, in terms of access to influence, to her "friends": her brother the risen and rising Mosby, his gentle lover (and Susan's mistress) Alice (who confers separate elevation on Mosby), and Alice's own network of relations, including both her gentle family of origin and her affinal capacitations (social, economic, structural) as Arden's proleptic (and would-be) widow.[59] Likewise for both suitors, contractual service itself (in this case, the arranged murder of master, superior) affirms, coaffirms, entry into the same web of relations: trusty service makes for brotherhood, kinship. They strive for *affinal relation* with Susan (thus to Mosby; and thus further, potentially, to Alice), and for relations of clientage with her brother and mistress. Each relational mode is a means to the other. In the world of this play, contractuality and kinship constitute and structure each other.

What evaporates in the motion here in *Arden* is any sense of their relative priority – and thus any sacramental force that attaches to such prioritizing. Yet Michael and Clarke continue to attempt to seize just such force, in the transcendental energy of swearing, to control Mosby and Alice, whose ideological wildness has nowhere been more clearly manifested than in their repudiation of such proprieties. And the suitor-servants' own wildness, as agents of murder (in Michael's case, treasonous master-murder and quasi-treasonous heir-murder), is to them a mobilizing toward the substantiating, ascribing, achievement of the solid positional identities of client and husband. Such a deconstructive sea of contradictions very closely resembles the ascriptive marital hypotheses of Alice and Mosby, emphasizing the dispersion of new confusions about the logic of social and thus personal identity.

Since Clarke's hoped-for confirmation of parity never quite comes, he settles for endorsing his betters' act, trying to speak as if a peer:

> . . . trust me, you show a noble mind,
> That rather than you'll live with him you hate,
> You'll venture life and die with him you love.
> The like will I do for my Susan's sake. (i.269–72)

The painter both presumes to judge them (however positively), and claims an explicit parity of worth. But further, he also uses the language of *venture* that Michael employed above (venturing upon house and land, with a right-down blow; see i.174–75), a term that helped enable the bourgeois or mercantile annexation of the aristocratic language of venturesome chivalry as a vehicle for commercial expansion. In *The Merchant of Venice*, Shakespeare's Christians thus confer a moral force on the "pursuit of the Golden Fleece."[60] But here the venture gilded is double. It includes commerce as much as *Merchant* does: increased access, by marriage, to the symbolic capital of linkage and influence, themselves means to more literal forms of capital. (Bassanio's commerce rather than Antonio's shipping, so to speak.) But Michael and Clarke's use of the rhetoric also gilds murder. "Showing a noble mind" is a rhetoric now appropriable not only by notable county gentry such as Arden, but by lesser men, and for even more disturbing purposes than Arden's. It is also now more open to a less class-categorical use, deeply personal, extra-social, a personal integrity that risks life rather than live it subjected in such a self-defining territory as that of mate selection. The claim – and the murder – are denials of such subjection; perhaps better to say, mate selection is beginning to be seen precisely as individually self-defining, rather than as the zone of familial recruitment and perpetuation. Finally, its expressive equivalents in action have also become distributed across a wider range of ennobling definition, extending "death before dishonor" to "petty treason before dishonor," that is, murder before the loss of what one desires – here, a wife. Along the way, such a posture provides too a vehicle for something like status revenge.

Alice responds to Clarke's assertion of clarity and identity in what by now will seem a typically mixed way.

> ALICE Yet nothing could enforce me to the deed
> But Mosby's love. Might I without control
> Enjoy thee still, then Arden should not die;
> But seeing I cannot, therefore let him die.
> MOSBY Enough, sweet Alice; thy kind words make me melt.   (i.273–77)

Alice claims a committed (presumably wifely?) loyalty to Arden that only Mosby's titanic love could dislodge, thus participating in both nobly conservative and magnificently independent postures at once. The dream is one of uncontrol, of radical liberty; if she may not have it, Arden must lose his; what is not given, she will seize. And just this violating posture (her "kind words") is "melting" to Mosby: he feels orgasmic, perhaps even "feminized" by her power (given the traditional associations of such liquidity), certainly overwhelmed ("Enough!").

One other moment in the career of the servant-lovers ought to be stressed at this point. Like Pedringano, Michael is developed with a detail considerably in excess of his plot requirements, providing a window into a territory of submissiveness and desire that is remarkable for its time (or any). The chief showpiece in this development is his guilty soliloquy in scene iv, when he is to aid the murderers by leaving Franklin's door unlocked in London. Like Tamburlaine's warring elements, several pressures toil for mastery within Michael. Arden's kindness (Michael is our only source for this), experienced as an external moral force, obligates him: "My master's kindness pleads to me for life / With just demand, and I must grant it him" (iv.62–63). The fealty implicit in Michael's subjection to his master jostles with a sense of his allegiance as given, chosen, by a willing subject bound originally and here again to his own sense of himself. Michael has *sworn*, willfully subjected his own will, and from his position as one empowered (to betray or save his master) he feels a clear sense of obligation.

This debt is opposed not only by his fear of the murderers, but also by a conflicting oath: "My mistress she hath forced me with an oath, / For Susan's sake the which I may not break, / For that is nearer than a master's love" (iv.64–66). First of all, note how the autonomy behind his oath has been relocated. If oaths are social machinery by means of which the individual harnesses his will publicly to a particular obligation, the effectively deconstructive presupposition is that one so harnessed must begin by being free to do so. Oaths thus function as a dual sign, of freedom and commitment. But Michael experiences his oath as unfree, *coerced*, by the demands of his mistress. (This ownership eventually transfers to Black Will and Shakebag.) Of course, the coercion derives originally from his prior desire for Susan, though his exact locution regarding her is a bit obscure: he may not break his oath lest he lose her, obviously, but "for her sake" might imply something of a debt to her, a responsibility for her, an owing of himself to her – lest *she* lose *him*. However, Michael principally experiences the *agent* in all this as Alice: the oath she forced from him was extorted, meant to arouse, reify, and entrap his will. Such obligations entail (by presupposing logically) the responsibility for the commitment; but it is exactly this responsibility that Michael cannot or will not feel, struggling to retain enough autonomy to keep a grip on his commitment to his loving master, itself a profound source of self-meaning to him. Unlike the superserviceable Oswald or Iago, Michael feels a divided loyalty (a reflex of the division between Alice and Arden), and his "own" private ambitions cannot fully transform his loyalty to his master-victim into a merely technical fact, to be edited at will.[61]

But then, his tortured mind says, the absent untouched Susan comes nearer, who will somehow give him something he cannot get from Arden's love. And even here, the principal sense is of Michael dangling between the freely given allegiances to Arden and Susan, but trapped intolerably in the middle by his own oath, unfreely given (or is that his own remystification?), at least extracted with a mind to unfreedom and a permanent imposition of culpable responsibility, to – or is it by? – his master's mistress. Even these unstable prepositions are evidence of the obscurity of that which the play is trying to capture or create. Who is in charge? What is "in charge"?

Looking back on the two suitors and the two lovers, let me reemphasize the Arden author's modal concentration on the sense of the ideological friction, of the restless dual cathexes of conservative socialized authority and licentious seizure – of mate, of life, of personal identity. Such fantasies as drive these characters have yet to develop a fully coherent voice. Mosby and Alice consistently feel abraded by the structures that restrain their desires, yet they derive strength and shape from them over and over. The pattern repeats continually. Alice measures the strength of her love for Mosby by its capacity to overcome her deep loyalty to Arden. Mosby firmly deploys his traditional and rightful male authority over Susan's marriage to set the suitors in a murderous competition to kill Alice's husband. Michael struggles with the conflicts between his heartfelt loyalty to Arden as master, his own given and taken word, and (as we shall see) his ultimately clear sense of the joy of a sheerly structural acquisition of Susan. The painter declares a noble mind, as a favor, to poison one not even a rival in exchange for Mosby's familial endorsement. The dissonant relations here between happily received social value and behavior profoundly erosive of its underlying logic may well be largely inaudible to the participants in this drama of the transformation of social reality. Perhaps the slippery tone can be captured in Alice's final oath to the painter when he promises the poison for Arden's broth: "As I am a gentlewoman, Clarke, next day / Thou and Susan shall be married" (i.286–87). Mosby of course promises a fine if unspecified dowry.

We can usefully end this section as we began, thinking further about oaths. They not only tie the masters and servants together in an unstable net of reiterated rights and obligations, but also mediate in the same volatile way the giddy relations between the so-called masters themselves. After the broth-plot miscarries, the lovers lament its failure:

> MOSBY But had he eaten but three spoonfuls more,
> Then had he died and our love continued.
> ALICE Why, so it shall, Mosby, albeit he live.
> MOSBY It is unpossible, for I have sworn
> Never hereafter to solicit thee
> Or, whilst he lives, once more importune thee.
> ALICE Thou shalt not need; I will importune thee.
> What, shall an oath make thee forsake my love?
> As if I have not sworn as much myself,
> And given my hand unto him in the church!
> Tush, Mosby. Oaths are words, and words is wind,
> And wind is mutable. Then I conclude
> 'Tis childishness to stand upon an oath
> MOSBY Well proved, Mistress Alice; yet, by your leave,
> I'll keep mine unbroken whilst he lives.   (i.426–40)

Mosby had been drawn earlier to swear to Arden, "As I intend to live / With God and His elected saints in heaven, / I never meant more to solicit her" (i.326–28), parading for the audience his readiness to swear on the most sacred things for a good cover story. (These are the effective words that finally led Arden to set rancor aside after the "mandate for my wife" speech.) Yet now, alone with Alice, Mosby seems more bound by his oath than we expected. Has he been frightened by the experience of the murder attempt? Has some sense of reality in the oath finally gotten to him? Or is this more testing of Alice?

Her first reaction is a legalistic, letter-over-spirit one: she'll do the importuning, so that he needn't break his oath. But then, of course, she realizes what his words meant, and flings a bitter reproach. I've sacrificed my word (and, once again, hand), given in church! Can't you do the same? The seriousness of her commitment is again measured by the magnitude of her sacrifice of commitment. Mosby's failure to match her own words she feels as a betrayal. But then her very measure of seriousness is itself radically demystified, as she seems to decide that he needs instruction, not confrontation. For with the eye-rolling "tush" she deflates what he takes seriously, explaining slowly (for the Realpolitik-impaired), condescendingly, technically, that oaths are but wind.[62] However, the insulting reference to childishness goes too far, and Mosby says "well proved," yet stands by his oath – by the most recent one, of course, to Arden, for he has certainly sworn solemn oaths earlier in the closet (i.185). (Where his repeated oaths to Clarke stand, or lie, is unclear. Elsewhere, obviously.)

At this stage the lovers' actions seem restlessly to float between polarities of personal, extra-social, magical, transcendental utterance and the sense that oaths are mere words. Sometimes each stands for a different sense; other times both senses jostle uneasily (or unconsciously) in the posturings of each condescending yet insecure individual. Such obscurity is not quite so thematized in the actions of Black Will and Shakebag, to whom we now turn, though they swear the most, and are not the less interesting for it.

IV

The playwright introduces the thugs through the interesting medium of Bradshaw, the innocent man who dies by proximity at the play's end. It is from him that we get the initial impression of Black Will's debased savagery, in his recollection of their shared military service:

> ... such a slave, so vile a rogue as he,
> Lives not again upon the earth. ...
> ... all the camp feared him for his villainy.
> I warrant you he bears so bad a mind
> That for a crown he'll murder any man.   (ii.5–6, 10–12)

The language is standard in its condemnations: Black Will is vile, a slave, a rogue, a villain, willing to murder anyone for next to nothing (or – the other oxymoron – to crown his absolute will). The overtones of partly moralized social rank are mostly obvious, but it is worth saying that most of them operate through some kind of egregious deprivation or expulsion: the unmastered rogue who lives outside of the accepted bounds, the villain at the bottom of things, the owned slave without even the human status of self-determination, the feral man so wild as to frighten the entire camp of soldiers, the man so bad (and poor) that murder is cheap for him. The picture rouses fear and horror in Bradshaw, but I want to stress how his picture is founded logically and causally on the villain's pain and isolation.

Will confirms this emphasis at once, calling out to "fellow Bradshaw" in his first line; but Bradshaw will not accept this fearful status, replying, "Oh, Will, times are changed; no fellows now, / Though we were once together in the field" (ii.15–16). Will's striking reply is worth repeating at length:

> BLACK WILL Why, Bradshaw, was not thou and I fellow soldiers at Boulogne, where I was a corporal and thou but a base mercenary groom? "No fellows now" because you are a goldsmith and have a little plate in your shop? You were glad to call me "fellow Will" and, with a curtsey to the earth, "one snatch, good corporal," when I stole the half ox from John the victualler, and domineered with it amongst good fellows in one night.
> BRADSHAW Ay, Will, those days are past with me.
> BLACK WILL Ay, but they be not past with me, for I keep that same honourable mind still.   (ii.18–28)

This picture of the dissonance of battlefield versus peacetime social relations rings complex bells with *The Spanish Tragedy* and later plays such as *Henry V*, and might be parsed along these lines, but I want instead to stress Black Will's fondest memory, the author's explicit and remarkable addition to Holinshed. This retrospective fantasy magnifies and elevates Will's social rank, his worth, but its highly specific vehicle is remarkable. Will treasures the delicious time he was able to *dispense hospitality*, to *give* to his fellows and be sought out for it, to be able to "domineer" by generosity – to be, in short, *wanted*. There is a comic tone, as so often, to this youthful memory counting as the touchstone of Will's "honourable mind," but how powerful it is that *this* is his touchstone![63] It is well known, of course, how important such hospitable gestures were for the Elizabethan aristocracy, as performatives of rank,[64] and it is easy to read this detail solely as ambitious or self-inflating. But I find such a reading easy and ungenerous: we need to register how softness and anguish survive within this brutal and degraded man before we can hear him truly. As will prove common, such clues must be skimmed out of Will and Shakebag's typical braying and clamorous tones of self-announcement and bragging and threatening. This means that they will be easy to miss, but to miss them is to miss the playwright's striking acknowledgment of the *origins* of those tones, and the brutality that accompanies them and gives them life, in pain and starvation. This starved man usually toils for vengeful deprivation of others in return, but here at the outset, as a foundation for this despised subject-position, the playwright gives us Will's dream of healing self-deprivation through giving – unexpected, and breathtaking.[65]

The more frequent vehicle, of course, is rage, but a rage that is subjected to striking permutations by an author who is no more satisfied with cartoon strokes for this rank than Shakespeare was with Falstaff and his fellows. Greene offers Black Will and Shakebag twenty angels for the job, and they fill up this enormous sum with their own striking meaning:

> BLACK WILL How? Twenty angels? Give my fellow George Shakebag and me twenty angels, and if thou'lt have thy own father slain that thou mayest inherit his land we'll kill him.
> SHAKEBAG Ay, thy mother, thy sister, thy brother, or all thy kin.   (ii.87–90)

The stupendous value of twenty angels resides in the degree of horror it will buy: the measure of such horror takes kinship-structure form, as it did with Alice earlier (whose love for Mosby was measured by its capacity to destroy her bounteous loyalty to her husband). We have already seen Bradshaw speak of Will as ready to kill "any man" for a crown, the vagueness marking a general disregard for such particularities of identity as might give a normal man pause. Here the particularities are made concrete: the money buys the rupture of the deepest and most basic bonds the men can imagine, the bonds of family. Twenty angels buys parricide, the father exchanged for the inheritance he refuses to fork out; it buys the murder of heirs (such as Michael fantasizes to lure Susan); and it buys the murder of mothers. Is this last a fantasy of retaliatory murder of the original failure of love, or just the reverse: of the first taste of what life has so utterly, maimingly failed to supply since? Either way we glimpse a wall of pain. Black Will's blackness perhaps had its first birth in fear of the dark, the fearful negative of Falstaff's plaintive childlike "I would 'twere bedtime, Hal, and all well" (*Henry IV Part One* 5.1.125).[66]

We must not rest with some simple moralism about the incommensurability of money and the most sacred of human lives: what we have to face is precisely that for these men they *are* commensurate. Indeed, the need goes further, since this would be a case of *vicarious* parricide or mother-murder: the relations in question are imported by the killers. Whether this is a matter of imputing such extreme motive to Greene on the basis of the size of the fee (extraordinary to them), or of the deed finding niches already shaped by their impoverishment, perhaps cannot be decided; both possibilities produce a similar effect. What remains central is how such riches at once call up a ready fantasy of violation of the culture's deepest bonds, a readiness that must surely derive from their own repudiations, repudiations that in turn bespeak their origin in damaged and radically placeless lives.

This causal chain was very frightening to many early modern Englishmen and women, as tireless homiletic injunctions against civil disorder suggest. The social, political, and economic dislocations of the
times had mustered a huge army of restless uprooted men and women,
whose incendiary potential threatened not just the queen and her narrow
elite but those many others who felt themselves located and substantiated, like Arden, by her order.[67] However, if the author of *Arden of
Faversham* shows himself willing to engage one version of the phenomenological reality of these restless lives, he also seems to cushion the impact
of his engagement. For the force of Black Will and Shakebag's purchased
anger is diluted by the repetitions of their attempted murder of Arden.
The pair try four times before succeeding on number five in the final
scene of the play: (1) the London street murder foiled by the prentice
letting down his window (scene iii); (2) the midnight attempt at the
London lodgings when Michael gives the alarm (iv); (3) the Rainham
Down attempt interrupted by Lord Cheiny (ix); (4) the attempt foiled by
the foggy night (xii); (5) the actual murder at the dinner-table (xiv).[68]

This pattern, easy to see as failure, has at least two sides. First, it is
often read as *comic*. The sheer fact of repeated failure seems ineptitude;
furthermore, as Frances E. Dolan points out, the events sometimes have
a slapstick quality, and in any case such lower-class characters are
traditionally tied to the comic.[69] Such "literary" qualities are easily
associated with a political effect: as Paul Brown observes of the revolt in
The Tempest, laughter at lower-class fury can serve to trivialize it, to
produce "the ludicrous revolt of the masterless."[70] In *The Tempest* the
laughter is given to the reformed aristocratic rebels, as a displacement
which the audience is invited to share. Here in *Arden* the laughter seems
reserved to the audience, possibly making for a simpler piece of
ideological manipulation, unplaced by the text (as is perhaps not the
case with *The Tempest*). Whether we laugh with comic distance at the
inevitable ineptitude of such ludicrous rebels or roar, with temporary
anarchic identification in the world of pratfall fantasy, for them to get
on with it and kill their man, subversion is easily recaptured. Except, of
course, for the fact that they only fail four times, not every time.
Comedy and superiority burn away when Arden's blood and brains
spread on the parlor floor. Unrest becomes unfunny, and is not
recuperated by the lamenting palinode of repentance and reported
judgment at the play's end.

Furthermore (the second side of the pattern of repeated failure), the
incapacity of Black Will and Shakebag to carry out their dream job is
probably a *demystification* of their own mystifying of the material as an
epic venture, a mental effort carried out by endless oaths and similes and

claims. The material world they inhabit is highly recalcitrant to any practical rewriting of their exclusion from the social body. For most such masterless men, throughout both the drama and the period, "will" (desire, wish, determination, spirit, swearing) is simply not enough. The material world endlessly blocks the glorious fantasies of elevation these men have. Tamburlaine is, for the most part, *only* a fantasy.

The practice (of self-fashioning by murder) seems to have problems of both means and ends. The enactment of murder is itself of some considerable difficulty, as Black Will and Hamlet both find. To wade through the sea of troubles to a practical end is much harder than the language of epic voyaging makes it seem. Yet the controlling link between means and end, act and result, is tenuous too, as the Player King reminds us. Our plans may be ours, but their ends are not. Assuming logistical superiority, gentleman Greene offers to "lay the platform" of Arden's death, but the two thugs have no patience with him. For them the act is the thing; Will brooks nothing cerebral, indeed allows no gap between thought and act at all: "Plat me no platforms! Give me the money and I'll stab him as he stands pissing against a wall, but I'll kill him" (ii.96–97). This fetish of boldness, like Michael's downright blow, marks the act as in itself self-establishing, its own reward, beyond any fee. Will wants direct action; no end runs for him. His act is also quite like an oath. The effect of "pissing against a wall" (no stopping for *any* decorum) conveys "I'll kill him no matter what; nothing can stop me."[71] Alas, Will is all too vulnerable to thwarting: onstage, hired murderers tend almost always to end up dead, or at least to disappear back into the outside whence they came. Perhaps murder doesn't work so well as a tool for self-fashioning. Perhaps for such men nothing will ever work.

Shakebag brings the full force of murder as self-institutionalization into view: "He's dead as if he had been condemned by an Act of Parliament if once Black Will and I swear his death" (ii.100–01). This claim combines something of the effect of Tamburlaine's "I have said" with a kind of seizure of the authority of the highest legislative authority in the land. (Presumably to speak of Parliament rather than King is to summon *collective* ratification.) Will carries the fiction revealingly further:

> My fingers itches to be at the peasant. Ah, that I might be set a work thus throughout the year and that murder would grow to an occupation that a man might without danger of law. Zounds! I warrant I should be warden of the company. Come, let us be going, and we'll bait at Rochester, where I'll give thee a gallon of sack to handsel the match withal. (ii.104–09)

As we have seen repeatedly, the fantasy of personal domination invariably erupts in a language of the social debasement of the victim:

such contempt glorifies the self, a deeply desired by-product. But such elevation becomes far more concrete, for Will dreams here, stunningly, of a steady job! He hates hand-to-mouth piecework, apparently, and dreams of a gradual social change that would confer upon him the status of one with an *occupation*. For an occupation can breed a socially acceptable identity; debasing, self-irrelevant labor can establish a self. Black Will knows but doesn't care why he's to murder Arden (unlike, in different ways, both Pedringano and Webster's Bosola); he dreams of extracting a different sort of self-institution: the dream of ordered work within the law. If things were properly arranged, he seems to say, he'd be the ideal legal murderer. (No Bosolan reluctance here.) Black Will's dreams reveal the have-not's envious desire beneath anger at the established, as can be seen in the treasured memory of the half-ox. The desire precedes the envy, and is not swallowed by it in this play. Will dreams of a steady life, not fueled by envious rage, but by methodical, bourgeois competence at his trade. What for Falstaff is a joke ("Why, Hal, 'tis my vocation, Hal. 'Tis no sin for a man to labor in his vocation" [1.2.105–6]) is at some level a real fantasy, as it were, for Black Will.

The mention of Falstaff takes us to the final line of the speech, where sack becomes a symbol. Black Will proposes the bonding contractual gesture of the *handsel*. Technically, this oath-like material gesture was an inaugural gift, a piece of homeostatic magic designed to bring on more such success in a venture. But there is perhaps an echo of *sealing*, the Renaissance equivalent of putting one's identity on the dotted line, something of witnessing. And of course most deeply Black Will again makes himself the giver, the hospitable nourisher, as with the ox. (Is it ultimately some kind of infolded pathetic lament, inescapable even in the heart of this precious memory, that it was a *half*-ox?)

Rising by degrading self-subjection becomes a time-honored practice (and subject) in Renaissance drama, and we have already watched Pedringano assess its costs. But nowhere else is there such a detailed exploration as here of deprivation as the root of such ambition. Pedringano and Bosola seem less entitled to sympathy because of their prior locations, as main servant to the blood royal, university man and servant to a cardinal, and so forth. Black Will, I suggest, comes from the Elizabethan underclass, a placeless vagrant, far from the court and its highly unusual set of opportunities. When his fingers itch to be at Arden the peasant, he inverts, retorts, his own fate upon his victim, speaking from the dirt. It is dirt left behind, it is true, for London and the Netherlands, classic regions of opportunity for the placeless. However, the striking images of destitution that position Will and Shakebag before us indicate a presumptive zone of origin well below most of the dramatic villains we get to know so well.[72] For such men, there was nowhere to go but up. Will's violent refusal of that world makes a virtue of necessity: he *uses* the violence that perhaps began as an inchoate gesture of defiance and hatred, to reach out toward somewhere else in the social world. He reached his greatest elevation, as corporal (ii.19), in wartime, when peacetime social controls are most set aside, sudden elevations are most possible. ("Ancient" Pistol's comparable career is instructive both for lows and highs.)[73] When he returns, he dreams of being the Warden of the Worshipful Company of Murderers, after all: a thoroughly bourgeois fate, beyond the yeomen like Michael, leaping past one group of oppressive superiors, but beyond he cannot dream.

In the next scene Will and Shakebag fail for the first time to kill Arden, defeated by a prentice who lets down the shutter of his stall and breaks Will's head. He is utterly unconcerned by the ruffians' threats: "if you get you not away all the sooner, you shall be well beaten and sent to the Counter" (iii.57–58). Though Will is terrifying to Bradshaw, he is a pest to a London prentice, another evidence of Will's stature in his world. (Perhaps more specifically in regard to the worlds of war and peace: in war Will was a sanctioned killer, in peace he is always nearly a buffoon.) Aside from his impotent fury (he swears he will pull down all the shop signs), Will regrets a professional failure, and he and Shakebag allude repeatedly to the goodness of their word. "Were my consent to give again we would not do it under ten pound more ... But that a bargain is a bargain and so forth, you should do it yourself" (iii.65–66, 68–69). Their good name is at stake. "Forbearance is no acquittance; another time we'll do it, I warrant thee," Shakebag reassures Greene (iii.75–76).

Still, as with the insecure affirmations of Alice and Mosby, such occupational responsibility is mixed uneasily with the half-visible deconstructive praxis of these disruptive killers for hire. Greene makes the mistake of reminding Will, saying, "Remember how devoutly thou hast sworn / To kill the villain; think upon thine oath" (iii.80–81), and uncorks a furious rejoinder from Will:

> Tush, I have broken five hundred oaths!
> But wouldst thou charm me to effect this deed,
> Tell me of gold, my resolution's fee;
> Say thou seest Mosby kneeling at my knees,
> Off'ring me service for my high attempt;
> And sweet Alice Arden, with a lap of crowns,
> Comes with a lowly curtsey to the earth,
> Saying 'Take this but for thy quarterage;
> Such yearly tribute will I answer thee.'
> I tell thee, Greene, the forlorn traveller,
> Whose lips are glued with summer's parching heat,

Ne'er longed so much to see a running brook
As I to finish Arden's tragedy.
Seest thou this gore that cleaveth to my face?
From hence ne'er will I wash this bloody stain
Till Arden's heart be panting in my hand.[74]   (iii.82–97)

The very act of calling on his given word (of *reminding*, as Alice and Michael do above) drives Will into a frantic rage. The questioning of his potency latent in the reminder calls up his deepest resource of self-respect: his insistence on disorderliness, on oath-breaking, defacing the normative structures that bind others and keep him down. Instead, he demands, charm me with allure; seek not to threaten me, or I strike. Give him gold, his resolution's fee: gold ratifies him, recognizes him, confers himself on him, as changeless, relentless, remorseless, absolute.

He also fantasizes what he thinks gold buys – status. Heroic oath-breaking leads to the vision of his employers kneeling before him, Mosby offering abjected acknowledgment of superiority, and not only inferiority but service, not only inverting his hire-status but enabling its recursive movement toward ascriptive force. For her part, Alice with her sweet lap lowers herself socially (curtsey) and offers socially elevating wealth (the tinge of *crowns*) within highly legalist language (quarterage, tribute – this last also heroic). Such a spectacle is erotically perceived, too, a signal that becomes a pattern in time (as I think Alice herself intends, but that also speaks to Will's libidinal relation to these needs).

However, the very touch of these images of gratification and satisfaction arouses another image of emptiness: Will compares his hunger for Arden's death to that of a forlorn traveler, "whose lips are glued" shut, for a running brook. Once again Will's deprivations leak into view. The traveler is forlorn, lost, abandoned, unfriended; and not only a placeless wanderer but also an unemployed worker, a sturdy vagrant, a masterless man. For him Arden's murder is a way out (or rather, in), a self-institutionalization, a self-interpellation.

At the same time such deprivation and reparation occurs in the physical as well as in the social body. This typifying pain takes a precisely *oral* form, a mark that, having begun with the mythical half-ox, now becomes a leitmotif for this pattern, resonating variously between the pain of an absent or betraying maternal nourishment and a wounding bite. Here the traveler's lips are glued, seemingly with the gore from Will's broken head, now cleaving to his face. With an oath he turns this pain to use, as habitually, making it, as does Kyd with Bel-imperia's bloody scarf, a talisman or charm that handsels or self-determines or dedicates.

And what is his goal? Once again, to occupy a socially accepted and self-defining niche, performing a determining act of the judicial torturer and hangman. Black Will keeps dreaming of an institutional identity, perhaps historically the only one of this kind to be had (though we have more modern applications). Such positive identity, though, however reified (Will's dream), was itself another instantiation of the category of outsider. Pieter Spierenberg, historian of executions in early modern Europe, begins his history with the widespread public detestation of the hangman, who was nearly literally a kind of untouchable, marked as *infamous* (a technical term).[75] He was subjected to frequent daily abuse in the streets (usually stoning, so that one's hands might not be soiled by direct contact); money was unsafe to take directly from his hands (he had to put it on the counter before the merchant would touch it); he could not finger the fruit he considered buying; boatmen and funeral guildsmen refused to carry him in life and in death; those who drank with him unwittingly were sometimes even reported to kill themselves. (See Spierenberg, *The Spectacle of Suffering* 19.)

> It is not surprising therefore that the hangman's touch was considered as a penalty in itself. The ensuing infamy constituted an important ingredient of the injury that punishment should be. In popular tales this touch emerges as the most dreadful of all for the condemned. Consequently, it is a means of showing mercy if the judges determined that a person to be beheaded was not to be touched by the executioner (ibid.).

He was subjected to various literal, spatial marginalizations: the location of his home was stipulated, he had his own pew in church, he was the last participant at communion (in both Protestant and Catholic countries), he might be required to drink alone at his own isolate table at the tavern, or only at one tavern, or even in the street. He had a hard time finding godparents for his children; then his sons were barred from acceptance as apprentices to most guilds, and his daughters were hard put to find husbands (19–20). Only later in the early modern period was he entitled to burial in consecrated ground, with a normal church funeral (32–33). Such contemptuous views certainly obtained in early modern England. In *Measure for Measure* Shakespeare names his executioner Abhorson. The bawd Pompey must choose between helping Abhorson with his work and being whipped (see 4.2.8–14). In Fletcher's *The Woman's Prize*, or *The Tamer Tamed* (1604, a sequel to *The Taming of the Shrew*), a tormented, remarried Petruchio exclaims, "I would do any thing below repentance, / Any base dunghill slavery; be a hangman, / Ere I would be a husband" (3.5.127–29).[76] No wonder that Spierenberg speaks of "the precariousness of the hangman's existence among his fellow citizens" (13). And what a wonder that for Black Will such positionality is an object of desire![77]

At this point Shakebag contributes his own echo of Will's self-willed posture, significantly advancing the pattern of predatory suffering orality.

> Such mercy as the starven lioness,
> When she is dry-sucked of her eager young,
> Shows to the prey that next encounters her,
> On Arden so much pity shall I take.   (iii.103–6)

Again there is the mixture of oral suffering, maternal nourishing, and violent domination. Now the murderer is a mother, and for a good and selfless cause. She lives up to her obligations, feeds her young, and is relentless.[78] What Will sought for as a socially sanctioned, albeit rare, occupation, Shakebag construes as a natural and universal display of ordered and nourishing violence. Disruptive characters invariably construe their own actions self-confirmingly. The discourse of traditional order repeatedly serves this function locally, however much such usages may eventually corrode its foundations.

Michael now enters, and the killers seize him. Black Will, impatient with the discursive chat of Greene, calls for a more efficient brutality than Greene has used: "You deal too mildly with the peasant" (iii.136). He grabs Michael by the lapels, preparing, we expect, to impose his will on him and use him for their plot; the result is somewhat different:

> 'Tis known to us you love Mosby's sister;
> We know besides that you have ta'en your oath
> To further Mosby to your mistress' bed
> And kill your master for his sister's sake.
> Now, sir, a poorer coward than yourself
> Was never fostered in the coast of Kent.
> How comes it then that such a knave as you
> Dare swear a matter of such consequence?   (iii.137–44)

Will seizes the power that comes with knowing a man's inmost secrets, but he seems most concerned not with the treasons, petty and otherwise,[79] but with the effrontery of Michael's oath. Such swearing, it seems – to Will anyway – is not a matter for ordinary men to meddle with, but only for men of worth and mettle, like himself. He has devised "a complot under hand" with his confederates to control any wandering ideas Michael may have in the practical realm (such as revealing the murder plan), but the important thing he wants to get clear is a more metaphysical (or perhaps meta-social) demonstration, of who is the real recipient of the oath's magical or transcendental empowerment:

> ... I am the very man,
> Marked in my birth-hour by the Destinies,
> To give an end to Arden's life on earth;

Thou but a member but to whet the knife
Whose edge must search the closet of his breast.
Thy office is but to appoint the place,
And train thy master to his tragedy;
Mine to perform it when occasion serves. (iii.152–59)

Will's service began in employment, underwent great imaginative magnification with the aid of the twenty angels,[80] and has now emerged as his divinely appointed destiny. He is destined, or rather, has destined himself; for is not this too a seizure like Hieronymo's "all the saints do sit soliciting for our revenge"? Will (by this time his name rings uncontrollably as a sign) is to become *par sibi*, like himself,[81] by virtue of the ascriptive power (he has) vested in this murder. By this time he seems to be speaking mainly to himself, though declaiming to those present too; voicing a fantasy, perhaps, rather than making a claim. Or maybe Will claims a predetermining audience of the Destinies, whose voice he feels himself to be.[82] For contrast, Michael may not intrude beyond his proper role. (A greater man than I cometh after?) Michael, seized by the lapels, serves as a prosthesis, a member, a tool with (limited) function (office), to whet will's edge, an earthly extension of Will's will, just as the Destinies are in heavenly terms.

The copresence of "member" and the searching of the closet of Arden's breast calls out for intratextual comment. This is a clear intrusion or invasion, as with Alice's invitation to Mosby (into what after all is Arden's closet too, as householder and husband). We also have the overlay of the oath sworn there, the "decree" before the heavens that Arden must die, as here, as proof (indeed, guarantee) of the lovers' love. Finally, there is what might be termed the pre-echo of Will hidden in the counting-house in the final scene, from which he only exits to kill. (Surely the counting-house is even more Arden's closet.) It is no surprise that houses and bodies alike have closets which hold infinite riches, on which much may be sworn, more may be built. The act that founds the love of the lovers is both erotic and violent; the same is true for that act that founds Will's achievement of significant identity, again both violent and libidinal. Michael is handmaiden to both acts.

The scene ends with Michael's soliloquy, wherein he once again laments his double bind, and works his way through it to some rudimentary peace of mind – or at least dismissal. He begins with yet another iteration of a now-familiar trope:

Thus feeds the lamb securely on the down
Whilst through the thicket of an arbour brake
The hunger-bitten wolf o'erpries his haunt
And takes advantage to eat him up. (iii.184–87)

For Michael, if for no one else, Arden is a lamb, ripe to sacrifice by the hunger-bitten wolf (though a lamb that appropriately feeds on the downland, as Arden the engrossing landlord may be said to do).[83] Yet the wolf, though savage, is marked even by fearful Michael as himself (or herself) a bitten victim, driven by a pain natural to all living things. (Indeed, "hunger-bitten" is, like so many other details in the play, doubled, doubly oral; or perhaps instead hunger gnaws the wolf's innards, like the eagle of Prometheus. Will would certainly like this reading.)

Michael ends his hesitations by acknowledging the powers of oaths, in the usual disordered way:

> So I have sworn to Mosby and my mistress,
> So I have promised to the slaughtermen;
> And should I not deal currently with them,
> Their lawless rage would take revenge on me.
> Tush, I will spurn at mercy for this once.
> Let pity lodge where feeble women lie;
> I am resolved, and Arden needs must die.   (iii.196–202)

He is bound by his oaths (separate ones to all four), and is thereby at the mercy of their "lawless rage," unconstrained by what binds him. So their lawless mercilessness summons up an answering mercilessness of his own, introduced by their favorite despising particle "tush," accompanied by resoluteness and spurning.

The line banishing pity, so banal in its discursive familiarity, nonetheless opens up a striking linkage with the final image I will deal with of the deprivations of brutes. In scene v, after Michael has failed to overcome his fears, and thus disrupted another of the murder-plots, the killers rage at their prevention, presuming that Michael has betrayed them as a mockery. Will swears revenge by inviting his own impotence:

> Ne'er let this sword assist me when I need,
> But rust and canker after I have sworn,
> If I, the next time that I meet the hind,
> Lop not away his leg, his arm, or both.   (v.42–45)

Shakebag swears likewise, in a stunning mixture of active and passive violence and pain:

> And let me never draw a sword again,
> Nor prosper in the twilight, cockshut light,
> When I would fleece the wealthy passenger,
> But lie and languish in a loathsome den,
> Hated and spit at by the goers-by,
> And in that death may die unpitied
> If I, the next time that I meet the slave,

Cut not the nose from off the coward's face
And trample on it for this villainy. (v.46–54)

Like Will, Shakebag builds in a self-coercive negative (as Pedringano also did in similar circumstances): Will brandishes a self-castration, but Shakebag imagines, much more powerfully, what surely must be a *return*, to a life all too well known and hated, the forgotten and despised and rejected life of those at the real bottom of the social order. Such a hated life is flown from at all costs, most satisfyingly by just such a venture as this murder. For murder, as an action, especially as a violent act, strikes at the contemptible (and terrifying) helplessness and passivity of lying and languishing, at the feebleness of the women in Michael's line ("Let pity lodge where feeble women lie"), who for men like Black Will and Shakebag are not only prostrate but false, and deserve to be spurned on both counts (as the play's ending will reveal). Such life is a death, and a death unworthy even of pity (the necessary denizen of such a wasteland, but banished proleptically here as in Pedringano's similar speech) unless one can summon the worthy manly rage necessary to enable a displacement of responsibility onto another. Again dismemberment, the law's penalty for so many poor men's crimes, threatens. Shakebag, unlike Will, seizes it and threatens Michael with it, escaping its edge for himself. Finally it seems that dismemberment awaits such men at either end, whether they lie impotent and languish like feeble women, spat on by such manly goers-by as themselves, or take arms against a sea of troubles, and end them on the scaffold. But what seems preconditional for these men, and most hated, is passivity and weakness, the originary condition of such culturally feminized starvelings, and they threaten themselves with it, swearing by it, as a way of continually repudiating selves so interpellated. Such deprived weakness fuels enormous rage. No wonder that the hegemonic Henry V, so well-informed about the powers of the lower strata, says of another poor man with a notable nose, "We would have all such offenders so cut off" (*Henry V* 3.6.107).

V

A second movement in the lovers' dissonant relation begins soon after, in scene viii, with Mosby's soliloquy of depression. Once again, only through negations can they seem to work toward the foundation of their new positive bond.

Mosby's disturbed thoughts, like excess of sack (a surfeit after intoxicating desire?), enfeeble his body (that is, render him passive and feminized, continuing parallels with Michael and Shakebag) and "nip" him "as the bitter north-east wind / Doth check the tender blossoms in the spring" (viii.5–6). The parallel with Don Andrea is ominous.[84] Here too the discontent is a function of upward sexual mobility. Yet how distant Mosby is here from any libidinal sense of this path: "My golden time was when I had no gold. / Though then I wanted, yet I slept secure; / My daily toil begat me night's repose, / My night's repose made daylight fresh to me" (viii.11–14). His dream, from which he has awakened unrested, seems now of wealth, and of a "nest among the clouds" (16); like Hal, he is on the way to despising it:

> But whither doth contemplation carry me?
> The way I seek to find, where pleasure dwells,
> Is hedged behind me that I cannot back
> But needs must on although to danger's gate.   (viii.19–22)

Anticipating Macbeth, Mosby wearily says "*retro me*" to his pastoral nostalgia, feeling no choice but to go forward. And the goal is similarly withered: Alice is now a nameless place, "danger's gate." All pleasure seems unreachably past; only process survives.

Yet such motion can still reassert purpose: "Then, Arden, perish *thou* by that decree (viii.23; my emphasis). From the original goal Mosby recovers a sense of telos, if no longer along a trajectory quite shared with Alice. The word "decree" (plucked from its origin in Alice's closet) reengages the will, and the sense of empowerment that having, exercising, a will conveys. Indeed, the hedge itself becomes the decree, passive becomes active. The plan that seemed in the preceding lines to have entrapped Mosby, to have deprived him of the peace that comes with unconstricted unplanned living, he reorients, as a deprivation of *Arden*, seizing agency from that oath and obligation, the reified, embodied, externalized fantasy that he experienced as a hedge. This gesture of escape suggests that Mosby, like Michael, feels himself to have been "forced with an oath" (iv.64). He struggles to recapture a sense of autonomy, fighting the depression that accompanies a felt loss or alienation of control, originally willed as a commitment, a seizure.

Once restored, he works his way through the other agents in play, assessing their power over him, their potential for danger, and recapturing from each a quantum of his own freedom and power (freedom from and freedom to), unfastening himself from the contractual and occasional bonds by which he is subjected, by which he had originally felt enabled. First Greene:

> For Greene doth ear the land and weed thee [Arden] up
> To make my harvest nothing but pure corn.
> And for his pains I'll heave him up awhile
> And, after, smother him to have his wax.[85]   (viii.24–27)

Mosby employs this nostalgic vegetative language to seize the very power to which he had felt subject at the outset of his speech:[86]

> Then is there Michael and the painter too,
> Chief actors to Arden's overthrow,
> Who, when they shall see me sit in Arden's seat,
> They will insult upon me for my meed,
> Or fright me by detecting of his end.
> I'll none of that, for I can cast a bone
> To make these curs pluck out each other's throat,
> And then am I sole ruler of mine own.   (viii.29–36)

As with Henry IV and the Percies, Mosby's elevation will subject him to those below him (over whom he now has authority as the master of Susan's body). By making them destroy each other, he subjects them to subhuman (i.e., canine) status, reduces the dispersions of power, to the self, the individual, reeling in his vulnerabilities.

Once again, as with Lorenzo, bonds become vulnerabilities:

> Yet Mistress Alice lives; but she's myself,
> And holy church rites make us two but one.
> But what for that I may not trust you, Alice?
> You have supplanted Arden for my sake,
> And will extirpen me to plant another.
> 'Tis fearful sleeping in a serpent's bed,
> And I will cleanly rid my hands of her.   (viii.37–43)

Sole ruler cannot abide a coequal wife, apparently. To say Alice lives is to think of her dead. She is to some degree incorporated, through the rites of the church; but while there is technical safety in this, he really feels penetrated, knowing now what founds their bond. For the irony is that Mosby moves instantly from this most direct reference to seized ascription, to (can this be *causal*?) explicit doubt of Alice, and the decision to get rid of her himself, in self-protection from exactly the behavior on her part that has resulted in his own opportunity for elevation. Mosby says Alice has supplanted Arden: literally, she has not put Mosby in Arden's place so much as herself in Arden's place – and thus Mosby in hers, as "wife." (Her autonomy already conspicuous, Alice will not be a wife subordinated to his appropriate spousal authority, but a more modern mate, coequal if not better – that is, worse.) Now Mosby "realizes" that this seizure of autonomy and will and initiative will be repeated, replacing him with another – literally, *planting* another, an insemination which leads to thinking Alice as a *serpent* in bed, i.e., masculinized and phallic, beside Mosby sleeping there unaware, vulnerable, feminized.[87] After this half-erotic fantasy he swears he will "cleanly rid his hands" of her. Why hands? Partly, perhaps, because he can thus make her a tool he can use and then dispose of. But in light of the previous line, if she is something (phallic) that dirties his hands, this may be some jumbled sexual image, perhaps post-masturbatory. Perhaps enjoyed no sooner but despised straight, thus savage, extreme, rude, cruel, not to trust.

Such mutual soiling leads once again to mutual negations, beginning with Alice too using vegetable language, not inseminating but the reverse: "let our springtime wither; / Our harvest else will yield but loathsome weeds" (viii.66–67). Like Mosby, she too has been feeling the bitter north-east wind, and like Mosby she tries to control it by turning its destruction on another. Also nostalgic, Alice would return to her old situation, leaving the "title of an odious strumpet's name" (72) for the name (of proper wife) that Mosby has "rifled" her of, having "made [her] sland'rous to all [her] kin." "Even in my forehead is thy name engraven, / A mean artificer, that low-born name" (viii.74–77).

These words engender Mosby's fury anew; indeed, such bitter states of mind seem to be the necessary prelude to affection between the pair, and to be sought as such. "Nay, if thou ban, let me breathe curses forth," he cries, raining out oaths of negation and unbinding, speaking of better opportunities he has left behind, such as marriage to an honest maid "whose beauty and demeanour far exceeded thee. / This certain good I lost for changing bad, / And wrapped my credit in thy company" (viii.90–92). But now he swears he will see her as she is, "a copesmate for [her] hinds" (viii.104). If Alice has lost her good name, he says, look what he has lost: credit, opportunities for advancement, a proper marriage (dowry, beauty, carriage), and again credit. (These, of course, are exactly equivalent to Alice's loss, not worse.) Thus deserving, he sends her off to muddy Hodge, fit mate for one with such tastes (an insult that occludes his own inferior status by appearing to come from above): "I am too good to be your favorite" (viii.105).

Alice replies in kind:

> Now I see, and too soon find it true,
> Which often hath been told me by my friends,
> That Mosby loves me not but for my wealth,
> Which too incredulous I ne'er believed.   (viii.106–09)

This "friends'" view of Mosby is, remember, her *family's*. This line provides some evidence for the enforced-marriage reading of the relationship. Alice's friends have discussed Mosby with her and offered opinions for some time ("often"), perhaps since before her marriage. But the very mention, it seems, of her friends' disapprobation and their idea of

Mosby's mercenary motives recalls her in panic to her original anti-social allegiance:

> Look on me, Mosby, or I'll kill myself;
> Nothing shall hide me from thy stormy look. . . .
> I will do penance for offending thee
> And burn this prayerbook, where I here use
> The holy word that had converted me.
> See, Mosby, I will tear away the leaves,
> And all the leaves, and in this golden cover
> Shall thy sweet phrases and thy letters dwell,
> And thereon will I chiefly meditate
> And hold no other sect but such devotion.   (viii.112–13, 115–22)

Alice dreads Mosby's denial of recognition; better his anger than dismissal. Somehow his love, she says (better, really, her investment in the project), makes her exist, like God or Satan's love. She pleads for penance rather than have him turn his face away from her. This sounds like a permutation of Faustus' terrified appeasement of Lucifer, "I'll burn my book." However, instead of fending off a punishing deity, Alice's idolatrous offering strives to bind an abandoning Mosby, tying the proof of her new-forged reality to an oxymoronic rebellious counter-devotion or submission that originally seemed the guarantee of liberation. For a Protestant audience such self-gift (willful and submissive at once) would have been frightful idolatry.

Still, Mosby will not so easily relent:

> Oh, no, I am a base artificer,
> My wings are feathered for a lowly flight.
> Mosby? Fie, no! not for a thousand pound.
> Make love to you? Why, 'tis unpardonable;
> We beggars must not breathe where gentles are.   (viii.135–39)

He hangs on, extorting apologies, already playing the husband, till finally she finds the right thing to say, ending the scene recursively with a latter spring of mysterious mendelian legitimacy:

> Sweet Mosby is as gentle as a king,
> And I too blind to judge him otherwise.
> Flowers do sometimes spring in fallow lands,
> Weeds in gardens, roses grow on thorns;
> So whatso'er my Mosby's father was,
> Himself is valued gentle by his worth.   (viii.140–45)

The main impression this speech gives is that of the sheer application of pressure, praise that is incoherent but gets the job done. Mosby's worth overcomes any limits of parentage, which in any case is non-determining (if flowers in fallows, also weeds in gardens – is this, if Mosby, also Alice?). Besides, she seems to say, I'm so crazy about you that I can't see straight, but you look like a king to me. Mosby is gentled, tamed, by being made gentle; and the transformation to or achievement of gentility occurs in despite of its usual determination by lineage. Like Clarke's murderous noble mind (see i.269), Mosby's gentility is individually transcendent; the absence of social foundation becomes a transcended ground.

Such insinuation, as Mosby calls it, does the trick: "I'll forget this quarrel, gentle Alice, / Provided I'll be tempted so no more" (viii.148–49). "Then," she replies, "with thy lips seal up this new-made match" (150). When a second later he rejoins, "Ay, to the gates of death to follow thee" (viii.165), the sense of echo is strong, for first, of course, he had begun the scene in near-despair, feeling he had lost all autonomous telos: "I cannot back / But needs must on although to danger's gate" (21–22).[88] More obscurely, this new forwardness sealed with lips speaks of wasteland, echoing across the narrative to the forlorn traveler's lips, glued like Will's broken head with gore. The running brook that beckons Will seems now to flow with Arden's blood, and beckons the lovers too, from beyond their increasingly forlorn and fallen world. Such continual reconsecrations to heterodoxy as we witness, ever more extravagant, speak more to denied and arid absences of the social orders they have left behind (Alice's good wife's name, Mosby's credit and marriage with an honest maid) than they effectually reaffirm the new society the lovers have been dreaming.

VI

A pair of gestures by Will in scene ix and a movement by Alice in scene x carry the play to the point of the actual murder. First, though, consider that there are *two* assassins: such haunted and abandoned men, enclosed as well as expelled by a society of Others, have great need of someone the Same. Though they seem continually to quarrel, I think we need to read this as a mutual and satisfying provision of audience, for demanding expressions of their own worth, so generally denied by everyone else – as by Bradshaw, for instance. When one of *them* denies the other, though, the effect is something like that of a sonnet-lady's refusal: it invites reiteration, itself a self-pleasuring and nourishing process.

As Black Will and Shakebag prepare in scene ix to take another shot at Arden, they quarrel as usual about their relative status and honor. Like a professional teammate, Shakebag has encouraged Will to check his powder, but (or perhaps we should say, so) Will takes offense. This active verb is especially appropriate here (though perhaps it is always revealing). "Then ask me if my nose be on my face" (ix.3), he snaps back, reminding us of Shakebag's threatened rhinectomy in response to Michael's offense earlier. "You were best swear me on the intergatories" (6), he says, as to how many pistols I have discharged, etc. Shakebag retorts that his total career take is more "than either thou or all thy kin are worth" (18). These typical jabs make the usual phallic and legalistic and kinship claims and denials – each claim entailing a mutualist denial, and *vice versa*. Will finds such words agreeably "intolerable" (as Arden did in scene i), and this time they fight, enacting (as Greene notes) the very "two dogs and a bone" scenario that Mosby plans to use to dispose of Michael and the painter. Greene calls a halt, from which Will extracts one final unit of divinely-countenanced self-fashioning: "I do but slip [the quarrel] until a better time. / But if I do forget – / *Then he kneels down and holds up his hands to heaven*" (ix.36–37). As so often, he both enjoins heaven's supportive attention and casts it as threatening. The traditional language of order is wrested to many disorderly utterances, but it always carries with it a trace of its originally judgmental vector, by which Will seems, behind it all, mesmerized.

A moment later they are about to spring the trap on Arden on Rainham Down when Lord Cheiny intervenes and they are foiled again. Greene, labeled earlier as "a man of great devotion" (i.587), says "The Lord of Heaven hath preserved him" (ix.142). Greene seems to convey no sense that such divine interference has anything to say to the killers. The observation seems to have the force of a technical note, marking, as modern insurance policies say, an act of God. But Black Will will have none even of this transcendentalism, however secular: "The Lord of Heaven a fig! The Lord Cheiny hath preserved him" (ix.143). Perhaps what Greene failed to hear was audible enough to Will to require (like Michael's nose) trampling. And the terminology of the gesture (the fig – again like Michael's nose) is expressly phallic. The uses of the phallus for anger seem endless in this play. However much Will may be able to use transcendental categories for self-dramatization, he cannot abide their presumptions of human limit. In the face of his repeated failures, such relentlessness (also hard-bitten professionalism, of course) is a bulwark sorely needed.

Scene x begins with Alice's equivalent of Black Will's phallic gestures. Arden departs for dinner with Lord Cheiny. Alice feigns resentment, but Arden insists that his attendance is obligatory: "For so his honour late commanded me" (x.11) perfectly exhibits his submissive and deferential tone (expressed even in private). Alice seizes this obedient tone as feminized, by a belittling erotic response: "The time hath been – would

God it were not past – / That honour's title nor a lord's command /
Could once have drawn you from these arms of mine" (x.14–16). (Can
this reference be meant to suggest that Arden is "past it"? – a shadow of
the oral tradition's age difference?)

It seems clear (and becomes clearer throughout scene xiv) that Alice
sometimes eroticizes her relations this way as a means of controlling
them. When she first enters the play, she is reproaching Arden for rising
early from bed: "Had I been wake you had not risen so soon" (i.59).
Arden takes this expressly as erotic, remembering "Ovid-like" occasions,
but says that this night she has "killed [his] heart": "I heard thee call on
Mosby in thy sleep" (i.65–66). We cannot tell if her reproach is not also
sadistic, or even if it is just a matter of dislike of what Franklin stands for
in Arden's life, but the brandishing of the erotic is clear. So it is more
nakedly a moment later, when in the same tones she begs Franklin to
bring her man home soon, and says, "In hope you'll hasten him home I'll
give you this. [*And then she kisseth him*]" [i.411]). To Arden she breathes,
"Stay no longer there / Than thou must needs, lest that I die for sorrow"
(i.406).

Such false fainting dependency is but the mask for an eroticized
concern with power that becomes increasingly explicit as the murder
approaches. Soon after Arden leaves for Lord Cheiny's, Alice says
contemptuously, "Why should he thrust his sickle in our corn, / Or what
hath he to do with thee, my love, / Or govern me that am to rule myself?"
(x.82–84). By this time the vegetable imagery has become quite multi-
valent: Arden's thrusting phallic sickle (so little in evidence when we last
saw him, yet still so offensively swollen for Alice) now threatens their
harvest, so long awaited, and perhaps even summons up the grim reaper
and the urge to *carpe diem*. The image also suggests agrarian theft: Arden
is the bourgeois usurper again. Finally, her reaction to Arden's invasive
sexuality bodes ill for Mosby too, as Alice seems to deny even his
potential right to interfere with her own will. It is no wonder that Mosby
uneasily replies by asking, "what's love without true constancy?" (x.90),
which he images as another phallic image, a pillar that, being touched,
falls, without the true bonding of mortar or cement (a pun on "semen"?),
"and buries all his haughty pride in dust" (x.96).[89] "No," he says
subjunctively, "let our love be rocks of adamant" (x.97): the spectacle of
Alice's reactions to Arden appears to rouse thoughts of doubt for
Mosby, which he must avert with wishful protestations.

As the climactic moment approaches in scene xiv, Alice expends
eroticism on another object. After Black Will explains the most recent
failure (in a passage that looks forward strikingly to Falstaff's account of
the Gadshill robbery), she says,

Ah, sirs, had he yesternight been slain,
For every drop of his detested blood
I would have crammed in angels in thy fist,
And kissed thee, too, and hugged thee in my arms.   (xiv.70–73)

And a moment later she makes it present:

Come, Black Will, that in mine eyes art fair;
Next unto Mosby do I honour thee. . . .
My hands shall play you golden harmony.
How like you this? Say, will you do it, sirs?   (xiv.112–13, 115–16)

The thought of Arden's death makes Alice melt too (as it did Mosby above at i.277). The Marlovian trope of emphasis by the compressed violence of opposed extremes (*drop* and *crammed*) bears here a sexual freight, explicit in the kisses and hugs, but with crammed fist suggesting too (as with Alice's hands playing harmony) a submerged masturbatory fantasy. And in each case the drops (the cement, Mosby would call them) are joyful gold, sexual commodities like Franklin's kiss.

The underlying reality-function of these images (and thus proof of their inflammatory surface) seeps out when she adds, thinking forward to post-murder plans, "Michael will saddle you two lusty geldings. Ride whither you will" (xiv.129–30). If she has aroused their passionate desire for the murder by a kind of metonymic allure of her own, it has been ultimately for an appropriation of that passion. And once Black Will and Shakebag, now seeming precise embodiments of "savage, extreme, rude, cruel, not to trust," have enacted that joy proposed, she will send them on their way, lusty but gelded, bearing the responsibility for her bliss. Having aroused herself while she was at it, after the killers leave she indulges in a highly explicit Ovidian sexual fantasy about Mosby (at xiv.142–53), probably functionally a prothalamion looking forward to the closeted bloodletting of the coming wedding night. She can't wait.

Such consummation is preceded by a final programmatic institutional-ization, a bizarre and sadistic ceremony of pledging and toasting that is Alice and Mosby's equivalent of *wedding*. Alice ironically berates Arden for bringing Mosby home to dinner: "his company hath purchased [her] ill friends" (182), she says, and she would have him gone. After the guilt-inducing fiasco of scene xiii, Arden is (once again) anxious to show how unjealous he is, and now such talk makes him unwittingly play the role of priest at their marriage. (If the lovers went to London to use one priest, as Holinshed tells us, perhaps this secret charade counts as a similar appropriation, something like Jessica stealing her dowry from a father who would never bless the match.) "Sirrah," Arden says to Michael, "fetch me a cup of wine; I'll make them friends" (199). "You may

enforce me to [welcome Mosby] if you will" (180), she has said, but the
enforcement of this marriage flows the other way. "I am content to drink
to him for this once" (206), she now says, and addresses Mosby with
these words: "Be you as strange to me as I to you" (208), a mutual
pledge that encodes their strange foreign bonding simultaneously within
and outside of the conceptual confines of traditional matrimony. Thus
strangered with a pledge, Mosby responds with an openness that almost
courts exposure – as befits such a public declaration:

> M O S B Y I'll see your husband in despite of you.
> Yet, Arden, I protest to thee by heaven,
> Thou ne'er shalt see me more after this night.
> I'll go to Rome rather than be forsworn.
> A R D E N Tush, I'll have no such vows made in my house.
> A L I C E Yes, I pray you, husband, let him swear;
> And on that condition, Mosby, pledge me here.   (xiv.213–19)

The lovers carry out their inverted ceremonial of bonding, flirtingly
secure in the truth-like effect of saying it all before Arden's face, a
pleasure Shakespeare is to turn to black-humor use with Iago, who
continually thus plays with the literal, seeming ironic without being so.

The moment of the murder finally arrives, the seizure of life ushered in
by an appropriate watchword:

> M O S B Y Ah, Master Arden, 'Now I can take you.'
> A R D E N Mosby! Michael! Alice! What will you do?
> B L A C K W I L L Nothing but take you up, sir, nothing else.
> M O S B Y There's for the pressing iron you told me of.
> S H A K E B A G And there's for the ten pounds in my sleeve.
> A L I C E What, groans thou? Nay then, give me the weapon.
> Take this for hind'ring Mosby's love and mine.
> M I C H A E L Oh, Mistress!   (xiv.232–39)

Mosby's use of the watchword seems to be doubly meaningful, not only
as the ultimate embodiment of the theme of seizure, but also as a
statement of control from within the fictive world of the dice-game, a
final invisible sadistic practical joke, unseen as a real-world move until
too late. Like Horatio at a similar moment in *The Spanish Tragedy*,
Arden is totally stunned by his own murder, and cries out for an
explanation, unable to believe what is happening. Each participant offers
something like an account of the action from his or her own particular
point of view.

Black Will begins, savoring his long-awaited ascension (actually,
pulling Arden down) with an olympian mock explanation, just holding
Arden to be struck. The end, the blows, have not landed yet, and Will is
just quietly eating Arden's will. There is a strange horrible calming effect

quite like that of Lorenzo's words to Horatio: "nothing much, just dealing with you."

Mosby offers a major contrast, speaking and acting with the utmost cathartic violence. So White suggests, at any rate, citing Holinshed's account that Mosby, "hauing at his girdle a pressing iron of fourteen pounds weight, stroke him on the hed with the same, so that he fell downe, and gaue a great grone, insomuch that they thought he had been killed" (see Wine edition 155). This act inverts the many status insults Mosby has borne from Arden, and enacts the inversion with the very tool mocked in scene i (313). "There's for" is also exchange-talk, quasi-contractual and oath-bound, as well as a matter of "getting even." We may even parse the particular manner of death, as one can with Lorenzo's sardonic caption for Horatio, "Yet is he at the highest, now he's dead." As hanging mocks Horatio's rising, smashing with the iron flattens the superior Arden. And consider the phallic force of this iron, dangling from Mosby's belt like a six-gun (if the players troubled to follow Holinshed).[90]

Shakebag's intervention reminds us of the money which has bought this event: for Shakebag the ten pounds quite reasonably equals the life crushed out of Arden, though perhaps for us a difference is supposed to be visible, an incommensurability. But it is Alice's reaction that is most striking of all. She is unwilling, in the end, to leave the actual killing to her hirelings or even to Mosby. Arden's groan seems to infuriate her: perhaps she is angry that he still needs killing, or perhaps it is his agony and its uncomprehending claim on her that enrages her. For whatever reason, she seizes the weapon in her own hands, and curses Arden as she strikes, for *hindering* her: his greatest offense is that of having dared to think to limit her will, to exercise marital authority over her (who is to rule herself). This is the core detail, of felt control, blockage, restriction. Indeed, Arden has in fact been most cooperative and manipulable, both with Franklin's advice early on, and of late with the trick in scene xiii of Mosby's wound and Alice's playing on it. But she has hated not being able to act, to have her will *enacted directly*, and even successful back-door sex with Mosby has presupposed a limit of will; she wants it all, absolutely, without hindrance, and so finally cannot rest with less than hands-on unmediated action. If this hated authority was devised (by the enforced marriage) to inhibit precisely this desire, so much the clearer is her irresistible explosion.

Indeed, maybe Alice is to be enlisted in Mosby's own expressive violence, for though Holinshed tells us that she stabbed Arden ("with a knife gaue him seuen or eight p[r]icks into the brest," Wine edition 155), the text before us does not say which weapon she seizes to deal her own

blows. I suggest that it would be quite fitting for her to take the iron
from Mosby and use it. For surely the central affect for her is of total
frustrated violence finally unleashed: in my mind's eye she shatters,
smashes, defaces, demolishes, her constricting bond to Arden, that so
hatefully authorized his control of her.[91]

From this blast of affect it is surely no distance at all to Michael's
appalled whimper of shock and grief. Yet it must also be acknowledged
that his grief is succeeded at once by a world-upside-down and apocalyptic elation, as he finally turns to his bride, to be his at last. When the
assembled company seat themselves, preparing to act out the cover story,
Alice puts Mosby in Arden's chair, as if her new husband. Michael says
aside, "Susan, shall thou and I wait on them? / Or, and thou say'st the
word, let us sit down too" (xiv.288–89). The successful petty treason
reorients not only the marriage (the wife replaces Arden with Mosby),
but the relation of servants to masters (Michael and Susan become peers
of their [former] masters). Indeed, it is even more complex: the sister also
no longer has to wait on her brother, who originally owned the gendered
right of sexual disposal of her. Kinship, rank, and gender determinations
are suddenly all in flux.

Susan thinks to wait: everything seems so crazy. "Peace, we have other
matters now in hand. / I fear me, Michael, all will be bewrayed"
(xiv.290–91). But nothing, it seems, can spoil his satisfaction in the event:
"Tush, so it be known that I shall marry thee in the morning I care not
though I be hanged ere night" (xiv.292–93). With the ejaculatory word
that has dismissed so much of traditional importance in this play,
Michael tosses away his wedding night. Perhaps there is some hyperbole
here ("a day of love with you is worth a lifetime"), but the achievement
of Susan, really the *publication* ("so it be known") of his sheer *entitlement*
to marry Susan, seems full harvest to Michael. Perhaps this is just
dramatic shorthand, a cartoon of an unwritten plot; or perhaps what has
gone before was enough to put anyone off thinking erotically of the
body. However this detail works, we must enroll Michael too in the list
of those transported by Arden's death, one way or another.

What remains of the tale is very familiar: Alice's brief anticipation of
consummation ("We'll spend this night in dalliance and in sport"
[xiv.339]); the sudden access of blood-guilt on Alice's part; the search for
the body, the brazening, the discovery, the confessions, the judgments,
and Franklin's report of the final image of Arden's body, printed on the
ground he stole from Dick Reede the forlorn sailor. Black Will,
allegorical to the last, was burnt in Flushing, on a stage. The grief, guilt,
mutual recrimination, and repentance are rehearsed as Epilogue by

Franklin for the stage audience, as a framing, whether earnest or wry and weary we cannot tell, to place, to interpret, to cast a net over, to focus the disruptive energies the playwright has so carefully made available to us.

Instead of reviewing these well-known moralistic details, I conclude with a coda, the closing of a loop, Shakebag's passage from the murder to the Lord Protector, Arden and Franklin's patron, with whom the play began. No sooner is Arden dead than Shakebag thinks of his escape:

> In Southwark dwells a bonny northern lass,
> The widow Chambley; I'll to her house now,
> And if she will not give me harborough,
> I'll make booty of the quean, even to her smock.   (xiv.243–46)

He moves immediately for a hideout, a place of protection, the opposite, in short, of the loathsome den. It is first of the London suburbs he thinks, but his fantasy there is full of country affect. The Widow Chambley – bonny (dialectal, uncentered), northern (traditional, *contra* the city South of London), a lass (young and light-hearted) – seems an old-fashioned country girl, like Queen Elizabeth's alter ego the milkmaid. So plain a nostalgic dream, tonally rather like Will's inaugural memory of the half-ox. Yet Shakebag is helpless to resist the habitual transformation of the dream into his usual fear of denial, rejection, and betrayal, arousing his own pugnacious readiness to despoil in (re)turn.

And sure enough, the world rewards his expectations in scene xv:

> The widow Chambley in her husband's days I kept;
> And now he's dead she is grown so stout
> She will not know her old companions.
> I came thither, thinking to have had
> Harbour as I was wont,
> And she was ready to thrust me out at doors.
> But whether she would or no I got me up,
> And as she followed me I spurned her down the stairs
> And broke her neck, and cut her tapster's throat.
> And now I am going to fling them in the Thames.
> I have the gold; what care I though it be known?
> I'll cross the water and take sanctuary.   (xv.1–12)

The bonny northern lass is recast as a woman he kept during her marriage, i.e., as adulterous and secret and treacherous, however bonded to Shakebag. But she has changed, is no longer pliant and ready. Further, a widow now, she is no longer owned. Indeed, she is now grown stout to the point of willfulness, even scorn (or fear, like Bradshaw's with Black Will in scene ii), of men such as he. Shakebag's dream of home, safety, protection, love, of *harbor*, is finally betrayed by the widow, who would have him thrust out, not taken in (as Frost says we must be at home). So he forces his way in, physically: the principle seems to be, "if no embrace, then rape." This forced entry is followed by spurning down stairs, breaking her neck (an accident? if such a word can be used of such circumstances), and the amazing "cut her tapster's throat." The parallel of "her ... her" invites the reading that Shakebag cut the widow's own throat – an embraced and hopeless rage enacted on her dead body, from which others drank, but not he. But of course the tapster is a servant (the reading demanded by "fling *them* in the river"), as innocent as Hal's Francis may be, as innocent as Shakebag himself may once have been. (The Falstaffian affect here is very strong, though much more harsh than in Shakespeare, where it is cold-hearted enough.) In the end Shakebag is left still homeless, but with the aid of Pedringano's test he concludes, "I have the gold," still such an amazing thing. With gold in hand all other matters disappear, for a while. He departs again across the water for sanctuary, though, as Wine points out, if he is in Southwark he is already across the water, already where sanctuary is to be found – if anywhere. Perhaps this is why, according to the Epilogue, he does not remain there, but, "being sent for out, / [he] was murdered in Southwark as he passed / To Greenwich where the Lord Protector lay" (Epilogue 3–5). The play ends as it began, with the Lord Protector's obscure presence. The land he gave Arden was not in the end sufficient consolation for his marriage. Likewise, if Shakebag left the safety of sanctuary (such as it was) in hopes of something turning up in Greenwich, he never arrived. Perhaps, as Falstaff hoped to be, he was sent for soon at night.

The ideology of prodigality in *The Miseries of Enforced Marriage* and *A Yorkshire Tragedy*

> ... being Wives,
> They are Sovereigns: Cordials that preserve our Lives,
> They are like our hands that feed us, this is clear,
> They renew man, as spring renews the year.   (*Miseries* 142–45)
>
> O Gentlemen, I am undone, I am undone, for I am married, I that could not abide a Woman, but to make her a whore, hated all She-creatures, fair and poor, swore I would never marry but to one that was rich, and to be thus cunnicacht.   (*Miseries* 2158–60)
>
> A perilous gash, a very limb lopped off.   (*Henry IV Part One* 4.1.43)

In 1605 mass murderer and former ward Walter Calverley was pressed to death, refusing to plead guilty or innocent for trying to annihilate his family. His violent story caught the public eye, and two pamphlets, a ballad, and two plays appeared in the next three years. Three of these texts survive: the first pamphlet, the anonymous *Two Most Unnatural and Bloodie Murthers* (1605), George Wilkins's play *The Miseries of Enforced Marriage* (1607), and *A Yorkshire Tragedy* (1608), by "William Shakespeare," as the title page has it.[1] Contrary to common assumption, this discursive field does not center on Wilkins's famous titular rubric: in Calverley's life, in *Murthers*, and in *A Yorkshire Tragedy* the marriage in question is *not* enforced. Enforcement is Wilkins's crucial defining supplement to the story, amplifying and focusing its lines of force. I propose to follow Wilkins's refraction of Walter Calverley's violence across an extended spectrum of family practices. Here we can discover capacities and costs otherwise submerged in unspoken practical knowledge, and watch various elements of the aggregate of controls on status, generation, gender, and kinship which we now call patriarchy come into detailed contest.

Wilkins's crucial move is to *trope* enforcement, both term and concept, across a variety of subject-positions:

> ... the young puppet, having the lesson before from the old Fox, give[s] the son half a dozen warm kisses, which after her father's oaths, takes such

Impression in thee, thou straight callst by Iesu Mistress, I love you: — When
she has the wit to ask, but Sir, will you marry me, and thou in thy Cox-
sparrow humor repliest, aye (before God) as I am a Gentleman will I, which
the Father over-hearing, leaps in, takes you at your word, swears he is glad to
see this; nay he will have you contracted straight, and for a need makes the
priest of himself ...   (105–13)

You will not enforce me I hope Sir?   (233: daughter to suitor)

... to prevent [debauch], we'll match him to a wife,
Marriage restrains the scope of single life.   (356–57: guardian to uncle)

[LORD] You that will have your will, come get you in:
I'll make thee shape thy thoughts to marry her,
Or wish thy birth had been thy murderer.
SCARBORROW Fate pity me, because I am enforced ...   (490–93)

... I am my father's only child, ...
And though that I should vow a single life
To keep my soul unspotted, yet will he
Enforce me to a marriage ...   (830–36: daughter's apostrophe)

I Frank Ilford, Gentleman. ... was Enforced from the Miter in Breadstreet, to
the Counter ... (1171–76)

... the extremity of want
Enforceth us to question for our own,
The rather that we see, not like a Brother
Our Brother keeps from us to spend on other.   (1225–28)

To comprehend these variations of his defining trope Wilkins elaborates
the Calverley record. He devises an extended affiliate network for the
youth he calls William Scarborrow,[2] characterized not only by extension
but by densely specified relation. He links enforcement (for both victims
and agents) to happily unattached London gallants; to a serious fatherless young heir approaching his majority; to a brotherless and betrothed
virgin; to a sonless father; to the younger brothers of a prodigal heir in
wardship; to a virgin with such brothers; to a ward's guardian; to a
guardian's unmarried niece; and to a guardian's similarly distanced but
familial double, the trusted family servant.[3] Wilkins's work and ours is to
explore and parse these variations of relation and practice, and to
construe what they permute: a systemic critique of recruitment and
reproduction strategies among the Jacobean elite.

Wilkins positions his play at the most overdetermined intersection of a
set of generational, status, and gender frictions arising from social
control over marriage as the institutional transition to adult status. He
begins from the sharpest-edged parental-authoritarian picture of elite
marriage, a picture based on extremes. In early modern marriage both
theoretical usage and practical behavior were actually quite various. The

category of "enforced marriage" was generally used in a loose and non-technical way, as we now tend to say "arranged": to signify marriage parentally arranged for familial purposes, with minimal or secondary regard for the children's preferences. But there was in fact much flexibility and parent–child negotiation throughout the social scale. For most cases, as Keith Wrightson judiciously argues,

> the key to the situation may well have been less parental "arrangement," with or without subsequent consultation of the child, than the seizing of the initiative by one of the parties concerned and the subsequent securing of the consent of the other.[4]

However, selection functioned in terms of *generational* relations (the parents as one "party," the children as "the other"), rather than *erotic* relations between the lovers. This construction, however flexible, establishes a conceptual floor rather different from our own sense of choice. The variable of *rank* further specifies the marital experience: "the aristocracy, upper gentry and urban plutocracy" maximized the factor of authority. Despite otherwise widespread flexibility, Wrightson argues, for the elite "the 'arranged match,' initiated by parents, which left the child with nothing more than a right of veto was undoubtedly a reality" (71, 74).

Elite sons and daughters here seem, from our modern vantage point, fairly similarly placed – as instruments – in such alliances. Their parents usually pressed such marriages toward the instrumental goals of the family: "the safeguarding of property, the assertion and advancement of status and the forging of alliances between families" (Wrightson, *English Society* 80). Individual needs and desires of children were often ignored. Daughters were readily experienced as financially burdensome, needing dowers. And sons, even heirs, might sometimes be sold for the family's financial gain. According to his daughter, Sir Henry Cary, Viscount Falkland, was estranged from his heir Lucius Cary, "with whom he was very angry for his marriage [without parental consent], for this regard only, that he was by it frustrated of that supply which his estate (otherwise desperate) did necessarily require for the disengagement of it, he having always much outgone what he had."[5] Sons and daughters both rebelled against such parental objectification. Nonetheless, the management process was further, I suggest, experienced as significantly *gendered*.

For this, it seems to me, is the initial function of Wilkins's terminologically canonical emphasis on *enforced* rather than *arranged* marriage. Despite its earlier loose usage, as the drama progresses, and as the depredations of the Court of Wards upon the elite marriage market grow more scandalous, the term undergoes theoretical evolution, in terms both of gender and of wardship. The first thing to see about the developed sense of the term is that it now tends to name the subjection of a specially privileged male to a kind of treatment typically confined to women. Elite marriage seems more often to be called "enforced" when a choice of mates is imposed against a son and heir's will, but is more often experienced as "arranged," that is, *ordinarily*, when imposed upon the daughter. The male normally has some influence, the promise of future power; the female more often only a limited right of refusal.[6] This notion of *enforcement* makes explicitly present an implied but quite significant obstacle, the young man's masculine will. The daughter's will so much more often seems felt as "merely" feminine, disordered and immature rather than substantiating. Ascham exhibits this distinction negatively, commenting upon modern deterioration into marital freedom:

> Our tyme is so fare from that old discipline and obedience, as now, not onelie yong ientlemen, but euen verie girles dare without all feare, though not without open shame, where they list, and how they list, marie them selues in spite of father, mother, God, good order, and all.[7]

For Ascham such hypertrophy of will grows from the distressing to the absurd, even apocalyptic, when extended from young gentlemen to "verie girles," very triviality gone wild. Normal "arranged" marriage seems to presume "simple" supervisory management, minimally acknowledging daughters as willing subjects. (Escape to greater agency in marriage thus had much appeal for them.) Their situation contrasts strongly with the incipient status of the heir, marked from birth as a problematic repository of family power.

"Ideally," Houlbrooke remarks, "the relationship between father and eldest son was a particularly close one. The father was supposed to prepare his heir for his responsibilities by gradually taking him into his confidence." Yet, as Macfarlane observes, "the degree of tension, authority, and intimacy present in the father–son bond" was a "general problem." Sir Henry Cary and his heir Lucius diverged bitterly over Lucius' responsibility to the succession. For the opposite mercenary stance, consider the sober Ralph Josselin, who felt that in some families, "parents [were] neglected by children, their deaths gapd for to enjoy that they have."[8] Reginald Scot cites Fleming's Ovid, concerning cases when "the sonne too soone dooth aske how long his father is to live" (*Discoverie* 68). The father–son relation was a nexus intensely overdetermined for ideological crime, not only for its internal structural conflicts but also by analogy with other such nodes. Ovid names this sin as one of a set of what I described generally as "betrayals of relation": between host and guest, father and son-in-law, brothers, husband and wife, step-relations (see *Metamorphoses* 1.144–48). Some of these betrayals arise specifically in *Arden of Faversham*, as petty treason. Scot, however, cites the Ovid when arguing "That women have used poisoning in all ages more than men" (*Discoverie* 67–68): the classic "weapon of the weak," of the subjected and angry. Such inscriptions mark the son and heir as a problematic and consequential player in his own right, sharing an intense subjected rivalrous alliance with familial decision-makers.

Wilkins further sharpens the edges, for with this newer sense of enforced marriage we are also not simply dealing with sons – not sons, anyway, of those doing the managing – but with *wards*. This is the crucial element of the newer signification: the insertion of a galling distance between marriage-maker and heir. For the founding condition of such enforcement as a violation was a problematic sense of (betrayed) family unity. Even with parents and daughters considerable bonding was common, despite the divisive obligation to dower them. But with heirs important community of practical as well as emotional interest existed, between successive heads of the family as it were (though this very formulation marks the region of disputed resources).

The institution of wardship disrupted this community, substituting a very different relationship. Under this system of management, richly traced by Joel Hurstfield,[9] any underage heir of a deceased gentleman became a ward of the crown, which then might sell the wardship (with its right of disposal in marriage) to the highest bidder. For the penurious government of Elizabeth I the arrangement was mainly financial, a form of class-specific taxation. But then as now taxation was unpopular with the well-to-do, and thought by many of its victims to be ideologically unsound. For many high bidders were speculators, trading in wardships, mulcting penalties and gratuities, extracting surplus value without regard to the family lives involved. And since the institution made the privileged vulnerable, in the crucial arena of family reproduction and transmission of resources both material and symbolic, there was much complaint. Sons were no longer subjected even to their fathers, to those with some version of the "same" interests in mind. Instead, they were trafficked in, used as cash cows, exploited, legally rebuked and fined for attempting to exert wills of their own. The freight of wincing violation so often conveyed by such "enforcement" of a son surely thrives, unsurprisingly, on the use of "enforce" to mean *rape* (*OED* II.9). Pain might be shared, by heir and his family alike, deprived of lineal self-determination. For the son, however, such enforced marriage additionally imposes a feminizing degradation: the man enforced to marry, his will crushed, feels raped.

Obviously, then, these young men were in certain complex ways subjected to the powerless condition of daughters (in a doubly alienated form, as if daughters without familial relation, unloved daughters, others' daughters). And here more general conceptual operations become possible. First of all, enforced sons' positionality can be simultaneously defined by likeness and unlikeness to daughters'. Young men can feel both feminized and infantilized; our perspective will vary with a focus on gender or generation. If fatherless elite male heirs were structurally feminized by this institution, we can peer into processes of gender interpellation active not only in marriage but throughout the cultural field. Men and women were allowed complexly different access to capacities for self-definition and self-determination, utilized them differently, and experienced their limits differently. When heirs, especially privileged young men, experience "female" limitations that grow precisely from their own patriarchal interpellation, as elite heirs, informative dissonance results. The daughters in this play embrace their cultural destination, offering a rich normative contrast. Yet there are two kinds of sons here: one blocked from his love-choice, and a set of others who resent having to marry at all to escape an intensely felt cultural infantilization. And all of these youths, male and female alike, pass through serious and often destructive ambivalence regarding the marital transition to adulthood. Their frantic responses sometimes reveal, by differences in kind as well as excessive degree, deep structures that seldom break the surface of awareness during the calm flow of quotidian social relations.

In *The Miseries of Enforced Marriage* and its accompanying texts, then, we can begin to trace such structural features by asking what happens to young men, to young women, and to fathers, when an heir gets treated like a daughter. In the play's central event young William Scarborrow responds to his enforced marriage by repudiating his new wife and vowing to waste his inheritance and family name in London, as a vengeful prodigal. In the hungry responses of his friends and siblings to this retributive spew Wilkins conducts a double critique of early modern English kinship structure, from within and without, seen as a strategic practice for regulating the transmission and possession of such resources of material and symbolic capital. Scarborrow's predatory gallant friends beckon him to repudiate kinship obligations altogether, and move to London; his impoverished siblings rage at the exploitive capacities conferred upon him by the operation of primogeniture.

Wilkins's critique proceeds cumulatively, eventually across four scenes of the management of marital will: (1) a grotesque *per verba de praesenti* betrothal, where the groom is ambushed; (2) a woman's wary interrogation and acceptance of an inexperienced suitor; (3) a classic enforcement of marriage by a guardian upon a ward; and (4) a similar compulsion of a daughter to marriage by a sonless father. As these scenes unfold, an ensemble of further critical aims comes into view. Wilkins accents the discontinuities among individual and group needs and desires that early modern marital machinery was meant to channel and gratify. He highlights the frames that define such affect, whether by gap or coincidence: familial and extrafamilial loci, transgenerational or parent–child positions, the cooperations and rivalries of siblings, the private–public mixtures of the erotic. He presents an accounting of opportunities and prices paid. And he proposes regulative possibilities for renegotiating enforcement flashpoints. Finally, at the last hopeless instant before the historical Calverley's murderous paroxysm, Wilkins turns his play away, to a fifth, city-comic, enforced-marriage scene and a peacemaking *deus ex machina*, evading the fullest confrontation with the contradictions of early modern English social regularity. To explore Calverley's final revenge on the social system, and to look for what Wilkins found intolerable, I will close with *A Yorkshire Tragedy*, which completes the depiction of the Calverley murders, but resorts nonetheless in the end to similar gestures of social denial.

I

Wilkins initially frames his subject by juxtaposing two versions of marital negotiation: a caustic and frightened gallant's fantasy proposed by Frank Ilford, apparently to entertain his friends Wentloe and Bartley; and the subsequent conversation of mutual assessment and wary betrothal between their friend William Scarborrow and Clare Harcop. The first provides a programmatic instance of the trope of enforcement (that is, of a violating denial of autonomy); the second, the play's closest approach to intersubjective mutuality. Together the two scenarios describe a horizon of possibility for marital selection among gentlefolk.

The young gallants enter to the Harcop manor in Yorkshire, in search of their mate William Scarborrow, who is visiting there. Secretly unsure of their welcome, they discuss techniques for making contacts and presuming on their status, which they affect to suppose apparent:

> I tell thee Wentloe [says Ilford] thou canst not live on this side of the world: feed well, drink Tobacco, and be honored into the presence, but thou must be acquainted with all sorts of men, aye and so far in too, till they desire to be more acquainted with thee. (19–22)

Ilford's ironic lecturing tone marks him as the familiar Jacobean fetishist of knowing intrusion, a self-conceived insider who knows how to see

through the forms to the sweet iron reality of gratifications beyond, how
to get in and stay in. When Scarborrow enters Ilford goes forward in his
art, offering candid guidance for anyone delicate or doubting:

> And well encountered my little Villain of fifteen hundred a year, 'Sfoot what
> makest thou here in this barren soil of the North? ... nay I know thou art
> called down into the country here, by some hoary Knight or other, who
> knowing thee a young Gentleman of good parts, and a great living, hath
> desired thee to see some pitiful piece of his Workmanship, a Daughter I mean,
> Is't not, so?   (51–53, 65–68)

When Scarborrow admits to being "about some such preferment"
(69), Ilford delivers his full cautionary set piece, on how "marriages are
made up nowadays":

> ... the father according to the fashion, being sure you have a good living, and
> without Encumbrance, comes to you thus: — takes you by the hand thus: —
> wipes his long beard thus: — or turns up his Mustachio thus: — Walks some
> turn or two thus: — to show his comely Gravity thus: — And having washed
> his foul mouth thus: — at last breaks out thus: —
> ...
> Master Scarborrow, you are a young Gentleman, I knew your father well, he
> was my worshipful good Neighbor, for our Demesnes lay near together. Then,
> Sir, — you and I must be of more near acquaintance. —
> ...
> Sir, my self am Lord of some thousand a year, a Widower, (master Scar-
> borrow) I have a couple of young Gentlewomen to my Daughters, a thousand
> a year will do well divided among them? Ha, will't not Master Scarborrow, —
> At which you out of your education must reply thus. — The Portion will
> deserve them worthy husbands: on which Tinder he soon takes fire and swears
> you are the Man his hopes shot at, and one of them shall be yours.
> ...
> Then putting you and the young Puggs to in a close room together.
> WENTLOE If he should lie with her there, is not the father partly the Bawd?
> ILFORD Where the young puppet, having the lesson before from the old Fox,
> give the son half a dozen warm kisses, which after her father's oaths, takes
> such Impression in thee, thou straight callst by Iesu Mistress, I love you: —
> When she has the wit to ask, but Sir, will you marry me, and thou in thy Cox-
> sparrow humor repliest, aye (before God) as I am a Gentleman will I, which
> the Father over-hearing, leaps in, takes you at your word, swears he is glad to
> see this; nay he will have you contracted straight, and for a need makes the
> priest of himself.   (76–113)[10]

This tale is uttered "humorously," and in fact by an unreliable source,
but the audience does not yet know that Ilford will prove as parasitic and
manipulative as the fantasy father–daughter team. Right now he seems
just a young single man, perhaps loose, perhaps harshly witty, not yet
shown to be corrupt. The audience, waiting to learn where to stand, is
probably led to take his fantasy spectacle as the "enforcement" of the

title – manipulation of the suitor by the bride and her father. Such leading might be expected: other plays such as *All's Well that Ends Well* and *The Duchess of Malfi* manifest the ready cultural preoccupation with such marital ambush, with desiring, fearing, needing the trapping or seizure of husbands. And indeed, *Miseries'* pamphlet source, *Two Most Unnatural and Bloodie Murthers*, specifies Scarborrow (Wilkins's name for the historical Walter Calverley) as just such a target:

> ... his course of life did promise so much good, [p.2] that there was a commendable grauity appeared even in his youth, he being of this hope, vertuous in his life, and worthy by his birth, was sought unto by many gallant Gentlemen, and desired that he would unite his fortune into their families, by matching himselfe to one and the chiefe of their daughters.
> Among which number it happened, being once invited for such a purpose, (a welcome guest) to an antient Gentleman of cheefe note in his Country ....[11]

Given Scarborrow's placement in the marriage-market, various interpretive nodes stand out in Ilford's fantasy. The daughter is a "puppet," a darling, but perhaps also (or merely?) an agent of the foxy paternal will. The father's oaths and his daughter's warm kisses constitute alternative but parallel forms of coercive intensification: alliance, wealth, and sex. The direct erotic lure angles for the binding words of the betrothal *per verba de praesenti*, then supposedly "overheard" by the father as a hidden and most offendable witness. He "leaps in," forcibly transforming inner and private arousal to outer and public commitment by "taking" the panting youth at his unfortunate word.[12]

The witnessing was not, of course, technically required. "An indissoluble union could be created solely by the consent of the two parties expressed in words of the present tense – a contract of marriage or spousals *per verba de praesenti*. ... Neither solemnization in church, nor the use of specially prescribed phrases, nor even the presence of witnesses, was essential to an act of marriage."[13] Still, the gesture of what amounts to exposure, if not repudiated at once, will transform the private utterance to the closure of a public acknowledgment. This device thus overlaps interestingly with the so-called bed-trick, sharing an exploitation of private enactment of commitment, whether verbal or bodily. Here and in structurally similar instances (in *Measure for Measure*, *All's Well that Ends Well*, *The Duchess of Malfi*, *The Changeling*, and *A New Way to Pay Old Debts*), the emphasis falls on such devices as manipulations of arousal (bodily or verbal) that are designed to entrap (potential) husbands.

It is worth noting that some other sixteenth-century commentators emphasized the reverse abuse: men's abuse of clandestine contract for lustful purposes. Richard Whytford, in *A Werke for Housholders* (1530, 1537), voices this lament:

> The ghostly ennemy doth deceyve many psones by ye pretence & colour of matrymony in pryuate & secrete contractes. For many men whan they can not obteyne theur unclene desyre of the woman wyl promyse marryage, & thervpon make a contracte promyse eche vnto other sayenge. Here I take the Margery vnto my wyfe, I therto plyght the my trouth. And she agayne, vnto him in lyke maner. And after that done, they suppose they maye lawfully vse theyr unclene behauyour, and somtyme the acte and dede doth folow, vnto the great offence of god & theyr owne soules.[14]

F. J. Furnivall similarly cites seventeen troth-plights disputed at law, of which ten concern men who try to "sneak out of their contracts when they've had their fill of pleasure with the women."[15]

These various instances have a number of different controlling purposes: the "simple" gratification of sexual desire, whether premarital (Whytford and Furnivall) or adulterous (Middleton and Rowley); the disciplining of wayward and unworthy husbands (Shakespeare); the "liberation" of shy ones (Webster); or implementing "the traffic in women," a usage that discovers the processual network of homosocial bonding among males.[16] Ilford's fantasy is, structurally, a deeply different one. For one thing, it claims to be generic (how "marriages are made up nowadays"), as opposed to atypical (as in the dramatic instances from Shakespeare, Middleton and Rowley, and Webster). We hear a claim about an institution. Yet it is also not shaped around the simple gender binary of male and female, as are, in different ways, the concerns of the Tudor moralists and of Rubin and Sedgwick (and Massinger).

Ilford's fantasy is ultimately a critique of marriage as the engine of the kinship system of early modern England. The traffic he fears is in vulnerable young men, the alliance not gendered and homosocial but *familial*, fathers and daughters scheming together to nourish the ongoing structure of family at the expense of innocent male youth. This paranoid fantasy allies rather separate antagonists in a unifying grand conspiracy theory; however, its logic helps explain the social functions of some very idiomatic Renaissance behaviors. Let's follow it further.[17]

Wentloe asks archly if the father would be so willing thus to betroth his daughter if he knew that the young man "breathes himself at some two or three Bawdy houses in a morning" (120). Ilford replies, "Oh the sooner, for that and the Land together, tell the old lad, he will know the better how to deal with his Daughter? *The Wise and Ancient Fathers know this Rule, / Should both wed Maids, the Child would be a Fool*" (121–24). Part of the force of this rejoinder is ironic, a piece of would-be table-turning on the controlling father. But Ilford's reply recaptures some independence by another route (and also recuperates some male solidarity with those oppressive fathers) by a transgenerational legitimation of *whoremongering*.

This move is extremely fruitful for the bachelor gallants. So far they have been attempting to pull the fangs of what they experience as the threat of family and marriage by mockingly instructing one of their nominally weaker brethren in his fearful fate, thus facing and transcending its risk themselves. The whoremongering jokes enact a different defensive reduction, however, not of one of their own to a scapegoat, but of women – in two ways. First, of to-be-duped *wives* who think to own the men they snare: the move parries the disabling pressure of the marriage-trap, sprung on unwary young men by the old (fathers) and the grasping seizing engulfing women who are daughters to such fathers, dispensing warm kisses while coolly retaining the wit to ask the right trick question at the right time.

The second reduction constructs women not as duped wives but as *whores*, defanged anti-types to the marauding daughter. Prostitutes are used rather than using, bought instead of owning, thrown away as disposable instead of sticking like pitch,[18] sexually arousing and entertaining and enabling and satisfying as opposed to frustrating and castrating. Furthermore, punks are cash-nexus creatures, entailing no masculine obligations (of protection etc.) such as Clare later requires of Scarborrow, obligations that authentically bind him, that entail and contain both "love" and the mutual seriousness of intersubjectivity. (Think how Cassio mocks Bianca's fantasy of marriage.) The most frightening thing about women is that "being Wives, / They are Sovereigns" (142–43) – that is, figures of power; that's why the gallant wants a whore. The man owns the woman's time and body, a limited contractual bond that frees him when he pays. These are the women for gallants, as Ilford later acknowledges: "I could not abide a Woman, but to make her a whore" (2159–60). (Note that the words Wilkins gives Ilford grasp the whore as a product, transformed from a prior status, perhaps of agent. Women's agency is what Ilford seems to hate above all.)[19]

Scarborrow, having come home to the family country of Yorkshire (where he was born, where his father died) for marital "preferment," is not ready to accept these formulations, disabling him as they do. His project rests, at the self-aware level anyway, on the idealist plinth cited as my second epigraph, of wives as sovereign in the sustaining virtue of their cultural place, as preserving cordials, nourishing hands, fertile renewers of mankind (142–45). Scarborrow recovers his ground with a different misogynist joke (that change of women makes for "bald

Knaves, Sir Knight" [129]), offloading the contempt onto whores as a way of relegitimating his marital ambitions. This allows Ilford to reply with *cuckoldry jokes*, which once again voice, from the other side, the male fear of marriage as subjection and humiliation, concluding "marry none of them" (147, 150). Despite the logical alternation, cuckoldry jokes are parallel in deep structure to whoremongering talk. The latter makes ostentatious claims to potency, coupled with independence from emotional bonding or subjection; cuckoldry jokes, however, voice a self-preserving scorn of less potent men. Such "weak" men cannot control (by satisfying or intimidating) precisely what the whoremonger buys – the female part. Whoremongering talk exhibits the positive version of self-inflation; cuckoldry jokes condescend to the supposedly negative or defective.

One other discursive permutation concerns us here: the scapegoating not of the weak young victim such as Scarborrow, nor of the cuckolded husband too impotent to keep his wife in check, but of the old father himself: instigator of marriage, disposer of daughters, long-term bearer of the withering effects of marriage. In short, we must consider Ilford's feminized father-figure. The original threat, gendered and generational, is of Harcop and Clare as sucking, enveloping, controlling, birdliming. The father "wipes his long beard thus," "turns up his Mustachio thus," and "having washed his foul mouth thus," begins his spell (79–82). Though it is hard to be positive quite how to take these repulsed and repulsive lines, I suspect that Ilford experiences them as *vaginal*, as in Lear's sulphurous pit. Wiping and washing activate dirt-thoughts for him, anyway, already there in "foul," and danger comes out of the filthy hole. All of this seems a processing of threatening feminine affect, attracted *from daughter* (whose individual agency is first specified by the "half a dozen warm kisses" – and is "warm" somehow directingly particular, i.e., oral, maybe sticky?) *to father*, the fantasy recognizing him as the source *by* making him filthily feminized. Such feminizing would serve Ilford as a censoring mechanism, preserving masculine solidarity by feminizing a very significant (male) departure from it.

This reading of old Harcop's strangely prominent mouth seems the more likely if we derive a generalization from these three defensive tropes (whoremongering talk, cuckoldry jokes, and effeminized old men). I suggest that the mere presence in fantasy of sons being maritally feminized (manipulated, subjected, trafficked in, here by the team of father and daughter) arouses the defensive response of *misogyny*. These sons, in fear of becoming daughterly, abuse a version of themselves, whose weakness is amplified and demonized. Blame is attached to the *female*, and not to the (masculine) father. Yet it is conspicuously true that the father's agency is, both historically and in the fantasy, the central and powerful one; daughters are really precisely subjected to the parental will in marriage. That is to say, this is *not* a site of daughterly agency, but of daughterly subjection. Yet the prospect of such male subjection to feminine fate seems to generate, as its typical defensive maneuver, rage at women and feminized men. (Still, alongside such gendered rage we must not lose sight of the status that sons and daughters also share, the status of *children*, for whom marriage offers – both happily and infuriatingly – what seems a highly controlling escape to adulthood from what comes to seem more and more a state of infantilization.)

If such youthful male misogyny defends against powerful fathers, it does so precisely by misrecognizing and thus concealing the more potent portion of the systemic agency (male seniority) by assimilating it to the female part. This move enables the conflict to be posed as simply gendered, and masks the frictions internal to the masculine, which disrupt patriarchy. This strategic misrecognition – linking maleness with youth, unmarried freedom, and bonding; femaleness with age, familial inscription, and bondage – is carried out by the gallants and interrogated by Wilkins throughout the play in a central and highly nuanced discourse of *orality* based on a complex social opposition between *drinking wine* and *eating food*. This discourse instantiates materials from an increasingly theorized zone of culture. "Food," says Mary Douglas, "is a field of action. It is a medium in which other levels of categorization become manifest ... Food choices support political alignments and social opportunities."[20] Likewise, "drinks give the actual structure of social life ... [and] act as markers of personal identity and of boundaries of inclusion and exclusion."[21]

Two specimens of such structuration are relevant to *The Miseries of Enforced Marriage*. Douglas distinguishes between inclusive and selective hospitality. When everyone in a territorial unit gets invited to a feast, inclusive hospitality both demonstrates community solidarity and reaffirms the general horizon of mutual aid. Selective hospitality affirms both relation and exclusion, for instance through "ego-focused categories: kin, workmates, and neighbors are selected for their closeness to a particular person among the hosts."[22] Joseph Gusfield examines a related differentiation, showing how coffee and alcohol function as transitional markers between the realms of recreation and worktime, a segregation of fairly recent naturalization, and one "that holds across classes and sexes and occupations." Gusfield points out, however, that

... in the pre-industrial work pattern men worked in all-male teams, as construction workers still do. In that pattern, the dominant cleavage is between work and home, work being associated with males and home with females. In this case, drinking alcohol, strong drink at that, is not separated from work, and by that token, it does not belong in the home.[23]

In combination, and with appropriate historical adjustment, these patterns can help us formulate Wilkins's agenda for using such markers. I propose that the ideological opposition he constructs between food and drink is a struggle between two hospitalities (one extrafamilial, male, selective and exclusive; one familial, female, inclusive or imperialist). These hospitalities function as competing interpellating matrices or sources of identity for William Scarborrow. Furthermore, this struggle is experienced by the characters as severally categorical: not only in terms of social grouping and residence, but also as providing alternative contents for gender identity.

Wilkins's discourse links *drinking* with whoremongering, with liberated youthful gallant vigor, and with waste; *eating*, with family, security, nourishing investment, corrupting dependency, and a repulsive interior or alimentary physicality. This binary makes frequent resort to tropes of prodigality, in both Biblical and Circean forms, both frightened and frightening.

When Harcop and Clare first enter, for instance, Ilford says to Scarborrow,

> But soft, here comes a voider for us: and I see, do what I can, as long as the world lasts, there will be Cuckolds in it. Do you hear Child, here's one come to blend you together: he has brought you a kneading-tub, if thou dost take her at his hands.   (164–68)

A voider is a vessel for dirty dishes (like a bus-boy's tub), or the person who wields one, a bus-boy or waiter.[24] The kneading-tub is for bread-making, blending of ingredients. Clare is thus an open yeasty container, either for garbage or for as yet inedible food; Harcop a lowly servant waiting to pick over the orts, or a baker up to the elbows in dough; and Scarborrow (the object of Ilford's cautionary ideologizing) about to become blended, adulterated, degraded, finally perhaps submerged in female dough, even consumed. Wilkins seems here and hereafter to disturb the sexual baking imagery of *Troilus and Cressida* from the perspective of *Hamlet*: this premarital scene is not where you eat but where you are eaten.[25]

Similar discomfort appears when Ilford is recommending whores over wives: "let's to London, there's variety: and change of pasture makes fat Calves" (127–28), he says. A first reaction may be to hear "makes" as "makes for," women as whores being desirably felt as bovine, sub-humanized and thus further non-entangling and powerless. However, the figure actually casts the *men* as the calves; and then one hears of the weakly young, immature and bound for the slaughter. This is distinctly not the effect of Vernon's admiring description of Hal and his comrades before Shrewsbury, as "wanton as youthful goats, wild as young bulls" (*Henry IV, Part One* 4.1.103). (And surely, too, there is a shadow of calves on the way to becoming horned creatures, once again victimized by women in marriage.)[26] The calf as vehicle is more revealing than as tenor; Ilford voices more insecurity than he means to. Indeed, the puerile jollity seems attracted from prodigal-son territory (fatted calves are killed and eaten when dissolute young men come home). Coming home is just what is being banned in this anti-marital jab, but once again the troping seems to argue that if the men are calves (which is, I suppose, to say that they are boys), homecoming is a feast upon them.

Harcop's first words to the youths continue in this vein: "Nay no parting Gentlemen: *Hem*." Wentloe obscurely wonders, "'Sfoot does he make Punks of us, that he Hems already?" (171–72). Now it is not at once clear how ritual "hemming" (clearing the throat for drinking) makes punks of the young men. Is this brothel behavior? Do women there serve first a drink and then themselves? (Scarborrow's disinherited sister is later to fear a future in which she must pursue "the old trade, Filling of small Cans in the suburbs," a life she exactly equates with that of "a common road" traveled by every beast who can pay [1390–92].) But it turns out actually that Harcop, far from degrading his guests, is in fact claiming common ground with them:

> Gallants,
> Know old John Harcop keeps a Wine-cellar,
> Has Traveled, been at Court, known Fashions,
> And unto all bears habit like your selves,
> The shapes of Gentlemen and men of sort.   (173–77)

He insists at once on being treated as one of the youths, rather than being set against them as their marriage-fantasy would shape it. Ilford asks one more testing question, to make sure, and Harcop replies with a self-constructing sentence (toned as if much repeated) that at once resignedly concedes distance and yet brags about continuity.

> ILFORD Prithee tell me hast not thou been a Whoremaster.
> HARCOP *In youth I swilled my fill at Venus cup,*
> *Instead of full draughts now I am fain to sup.*
> ILFORD Why then thou art a man fit for my company:
> Dost thou hear that he is a good fellow of our stamp,
> Make much of his daughter.   (184–89)

This striking passage precisely opposes the "heavy father" trope so familiar from both plays and "history." Miriam Slater's description of Sir Ralph Verney, "the very antithesis of that nightmare of the propertied classes, the profligate heir," provides the supposed norm of the dominant ideology.

> By training and temperament Sir Ralph was extremely well suited to carry on in his father's place. He was intelligent, articulate, ambitious, and tireless in his efforts to preserve and improve his patrimony. Incapable of great depth of feeling for any but a few intimates, he was sufficiently perceptive about other men's weaknesses to make him a formidable business adversary. Totally humorless, he was not without sufficient tact to appear almost charming when charm was necessary to get what he wanted. Wholly lacking in spontaneity, he was careful, even calculating in his dealings with family and friends, though he prided himself on his scrupulousness. He was blessed with the extraordinary physical and emotional endurance often possessed by the exquisitely patient. Sir Ralph was the sort of man whom older relatives have difficulty remembering as a child.[27]

Harcop, though much concerned with lost childhood (youth, anyway), is also mercilessly committed to the transmission of patriarchy, as Clare later fears. Yet his means of pursuing this very goal, unlike those of Sir Ralph Verney, partake vigorously of *both* poles of the dialectic, iron-age and wild. He votes clearly on whoremastery, though his capacity has lessened. He identifies himself still with youth's rebellion against age and responsibility and the effeminacy of marriage, preserving male solidarity through misogyny and self-indulgence. Harcop, in other words, does not relish being the victim of the young men's construction, but claims his own continuing entitlement to full masculine status, with its misogynist and irresponsible pleasures. But at the same time in the same words when he marks himself orally (the references to swilling and supping full draughts at Venus's cup *oralize*, so to speak, the answer to Ilford's question about his expressly whoremongering *genital* exploits)[28] he subjects himself to the feminine. For we must hear not only a reference to the malevolent female transformations of Circe, but also to the prodigal son feeding on swill with swine. Above all, in his nostalgic tone, we must hear the *contented* pig (once-content, at least), Spenser's Grill, striving for permanent embrace of the libidinous life to which magic woman has called him: "Let *Grill* be *Grill*, and haue his hoggish mind," says Guyon.[29] In such an emblem of detranscendent investment we can see not only Odysseus' companion-victim to Circe from Book 10 of the *Odyssey* (Gryllos, i.e., lecherous hog), but surely also the gridiron – Grill named as what he's cooked on. Once again, marauder and prey, celebrant and sacrificial victim, gallant and monster, parent and youth, eating and eaten coalesce.[30]

It comes then as no surprise that when Scarborrow finally finds himself alone with Clare, he's scared of her. Presumably his initial silence is the track of Ilford's alarmist misogynist contamination; he wasn't talking this way before the lesson, but now he feels abandoned and frightened as well as excited:

> The Father, and the Gallants have left me here with a Gentlewoman, and if I know what to say to her I am a villain, heaven grant her life hath borrowed so much Impudence of her sex, but to speak to me first: for by this hand, I have not so much steel of Immodesty in my face, to Parley to a Wench without blushing. I'll walk by her, in hope she can open her teeth. — Not a word? — Is it not strange a man should be in a woman's company all this while and not hear her tongue. — I'll go further? — God of his goodness: not a Syllable. I think if I should take up her Clothes too, she would say nothing to me. — With what words true does a man begin to woo. (191–200)

Throughout he reverses the poles of capacity. For him taking initiative is displaying vulnerability, which makes him wish for absent steel to hide behind. Lacking that, he hopes for female impudence in her to get things rolling, but it is clear that he's very uneasy with such a proposition. Indeed, his terms for her capacity identify very directly the male nightmare of the sexually aggressive woman. For her to speak is to open her teeth, to wield her fearful woman's tongue. Indeed, if he lifts her skirts (a fantasy of very mixed valence), he thinks he'll find the notorious (but that's the point) *vagina dentata*, the fiendish face between her forks, saying "nothing."[31]

This passage elaborates Wilkins's discourse of orality by adding meanings to women's mouths, about which Peter Stallybrass has written so well.[32] His analysis focuses, following Lévi-Strauss, on women's mouths as conduits, points of forbidden or contaminating entry or exit, marking boundaries. These categories are extremely useful for comprehending the early modern praxis of male control of women. Here female mouths are a locus of different anxiety, specially pointed for the jumpy anti-marital youths of this play, for a self-conscious cohort of men whose noisy masculinity masks a rooted fear of familially conscripting effeminization.

We have repeatedly seen gestures of such fright at the prospect of something like *marital or familial consumption of the male* (self-consumption, in the case of the feminized old father). The dirty gaping old man, now a voider, the kneading-tub, Venus's cup of swill, the fatted calf on the grill, and now the imagined "nothing" beneath Clare's skirts (recalling not only Lear's sulphurous pit, but also Fortinbras sharking up lawless resolutes in the skirts of Norway): all speak of the female mouth not negatively, as a locus of escape or contaminating entry or passive infection, but as itself positively destructive of the male self. It is now Scarborrow who feels weak, shy, silent, blushing (a non-volitional and traditionally female gesture that announces the self as vulnerable; hearts on sleeves for daws to peck at). And it is – in Ilford and Scarborrow's discursive imagination – Clare whose teeth presage loss of manhood.

What a relief it is to step back from this disturbing ventriloquism of Ilford and Scarborrow's discourse of monster women. For this ancient fantasy does not, it turns out, accurately map Clare at all. Wilkins uses the manic misogyny to frame the actual wooing in a particular way. For however Scarborrow may cast Clare's responses in this matrix, it becomes apparent to the audience that she is involved in a very different activity indeed, though still aggressively securing a husband.

Her praxis has several components, but none of them involves the deft monstrous female puppeting of males by the strings of their own desires (as in the gallants' fantasy). Her central maneuver is instead a wary testing of Scarborrow's capacities. She has, presumably, the right of refusal to fall back on, but sooner or later she will have to agree to some specimen of her father's choosing. And she will not be able to compare the members of a set, or consider too long, but must instead vote *seriatim* for keeps on a case-by-case basis.[33] Her main chance, then, is to play her cards carefully, to keep interest alive in whatever candidate is before her, and to commit herself to the best possible man she is likely to get. This means a judgment call, in other words, of the nicest discrimination, given that she will never have enough information or choice to make the kind of judgments we now think usual. Clare is bound to submit, yet still in a sense free too, as Sartre said of the torturer's victim: free to decide not *whether* to submit, but *when* – which in this case means *to whom*.[34]

Thus we may detect a pattern of gaming that for her is probing, challenging, masochistic, sadistic, and tempting by turns; bullying, yet leaving room for the best final submission to her structural fate. Resigned to his own awkwardness, Scarborrow asks in self-exasperation what time it is; Clare replies smoothly that she has no watch but her eyes, and thus cannot tell. He begins off-balance, exhibiting a self-conscious struggle to woo, almost as if it's what is expected of him, what he feels appropriate, rather than what he's hungry for. There is something of the lost boy here, dealing with pressures his precepts have not prepared him for; but we certainly do not see the unwitting headstrong heated-up and self-committing mode of the fantasy suitor.

For her part Clare is watchful and wary, but flirtatious too, above all concerned to trump his wit (no great chore, though she does so interestingly), replying with more than he bargains for. Her nominal game of witty repartee has a continual undertone of surplus and turbulent independence, even pugnacity or anger, that exceeds the limits of dance-like flirtation. She seems to be testing his responses to a woman who is too much for him, indeed, who is almost her own person, if such a thought were thinkable. Such ontological thinking is by no means inappropriate, as the following passage shows.

> SCARBORROW Prithee tell me: Are you not a Woman?
> CLARE I know not that neither, till I am better acquainted with a man.
> SCARBORROW And how would you be acquainted with a man?
> CLARE To distinguish betwixt himself and my self.
> SCARBORROW Why I am a Man.
> CLARE That's more than I know Sir.
> SCARBORROW To approve that I am no less: thus I kiss thee.
> CLARE And by that proof I am a man too, for I have kissed you.   (208–15)

Though the tone is that of comic stichomythia, and results in a made bargain (and eventually in "true love"), Wilkins presents a wonderfully direct address to the authority of gendered subject-positions. Scarborrow presumably hopes to constrain his fractious interlocutor in a net of traditional definition ("are you not a woman?"). However, she turns his device back onto him before he can effect it. Her Burkean antinomy of definition ("I'm defined by what I'm not," that is, "I am what you're not") elbows Scarborrow into having to claim his own manhood. When she doubts this insipidity (or rather, declares herself ignorant of it), he kisses her to prove it, reaffirming both identities by a phallocentric physical gesture of erotic intrusion designed to mark the two selves by opposition, hierarchy, and power, in a relation of active and passive. Clare, however, is pretty fully his equal here, and makes him know it. She defies the antinomian and subjecting distinction by seizing the phallic marker for herself (signing with a steel-trap flourish for the audience the blank check of his precedent fantasy as to what's under her skirts). No wonder he began by doubting lexically whether she were a woman.

Scarborrow cannot keep this up, and recoils from the gaming, saying, "Prithee tell me can you love?" (Would one stage a pause before this line, Scarborrow taken aback?) He hears the defiance in her replies, and doubts he can summon up in her the compliant female posture he had hoped to elicit. She answers all too directly as he fears (in the mode of Prince Hal's "I do, I will"): "O Lord Sir, three or four things: I Love my meat, choice of suitors: Clothes in the Fashion: and like a right woman I love to have my will" (217–19). Clare declines to love a man, loving first instead her meat (the phallus? *her* phallus?), the capacity to do the choosing, to dress as she will (with a chime on clothes above at 1.200, as in "take them up"?), and (once again, in case he has forgotten) to have

her will, like a true woman. "This is what we're really like," she seems to
be saying, "none of your fantasies."

Having frightened him once more, and thoroughly, Clare now backs
away from her forwardness, leaving him suddenly to cope with the
vacuum of will, seeming finally to draw from him a string of compliances
ending in the marriage proposal, as if proving (that is, at least being able
to prove) a considerate manliness:

> SCARBORROW What think you of me for a Husband?
> CLARE Let me first know, what you think of me for a wife?
> SCARBORROW Troth I think you are a proper Gentlewoman.
> CLARE Do you but think so?
> SCARBORROW Nay I see you are a very perfect proper Gentlewoman.
> CLARE. It is great pity then I should be alone without a proper man.
> SCARBORROW Your father says I shall marry you.
> CLARE And I say God forbid Sir: I am a great deal too young.
> SCARBORROW I love thee by my troth.
> CLARE O pray you do not so, for then you stray from the steps of Gentility,
> the fashion among them is to marry first, and love after by leisure.
> SCARBORROW That I do love thee, here by heaven I swear, and call it as a
> witness to this kiss.
> CLARE You will not enforce me I hope Sir?
> SCARBORROW Makes me this woman's husband, thou art my Clare,
> Accept my heart, and prove as Chaste, as fair.
> CLARE O God, you are too hot in your gifts, should I accept them, we should
> have you plead nonage, some half a year hence: sue for reversement, & say the
> deed was done under age.
> SCARBORROW Prithee do not jest?
> CLARE No (God is my record) I speak in earnest: & desire to know
> Whether ye mean to marry me, yea or no.
> SCARBORROW This hand thus takes thee as my loving wife.
> CLARE For better, for worse.
> SCARBORROW Aye, till death us depart love.
> CLARE Why then I thank you Sir, and now I am like to have that I long
> looked for: A Husband.
> How soon from our own tongues is the word said
> Captives our maiden-freedom to a head.   (220–48)

By now the cues in this graduated exchange will be apparent. Clare
excites his desire with hers for a "proper man," and he cites her father,
seizing entitlement to her. She sardonically denies his claim with a
critique of lustful and materialistic aristocratic loving, and he once again
(but this time much more carefully) presents a kiss as an oath or
affirmation. Clare reconstrues it as an enforcement (again activating the
play's title), surely as a rape – this time not standing her ground and
replying like a man, as she did with the last kiss, but embracing the
violating meaning and extracting the gesture of legitimation in return.
The performative "makes" (234) follows from the oath-kiss, once again

making *him* (rather than her), making him her husband. He presents her with his heart (the signum/phallus/kiss, as her "your gift is too hot" shows), and exhorts her to be chaste (meaning "keep my heart well"?, perhaps equating his heart with her nothing?). As with *The Merchant of Venice*'s Gratiano on his wife Nerissa's ring (again a *nothing*), marriage instantly inaugurates the world of male fear of, vulnerability to, aggressive defense against, female power in cuckoldry. ("So long as I live I'll fear no other thing / So sore, as keeping safe Nerissa's ring" [5.1.306–7].)

Clare directly experiences this defensiveness as violating, and is not about to accept and remunerate the "gift" of his heart when it reverses or uses up her freedom in the guise of a gesture of honor. She suggests instead that he speaks from a position of simple and irresponsible greed that a few months of possession will lead him to tire of and toss aside, leaving her marred in substance for the only market she can succeed in. (The *per verba de praesenti* betrothal can still function as exploitive of women, it seems.) But Scarborrow perseveres in reassurance, and she finally judges it wise to accept him, as the best offer she thinks it likely she'll get. Still, in her "For better, for worse" we must hear resignation, a shrugging in the face of a negative; this is not satisfaction, but acknowledgment of the accomplishment as both minimal and maximal; the best under the circumstances, but calling for resolve to meet and bear whatever follows. Getting what she has longed for, she laments the mortal feeling of having given herself; she feels more loss of freedom than gain of husband – her maiden independence, such as it was, now captived, subordinated, to a new body, a new head.

For his part Scarborrow begins his dominion with some hesitant relief and a consolidating lecture: "you are now mine, and I must let you know, / What every wife doth to her husband owe" (249–50): dedicated obedience, prosthetic identity. Women have two of everything (eyes, hands, feet), one of which is the husband's – except for their chastity, which is single, and all his. "Their very thoughts they cannot term them one, / Maids being once made wives, can nothing call / Rightly their own; they are their husbands all" (262–64). The transfer of genital ownership ends Clare's threatening freedom: he has it now, it cannot threaten him because it is his, not hers; in effect (a consummation obviously wished for), betrothal has finally *castrated* Clare. Thus formally chastened, Clare replies, "We being thus subdued, pray you know then, / As women owe a duty, so do men" (267–68), and calls for gentle husbandly protection. She uses notably domestic metaphors: of branch and bark protecting trees, ewes protecting lambs, hens their chicks. But two of her three figures call for female modes of protection. If she must relinquish her masculine potency, she hopes he will retain some positive effeminacy from the reeducation-by-fire to which she subjected him before subjecting herself to him. If you can so behave yourself, she says in coercive judgment, "I am your Clare, and you are fit for me" (282).

Thus ends Clare's careful achievement of a husband – only it does not, of course, for all of her studied effort soon vanishes in the wind of the Guardian's authority. Scarborrow must shift for himself without Clare's hard-earned skill. (She always knew herself destined for submission.) With his subjection we reach the heart of the play, now equipped to measure and judge with Clare's yardstick.

II

In Wilkins's transition from wooing to wardship the principals act to reify what has passed. Harcop enters with the youths (and the silent Butler).

> HARCOP Now master *Scarborrow*.
> SCARBORROW Prepared to ask how you like that we have done,
> your daughter's made my wife, and I your Son.
> HARCOP And both agreed so.
> BOTH We are Sir,
> HARCOP Then long may you live together, have store of sons.
> ILFORD 'Tis no matter who is the father.   (294–99)

The betrothal transforms both identities and social relations. Clare passes from child to adult woman, from father's adjunct to husband's. Scarborrow himself has become Harcop's son and heir. Such a construction may have some force of appeal or bargain, since Harcop has entered as to an accounting. But most noteworthy is how Wilkins introduces the variable of wardship, precisely by its conspicuous absence. For Scarborrow presents a non-relational construction of himself ("I"), transformed to child/heir of Harcop, silently detaching himself from his yet unmentioned Guardian – switching fathers, as it were. This silence constitutes a crux, but for the moment let us submit to the text, which carries us rapidly on, first to its juxtaposition of Harcop's licensing affirmation of the patriarchal mission – "have store of sons" – and then to Ilford's caustic aside on this project of marriage. He is at once familiarly hostile, to father (whose "naive" words he appears to comment on), to daughter, inevitably unfaithful, and to pliant fiancé.

Such phobic sarcasm on unstable fathering is prophetic, however. For next the Butler recalls Scarborrow to London and his guardian, of whom we now first hear (though an original auditor *might* already know that Scarborrow is a ward).[35] With the guardian's arrival the next stage of the play begins, frontally posing the titular issue of enforced marriage and confusing any preliminary sense that Harcop's supposed "plot" constituted that enforcement.

Scarborrow was initially situated for us between Ilford and Clare's constructions of gender relations. In seizing his love-match, he tried to embrace the specific identity constituted by the model of relation he chose – and was chosen by. But the two moments of this interpellation, constitution of self by the ideologically prior and by the self as a conscious agent, involve an unstable dialectic.[36] Now, after seizing his love-match and the self it was supposed to bring, Scarborrow finds himself under differential obligations to patriarchal authorities much more varied than he anticipated. The essentializing alignments of Scarborrow's identity begin with the betrothal (hardwrought against the Ilford discourse and sponsored by Harcop's own twice-placed relation to it), but its eventual results are shattering. For no sooner has Scarborrow pledged himself, with all save a ward's propriety, to Harcop as to a (new) father, than Wilkins complexly resubjects him to a triple prior father-figure: *the guardian*, himself an unequal substitute for the *dead blood father*, and the intermediate parental locus of *the crown*.

Sacramental energy is supposed to circulate comfortably along this pathway of substitutions, reaffirming individual and systemic ontology at every step. Instead Wilkins destabilizes them all, as reascriptive, disenchanted, weak, fragile: the dead blood-father Scarborrow Senior, the implicit (and economic) mediation of the crown, the guardian Lord Faulconbridge, and father-in-law-to-be Harcop. Each figure should produce patriarchal authority: by *blood*, by legal *default*, by legal *purchase* (as typically in the protesting discourse detailed by Hurstfield, though the play is silent on this score), and by *marriage* (actually, *betrothal*; also in effect, by reference to Lord Faulconbridge, by *elopement*).[37] These loci are presumptively reinforcing in early modern England, but here they distribute, and disrupt.

This set of equations frames our introduction to the guardian in scene ii, where Lord Faulconbridge explains things to Scarborrow's uncle William. The former wishes he had such a son, and the latter replies, "His friends are proud, to hear this good of him" (345). This particular guardianship, unlike the cliché, seems welcome, as socially elevating, rather than a hateful displacement of familial and financial authority. Acknowledging Scarborrow's worth, Lord Faulconbridge proceeds to "protect" it:

> And yet Sir William being as he is,
> Young, and unsettled, though of virtuous thoughts,
> By Genuine disposition, yet our eyes

See daily precedents, hopeful Gentlemen,
Being trusted in the world with their own will,
Divert the good is looked from them to Ill,
Make their old names forgot, or not worth note
With company they keep, such Reveling
With Panders, Parasites, P[r]odigies of Knaves,
That they sell all, even their old fathers' graves.
Which to prevent, we'll match him to a wife,
Marriage Restrains the scope of single life.   (346–57)

No reference is made to the near-dementia of *A Yorkshire Tragedy* and
Two Most Unnatural and Bloodie Murthers. Scarborrow appears a
generically unstable youth, culpably but typically indifferent to the filial
obligation to care for family name and reputation. They fear prodigal
waste of the family inheritance, not marriage outside the guardian's
wishes (as with Burghley's warning, "marry thy children in haste lest they
marry themselves").[38] Indeed, marriage is to be precisely a restraining
device, against prodigality.[39] In this plan Sir William finds "My Lord ...
like a father for my Kinsman" (358), the ideal lieutenant-guardian.

Yet his choice for his ward may remind the audience of the guardian's
possible profit:

LORD And I have found him one of Noble parentage,
A Niece of mine, nay I have broke with her,
Know thus much of her mind, what for my pleasure
As also for the good appears in him,
She is pleased of all that's hers to make him King.
WILLIAM Our name is blest in such an honored marriage.   (359–64)

He may wish, as guardians often did, to marry off a spare relation of his
own; or he may seek more permanent access to the heir's inheritance.
However, the text says nothing overt of this, and Uncle William (who
seems present exactly for this purpose) extols Lord Faulconbridge's
generosity and care in providing the advancement of a noble match. In
any case, Lord Faulconbridge has power to dispose: negotiations have
already begun, Katherine honoring both his pleasure and Scarborrow's
reported virtues. Indeed, Doctor Baxter, Chancellor of Oxford, is here
"To see the contract 'twixt [his] honored Niece and master *Scarborrow*"
(371–72). No resistence is expected, and Scarborrow is quite dutiful –
until he realized that a wife is what he's being given, not some vague
favor.

[SCARBORROW] Nothing can from your honour come; prove me so rude,
But I'll accept to shun Ingratitude.
LORD We accept thy promise, now return thee this,
A virtuous wife, accept her with a kiss.
SCARBORROW My honorable Lord.

LORD Fear not to take her man, she will fear neither,
Do what thou canst being both abed together.
SCARBORROW O but my Lord.
LORD But me a Dog of wax, come kiss, and agree,
Your friends have thought it fit, and it must be.   (394–403)

The dance of authority and submission between Scarborrow and Lord
Faulconbridge bespeaks power even though its subject is nominally that
of gift, as terms like *prove, promise, return, accept, ingratitude* show. Lord
Faulconbridge at first construes the resistance as fear ("Fear not to take
her man"). What is this fear? That the boy fears to become a man? That
he fears to give up his bachelor freedom? A fear of hurting the frail thing
he's to marry? Is this an investment in the mythology of female shyness
and virgin fear, so often a disguise for its male equivalent? Sometimes in
the drama, when a guide-figure surveys the prospect of marriage for his
(male) charge he enjoins the young man to marry and "spare not." So
the Butler says to Ilford below (1788), and the phrase is used in *The
Witch of Edmonton* as well.[40] There it seems to mean "Don't take her
fear seriously," or "Make your mark," or "She's yours for what you
will," or even "She wants it too, never fear" (399: "she will fear
neither"). It obviously calms the boy's fears to be reminded that he can
hurt his bride. What seems foremost here is that Lord Faulconbridge
weighs what he deems boyish fears and girlish pains as trivial, and
jovially pushes past them.

However, when real resistance to the patriarchal will hoves into view,
the guardian bristles, "How Sauce-box" (405): opposition arouses feminizing (i.e., castrating) infantilization, reversing the encouragement to
manliness. Scarborrow tries to appropriate this diminished role, pleading
"the unripeness of [his] years" (406),[41] but Lord Faulconbridge claims
the injured rights of the hard-working parent:

O Jack.
How both our cares, your Uncle and my self,
Sought, studied, found out, and for your good,
A maid, a Niece of mine, both fair and chaste,
And must we stand at your discretion.   (412–16)

To such offendedness Scarborrow can only reply with the worst: his faith
is given to "Sir John Harcop's daughter." To her he has "made an oath"
(423).

[SCARBORROW] Such power hath faith and troth 'twixt couples young,
Death only cuts the knot tied with the tongue.
LORD And have you knit that knot Sir.
SCARBORROW I have done so much, that if I wed not her,
My marriage makes me an adulterer,

In which black sheets, I wallow all my life,
My babes being Bastards, and a whore my wife.[42]   (426–32)

Often any betrothed woman whose marriage was even delayed was so judged (premature consummation being supposed), and if her betrothal was broken, thought "fit for no other." [43] For Scarborrow this is *not* a double-standard case: the damage extends beyond gender. He tries to seize his married identity by appeal to the imminence of penalty. The threats make a claim not on the speaker's determination, as with Black Will, but on the listener's: "*my* sin be on *your* head." Lord Faulconbridge, however, will not hear, pouring retribution on the sinner with a vigor that disrupts any notion of selfless guardian:

> LORD Ha, is't even so, My secretary there,
> Write me a letter straight to Sir John Harcop,
> I'll see Sir Jack and if that Harcop dare,
> Being my Ward, contract you to his daughter.
> My steward too, post you to Yorkshire,
> Where lies my youngster's Land, and sirrah,
> Fell me his wood, make havoc, spoil and waste.
> Sir you shall know that you are Ward to me,
> I'll make you poor enough: then mend your self.
> WILLIAM O Cousin.
> SCARBORROW O Uncle.
> LORD Contract your self and where you list,
> I'll make you know me Sir to be your guard.
> SCARBORROW World now thou seest what 'tis to be a ward.
> LORD And where I meant my self to have disbursed
> Four thousand pound, upon this marriage
> Surrendered up your land to your own use,
> And compassed other portions to your hands,
> Sir I'll now yoke you still.
> SCARBORROW A yoke indeed.
> HUNS [Lord Faulconbridge].[44] And spite of [*sic*] they dare contradict my will,
> I'll make thee marry to my Chambermaid. Come coz.   (433–54)

The challenge implicates both Scarborrow and Harcop, and Lord Faulconbridge responds to each. Harcop is treated pugnaciously, as a transgressor of Lord Faulconbridge's honor: he is challenged by letter, to see if he *dare* take this contractual action. Scarborrow is to be punished by being despoiled of his lands (not proposed or queried, but ordered as present fact). If "fell me" is not the so-called "ethical dative" but equal to "fell his wood and sell it for *my* profit," Lord Faulconbridge proposes explicitly to behave as the classic exploitive guardian rather than as a true caretaker. If Scarborrow insists on being an undutiful ward, his guardian will do likewise. Indeed, he goes further: where he had planned, he says, to make Scarborrow's marriage an enfranchisement (to adult status) – possession of real money, control of his own lands – he will now activate a further disenfranchisement, by disparaging Scarborrow in marriage to his chambermaid (expressly forbidden by the wardship statutes).[45]

Scarborrow begs his uncle for sympathy, but William only reaffirms Lord Faulconbridge's entitlements. Scarborrow continues to lament: "that I a Gentleman should be thus torn / From mine own right, and forced to be forsworn" (470–71). What exactly is this right? What takes precedence, in a class-specific way ("I a Gentleman"), over the legal right of Lord Faulconbridge? Perhaps some right to honor his oath, not to be forsworn. I suspect a noble traditionalist hostility to the technology of the law, perhaps as new-fangled. Compare John of Gaunt's "England, ... is now bound in with shame, / With inky blots and rotten parchment bonds" (*Richard II* 2.1.61–64). Perhaps a marriage forced across an honorable precontract feels like a degradation, perhaps a disparagement, an *enforced falsity* to full gentle identity. Perhaps it also destroys honor like a rape. This mix of personal and aristocratic resentment exhibits both the shape of the elite's resentment of commodified wardship, and the ways that marital control generated (and deformed) identity.

Such emotion funds the temporary culmination of immediate reaction:

> [LORD] You that will have your will, come get you in:
> I'll make thee shape thy thoughts to marry her,
> Or wish thy birth had been thy murderer.
> SCARBORROW Fate pity me, because I am enforced,
> For I have heard those matches have cost blood,
> Where love is once begun and then withstood. (490–95)

The collision of wills clearly sucks in and renders vulnerable each man's sense of primal identity, and seems to presage the anarchic affirmations of *A Yorkshire Tragedy*. Wilkins's purposes eventually go another way, but at this point the future is ominous.

III

Having brought about the enforced marriage, Wilkins now initiates his critique, sorting those affected by it in two ways: by principal or affiliate status, and by location inside or outside the marital orbit. He also takes pains to show how men and women face these pressures differently.

The triad of marital principals (Scarborrow, his betrothed Clare, and his enforced wife Katherine) are severally embittered by the abjecting transformations of the enforcement. The two women experience the degradation similarly, as making them *whores*, a term of erotic subjection Wilkins foregrounds for considerable interrogation. Scarborrow himself is feminized in a cognate way, replying to his marital rape with a highly rhetorical posture of *dissolution*.

In the struggles of Scarborrow's affiliates (his friends and siblings) Wilkins probes not only enforced marriage but primogeniture, an allied subjection of personal to familial interests. He juxtaposes the Prodigals to Scarborrow's equally fictitious siblings, whom we now meet for the first time. (Both groups are entirely of Wilkins's invention.) Each group enacts an attack on a central patriarchal structure (the fidelity–cuckoldry binary for the prodigals, primogenitural asymmetry for the agnates), and proposes an alternative distribution of material and symbolic resources. Each case resolves in favor of the family orbit, through the agency of the Butler. This old family servant is the play's final instantiation of father-hood, this time benign and productive. His comic schemes provide closure for both affiliate networks (mixing Middleton and the Shake-speare of *As You Like It*), clearing the way for Lord Faulconbridge's deathbed repentance, which relieves things for what is left of the principal triad and produces the play's terminus.

For the affiliate groups the enforcement transforms the heir into an object of material desire. First Ilford unmasks for us: he is in the business of undoing young men. He itemizes his current score –

> ... four by Dice, six by being bound with me, and ten by queans, of which some be Courtiers, some Country Gentlemen, and some Citizens' Sons. Thou art a good Frank, if thou pergest thus, thou art still a Companion for Gallants, mayst keep a Catamite, take Physic, at the Spring and the fall.
> *Enter Wentloe*
> WENTLOE Frank, news that will make thee fat Frank.
> ILFORD Prithee rather give me somewhat will keep me lean, I ha' no mind yet to take Physic.   (511–20)[46]

This is a defining moment for Wilkins's prodigals. Ilford turns out to be not only a London gallant but a parasite, of conventional profile. His victims are the usual suspects, upwardly mobile young men of all kinds, his tricks the usual mixtures of money, sex, and gambling. But special emphasis falls on the interpenetration of the categories of parasite and victim. These gallants' pleasures, like those of so many Jacobean gallants, contain simultaneously the urge to play (or waste) and the urge to exploit, to waste others. If youthful praxis experiments with "wild oats," it is, culturally speaking, instrumental to planting and harvesting full crops later. The Prodigals waste this resource of experience by not *using* it, but choosing it as an *end*.[47] Ilford and his friends fear exploitation by the world of Family, and seek to make a culturally temporary stage permanent, outside it. What we need to realize is that this posture will also prove culturally strategic.

Wilkins treats it as a fixation, though, and marks it as such with rich language of piggery. Ilford's first name now comes alive as the common noun (meaning "pigsty") familiar from *Henry IV, Part Two*: "Doth the old boar feed in the old frank?" Hal asks about Falstaff (2.2.138–39).[48] When Ilford congratulates himself for his exploitations ("thou art a good Frank") he reads himself as a pen for heirs undone. And undoing them seems oral or alimentary, if "pergest thus" means "purgest thus," something like consuming them, sucking them dry, voiding them when finished. Scarborrow's marriage will feed Frank fat.[49] The predatory gallants' blocking of the reproductive trajectory is thus obviously linked to the language of prodigals and pigs. And undoing heirs itself blocks the usual process of cultural reproduction, laying waste to the family's landed identity. This practice also constitutes a more pointed redirection of energies: an exclusive companionship with gallants, which Wilkins marks here with the casual reference to the catamite. It is unclear precisely what freight to attach to this term;[50] I will only reiterate, from this reference (an isolated one in *Miseries*) as from what has gone before, that Ilford represents a social category founded on a thorough-going cathexis for young unmarried men and as relentless a recoil from women and the family. Until the mechanistic ending, deviations from this line occur only for exploitation.

News of Scarborrow's marriage offers such an opportunity: he is now a rich man. Lord Faulconbridge has voided his punitive wishes, and has conveyed his full promise, including the £4000 of Scarborrow's own money. Note in passing, as a mystery, that Scarborrow's submission to the marriage is accomplished offstage. We do not witness his being either cowed or bought, by stick or carrot. This silence, like that about the betrothal and the guardian's probable reaction, seems strange. Perhaps Wilkins could not negotiate these transitions; perhaps he was not interested in them. Such deciding moments certainly attracted the authors of *Doctor Faustus* and *Macbeth*, whose lingering attentions have so defined our sense of the shapes of event, but Wilkins actively excludes them from his narrative stream, directing our attention elsewhere. The sufficiency of Lord Faulconbridge's pressures is simply given.[51]

Note too that the wolvish energy that Scarborrow arouses in Ilford may be displaced from the canonical grasping financier-guardian, from whom Lord Faulconbridge is distinguished. This relocation can be paired with the general conversion of the story to the tragicomic, via the deathbed recuperation of Lord Faulconbridge, an evasion of the monstrous rage enacted in *A Yorkshire Tragedy*. Perhaps Wilkins sought by such deflections to generalize or structuralize his concerns, fearing an evasive dismissal along the lines of transcendent (that is, individually ontological) evil. Perhaps instead he feared to insult a censorious *status quo*, or to side with a known mad murderer. I will return to this problem below.

Finally endowed against his will (so far as we are allowed to see) not only with wife but also with estate, Scarborrow is given over to "cashiered Captain discontent" (564), his reaction to "enforced sheets" (584). For Ilford this result spells opportunity:

> SCARBORROW I will not lie with her.
> ILFORD *Cetera volunt* she'll say still, If you will not, another will.
> SCARBORROW Why did she marry me, knowing I did not love her.
> ILFORD As other women do, either to be maintained by you, or to make you a Cuckold.   (594–98)

Ilford's strategic misogyny offers some supposed reality-testing, a proper distance on the generic miseries of marriage. See women as they are, he seems to say, and you won't be so vulnerable to them. This view is very much a categorical construction, of all wives. Scarborrow has fallen into a machine that only behaves in one way, that is ontologically hostile to and parasitic on men. Likewise, wives see no difference in men. If you won't another will: a wife wants maleness – sexual, financial service – not "you." She won't mind not being loved (that is, individually cathected) by you, because her relation to you is not individual either.

Here the clown enters, bringing letters from Harcop and Clare. Scarborrow, unswayed by Ilford, still laments his oathbreaking, considers his reply, elects brief despair:

> ... shall I say, my marriage was enforced,
> 'Twas bad in them, not well in me to yield,
> Wretched thee to whose marriage was compelled,
> I'll only write that which my grave hath bred,
> Forgive me Clare, for I am married....   (638–42)

He writes the note, turns to the gallants and says, "Gentlemen, I'll take my leave of you, / She that I am married to, but not my wife, / Will London leave, in Yorkshire lead our life" (651–53), and exits.

The scene now shifts, while Scarborrow's letter is in transit, to Scarborrow's younger brothers' arrival at Harcop's manor to initiate their share of affinal relations – like Ilford's friendship, very highly commodified. Juxtaposing Scarborrow's siblings to the prodigals, Wilkins almost technically foregrounds the relations between agnates and affines. Yet he does so with ever more noxious material:

> HARCOP Brothers to him [who] ere long shall be my son,
> By wedding this young girl: You are welcome both,
> Nay kiss her, kiss, though that she shall
> Be your Brother's wife, to kiss the cheek is free.

THOMAS Kiss, 'Sfoot what else? thou art a good plump wench, I like you
well, prithee make haste and bring store of boys, but be sure they have good
faces, that they may call me uncle.
JOHN Glad of so faire a sister, I salute you.
HARCOP Good, good i'faith, this kissing's good i'faith,
I loved to smack it too when I was young,
But mum: they have felt thy cheek Clare, let them hear thy tongue.
CLARE Such welcome as befits my Scarborrow's brothers,
From me his troth-plight wife be sure to have,
And though my tongue prove scant in any part,
The bounds be sure are large, full in my heart.   (662–76)

This passage painfully recombines much we have seen: where Harcop
offered the Prodigals wine, he offers the new "cousins" his daughter. The
father marks the homosocial transformations from the start: the woman,
a transformative reagent, makes the groom her father's son, and his
brothers are thus made welcome. They turn as by such right to affirm
masculist possessiveness. Rakish Thomas emits vicarious cuckoldry talk:
be sure you imprint your "store of boys" (recall Harcop's original
product-orientation at 298) with my brother's face (i.e., with the family
features) – which is to say, be faithful. John, more polite, still judges her
beauty an affinal acquisition.

These constructions, however, pale beside Harcop's hand-rubbing
pleasure in the copped kissing. Just how should one describe the licensing
licentiousness, the "enjoy her, boys," feel of this moment? The father
invites an explicitly erotic savoring of what would otherwise be more,
perhaps only, a formality. And the erotic commodification, vigorously
depersonalizing, objectifies Clare almost as if she weren't present. One
thinks of a humiliating version of the Sartrean caress, which "reveals the
flesh by stripping the body of its action," making unbearably real by
stroking against the will.[52] (Such negation is a form of Torture.) Harcop
certainly loves the specularity of it; note the repetitious fondling,
addressed more than half to himself. Similar moments elsewhere come to
mind. Justice Shallow and Shylock are both fetishistic old men of related
stamp and verbal habit, but their repetitions seem to be withholding,
stalling, enumerating. Here the mumbler has an active role. Harcop
caresses the process of watching these young men kiss his daughter: an
anti-Lear, a fatherly wittol. He enjoys giving "it" (71) to them, a parody
of the father giving away the bride. Perhaps he savors "it" as one past
"it." To "smack it" certainly recalls "swilled at Venus cup" (185), an
impersonal eroticism once again gone but not forgotten (or almost gone
– he still sups [i.e., sips]). He can still enjoy watching *them* swill at Venus'
cup. (Note the directly parodic reference later by Wentloe: "We'll but

taste of his Beer, kiss his Daughter, and to horse again" [929]. Presumably Harcop spoke so with the gallants, and was found absurd.)

Consider that the males dance this out in front of Clare: it is not sneaking male-bonding behavior, though patently homosocial.[53] The open depersonalization is all the more intense. If we imagine it, at least in theory, as a group fertility affirmation the instrumentality is not lessened. No wonder that when Clare ritually assures the brothers of her full-hearted welcome she affirms a distance, putting them in their place, a place a good deal more constrained than that which Harcop has just pried open for them. Clare rather says, "I love you according to my bond, no more." The disturbing fatherly behavior here is quite similar in its self-centeredness to Lear's quasi-incest,[54] but in this case the young woman feels excessively proffered rather than withheld, the father's action homosocially rather than oedipally exclusive. Harcop seems indeed the whoremaster, as he originally claimed.

Having gone, it turns out, through these motions (a further evacuation), brother Thomas gets down to business.

> [THOMAS] ... do you hear Sir John, what do you think drew me from London, and the Inns of Court, thus far into Yorkshire?
> HARCOP I guess to see this girl, shall be your sister.
> THOMAS Faith, and I guess partly so too, but the main was, and I will not lie to you, that your coming now in this wise into our kindred, I might be acquainted with you aforehand, that after my brother had married your daughter, I his brother might borrow some money of you. ... Besides Sir, I being a younger brother, would be ashamed of my generation if I would not borrow of any man that would lend, especially of my affinity, of whom I keep a Calendar. And look you Sir, thus I go over them. First o'er my Uncles, often o'er mine Aunts, then up to my Nephews, straight down to my Nieces, to this Cousin Thomas, and that Cousin Jeffrey, leaving the courteous claw given to none of their elbows, even unto the third and fourth remove of any that hath interest in our blood. All which do upon their summons made by me duly and faithfully provide for appearance ...   (677–97)

For this forthright sibling the marital transformations generate a linkage that principally entails access to (borrowed) money. Thomas bares the social device of marriage as a machine for managing and circulating literal and symbolic resources. The raw quality of his self-presentation not only marks the material function (which no one would have denied), but, as it were, materializes what is left: the symbolic (present in the as-yet-unexplained "appearance"). It also links marital and sibling relationality with other financial structures already in play: the canonically abusive guardian–ward relationship (sale and purchase of heirs as investments), and the cultural sore of primogeniture, seen as younger-brother disinheritance (over-provision to the eldest son as the maintenance of family-estate integrity). All three structures foreground acquisitive economic managements deemphasized within the familial reproduction of the social body. Alongside them we may log the emergent credit-institution of usury, the proto-*bank*. In a context where most dealings in finance and credit were traditionally conducted within the patronage networks of family, the usurer takes on a technically extrafamilial or even counter-familial status. The usurer who preys on heirs is a (Family) stereotype; what is less obvious, even masked, is that they often functioned as resources for *independence* from family, even as (dare one say) friends – though tenor and vehicle shift a good deal here.[55]

Such financial grazing can take place, as it were, either directly or indirectly. Both Thomas and Ilford ask the same self-introductory question: what on earth, save gain, could draw one from London and the Inns to this barren soil of the North? Both the siblings and the prodigals hope to feed on Scarborrow, in a conspicuously structuralized fashion. Ilford and company itemize their victims by number and type (see 511ff.), while Thomas has a chart by relation (mindful of kinship charts for specifying incest),[56] of uncle, aunt, nephew, etc., "even unto the third and fourth remove" (695–96). The heir is a locus of sustenance for all comers: siblings, guardians, fathers, daughters, parasites, servants yet to come. No wonder Scarborrow feels beleaguered.

Harcop chooses to take Thomas's talk as a joke. Perhaps it is. Is Thomas baring the device out of cheek, bullying with a pseudo-joke, or does he think he doesn't really mean it? Whatever the case, Harcop calls for drink, to "wash this chat with wine" (710). He seems to think it needs washing, and anyway, he never misses a chance to do Justice Shallow. (As usual Wilkins sites Harcop between youthful prodigal swilling and feminized nostalgic orality.) The men exit to the bar, and proceed to get drunk, much to Clare's disgust. She briefly remonstrates with Thomas against drunkenness (a standing reaction to her father's habits?), but to little avail. However, the Clown has brought in Scarborrow's fateful letter, to which she now avidly turns, initiating yet a third reaction to the enforced marriage, this time of the excluded principal:

> Methinks I guess how kindly he doth write,
> Of his true Love to me, as Chuck, Sweet-heart,
> I prithee do not think the time too long,
> That keeps us from the sweets of marriage rites ...
> With like desire methinks as mine own thoughts ...   (767–73)

Clare's last minute of earthly happiness is notably both sexual and domestic, the former imputed first or literally to Scarborrow as to a doting lover, but expressing her own fantasy throughout in the fluid

boundaries of new love. When she reads the awful news, and at first
denies her eyes, she returns to this expectant fantasy-position: "I know
... That I shall kiss him often, hug him thus, / Be made a happy and a
fruitful Mother / Of many prosperous children like to him ..." (787–91).
It seems crucial to note that she dreams in patriarchal terms, of
motherhood, "store of sons" who will prosper, and who will (in exact
and delighted accord with Thomas's wish) resemble their father. Clare
precisely fantasizes faithfulness.[57] We so often presume that fantasy is
irretrievably anarchic, always discontent with the enclosing paths of
civility. But culture also provides shapes for desire, shapes often happily
embraced as enabling and satisfying (in Therbörn's term, *qualifying*) even
by those aware of relevant limits and corruptions.[58] Though she was
wooed as one cramped and minutely controlled by gender disparities,
Clare still expects to become herself as a wife. Her pain is precisely that
of one deprived of this long-awaited and hard-earned fruition. Her
eventual response to that pain exactly reappropriates the self abducted
by Scarborrow's enforced marriage.

Here is the confrontation:

> He was contracted mine, yet he unjust
> Hath married to another: what's my estate then?
> A wretched maid, not fit for any man,
> For being united his with plighted faiths,
> Who ever sues to me commits a sin,
> Besiegeth me, and who shall marry me:
> Is like my self, lives in Adultery, (O God)
> That such hard Fortune, should betide my youth.
> I am Young, Fair, Rich, Honest, Virtuous,
> Yet for all this, who e'er shall marry me
> I am but his whore, live in Adultery.
> I cannot step into the path of pleasure
> For which I was created, born unto,
> Let me live ne'er so honest, rich or poor,
> If I once wed, yet must I live a whore.
> I must be made a strumpet 'gainst my will,
> A name I have abhorred, a shameful Ill
> I have eschewed, and now cannot withstand it
> In my self. I am my father's only child,
> In me he hath a hope, though not his name
> Can be increased, yet by my Issue
> His land shall be possessed, his age delighted.
> And though that I should vow a single life
> To keep my soul unspotted, yet will he
> Enforce me to a marriage:
> So that my grief doth of that weight consist,
> It helps me not to yield, nor to resist:
> And was I then created for a Whore? A whore,

Bad name, bad act, Bad man makes me a scorn:
Then live a strumpet? Better be unborn.   (812–41)

For Clare as for Scarborrow, his enforced marriage makes her a whore.
Her reaction unpacks an alternative ritual passage of marital transformation – not an organic fruition (the logic beneath the happy sexual
prosperous mother model), but a magical reconstitution of her own
identity by another's action, beyond her own will, relational by abandonment or absence or denial, as jilted. Her own experience of transformation (under construction before us in this speech) is not *passive* – which
would imply consciousness, resignation – but *inert*, immobile, unconscious, the transformation discovered as already completed, not endured
as process. (Such conversion is the goal of Ilford's programmatic desire
to whore all women – to strip them of subject-agency.)

Clare's new status is equally absolute and essentializing (as would the
status of wife have been), and radically contingent (on human action *not
her own*), mixing hitherto perfectly clear ascribed and achieved variables
in a mad and maiming fashion. She has not been prepared for this effect.
The horizon of her preparatory logic appears to have been something
like this. Avoid essentializing transformations (proscribed premarital
sexual events, though Clare is not inflexible here; witness her interlocu-
tory response to the kissing), find a man you can trust, and you'll
successfully become what you were always meant to be, full and happy in
your fate, both destined and earned. Unlike the adventuress Duchess of
Malfi (who lies about it), Clare did not set out to invent any new world.
She aimed for the received center, not the wilderness: for the authorized
and authorizing marriage bed. But she finds herself now made a monster:
her bed now incriminates any man who would touch her, look on her
basilisk virgin face. She is not only spoiled, but spoils others. And all of
this effective agency radiates from her untouched preserved and promised
status, now untouchable.

Like Auden's unloved joker, Clare now lacks a sense of ontological
substantiation; or rather, she experiences it as externalized, elsewhere
from the locus of her consciousness, yet inescapably and ontologically
true of *her*, her father's marketed daughter, who just accomplished
herself as thoroughly as she could, achieving the fate ascribed for her,
now only to have it count as a loss of that achievement. Tying her
identity to her self-transfer to Scarborrow, she has tied it not to what
fulfills it but to what empties it out, replacing it with its own negation.[59]
Clare has precisely not acted (since her betrothal), but she nonetheless *is*,
in her own mind, a *whore*, purely though without impurity, without
action. She is and is not Clare.

This internal abyss is intolerable. Its pressure drives Clare to suicide, to one last act of will to cut the Gordian knot of this impossible life and restore her to herself. For her final act will attempt to recover, to *seize*, her lost identity: not as chaste, like Lucrece, but as *wife*, by purely serving her husband's purity. If she was "created for a Whore," she says, "Better be unborn." (Not better to have been, but, as if it were possible, better to *be*; *present*, not past determination is what she wants.) If she was destined for this status, she will undo it all the way back to the origin, to deny the destiny that retroactively erases a thoughtfully lived life of virginity and happy sexual expectation of married chastity. This gesture will confer one last self-constituting gift of loyalty and commitment, clearing his name along with her own:

> ... Be judge you Maids
> Have trusted the false promises of men.
> Be judge you wives, the which have been enforced
> From the white sheets you lov'd, to them ye loathed ...
> My arms embracings, Kisses, Chastity,
> Were his possessions: and whilst I live
> He doth but steal those pleasures he enjoys,
> Is an Adulterer in his married arms,
> And never goes to his defiled bed,
> But God writes sin upon the Tester's head.[60]
> I'll be a Wife now, help to save his soul
> Though I have lost his body, give a slake
> To his iniquities ....   (852–66)

This palimpsestic suicide thus has two components, the erasing "better be unborn" and the self-reconstituting "I'll be a wife now [i.e., again], and cleanse my husband's soul." When she acts to cleanse her husband's soul by "giving a slake" to his iniquities, she echoes her father's response to other misbehaving Scarborrows. She washes her husband's words with blood, he theirs with wine. Such baptism returns her to herself, born again. (Her attraction to the beauty of this thought, and its monstrosity, are simultaneous.)

This martyrdom is addressed to two sympathetic and validating groups of witnesses: wronged maids who have believed men, and wronged wives who have been forced to marry away from prior love, as Harcop would have made her do. To and for each she offers a rewriting of the unwilled maimed identity she shares with them, produced by subjection to lovers and fathers.[61] How does Clare manage the transition from erasure to rewriting? If without invasion she became a whore, she will invade herself to purify the marriage, let blood to cleanse his soul, defy her constitution by another by constituting another, seizing autonomy in order to deny the subjecting ontologizing force of *whore*, reversing the poles of the vicarious construction. The summary force is this: by stabbing herself, she rewrites (really re-rewrites) the text of herself. Harcop says, "thou hast soiled thy self / With these red spots" (908–09).[62] Like a husband (thus both conventional and self-determining to the end), she has marked the sheet of herself, the spotted sheet proving her a true virgin and chaste wife. Such substantiation is obviously intolerably expensive, and also, from the patriarchal vantage, conveniently disciplinary; but it also provides, as suicide usually does, a vehicle fraught with enormous and efficacious vengeful energies. Wilkins leaves these to Scarborrow to voice, however, and thus may seem to sanitize the violation; but it is also possible that the horror of Clare's suicide is much more infectious if its rage is left implicit.

Another construction of Clare surfaces in this speech. Itemizing the different social weights beneath which she finds herself shaped, she also experiences herself as Harcop's *heir* – as, almost, a *son*. Her local need for this construction derives from her struggle with conflicting options for self-recovery and self-destruction, as virgin, wife, and whore. She briefly imagines remaining unmarried: "though that I should vow a single life / To keep my soul unspotted" (834). She presumes, however, that her father's unrelenting dynastic desire would overpower her. Let us compare this sense of being doomed to enforcement (noted at 836 and 854), with the other templates for enforced marriage that Wilkins has so far presented.

First we saw the betrothal trap of Ilford's initial fantasy, defined by the feminized and age-degraded father-figure both preying on and seeking reconnection with male youth; by deviousness (father–daughter conspiracy) – and by youthful paranoia and misogynist defenses. Second, recall the actual wooing of Clare and Scarborrow, marked by youthful male fear, defensive aggressiveness, female power and wariness, a concern for the specification of obligations, and some provision for women's initiative. Third, consider Lord Faulconbridge's legal-guardian enforced marriage of Scarborrow to his niece Katherine, marked so far by the absence of the guardian's canonical financial motive (except in the threatened punishment of stripping Scarborrow's lands); by the guardian's possible exogamic material motive in choosing his niece for the ward; and by the guardian's openly authoritarian and ego-driven posture regarding marital choice-making, endorsed by the representative Uncle William.

Fourth and finally we have Clare's presumption here about Harcop's non-negotiable requirement for an endogamic heir in body if not in name. This strategy was not unheard of, according to Houlbrooke. "Grandchildren who represented the main hope of continuing a family line were often regarded with particular affection. But such attachment

was not limited to members of the male line: some grandfathers looked
to daughters' sons to perpetuate their names" (193). Harcop's plan offers
a next-best consolation for the absence of the possibility that by Clare's
marriage his "name / Can be increased" (832). As a sonless gentry father
Harcop must reconcile himself to a dowering loss and (presumably) to
the family's eventual loss of named estate upon his death. Since his name
will die out ("increase of name" must mean grandsons named Harcop),
Clare must at least marry well, at least without disparagement (or
perhaps upward, as Scarborrow does, or must, or gets to). This allows
Harcop to retain in prospect a felt endogamic relation to the to-be-lost
name and estate if only through female-line succession. (That is, *felt* as
endogamic in estate-conservation, though exactly exogamic in outwardly
directed alliance; the constructions combine when Harcop dies and the
son-in-law inherits the Harcop estate.)[63] This plan also provides for the
father's old-age care and pleasure, the account of Clare's future that
Harcop himself repeatedly offers: see "I did beget thee for my comforter"
(887), and "The Treasure of his age, The Cradle of his sleep" (892). The
echoes of *King Lear* are strong, but in a gentry (that is, non-royal) and
sonless situation (with financial and dynastic limits) Harcop will resort to
direct enforcement.[64]

Wilkins thus situates Clare in relation to four social dispositions of
marital will: (1) in misogynist fantasy, as erotically corrupt and devious,
a transforming Circean temptress; (2) in hard-won realist wooing, where
choice is restricted to case-by-case half-hour tests; (3) in the evacuating
space of Lord Faulconbridge's ownership of "his" heir's will; and (4) as
compulsory instrument of her sonless father's frustrated dynastic *telos*,
the limiting horizon of such independence as option two provides.

Such richness justifies the text's relative economy regarding the other
principal, Clare's double Katherine, who enters with Scarborrow at 926
to learn of Clare's suicide. Like Clare, she is "made a whore" by the
enforced marriage. Both Scarborrow and Harcop, disputing blame,
construct her so. When she addresses Scarborrow as "Dear husband," he
cries, "False woman, not my wife, though married to me, / Look what
thy friends, and thou are guilty of ..." (951–52). This assimilates
Katherine to her friends, blaming them in her for the marriage and
death. As in the Ilford fantasy, a displacing misogyny is the response to
marital enforcement. Harcop of course blames Scarborrow, but also
makes Katherine a whore.

[HARCOP] Thy wife is but a strumpet, thy children Bastards,
Thy self a murderer, thy wife, accessory,
The bed a stews, thy house a Brothel.
SCARBORROW O tis too true.   (983–86)

Scarborrow blames everyone but himself; Harcop blames only Scarborrow, but in the same terms Scarborrow uses against Katherine. In the enforcement–betrothal split, it seems, each woman's existence or role or status must falsify the other's. This falsification, however internalized by the women, is really an instrument for masculine distributions of blame.

Katherine's sense of herself as voided echoes these views (and Clare's), though in a less radical key (speaking as married rather than as jilted):

> Thus am I left like Sea-tossed-Mariners,
> My fortunes being no more than my distress,
> Upon what shore soever I am driven,
> Be it good or bad, I must account it heaven,
> Though married, I am reputed not a wife,
> Neglected of my Husband, scorned, despis'd,
> And though my love and true obedience
> Lies prostrate to his beck, his heedless eye,
> Receives my services unworthily.
> I know no cause nor will be cause of none,
> But hope for better days when bad be gone,
> You are my guide, whither must I, Butler?   (1000–11)

Like Clare (with even less data?), Katherine is fully prepared to be an obedient wife. The ontological problem is less violent (lost at sea, she knows no cause), and she embraces its domesticated format: instead of the abyss, a virtuous and hopeful silence – and faith in the paternal, in the Butler. For her, as for Clare in another circumstance, this marriage is a fruition worth waiting and working for.

To this slight gesture of hope Wilkins opposes the large force of Scarborrow's repudiations, of the enforced marriage and the patriarchy that authorized it. True, we hear of it in softening indirect discourse (in the brothers' address to expelled Katherine), but the terms are extreme:

> [JOHN] My Brother having brought unto a grave,
> That murdered body whom he called his wife,
> ... thus he vowed,
> From thence he never would embrace your bed.
> THOMAS The more fool he.
> JOHN Never from hence acknowledge you his wife,
> When others strive to enrich their father's name,
> It should be his only aim, to beggar his,
> To spend their means, and in his only pride,
> Which with a sigh confirmed, he's rid to London,
> Vowing a course, that by his life so foul
> Men ne'er should join the hands, without the soul.   (1020–21, 1024–33)

Two vectors of rebellion appear here. The oath of physical denial centrally repudiates the mechanism that produces lineage. In frustrating the "false" wife's desires perhaps it also punishes. It certainly must deny a contamination of his own will (and desire).[65] The parallel gesture of prodigality wastes not bodily lineage but inheritance. Instead of enriching the family and father's name, he'll lay waste to it. And he addresses this symbolic protest to the fathers and guardians, the "men" (1033) responsible. As lineal self-destruction, it also echoes Clare's suicide (addressed to wronged women).

Once he is ready to waste, the Prodigals prepare to butcher him. Scene v begins the attack. As Wentloe puts it, "He's our own, he's our own, Come, let's make use of his wealth, as the sun of ice: Melt it, melt it" (1038–39). Ilford laughs, "To see that we and Usurers live by the fall of young heirs as swine by the dropping of Acorns" (1052–55). Wilkins returns us to his ideological discourse of waste, as usual keeping the terms circulating incestuously in a closed loop. Sons melt family wealth instead of conserving it; heirs fall like acorns, feeding parasites and gluttons instead of seeding oaks; and heirs, prodigals, and Prodigals, cannibals all alike, feed on the seed of the future. If women "renew man as spring renews the year" (145), these heterophobic men turn away to each other, living by the fall, the opposite season, turning inward rather than forward, both eating and eaten, not using, but using up. Hence Ilford's greeting to Scarborrow: "As many good fortunes as there were Grasshoppers in Egypt, and that's covered over with good luck" (1058–60).

The sting begins when Ilford has himself led in to Scarborrow by sergeants, as if arrested at the suit of Gripe the usurer. Ilford appeals to Scarborrow for security for bail, out of loyalty to their common status:

> How ill it will stand with the flourish of your reputations when men of rank and note communicate, that I Frank Ilford, Gentleman. whose Fortunes may transcend, to make ample Gratuities future, and heap satisfaction for any present extension of his friends' kindness, was Enforced from the Miter in Breadstreet, to the Counter ... if you shall think it meet, and that it shall accord with the state of gentry to submit my self ... [I'll] do't.
> WENTLOE Come, come, what a pox need all this, this is Mellis Flora, the sweetest of the honey, he that was not made to fat Cattle, but to feed Gentlemen.   (1171–83)

Ilford is enforced to prison for living the proper life of a gentleman, the prodigal life. Scarborrow is called by a *gradus* of choric argument from the boys to secure this life, out of shared identity (gentlemen both, Scarborrow enforced to marriage, Ilford to the Miter).

BARTLEY You wear good clothes.
WENTLOE Are well descended.
BARTLEY Keep the best company.
WENTLOE Should regard your credit.

BARTLEY Stand not upon't, be bound, be bound.
WENTLOE Ye are richly married.
BARTLEY Love not your wife.
WENTLOE Have store of friends.
BARTLEY Who shall be your heir.
WENTLOE The son of some slave.
BARTLEY Some groom.
WENTLOE Some Horse-keeper.
BARTLEY Stand not upon't, be bound, be bound.   (1184–96)

When Scarborrow finally succumbs, Ilford swears a like ironic oath aside, "To feed upon you as *Pharaoh's* lean kine did upon the fat" (1205).[66]

In this striking appeal Wilkins presents his fullest accounting of the ideology of prodigality as a repudiation of the imperatives of family. Two nets of prodigal tropes strive to oblige Scarborrow. First a familiar positive set: clothing, company (solidarity), reputation (credit *not* as financial), are to pressure Scarborrow, as binding status values to be upheld. Second, and much more important, a demystification or re-writing of normative pressures that would restrain Scarborrow's actions, in particular the pressures of obligation to family. Scarborrow has the money (by marriage), and so can spare/afford it. But the crucial pressure derives from setting up a direct conflict between (enforced, yet traditional) family obligations and "authentic" elective relations such as friendship.

This aggression is sited upon the theoretical absence, both individually and culturally agonized, of elective marriage.[67] Its first move is the ambiguity of "Love not your wife" (1191): is this an imperative or a declarative? Both have managing force, as does "have store of friends" (echoing the alternative "store of sons"): that is, "do so" and "since you do so," both argument and presumption. The next line, "Who shall be your heir," seems at first to follow from the preceding line: the friends shall or should be your respectful and loyal heirs. But the flow also reveals bitter forward reference, to the falsity and emptiness of the family-based, supposedly blood-based system of inheritance, so vulnerable to the supposed and female universal of cuckoldry. Your heir shall be the son of your cheating wife and some degraded and degrading slave.[68] Given this inevitable betrayal by women, low men, and the family system they hide behind and secretly constitute, you should disburse instead to your proper spirit-over-letter heirs – gentle young status-mates like Ilford – and serve the wholly masculine fraction of the system, turning your back on the contaminated and untrustworthily feminine portion resident in family structure. When Scarborrow agrees, Wentloe congratulates him precisely: "Now speaks my Bully like a

Gentleman of worth" (1199). The honorific *gentleman* is relocated and split to mark one who has repudiated the status of *genitor* in favor of that of exclusive *man*.[69]

What the Prodigals have argued here is that the ontological status ascribed to lineage – the core of ascription itself – is simply a genealogical fiction. Its only reality is the elective act of wife and cuckolder, which desperate family men have marked as exceptional out of sheer intolerable panic.[70] If blood not only does not transcend the will, but is really its mere misrecognized effect; if gender and status betrayal by wives and grooms is inevitable, the rule; then, they say, abandon this lineage of cuckoldry that calls itself Family, elope to the free state beyond its reach (which the play calls "London"), embrace the cleanest form of the elective, and bind yourself to love *us* – your equals, your like, your true-made mates in status and gender.

Such cannibal bonding, the Same feeding on the Same under the fiction of the transcendence of difference – "more than kin, less than kind," almost – culminates quite naturally in Ilford's inverted promise aside to feed on Scarborrow's fatness as Pharaoh's lean and hungry kine did on their fat brothers. When we consider other hovering Egyptian associations with the butchering of eldest sons, brothers selling privileged brothers into slavery, and plagues of locusts, not to mention prodigal grasshoppers, the Prodigals' enveloping linguistic miasma of destruction, of both heritage and descent, takes on the feel of a negative totalization.[71] Yet we should not therefore obliterate the creative force of the Prodigals' deconstruction of genealogy as a fiction. In the end Wilkins rejects it, in favor of an imperial familiality that embraces the homophobia of the Egyptian miasma. But he does first imagine what we might call postfamilial kinship, and such imagining is conceptually revolutionary. If the Prodigals' alternative bonding is a mere device here, a falsity, its metaphoric intelligibility shows that a literal version was thinkable. Achievement can give *freedom* from ascription – here not Anatomy but Family as Destiny. When core conservations of personal identity through significant others arise outside of the kinship system, especially in relations of friendship and sexual intimacy, we encounter a significant aspect of the rise of modernity, so often and inaccurately seen only as loss.[72] In a post-kinship world we must not sentimentalize nor reify the familial. When old certainties wither, new bondings become possible.

After the Prodigals' critique of the kinship order, Wilkins next presents a correlative address from within the family orbit.[73] Thomas and John lament together how Scarborrow is spending their portions along with his own, and they see this specifically in terms of rivalry:

... the extremity of want
Enforceth us to question for our own,
The rather that we see, not like a Brother
Our Brother keeps from us to spend on other.   (1225–28)

This is, of course, the same rivalry set up by the Prodigals, except that in
this opposed construction the family side consists not of seduced faithless
wife and bastard heir, but of seduced faithless heir and entitled siblings.
The divisiveness is now *internal* to Family. The sibs' enforcing extremity
of want (once again Wilkins's fetish term for irresistible need) turns out
to derive from actively courtly and potentially prodigal needs and desires
– that is, like those of Ilford:

> [THOMAS] Credit must be maintained which will not be without money,
> Good clothes must be had, which will not be without money, company must
> be kept which will not be without money, all which we must have....
>   (1232–35)

The brothers deal in the same coin of socialized value as the Prodigals,
even using the same jingle of terms – clothes, company, and credit (see
1184, 1186, 1187 cited above). One group insists that these markers
identify a shared status outside of family relations; the other, that they are
just what family relations should provide. The Prodigals claim fraternity
on the grounds of gentility and the brothers claim gentility on the grounds
of fraternity. The goals or needs – the familiar coin of city-gallant life;
that is, the signifiers of status identity – are the same. What Wilkins has
done is to split his players into these artificial groups (for of course the
Prodigals are simply of *occluded* family) in order to pit against each other
two kinds of rebellion against familial practice, thus demystifying any
notion of patriarchy as univocal or simply masculist, revealing competing
strategic interests both within and without that it fails to master.

Ilford and his mates encourage one kind of male rebellion against the
Father, here representing the hated and feared father–daughter,
husband–wife family system that plots to castrate and tame young men
like themselves – whose identity they construct for themselves in terms of
youth and unfettered masculinity. This last category they define through
a kind of misogynist and quasi-homoerotic homosociality, opposed to
the reproductively oriented family structure.

Thomas and John, on the other side, enact an internal rebellion
against a related kind of Father, normatively constructed by primogeniture in Scarborrow, *in loco parentis* over them. The parallel is usual,
if jussive: compare Margaret Cavendish's reference to her brother Sir
John Lucas, "who was heir to my father's estate, and as it were the father
to take care of us all" (*True Relation* 159). Behind this norm, before the
genitor's death, lay the childhood family rivalry of heir vs. everyone else,

living on after in the zero-sum predicaments of "younger brothers" (almost a technical term, describing a universal state of neglect and abandonment) and dowerless sisters. To probe this familial insubordination, balancing the gallant sedition against father and daughter, Wilkins again enlists both genders:

> JOHN Besides, we have brought our sister to this Town,
> That she herself having her own from him,
> Might bring herself in Court to be preferred,
> Under some Noble personage, or else that he
> Whose friends are great in Court, by his late match,
> As he is in nature bound, provide for her.   (1236–41)

The brothers need to maintain their gentle status; the sister needs either her portion to buy preferment from a noble person, or access to intercessors from among the Lord Faulconbridge network to get the same.

They reiterate these arguments when confronting Scarborrow directly, conceding if hating his right to self-destruction at the hands of the Prodigals, but claiming their own family birthright. For the next hundred lines Wilkins centers the food-and-drink terminology in the two groups' mutual abuse, the valence of value continually oscillating as each constructs the other fighting for access to the family goods. Though the strife is bitter, what strikes most is how both groups depend on the same discourse:

> [THOMAS] Our Birth-right good brother, this Town craves maintenance, silk stockings must be had, and we would be loath our heritage should be arraigned at the Vintner's bar, and so condemned to the Vintner's box, though while you did keep house, we had some Belly-timber at your Table, or so, yet we would have you think, we are your Brothers, yet no Esaus to sell our patrimony for Porridge.   (1288–94)

Scarborrow rejoins in kind:

> So, then you two my Brothers, and she my sister, come not as in duty you are bound, to an elder brother, out of Yorkshire to see us, but like leaches to suck from us. . . .
> You have been too saucy both, and you shall know,
> I'll curb you for it, ask why; I'll have it so.   (1300–02, 1308–09)

For the brothers, Scarborrow's London Prodigal life "consumes [his] body's wealth" (1282), transforming the solid food of heritage into the vintner's profits, leaving crumbs for porridge at best. He has become a hated withholding father and wolvish devouring guardian in one, the very figure he feared and hated in Ilford's fantasy (as well as in his guardian). As a result of his rebellion, though, his excluding allegiance is now to the gallant fraction rather than to the familial fraction of the patriarchy, and he now construes the siblings as sucking leeches[74] (like the dangerous female mouths early in the play, also like infant children who would feminize him and suck him dry).

As if to confirm his allegiance, Ilford calls Scarborrow to pledge a gallon of sack waiting for him in the fire. Scarborrow says, what do you think of my importunate brothers here, and Ilford answers, addressing them,

> You must learn more manners, stand at your Brother's back, as to shift a Trencher neatly, and take a Cup of Sack, and a Capon's leg contentedly.
> THOMAS You are a slave
> That feeds upon my brother like a fly,
> Poisoning where thou dost suck.　　　　　　　　　　　　　　(1333–39)

Ilford construes them as degradingly hungry too: servile waiters serving oenophiles and rewarded accordingly, with a capon's leg (both castrated cock and the limb for bowing, as in "make a leg"). Thomas retorts parasitic consumption to Ilford, *feeding* and *sucking* both abusive terms Scarborrow attaches to the familial fraction. John similarly accuses Ilford of living "like a Dog, by vomit" (1347),[75] and finds Scarborrow

> ... more degenerate
> Than greedy Vipers that devour their mother,
> They eat on her but to preserve themselves,
> And he consumes himself, and Beggars us.　　　　　　　　　(1377–80)

The sister receives matching treatment according to gender, when the siblings discuss how to live:

> THOMAS In troth sister, we two to beg in the fields,
> And you to betake yourself to the old trade,
> Filling of small Cans in the suburbs.
> SISTER Shall I be left then like a common road,
> That every beast that can but pay his toll
> May travel over, and like to Camomile,
> Flourish the better being trodden on [?]　　　　　　　　　(1389–95)

For the sister there is no space between options: her portion purchases preferment; its absence guarantees total subjection to the beastly Prodigal male world of the wine-trade, the literal embrace of whoredom.[76]

At this point the younger brothers and their sister seem doomed to the sodden future of Shakebag and the Widow Chambley, Pistol and Doll and the loathsome den. Wilkins will begin to turn aside now, but only after having marked the short slide from younger lower gentry to the gutter. The difference for the genders seems to be that the famished brothers will become highwaymen, the sister the pitiful highway itself, a common road. They will live *in* the drain, the ditch; she will *be* the ditch.

(As the 1611 Bible has it, "a whore is a deep ditch; and a strange woman is a narrow pit": Proverbs 23:27.) Starved, they will eat and drink vileness; adjunct to the end, she will empty herself to fill the beasts they have become. Worse, though, fallen brothers can still act: their degradation is not ascribed. They can come back. Her fate is ontologizing: she *is* (rather than *has*) fallen, absolute.

This discourse of food and drink embodies overall the conflicted logic of social-resource reproduction that Wilkins dilates under the multiple trope of enforcement. In its thick textuality we see scarcity and subjection, gender fright and misogyny, vengeful gorging, vengeful starvation, vengeful and pitiful waste. We may also dimly see positives: struggles, within limits but historically real for all that, for maturity and independence; persistent patterns of family loyalty; even perhaps among the Prodigals a shadow of elective bonding, an allegiance to possibilities of extrafamilial reality. In a time of dislocating social change, both survivals and inventions can serve to sustain those whose place and future have become obscure, or fallen into others' hands. Such potentialities remain shadowy behind the substance of Wilkins's social critique; his purpose, ultimately tragicomic at best, requires this. But neither are his characters simply benighted, crudely doomed. In his complex overlay of youth and age, male and female, family and other, "enforced" and "free," we need to listen for unseen options, cross-category pathways, emergent positionings upon which confused men and women might find their feet. Different auditors will hear different sounds, but it's clear that there is structural noise, waiting to coalesce into opportunity as well as loss.

IV

At this point the Butler enters, bringing news that begins a new movement of the play: Katherine has borne Scarborrow twin sons in Yorkshire. This structural event brings to a close the anti-patriarchal deprecations between brothers and Prodigals, and initiates a process of imperialist family containment, recovery, and fruition aptly heralded by such a comic sign as birth of twins. Indeed, the loyal scheming Butler replies to both challenges to family values from Scarborrow's affiliates: sustaining the brothers financially, marrying off the sister, in each case diverting extrafamilial resources to familial purposes. The brothers he teaches to be outlaws of the wood, dealing in highly appropriate echoes of *As You Like It*[77] (and in fact they rob Harcop, thus silently conserving Clare's promised dowry by a side door). The nameless sister he marries to Ilford (himself by then a new heir recuperated to familiality), by a cheating "enforcement" rather like Ilford's fantasy about Harcop as predator. In each case a "literary" tone sets in to enable such resolution, a phenomenon to which I shall return.

Note what dark possibilities Wilkins sidesteps in this news. Scarborrow is now twice over a father, not only to his angry brothers but of new and brother-displacing heirs. The twins themselves, of course, are guaranteed to feel the worst form of sibling rivalry, and for Scarborrow they repeat his unwanted pair of sucking brother-sons in the next generation. Indeed, to mime Bradley (or Ilford), are the sons Scarborrow's? Was there time to conceive them? When he swore not to embrace Katherine's bed, had he already begotten the sons? Or are they perhaps children of the groom? We might presume wedding-night consummation, but later Scarborrow will accuse the Butler of such usurpation. Still, the immediate effect of the Butler's announcement is to signal a positive shift in the play's course.

For his good news to Scarborrow about sons the Butler gets no thanks but blows; he reenters bleeding but only annoyed, patiently expecting the traditional order to right itself:

> Well I will not curse him: he feeds now upon Sack & Anchovies with a pox to him: but if he be not fain before he dies to eat Acorns, let me live with nothing but pollard, and my mouth be made a Cookingstoole for every scold to set her tail on.   (1396–1400)

The mixture here repeats with vigor the values that the preceding stretch has distributed agonistically. However, transformations are in play. Scarborrow's current diet is drink and appetizers, but he'll end up with acorns, the Prodigal's punishment. Up to this point prodigal eating has generally signaled victimization, suffered or exploited. Now, however, Wilkins begins to draw upon the motif's latent potential to figure transformation rather than loss, which becomes available at the Prodigal's canonical low-point, in the sty (associatively predicting its opposite and end, the fatted calf). The turn toward restoration is a turn away from a discourse centered on evil woman (the Prodigals' Circe) to one rewarding submission to the father.

Yet the Butler's oath recycles quite intensely some of the misogynist material used above to voice family hatred. Both of its terms are obscure. If "pollard" balances "Acorns," then it means "bran sifted from flour" (*OED* sb.2.II.4): that is, "if he doesn't dine ill, let me do so." But other senses are highly relevant. In particular, the term marks specific animal and vegetable figures for reproductivity, both precisely ambivalent. An animal pollard has lost his horns (*OED* sb.2.I.1): given cuckoldry jokes, this cuts both ways for humans. The vegetable form deserves quotation: "A tree which has been polled or cut back, at some height above the ground, so as to produce at that point a thick close growth of young branches" (*OED* sb.2.I.2). Scarborrow has surely been so cut off, yet this definition constitutes a pruning of the family tree, to foster richer growth. Not that these meanings form part of some thesis sentence, I hasten to say. They tend rather to float freely, like so much of the agonistic discourse in this play, generating tone and triggering thickening associations.[78]

Likewise with the "cookingstoole." The scold's cucking/ducking-stool is the basis, presumably: the coincidence of bad female mouth, forcible submersion, fouled male mouth, and stools (close-stools?) chimes with Ilford's early gagging vitriol. If the Butler's mouth is to be punished for speaking out, the oral punishment for scolds must lurk somewhere behind: the brank, with its maiming barbs and teeth.[79] "Let me be punished both *by* and *as* a scold," he seems to say. We must also count an association with cuckoldry (women unruly below as well as above), and a less common one (by spelling) with cooking. The culinary specificity is, above all, strikingly inexplicable except by reference to Scarborrow's bad food, acorns.

Perhaps what we see here is a kind of conservation of misogyny. The Butler will serve Wilkins's needs as agent of family reparation, but will do so by relocating inside the family fraction of the patriarchy much of what Wilkins has hitherto split off as rage and fear and positioned in the Prodigal sphere. Perhaps this counts as some kind of acknowledgment, of "the old Eve," as it were, conceptually necessary, even indispensable, but still needing policing. Perhaps the claim, a familiar one after all, is that the family is the only institution that *can* police her. There is certainly a pattern of increasing allusion to women outside family as unpoliced.

Or perhaps the claim will become more general: that family is really *all* after all, that there is no other space, even in London. The familial equivalent of secularization, in which living space opens up outside sanctified ascription, is doomed to failure – or at least must be denied. Family is not to be everything, but the only thing. The extensive demography of the *dramatis personae* works to confirm this. Scarborrow's many relations (brothers, a sister, a dead father, an uncle, an old family servant, a betrothed, a father-in-law-to-be, a guardian, and a wife) configure most of the possible modes of relation. His three "friends" are no more, perhaps, than the minimal number forming a group. Its leader is eventually recaptured, supplied retroactively with a father who transforms him into an heir, and married to Scarborrow's sister; its other two inhabitants evaporate. This looks suspiciously like an *imperialism of kinship*, a ramification of familiality not only to contain a specific subversion but with a view to enclosure of all the places in logical space. No commons are to be left in London for outlaws to gather in.

Within such a progression we may locate the Butler's manifold anti-feminism, as what seems for Wilkins's project a reappropriation of the powers of Prodigal misogyny. The key to this stretch seems to be *whoredom*. When the Butler decides, out of family loyalty, to care for Sister, he posits a certain dubious wonder at her personal desert, and a safeguard just in case:

> Well I do pity you, and the rather because you say, you would fain live honest and want means for it, for I can tell you 'tis as strange here [in London] to see a maid fair, poor, and honest, as to see a Collier with a clean face. ... Your father was my good Benefactor, and gave me a house whilst I live to put my head in: for I would be loath then to see his only daughter, for want of means, turn punk, I have a drift to keep you honest. Have you a care to keep your self so, yet you shall not know of it, for women's tongues are like sieves, they will hold nothing, they have power to vent.   (1445–57)

Such presumptions as to daughters' typifying looseness coexist painfully with this daughter's sense of what it takes to have a place rather than a cell in the family.

> [SISTER] Some husbands are respectless of their wives,
> During the time that they are issueless,
> But none with Infants blessed, can nourish hate,
> But love the mother for the children's sake.   (1419–22)

Such fulfillment as is to be had lies in a functional motherhood that buys esteem. No wonder that all of the women in the play embrace its placement so vigorously; it is the only game for them. (This impression is made the more intense by Wilkins's omission of any women characters associated with the Prodigals. Comparison with similarly placed characters such as Bianca in *Othello* and Courtesan in *A Trick to Catch the Old One* reaffirms the desire of women on the Prodigal side to change sides. Preferable life outside family seems much less imaginable for these women than for men.)

The husband who rejects this *telos* is cursed too:

> [BUTLER] He is your Brother & my master, I would be loath to Prophesy of him, but who soe'er doth curse his Children being Infants, ban his wife lying in Childbed, and beats his man brings him news of it, they may be born rich, but they shall live Slaves, be Knaves, and die Beggars.   (1411–15)

Such husbands' fate is just that Scarborrow embraced – life outside. Yet that place seems now not a brave new world but an arid wilderness, its inhabitants degraded isolate savages rather than a new nation. The term *slave* begins to take on a new and abusive prominence, marking negatively unattached men, men without family ties, or who have repudiated them, or who are wage-slaves. To be thus unattached is to be degraded and (the vector reverses, to hostile) morally repulsive. One is taken to have become a slave by choice, to be responsible for such a repulsive life.

Yet even such a self-determined (or at least culpable) damnation to outer darkness for men is laid at the door of female openness: groping for explanation, serious brother John says of unfamilial William, "But he that is given over unto sin, / Leprosed therewith without, and so within, / O Butler, we were issue to one father?" (1424–26). The frightening fate for women in this position is that their only hope is all too close to being defined as their inescapable doom, only to be platonic options, awaiting the chance to betray. Perhaps the raging Prodigal fear cannot really be domesticated.

Still, family loyalty propels the Butler to do what he can: "To keep you honest, and to keep you brave, / For once an honest man, will turn a Knave" (1464–65). His rhyme for the predicaments is striking. Penury means begging for the brothers, whoredom for the sister. Adequate maintenance means "bravery" for the brothers (silk stockings) and a reserved virginity (saleable in marriage) for their sister. It is hard to say which side of this simple parallel is more distant for us today: that the male equivalent of the female *eudaimonia* of virginity consists in silk stockings; or that begging, even homelessness (never mind the unthinkability of labor) is gentlemanly whoredom.

Back in the main plot for a moment, the Butler's gesture of pity for Sister's incipient whoredom is echoed by the other father, further recuperating the parental generation. Lord Faulconbridge meets drunken Scarborrow in the street, who with "much drink, [and] no money" laments to himself, "I were an excellent creature to make a Punk of, I should down with the least touch of a knave's finger" (1469–70, 1472–73) – linking drink, whoredom, and now a degraded feminization. (The feminine and degradation flutter back and forth now across the boundary of family.) Scarborrow, like Spenser's Red Cross Knight, is "poured out in looseness on the ground" (1.7.7.2). The guardian, however heavy-handedly, feels pity, but Scarborrow canonically returns the pity "i' thy throat" (1496) and threatens, since Lord Faulconbridge has "put a piece of turned stuff upon [him]," to "piss in [his] way" (1497–99). That is, he turns the pity to insult, deflects his own felt whoredom once again onto his wife Katherine, and threatens a posturing phallic revenge on his guardian, unpacking his heart like a drab.[80] Uncle William enters, and he and Lord Faulconbridge lament the disgrace, as "shame to our name" (1509). Mad with grief, Scarborrow draws, and even Ilford gapes with status-horror: "Hold, hold, do you draw upon your uncle?" (1522). Lord Faulconbridge and Sir William leave, unhurt by this rebellion and elevated enough to shake their heads in further pity at the sight: "he feeds on draff, / And wallows in the mire, to make men laugh" (1529–30).

This movement closes with one more discursive linkage of feeding and whoredom to family, that rescues the brothers and prepares resources to rescue Sister. Transforming abandonment to an active and unhelpless form of suffering (that is, conferring agency on younger brothers), the Butler leads Thomas and John to the trade of outlawry, though he finds them "sucklings, ... their mother's milk not wrung out of their nose yet" (1541–42).[81] Still, they fare well enough, robbing Harcop of £300, and Butler saves enough breath to greet the old man afterward with "you bear your Age fair, you keep a good house, I ha' fed at your board, and been drunk in your buttery" (1591–92). Repeating this experience after Harcop leaves, he calls this "Three hundred pound: A pretty breakfast" (1639). Yet, he enjoins the brothers, this money is spoken for (for Sister's marriage, we later learn). "Look you go not to your Gills, your Punks, and your Cock-tricks with it" (1646–47), he says, or he'll turn them in. If material adequacy propels women toward marriage, it appears to propel young men away from it; the risk is that the impoverished brothers will turn Prodigal, and spend their sister's dowry on whores. It takes a wise (or perhaps an old) father-figure to turn their thoughts from flesh to blood.

Scene ix prepares for resolution among the Prodigals: Ilford's father has died, reinscribing him in the economy of family that eventually results in the marriage to Sister. However, his first reaction is distinctly Prodigal:

> ILFORD Sure I ha' said my prayers, and lived virtuously a late, that this good fortune's befallen me. Look Gallants: I am sent for to come down to my Father's burial.
> WENTLOE But dost mean to go?
> ILFORD Troth no, I'll go down to take possession of his land, let the country bury him and they will: I'll stay here a while, to save charge at his funeral.
> BARTLEY And how dost feel thyself Frank, now thy father is dead?
> ILFORD As I did before, with my hands, how should I feel myself else?[82]
> (1656–65)

His father's death is centrally a financial gain, but he determines to marry, nominally in the same spirit, requiring only that his bride be fair, rich, and young.[83] He speaks of wanting an honest woman, to be "a countenance to [his] vices" (1678–79), and he disallows some categories

because "Ladies may lard their husbands' heads, Widows will Wood-
cocks make, & Chambermaids of servingmen learn that, they'll ne'er
forsake" (1682–84), so he may care about cuckoldry. However, he says a
moment later that "it's no great matter for her honesty, for in these days,
that's a Dowry out of request" (1688–89).

Whatever Ilford's stance, it offers the Butler the opening he needs, and
he proceeds to conjure up "two or three rich heirs" (1704–05) for the
gallants, itemizing them by county of origin and by income. Yet he first
plays hard to get, fearing that they have been whoremasters; Ilford
replies, can't one have been "a little whore-master" in his youth but you
must upbraid him with it?[84] "Why my father's dead man now, who by
his death has left me the better part of a thousand a year" (1716–18). The
Butler is supposed to take Ilford as seriously ready and fit to marry. A
man with an inheritance has responsibilities, must make plans. (Apparently nostalgia for whoremongering must await more mature years.)

Nonetheless, the heir is watched over by wise friends:

> BUTLER Now sir, she being but lately come to this town, and so nearly
> watched by the jealous eyes of her friends, she being a Rich heir, lest she
> should be stolen away by some dissolute Prodigal, or desperate-estated spend-
> thrift, as you ha' been Sir.
> ILFORD O but that's past Butler.   (1762–65)

Stealth is called for, because Wentloe and Bartley, out of "envy ... or
hope of their own advancement" might "make [Ilford's] labors known to
the gentlewoman's Uncles" (1778–79). He who would marry richly must
fear both Prodigals and Guardians, it seems, and the Butler proceeds to
deal for Ilford alone.

> BUTLER Which done, all's but this, being as you shall be brought into her
> company, and by my praising your virtues you get possession of her Love, one
> morning step to the tower, or to make all sure, hire some stipendiary priest for
> money: for Money in these days, what will not be done, and what will not a
> man do for a rich wife, and with him make no more ado but marry her in her
> lodging and being married, lie with her and spare not.   (1782–88)

The Butler emphasizes the acquisitive, as the door through which Ilford
decamps into family. Wentloe and Bartley are jettisoned, with relish: "I
will but shift off these two Rhinoceros" (1798). The church is for sale,
and for a rich wife any man would be equally beyond scruple. It only
then remains to seal the bargain, make her your wife beyond annulment,
by the unsparing transformative sexual act that Scarborrow determined
to refuse.

This plan is of course the play's final permutation of enforced
marriage, as comic reversal: it saves Sister from whoredom, and frees the
pseudo-father Butler of his responsibility.[85] It also enacts a reformative

reprisal: as Sister herself later says to Ilford, " 'Twas fitter for your self than for another, / To keep the sister, had undone the brother" (2116–17). There is irony too in the plot's resemblance to what Ilford feared at the play's outset. The Butler and Ilford enter above, and Butler laments, "God's precious Sir, the hell Sir, even as you had new kissed, and were about to court her, if her Uncles be not come" (1868–69). We have not seen the Butler giving Sister her lines, but he presumably designed this move to heat Ilford up, and then withhold the lure, just as the fantasy daughter does at the play's beginning.

For his efforts Ilford thanks him: "Honest-blest-natural-friend, thou dealest with me like a Brother" (1886–87; see also Wentloe's usage at 1838). Family has indeed begun to colonize Prodigal. Ilford now uses "brother" as a term of praise, but for Wilkins this use is ironic, marking the simultaneous accuracy and inaccuracy of Ilford's gratitude. In a primogenitural situation "brotherly" has as much cause to signify rivalry as mutual aid.[86] The Butler, not misled, replies aside, "These men like Fish, do swim within one stream, / Yet they'd eat one another, making no Conscience / To drink with them they'd poison" (1841–43). When Family and Prodigal begin to intermix we hear a kind of discursive friction, drumming in the Polonian dialectic of eating and being eaten, feeding and poisoning, penetrating and engulfing.

Ilford rejoices in his lucrative marriage: "I will practice all the Gallantry in use, for by a Wife comes all my happiness" (1933–34). The Butler arranges everything, requiring only detailed oaths, and Sister plays her part readily: "I am not Sir so uncharitable, To hate the man that loves me" (1974–75). The Butler then sends them off to "perfect [their] bliss" (2013) with the aid of the hired priest. "Then do clap yourself into her sheets and spare not" (2018–19). Looking on, as it were, he summarizes his project, shifting to choric verse.

> Down, down, 'tis the only way for you to get up.
> Thus in this task, for others' good I toil,
> And the kind Gentlewoman weds her self,
> Having been scarcely wooed, and ere her thoughts,
> Have learned to love him, that being her husband,
> She may relieve her brothers in their wants,
> She marries him to help her nearest kin,
> I make the match, and hope it is no sin. (2021–28)

This extended-family-values marriage will save them all from her disgrace in the suburbs, and provide the brothers with relational access to Ilford's wealth (Thomas's first thought with Harcop).

Such appropriation is of course Ilford's agenda. He and his wife reenter, as directly from the deflowering: "Ho Sirrah, who would ha'

thought it, I perceive now a woman may be a maid, be married, and
lose her maiden-head, and all in half and an hour, and how dost like me
now wench" (2041–43). His wife replies, "As doth befit your servant
and your wife, / That owe you love and duty all my life" (2043–45).
Then (ritual duties paid) Ilford must "kiss [his] portion out of [his]
young wife," and asks for the deeds to her lands. Instead she reveals the
truth: that she is poor, and "Sister to decayed Scarborrow" (2111).
Ilford of course responds furiously: "Do you hear Puppet, do you think
you shall not be damned for this, to Cozen a Gentleman of his hopes,
and compel your self into Matrimony with a man, whether he will or no
with you ... " (2120–23). Sister is challenged as herself enforcing
marriage ("puppet" abusively projected onto her from Ilford's own
sense of subjection),[87] cozening a gentleman of his legitimate mercenary
marital expectations. The tables are turned: Ilford is taken as he has
taken others, here by his own phobia, a father-daughter team. And
marriage detaches him from his former mates, as they recognize:
Wentloe says "Foe" (presumably the ejaculation "foh," though it is
tempting to read "foe"), "we shall have you turn proud now, grow
respectless of your Ancient acquaintance" (2144–45). Their anger at
Ilford's betrayal matches his own fury, which is directed typically
elsewhere, at women and family:

> I that could not abide a Woman, but to make her a whore, hated all She-
> creatures, fair and poor, swore I would never marry but to one that was rich,
> and to be thus cunnicacht. Who do you think this is Gentlemen? ... she
> proves to be the beggarly Sister to the more beggarly Scarborrow.   (2159–66)

The wicked pun on "cunnicacht" captures the infantilization of coney-
catching (a regression to childhood, the scene of helplessness) and the
sharpened fears of the *vagina dentata*. As usual, the misogynist ignores
male responsibility for the marriage (in this case the Butler's obvious
agency), focusing on degradation by women.

Another slant of light falls here, when Ilford says, "I could be made a
Cuckold with more patience, then endure this [enforced marriage]"
(2143–44). It is interesting to align these configurations. For Ilford, both
treat men as subjected mates, inverting the prodigal ideology for controlling women. The difference seems to be this. The Prodigal ideology
against enforced marriage is about how to dominate *women* (having only
controlling relations with them, contractual ones). Cuckoldry ideology is
about how to dominate *wives*, who have sworn overtly to be dutiful.
Both actions challenge male power. Enforced marriage threatens the
power of *single* males, who as heirs, prodigals, unbonded men (the
positive equivalents of "slaves") can try to situate themselves entirely

outside the realm of parental/guardian control, in "freedom." Cuckoldry threatens the power of *married* males (endowed with the cultural authority – and vulnerability – of husbands). Ilford seems to feel the loss of extrafamilial independence more grievously.

Once Ilford is married, the several hinges of Wilkins's dramatic plan now swing slowly shut. The neatness of the Butler's table-turning has a distinctly literary cast that increasingly dominates what remains of the story: such machinations begin to feel like tools for closing down a play. The Butler's trick is but the first of several gestures inflaming various angers which the climax will discharge. Ilford expels Sister as a whore (the familiar displacement), and exits in search of Scarborrow, to "draw his blood" (2193). When brother Thomas learns that Ilford has kept the jewels his stolen money bought for Sister (bait for Ilford), he too flies into a rage, with the same object: "Damnation on him, I will hear no more, / But for his wrong revenge me on my brother, / Degenerate, and was the cause of all" (2208–10).

Scarborrow too now rages, at himself for his own prodigality. "Spendthrifts, and such am I, / Like strumpets flourish, but are foul within, / And they like snakes, know when to cast their skin" (2248–50). He surely speaks here of both himself and the Ilford crowd: they are foul within, and cast him out when they've stripped him to the skin, but he too has been foul within, if merry without, and now stands stripped to his heart. At this moment of self-hatred Thomas enters: "Turn, draw, and die, I come to kill thee ... I do not wish to kill thee like a slave, / That taps men in their cups, and broach their hearts" (2251–60). The metaphoric linking of Scarborrow and his erstwhile drinking friends continues: the slave or unlinked man like Ilford makes a cowardly approach to his victim when he's drunk with wine; men are tapped and broached to be spilled.

The gallants now enter to attack Scarborrow and Thomas as they fight; Thomas calls them "slaves, worse than Fencers that wear long weapons" (2294–95), sides with Scarborrow, helps him beat off the attackers, and returns to raging:

> ... Our father sir,
> Left in your trust my portion: you ha' spent it,
> And suffered me (whilst you in riot's house,
> A drunken Tavern, spilled my maintenance
> Perhaps upon the ground with overflown cups,
> Like birds in hardest winter half starved, to fly)
> And pick up any food, lest I should die.   (2312–18)

Thomas packages Scarborrow's vice as a wine-spilling surfeit, contrasted to images of near-starvation, and proposes in a spasm of anti-familial destruction to kill him even if he were "clasped / Within [his] mother, wife, or children's arms" (2323–24). All that makes them pause is John's reproach: "Say who are you, or you, are you not one, / That scarce can make a fit distinction / Betwixt each other? Are you not Brothers?" (2333–35). John prevails, but Thomas flings away still enraged, and Scarborrow makes his final testament of responsibility:

> [I have] Undone my Brothers, made them thieves for bread,
> And begot pretty children to live beggars . . .
> My Brothers unto shame must yield their blood,
> My Babes at others' stirrups beg their food,
> Or else turn thieves too, and be choked for't,
> Die a Dog's death . . .
> The curse of heaven that's due to reprobates,
> Descends upon my Brothers, and my children,
> And I am parent to it, I am parent to it.   (2383–93)

His brothers must steal bread, his children beg for it or die the disgraceful death of hanging for stealing it – punishment in the throat. He accepts the language of the familial mode, even, perhaps even especially, when it cuts him most, naming his failure of primogenitural responsibility in that language itself.

His victimization, guilt, and shame are not yet absolute, however. The Butler enters to announce creditors:

> Snakes I think Sir, for they come with stings in their mouths, and their tongues are turned to teeth too: They claw Villainously, they have eat up your honest name, and honorable reputation by railing against you, and now they come to devour your possessions.   (2399–2403)

Next enter his wife and the twins, whom Scarborrow denies:

> [SCARBORROW] Who are you Gentlewoman.
> KATHERINE Sir your distressed wife, and these your children.
> SCARBORROW Mine? Where, how begot:
> Prove me by certain instance that divine,
> That I should call them lawful, or thee mine.
> KATHERINE Were we not married sir?
> SCARBORROW No, though we heard the words of Ceremony,
> But had hands knit as felons that wear fetters
> Forced upon them.   (2439–46)

The Butler challenges Scarborrow for this base blaming, comparing him to his "progenitor." This elicits typical master-rant from Scarborrow, who calls his servant "slave," but draws on him (2509) – degrading himself by treating his servant as a peer.[88] The Butler is ready to "prove itupon him even in his blood, his bones, / His guts, his Maw, his Throat, his Entrails" (2518–19), but Scarborrow withdraws the parity, calling Butler a "knave Slave-trencher-groom" (2524), and orders him out of doors.

The Butler exits, but returns like Kent to keep serving Family, now as Katherine's champion. Scarborrow responds with total apoplexy:

SCARBORROW Yes goodman slave, you shall be master,
Lie with my wife, and get more Bastards, do, do, do.
KATHERINE O me.
SCARBORROW Turns the world upside down, that men o'erbear their
Masters, It does, it does.
For even as Judas sold his Master Christ,
Men buy and sell their wives at highest price,
What will you give me? what will you give me? what will you give me?[89]

(2569–77)

He insists on the Prodigals' central critique, cursing rebellious servant and wife for cuckoldry, but the Christ/Judas comparison cuts unexpected ways. Its discontinuity of scale of course shrieks narcissism and self-pity, as so often, but the details also *self*-lacerate. As Judas sold Christ, so men sell their wives: all are bawds. He is not only the betrayed favored son, but pimp and Judas as well; Katherine both betraying whore and suddenly betrayed suffering wife. Scarborrow now struggles between victim and criminal status – trying, I think, to discharge suffering by augmenting, externalizing, and punishing it, like a furious child who breaks his toys.

Scene xii presents his final Prodigal paroxysm:

I'll parley with the Devil . . .
. . . I'll ask him
Whether a cormorant may have stuffed Chests
And see his brother starve: why he'll say aye,
The less they give, the more I gain thereby.
       Enter Butler
Their souls, their souls, their souls.
How now master? Nay, you are my master?
Is my wife's sheets warm? Does she kiss well?
BUTLER Good sir.
SCARBORROW Foe, mak't not strange for in these days,
There's many men lie in their masters' sheets,
And so may you in mine . . .

(2630–44)

Now Doctor Baxter, who married Scarborrow to Katherine, enters to crystallize all.

SCARBORROW These for thy act should die, she for my Clare,
Whose wounds stare thus upon me for revenge.
These to be rid from misery, this from sin,

And thou thy self shalt have a push amongst 'em,
That made Heaven's word a pack-horse to thy tongue.
Quotest scripture to make evils shine like good,
And as I send you thus with worms to dwell,
Angels applaud it a deed done well.   (2792–99)

Ready to murder everyone, Scarborrow is moved his closest to the final
violent fugue of Walter Calverley. But having aggravated Scarborrow's
rage from usable social critique into toxic hubris, Wilkins now redirects
the dramatic energy toward a different end, with a curative extended-
family intervention (as with a modern alcoholic). Agnates (uncle,
brothers, sister), friend turned affine (Ilford), the doubly parental servant
(who both served the father and served as father), all plead, finally
reinforced by the deathbed recantation of the noble guardian Lord
Faulconbridge. Instead of having Scarborrow kill his wife and children,
Wilkins kills off the guardian.

All gather – "your brothers and alliance Sir" (2807), as the Butler has
it – to call Scarborrow home:

WILLIAM Kinsman.
BROTHER AND SISTER Brother.
KATHERINE Husband.
CHILD Father.   (2811–14)

Sister and even Ilford are transformed: "WIFE And look Sir here's my
husband's hand in mine, / and I rejoice in him, and he in me" (2825–26).
Without ever receiving a name, Sister has become Wife, while Ilford has
undergone an even more miraculous, that is, totally stipulative, refresh-
ment, as a rejoicing affine. Meanwhile, a letter falls:

BUTLER ... Read but this letter.
WILLIAM Which tells you that your Lord & Guardian's dead.
BUTLER Which tells you that he knew he did you wrong,
Was grieved for't, and for satisfaction
Hath given you double of the wealth you had.
BROTHER Increased our portions.
WIFE Given me a dowry too.
BUTLER And that he knew,
Your sin was his, the punishment his due.   (2833–41)

The restorations seem all to have been accomplished, an unsympathetic
auditor might say, by magic and money. Just as we were not compelled
or allowed to watch Scarborrow abandon Clare and submit to Lord
Faulconbridge in marriage, so we do not see Lord Faulconbridge
interrogate his actions, and recant. Recalcitrant wills are concealed
behind a blooming family cathexis (especially the magical mutation of

Ilford's anger and the erasure of his companions Wentloe and Bartley), save for the finalizing financial and moral bookkeeping of the last will of Lord Faulconbridge and George Wilkins.

The final tableau works very hard to figure a satisfying embrace for everyone.

> SCARBORROW Then husbands thus shall nourish with their wives.
>   [*Kiss*]
> ILFORD As thou and I will wench.
> Brothers in brotherly love thus link together,
>   [*embrace*]
> SCARBORROW [query: BUTLER?] Children and servants pay their duty thus.
>   [*bow and kneel*]
> And all are pleas'd.
> ALL We are.
> SCARBORROW Then if all these be so,
> I am new wed so ends old marriage woe,
> And in your eyes so lovingly being wed,
> We hope your hands will bring us to our bed.   (2859–68)

Husbands and wives finally nourish, family embraces, everyone kneels to familial structuration. Clare, of course, is still dead, Harcop robbed. But that was in another plot, and besides ...

At one level of analysis one wonders what to do with an ending like this, so "unsatisfying," as we often say. Yet surely we should ask what it did satisfy, how Wilkins found it satisfactory to end things this way, who else it might have satisfied. What, in other words, does this ending accomplish? And we are the more fortunate, most unusually, to be able to compare its shape to other endings of the same story, those of *Two Most Unnaturall and Bloodie Murthers* and *A Yorkshire Tragedy* (and other trace documents), in search of what the culture sought to produce from this much-retold story. For like the tale of the death of John Kennedy, this tale could not end, could not rest or feed enough to finish. It kept speaking to early modern England. What was it trying to say, through all of its stutters and glottal stops?

I think Wilkins's aim in ending thus was to provide hope, correction, withdrawal from the edge. He invented the brothers, the Prodigals, and the Butler, and wrote at length of Clare. He distributed most of the energy of Walter Calverley's murderous rage among the principal character's affiliates. In the process he strove to engage larger social patterning, to locate enforcement's many scenes, to interrogate its tools and fields of interpellation. Then, I think, he sought to soothe the wounds he had opened, turning from social to dramatic structure, to the dissociative pleasures of comic intrigue.

V

With *A Yorkshire Tragedy* things are rather different. This utterly focused one-acter is nearly all edge. It does have a strange discontinuous opening scene (perhaps by another hand), all that remains of the Clare and Harcop strand to which Wilkins devotes so much energy. Otherwise *A Yorkshire Tragedy* is fundamentally a story of ending, the murderous ending of Walter Calverley and his family recorded in *Two Most Unnaturall and Bloodie Murthers* and elsewhere: the ending that Wilkins did not write.[90] In what follows I make two comparative suggestions. First, that though *A Yorkshire Tragedy* does actually stage the anomic murders that Wilkins deflects into tragicomedy, it also cannot finally resist such avoidance, and, like *Two Unnaturall Murders*, repeats it, a gesture that begins to seem to mark the subject of "enforcement" as a culturally intolerable contemplation. Second, that the only place where Walter Calverley's *telos* does not remain unspeakable is that other stage on which he died in the flesh, outside the law, unpleading and unsentenced, mute.

The most obvious difference between the plays is that, despite certain confusions, the Husband of *A Yorkshire Tragedy* has not explicitly been enforced to marry against his will.[91] Scene i seems unmistakably concerned with the jilted Clare figure of *Murthers* (though she never appears), but there is no reference of any kind to that plot in the remainder of the *Tragedy*. (Indeed, the distress is itself shadowy, more cited than explored. The servants' rehearsal of it is very much conducted *inter alia*, their sympathy authentic but half-attentive. What they are really interested in is the gifts their fellow Sam has brought from London.)[92] In *Murthers* the change of objects from "Clare" to the Wife is credited explicitly to Calverley, though his motivation is obscured:

> Maister Caverley came to London, and whether concealing his late contract from his honourable gardian, or forgetting his private and publicke vowes, or both I know not, but Time, mother of alterations, had not fanned over many daies, but hee had made a new bargaine, knit a new marriage knot, and was husband by all matrimoniall rites, to a curteous Gentlewoman, and neere by marriage to that honourable Personage to whom he was Ward.
>
> (*Murthers* 39–46)[93]

In the pamphlet the Husband's agency is clearly implied; in scene i of the play we find only the fact of the marriage (and its preconditioning jilt), without reference to any occasion for it. The young mistress grieves for his absence, but, say the servants, "he's married to another long ago ... beats his wife, and has two or three children by her" (i.37, 39–40). And in the next scene the Husband clearly says, "I hate the very hour I chose a wife" (ii.101), though it was "for fashion sake" that he married her, whom he "never could abide" (ii.74–75).

A moment later, however, a servant enters to tell the Husband that his "mistress was met by the way by them who were sent for her up to London by her honourable uncle, your worship's late guardian" (ii.117–19). This locates the Wife as the niece of Husband's guardian (and matches her to Wilkins's Katherine), approved if not chosen by him. But at ii.75 the Husband claims a supposedly original and long-standing distaste for her, implying that she was foisted on him. (*Murthers* describes the marriage as having been "made by honorable personages" [201].) All, it seems, that we can say with confidence is that though he probably chose her, she was an authorized choice, and he came to hate her as if he didn't choose her, as a figure and agent of his own subjection.

Wilkins's thematic of enforced marriage thus resides somewhere under erasure in *A Yorkshire Tragedy*. Perhaps Wilkins added it, or found it somewhere beneath his source-lode, submerged as its absent platonic center. But *A Yorkshire Tragedy* postdates *The Miseries of Enforced Marriage*, so far as the Stationer's Register dates mean anything (July 1607 and May 1608).[94] Even if the plays were "truly" separately written, though, their manifest intertextuality proposes a close structural relation as alternatives. Say that in the absence of enforced marriage as a specific stimulus, the Husband's rage takes on an existential quality, making a pair, as an *intensive* formation, with Wilkins's *extensive* ramification of generational and familial enforcement. Within the envelope of "enforced marriage" Wilkins compounds a variety of enforcements of will to which the existential stimulus of the Husband's totalizing Rage stands as immanent center, visible in *Miseries* more in discourse than action.

For the Husband's *rage* constitutes a second important divergence between the plays. He exudes a savage and all-encompassing passion, both deriving from and threatening violation, that is quite distinct from Scarborrow's enervated despair, born of deprivation.[95] This hypostatized Rage drives the enactment of the murders (and provides most of the great power of the play), from which runaway motive Wilkins perhaps necessarily had to turn aside in building Scarborrow, having opted for a restorative ending. The Husband is not passive, as Scarborrow is till his final paroxysm, but *out of control*. His rage is hot, isolate, myopic. His Wife finds him "half mad": "He sits and sullenly locks up his arms" (ii.13, 15) at the dejection of his state, "not penitent for those his sins are past, / But vexed his money cannot make them last" (ii.19–20). This closed withholding posture seems oxymoronic, a silent fuming cutting off that threatens explosion, and perhaps requires or authorizes its contrary of destructive *expense*.

It is thus fitting that the principal exhibitory discourse for the Husband's rage prior to the murders is his *gambling*, the third of *Yorkshire Tragedy*'s divergent correlatives, replacing Scarborrow's thematized drinking. That vice retains a soporific or slightly enfeebling aura, of leakage. The Husband's gambling is altogether different, a violent flinging away of his substance. When his Wife returns with, he thinks, more money for him to gamble away, he expresses this tone perfectly:

> Now, are you come? Where's the money? Let's see the money! Is the rubbish sold, those wiseacres, your lands? Why, when? The money, where is't? Pour't down, down with it! Down with it, I say, pour't o'th'ground! Let's see't, let's see't.   (iii, 34–38)

This business literalizes the release of expending, spilling, pouring, akin to Shakespeare's avidly sought expense of spirit. The gesture is not instrumental, as is Scarborrow's rhetorical drinking, performed as ideological commentary. Instead, I think, we can hear the lure of Sartre's for-itself, phenomenology by trapeze artist Karl Wallenda: "To be on the wire is life; the rest is waiting."[96] Perhaps, of course, this is true Prodigal behavior: adolescent thrill-seeking, rejection of responsibility, of the burdens of adulthood (seizing only its liberations). But this view focuses the act on its result; the obsessive repetitions suggest instead that he wants the moment of expense, of letting go, of discharge; wants it back, over and over, discharge as renewal. The roll of the dice denies imprisonment, confers the experience of freedom. This is another lustful seizure of the will, a counterseizure, as it were, fending off responsibility by means of expenditure. The Husband's inturned affect differs from Scarborrow's: the Husband does not say "Watch this!" but hunches alone with bated breath, waiting for his Wife to pour out, roll out, the coin of his substance. The moment seems, in its deepest core, not social at all.

But the play does propose a social side to this gesture: the Husband also (or perhaps elsewhere) feels his gambling to confer some kind of social identity or legitimacy: "Curbed in? / Shall it be said in all societies / That I broke custom, that I flagged in money?" (ii.79–81). These lines address some defining restriction or limit of will, in both the external clamp of "curbed" and the internal exhaustion of "flagged." Elsewhere the Husband growls, "That mortgage sits like a snaffle upon mine inheritance and makes me chaw upon iron" (ii.47–48). Gambling seems to undo some kind of felt social wound, a slur upon his sense of himself as a self-determining gentleman. Gambling enacts social and financial adequacy; its restraint establishes impotence and class degradation. He fumes equally at financial, social, and marital straits:

If marriage be honourable, then cuckolds are honourable, for they cannot be made without marriage. Fool, what meant I to marry? To get beggars? Now must my eldest son be a knave or nothing. He cannot live upo'th soil, for he will have no land to maintain him. That mortgage sits like a snaffle upon mine inheritance and makes me chaw upon iron. My second son must be a promoter and my third a thief, or an underputter, a slave pander. O, beggary, beggary ... Base, slavish, abject, filthy poverty!   (ii.42–50)

Such nihilistic fury evacuates familial placement, moving from the ironizings of the last passage to denying any ontologizing relation to wife and sons: "bastards, bastards, bastards; begot in tricks, begot in tricks" (ii.65). (Here the *Tragedy* rhymes briefly with Wentloe and Bartley's evacuation of blood kinship [*Miseries* 1198ff.]. If the plays are truly independent, the immanence of this kinship-hatred is all the more powerful, an attitude struggling into the light.)

Not only does the Husband hold his marriage responsible for these degradations, but he locates them as specific effects of his Wife's social and familial position. He repeatedly rages, as at insulting disloyalty, even exposure, at his wife's consulting of her friends, and their supposed condescension to him.[97] (Compare the adulterous Brachiano to his wife Isabella: "Have you learnt / The trick of impudent baseness to complain / Unto your kindred?" [*The White Devil* 2.1.172].) The Husband's personal status appears to be structured by activist opposition to his Wife's relations. His gambling defines him as it repudiates them: "Thinkest thou thy words / Shall kill my pleasures? Fall off to thy friends. / Thou and thy bastards beg, I will not bate / A whit in humour ... (ii.75–78). When he learns from her that the uncle-guardian proposes to find a place for the Husband at court (instead of bankrolling his gambling further), he responds furiously,

Was this thy journey to nunk, to set down the history of me, of my state and fortunes? Shall I that dedicated myself to pleasure now be confined in service, to crouch and stand like an old man i'th'hams, my hat off, I that could never abide to uncover my head i'th'church? Base slut, this fruit bears thy complaints.   (iii.50–55)

A moment later, an unnamed Gentleman confronts the Husband with his waste, the fall of his family reputation, and the abuse of his wife, "right honourably allied" (148). When the Husband responds with abuse, the gentleman beats him to the ground. Like the young men in *Miseries*, the Husband responds by blaming his wife, who somehow becomes the agent of his indigence:

I'm mad to be revenged. My strumpet wife,
It is thy quarrel that rips thus my flesh
And makes my breast spit blood. But thou shalt bleed!

Vanquished! Got down? Unable e'en to speak?
Surely 'tis want of money makes men weak.   (ii.181–85)

To his wife's degradingly well-placed alliance and his defeat at the
hands of this unrelated and unnamed gentleman (a sheer typological
representative, it seems, of class definition and responsibility), a third and
decisive socio-familial stimulus to rage is added, reiterating the link to
insolvency. The Husband is visited by the Master of the College, pleading
for the relief of his "university brother" who has "stood in wax" for his
elder brother (signed a bond as surety for a loan). Now, says the Master
to the Husband, "through your default and unnatural negligence [he] lies
in bond, executed for your debt, a prisoner" (iv.8–10). His brother's loyal
Master is the Husband's final provocation, voicing fraternal claims to
succor. All such claimants in *Miseries* are saved from Scarborrow by the
dead guardian's letter of repentance. The ward else would have made
"fat worms of stinking carcasses" all round (2802). *A Yorkshire Tragedy*
contains no such reprieve.

Instead, the Husband leaps winking into the abyss to seek the
totalizing murder of his family, the far from petty cultural treason at the
heart of the ending that Wilkins refused to accept. Scarborrow's elaborated miseries, searchingly dispersed by Wilkins throughout the social
body of his relations, seem to ordain the expressly ideological murder of
Family in general, but Wilkins turns back from the edge. Not so *A
Yorkshire Tragedy*. Scarborrow's distributed *telos* is refocused in the
Husband's obliterating psychotic snap, a spasm as ambiguous, as
schizoid, as breaking and as broken, as Othello's final self-slaughter,
insider and outsider at once.

Like his obsessional gambling, the Husband's murdering both affirms
and destroys elite familiality at every step. The totalizing negation is
clear: "Mine and my father's and my forefathers', generations, generations. Down goes the house of us; down, down it sinks. Now is the name
a beggar, begs in me" (iv.72–75). Yet each murder defends honor. "My
eldest beggar, thou shalt not live to ask an usurer bread, to cry at a great
man's gate, or follow 'good your honour' by a coach; no, nor your
brother. 'Tis charity to brain you" (100–103).[98] "Fates, / My children's
blood shall spin into your faces; / You shall see how confidently we scorn
beggary!" (iv.108–10). Struggling to seize his infant son from his wife, in
order to stab him, the Husband cries, "There are too many beggars"
(v.24). Stabbing his wife, he cries, "There's whores enow, and want
would make thee one" (v.32). Departing to find and kill the sole
remaining child, he tramples on the loyal servant who tries to stop him,
tearing him with gentlemanly spurs; "Now to my brat at nurse, my

sucking beggar. / Fates, I'll not leave you one to trample on!" (v.45–46).
The hammering reiterations are now writ with Clare's pen, in "red
Letters" brooking no misunderstandings.[99] ("This means you," as it
were.) Clare affirms and repudiates her identity at once, with the same
device: "here's my agent ready: Forgive me, I am dead. / 'Tis writ, and I
will act it" (851–52). So with the Husband, seizing autonomy by
repudiating socio-familial relation.

On the way to murder his child at nurse, the Husband is captured and
brought before the local magnate Knight. In a moment of final constancy
to his purpose he sums up his motives: "I have consumed all, played
away long acre, / And I thought it the charitablest deed I could do / To
cozen beggary and knock my house o'th'head" (ix.16–18). This raucous
disrespectful tone constitutes his iconoclastic signature as rebel against
familial sanctities. When confronted with his wife, however, the Husband
suddenly and conspicuously rewrites his tale, repenting his violence. The
jaunty tone is silenced, and the author turns to the ponderous didactic
register of moral placements. The Husband characterizes this transition
as the end of demonic possession:

> ... now glides the devil from me,
> Departs at every joint, heaves up my nails. ...
> Bind him one thousand more, you blessed angels,
> In that pit bottomless. Let him not rise
> To make men act unnatural tragedies.   (x.18–23)

His children's displayed corpses elicit similar sentiments:

> O, that I might my wishes now attain,
> I should then wish you living were again,
> Though I did beg with you, which thing I feared.
> O, 'twas the enemy my eyes so bleared!
> O, would you could pray heaven me to forgive
> That will unto my end repentant live.   (x.43–48)

Perhaps it goes too far to tear the author for the badness of these verses,
but there is some parallel with Wilkins's ending. Both authors delve deep
into bursting wounds, and then, when the risk of overflow is greatest,
both change the level of address. Wilkins turns to a literary *deus ex
machina*, Lord Faulconbridge's letter. The author of the *Tragedy*
detaches the Husband's violent disruptiveness from its specifically social
emplacement, explaining it as spiritual ventriloquism, the devil's work.
The Husband's will is recovered intact from the devil's puppet-strings,
and it repents. What human agency remains is contrite – and familially
communitarian as well: his wife will "number up all [her] friends / To
plead for pardon – [her] dear husband's life" (x.68–69), and the murderer
himself wishes for his children's intercession.

It is with this wish that *Two Unnaturall Murders* also ends:

> ...whereas before hee tolde Sir John Savill [the judge figure], he was glad hee
> had ridde the worlde of beggars, hee now imploves his houres in these words; I
> would I had those beggars, either I to begge with them, or they to aske
> heavens almes for mee.   (522–25)

The Husband's sentiments are the usual ones for the scaffold, where the
criminal obligingly provides the edifying caption that resolves and
explains his deeds. But more is to be found in the portmanteau of *respice
finem* than these various nostrums, however medicinal. All three authors
stop short of Walter Calverley's "actual" execution. Indeed, Cawley and
Gaines follow Baldwin Maxwell and Tucker Brooke in using this
narrative fact as historical evidence, to argue that the play was composed
before the execution. "Few Elizabethan chroniclers, ever eager to under-
score a moral, would have deliberately omitted the wages exacted for
such crimes," says Maxwell.[100]

However, there is another way to construe the nest of endings. Unlike
his fictional counterparts in the *Tragedy* and *Murthers*, the historical
Walter Calverley may in a disturbing way be said to have taken back
his repentance, to have had a different last word. For the actual
execution contained a final crucial gesture of textual aversion or
omission.

> ... [A]t the trial Walter stood mute and would make no plea. He was thus
> forced to undergo *peine forte et dure* ('strong and hard punishment'). British
> law, until well into the eighteenth century, required that a defendant arraigned
> of a felony enter a plea of guilty or not guilty before the trial could proceed. If
> he did not so plead, he was stretched out and pressed to death with heavy
> stone or iron weights until he either pleaded or died. So it was that Walter
> Calverley remained silent and was pressed to death on 5 August 1605. The
> Calverley estate was at the time vested in trust ... and was not liable to
> forfeiture, which would normally have been part of the penalty of a conviction
> for murder. By refusing to plead, however, Walter not only avoided such
> forfeiture but protected the stock upon his lands as well. His motives for
> standing mute at his trial are not at all clear. If he was repentant and
> concerned for his surviving wife and son, he thereby managed to preserve as
> much of his estate as possible to satisfy his creditors. On the other hand, if he
> really was convinced that his wife's children were not by him, he may have felt
> that he was saving his estate for the sake of his brother whom he failed to
> mention at all in his confession. Or, in fact, he may have been seeking the
> speediest way to end his life.[101]

In fact Walter Calverley himself was the first tale-teller to disrupt his
story's ending. His silence need not be read as a denial of communi-
cative meaning, of course: the editors hypothesize two possible material
effects of his silence, in regard to inheritance. But each, it may be

noted, constitutes a form of familial loyalty, assuring financial benefit to wife and son or to younger brother. These readings are certainly consonant with the dramatic gestures of *Miseries* and *A Yorkshire Tragedy*: all bespeak for Walter Calverley a final, and thus essentializing, conservation of the morality of kinship. But this, it seems to me, is precisely what the historically executed Walter Calverley chose *not* to say. In regard to his brother as well as the murders, he was expressly silent.

Having alluded to one ending of *Othello* (in the matter of Clare and the Husband's simultaneous affirmation and repudiation by death-dealing), I suggest that that play's other moment of ambiguous closure may offer a clue here. For Iago, the externalized insider to Othello's internalized outsider, ends as he definingly began, withholding information: "Demand me nothing. What you know, you know. / From this time forth I never will speak word" (5.2.311–12).[102] If this final gesture is meant to confer not rest but torment, if Iago's ultimate motive force is painful rage, may we not wonder if Walter Calverley's refusal to speak contained some similar energy? I suggest that he refused, in the last instance, the soothing that the plays serve up to their battered audiences. For he did withhold the consoling kiss for the rod of state, which Baldwin Maxwell insists early modern auditors so desired. The question Iago will not answer is Othello's "Why?" For "why" confers an ending, a resolution, enables the questioner to relinquish uncertainty. Answer soothes. That, I suspect, is as persuasive a reason "why" Walter Calverley refused to give one as a regenerate regard for the family piety he had so unambiguously defaced.

Whether a Yorkshire tragedy might have been felt to exhibit such Venetian rage must remain undecidable. Soon after the murder there appeared "a ballad on the murders and a second pamphlet treating the 'Araignment Condempnacon and Execucon of Master CAVERLY at Yorke."[103] These texts, like all others but Calverley's, probably offered explanatory judgmental accounts of the meaning of his deaths, given and received. But, as if to offer a final deferral, these texts themselves are lost. We are left only, as perhaps we should be, with the space into which texts appeared and disappeared, with the chosen, hard-wrought silence of Walter Calverley's pressed body.

4　Sexual and social mobility in *The Duchess of Malfi*

The real subject is not primarily sexual lewdness at all, but "social lewdness" mythically expressed in sexual terms.
Burke *A Rhetoric of Motives*

It may be compared to a cage, the birds without dispaire to get in, and those within dispaire to get out.
Florio's *Montaigne*

The Duchess of Malfi rewrites *The Spanish Tragedy* after *Hamlet* and *King Lear*. It echoes the early play's concerns with wandering royal women and hysterical royal men, with erotic mobility and killer servants. But it transforms these variables in crucial ways. The erotic mobility shifts distinctly, away from Bel-imperia's rebellious sexual raids and toward the emergent bourgeois and Protestant ideal of companionate marriage. Conversely, the tense fraternal defensiveness is even more embattled. Antonio's outrageous and successful invasion is far from heroic, his initial potency athletic rather than martial. Yet his achievement is, intolerably, fully *marital*. The Lorenzo figure attracts the lurid energy that his sister and her lover relinquish, and becomes himself uncontrollably eroticized. After Shakespeare's two greatest tragedies the figuration of status narcissism as incest has probably become inevitable. And Pedringano has come fully of age as well. The meditative qualities of the neglected malcontent have by 1614 been refracted among a host of pungent instances: Hamlet, Malevole, Iago, Vindice, Edmund, Kent, Webster's own Flamineo, all contribute to Bosola's strange mixture of calm knowing violence and puzzlement. The seminal issues of *The Spanish Tragedy* have now, after a full generation of Elizabethan and Jacobean drama, produced their curious bitter fruit. The ambitious scolding dancing madmen who sing the duchess to her rest finally fully externalize the panic of those early modern men and women trying to think the Jacobean court as cultural center, and failing.

I first consider the noble brother and sister in light of sexual mobility, folding together social categories of the strata of rank and anthropological notions of incest; and then the experience of their socially mobile servants Antonio and Bosola, as employees and social inferiors. In each case I seek to read Webster's interrogation of the highly charged boundary phenomena in dispute here, where the dotted line between royal-noble and gentle seems to stand in for the militarized zone separating the Jacobean court from its ever-tempted and peripheral onlookers, unsatisfied, tormented, grossly gaping on.

I

Incest is perhaps the central defining concept in anthropology. Intense debate continues regarding many issues: origin vs. structure and function, incest and exogamy (sexual vs. marriage regulation), and animal vs. human social behavior.[1] Still, a basic outline is visible. A narrowly psychological – that is to say, universalist – explanation of incest (via, for instance, "instinctive repulsion") is stymied by the diverse data available from non-western cultures. Jack Goody shows that the object of the defining "horror" that incest supposedly "inevitably arouses" varies greatly. Sometimes intercourse with blood relatives arouses the repulsion; on other occasions only relatives by marriage are forbidden.[2] Moreover, as Kenneth Burke notes, "psychoanalysis too often conceals ... the nature of exclusive social relations behind inclusive [i.e., universal] terms for sexual relations."[3] A vocabulary of "human nature" obscures crucial variations specific to different social formations. To deal with these we need to reconceive such "givens" of human psychology as *social products*.

Talcott Parsons conveniently summarizes the social conception of the incest taboo upon which my argument depends:

> it is not so much the prohibition of incest in its negative aspect which is important as the positive obligation to perform functions for the subunit and the larger society by marrying out. Incest is a withdrawal from this obligation to contribute to the formation and maintenance of supra-familial bonds on which major economic, political and religious functions of the society are dependent (19).[4]

Such public determination of private social structure is quite variable, as Raymond Firth noted long ago:

> I am prepared to see it shown that the incest situation varies according to the social structure of each community, that it has little to do with the prevention of sex relations as such, but that its real correlation is to be found in the maintenance of institutional forms in the society as a whole, and of the specific interest of groups in particular.[5]

The incest–exogamy dyad is seen as both strategic and flexible: "Where interest of rank or property steps in," says Firth, "the incest prohibition is likely to melt away" (340). "Exceptions" (such as those of ancient Egypt or Hawaii – and, I will argue, individual inclinations such as Ferdinand's) become as intelligible as the rule: both are social products, similarly determined by the pressures and limits of particular social formations.[6]

Intermarriage is the single most important device for ordering "the interpenetration of memberships among the different elements in the structural network" in traditional societies, in the absence of such social differentiations as class structure (Parsons, "Incest Taboo" 18). In the differentiated society of Jacobean England, strategic intermarriage remained central for the social elite, typically serving by both identification and differentiation to maintain and confirm distinctive group status (see Wrightson, *Social Order* 80). Owing to the custom of the dowry, "together with the great sensitivity to status and rank, ... it was inevitable that the great majority of marriages should take place between spouses from families with similar economic resources" (Stone, *Family* 60). Yet sometimes, owing to financial pressures or the decay of male lineage, elite families allowed useful recruiting marriages "beneath." For the unattached individual male this often created opportunities. As we have seen, Stone argues that "for a young man of gentle birth, the fastest ways of moving up the social scale were the lotteries of marriage with an heiress, Court favour, and success at the law. The first of the three is usually neglected or ignored by social historians, but it was probably the commonest method of upward movement for gentlemen" ("Social Mobility" 34–35). However authorized or excused case by case, such forays counted *en masse* as the familiar contamination of the ruling elite by invasion from below that Stone described in *The Crisis of the Aristocracy*. The elite generally responded with hegemonic contempt, but the friction between such contempt and the glittering opportunity of exceptions, however rare, fueled a widespread fascination. We have seen such friction between Lorenzo and Horatio: *The Duchess of Malfi* rearranges and intensifies both variables. The status-endogamy pressure specifies an outer frontier, over which the duchess trespasses not only erotically but maritally; the incest taboo marks an inner wilderness, where Ferdinand, intensifying Lorenzo, longs to dwell. But to grasp fully the symmetricality of these vectors of social force, we must mark the details of the play.

First, though, let us review the critical history of Ferdinand's incestuous desires. F. L. Lucas first addressed the possibility in 1927, though he thought it dubious.[7] Clifford Leech presented the view more fully in 1951, in *John Webster: A Critical Study*.[8] Leech's argument occasioned resistance from, for instance, J. R. Mulryne (in 1960), as implying too readily "the desire to consummate the passion."[9] In response Leech itemized his evidence in 1963, in *Webster: The Duchess of Malfi*:

> The grossness of his language to her in Act I, the continued violence of his response to the situation, his holding back from identifying her husband and, when that identity is established, from killing him until the Duchess is dead, his momentary identification of himself with her first husband, his necrophily in Act V – all these things ... seem to point in one direction.[10]

These items are widely thought to suggest incestuous desires, but they fail to address Mulryne's doubts, nor do they link the incest motif to other elements in the play. The anthropological view of incest, emphasizing not sex relations but the maintenance of institutional forms, allows us to add to Leech's evidence, incorporate Mulryne's logic, and integrate Ferdinand's behavior with the otherwise all-embracing issue of social mobility.

My core hypothesis can be briefly stated. I read Ferdinand as a threatened aristocrat, frightened by the contamination of his supposedly ascriptive social rank, and obsessively preoccupied with its defense. When coupled with Leech's evidence, this account construes Ferdinand's incestuous inclination toward his sister as a *social posture*, of extreme and paranoid compensation – a desperate expression of the desire to evade degrading contamination by inferiors. Muriel Bradbrook argues that the notion of Ferdinand's incest "can satisfactorily compensate for inaccessible Jacobean theological or social moods."[11] We are now more used to retrieving such social moods: I propose to read the two explanations as one, understanding the incest taboo as ideological.

An earlier version of this argument for conflation aroused readers' questions about the relative priority of the "sexual" and the "social" here, in terms of *gender vs. status* issues, or (differently) *incest vs. endogamy*.[12] So far as gender and status go, it has become much clearer to me that Webster's subject is the coincidence, the intertextuality and reactivity, of such categories. For my argument here, the crucial aspect of Ferdinand's hyperbolic reaction to his sister is that the sexual and the social – concerns with incest and with purity of status, rank, or blood – are *concentric* categories. They relate here as private and public, personal and political, "micro" and "macro" structural forms of the same praxis, which operates, I think, in the following way. The incest taboo calls for transfamilial bonding: by flouting the taboo Ferdinand violently refuses such relations. Such flouting constitutes an active but inverted employment of homosociality, self-defining not by identification but by differentiation, its symmetrical complement. Burke's work on definitions as mechanisms of boundary, on the element "-fin-" in "define," is crucial. "Here the intrinsic and the extrinsic can change places. ... to *define*, or *determine* a thing, is to mark its boundaries, hence to use terms that possess, implicitly at least, contextual reference. ... to define a thing in terms of its context, we must define it in terms of what it is not" (Burke's emphasis).[13]

In the normal ordering, in pursuit of the assertion and advancement of status, Ferdinand would wish to bond his lineage – his sister in marriage, thus himself in alliance – with an appropriately noble affine.[14] In the status-crisis environment of early modern England, Ferdinand is more threatened, needier, and more grasping. He strives actively to withhold the sisterly vessel of his honor, constructing her hyperbolically, in incest, as a figure for utterly incommensurable transcendence, radical difference in kind. This posture, however deranged, thus functions logically as a *radicalizing gesture*. Ferdinand's sexualization of the duchess enacts a transition from the wider to the narrower, from (licit) rank endogamy to (criminal) incest. This does not seem to me a shift from the social to the psychological or individual (a problematic distinction, to my mind). I read it as an *intensification*, to a level of something like social paranoia, of the familiar elite affect of boundary sensitivity – an affect growing to epidemic scale in a world full of ambitious social self-construction through erotic investment. Ferdinand's own highly eroticized investment, not just in status endogamy but family endogamy – in incest – is no less a self-constructing action than an "appropriate" marriage would be (or, for an invader, a fearfully common ambitious marriage upward). But it functions derivatively, as a reply to a threat, and seeks to impose *dis*continuity.

This is not to argue that Ferdinand has not somehow lost control. Such conflation of legitimate rank endogamy and proscribed family endogamy, "appropriately inward" and "too far in," is certainly socio-pathological. Yet, as Pitt-Rivers observes of the violent defense of aristocratic honor, such status-specific (ego)mania often has familiar warrant: the aristocracy is traditionally contemptuous of legality, and claims entitlement to "the tradition which makes them the leaders of society, arbiters rather than 'arbitrated' and therefore 'a law unto themselves.' The sacred quality of high status is demonstrated in freedom from the sanctions which apply to ordinary mortals." "The same principle," he suggestively concludes, "explains the incest of the Gods."[15] Like the closely linked boundaries of social rank, the boundary phe-nomena of early modern English kinship were frequently subject to editing, even erasure. Indeed, such conflation of class and family is sometimes even linguistically normative: idioms such as "family pride," "family name," "coming of an old family," are really *status* specifica-tions, claims to a *kind* of family. (It might be imagined that this displacing locution originates in an elite desire to *biologize*, as it were, their social distinction. It would also intensify kinship relatedness for them, relative to the rest of the populace.)

What we seem to have in the subject of incest in early modern England is a complex mixture of the doxic and the debated. Among the bulk of the population, according to Ingram's work on the church courts (the most recent detailed analysis), concern with "incest does not seem to have loomed large." There is "a relative paucity of [church-court] prosecutions," and "people do not seem to have spent much time or energy searching out suspected cases."[16] But Ingram regards this sense of things as implicit in "the relative weakness of kinship ties" characteristic of early modern England (save for the elite, as everyone agrees). Cressy disputes this larger view even for the general populace, citing over-reliance on legal evidence. Any reader of the drama must also dispute it, both regarding the weakness of kinship ties and the minimal concern with incest, *especially* for the stage aristocracy. The sheer quantity is instructive. Incest among the elite figures significantly in plays by Beaumont and Fletcher, Ford, Heywood, Jonson, Marston, Massinger, Middleton, Shakespeare, Tourneur, and Webster, just to name well-known playwrights. What is the social meaning of this outpour?

I suggest that this locus of intensity and fascination with incest is crucially specific to the elite, *doubly staged, as an object of envious scorn.* As the elite recoiled contemptuously from invasive contamination (and turned to increasingly privatized modes of self-identification, de-empha-sizing hospitality and large fleets of retainers, for instance), it was increasingly experienced as inturned, sterile, greedy, and irresponsible. (In comic terms, think of Sir Epicure Mammon.) It became more and more vulnerable to reproach and policing on such grounds, along the lines of Philip Slater's meditations on "the social limitations of libidinal withdrawal" in modern times:

> Although violation of the incest prohibition constitutes the nearest danger to suprafamilial collectivities, there are other and more extreme forms of libidinal contraction than that against which the taboo most specifically militates. If libidinal cathexis can be withdrawn from large collectivities and centered in the nuclear family, it can also be withdrawn from the family and centered in any single dyadic relationship, and finally, it can be withdrawn from all object relationships and centered in the ego, as in the classical psychoanalytic discussions of narcissism. All three are simply positions in a continuous dimension of social regression (113).

Slater goes on brilliantly to discuss social mechanisms developed to protect the larger bindings of social aggregates from usurping cathectic withdrawals, and to affirm "libidinal diffusion" throughout the larger community. He details the profoundly public "intrusion ritual" of the

wedding, the generations of social indebtedness of "showers" and
wedding gifts, the licensed and limited private indulgence of the honeymoon, complete with its own publicizing irritations ("just married" signs,
tin cans). What I want to derive from his work here is that early modern
stage representations of incest (and other intensified eroticisms) often
functioned as just such institutional policing, of what was perceived as a
status-group withdrawal from responsibility to the larger social body.[17]
They figure a cultural critique, of the embattled elite's compensatory and
destructive, even predatory, status narcissism, which combined all three
of Slater's forms of libidinal withdrawal. And behind the critique's
raucous hostility to such intensifications as Ferdinand's we find the aim
of Slater's equation of "libidinal diffusion with the de-eroticizing of the
sexual life of the individual – the transformation of hedonistic activity
into utilitarian activity" (119).

The elite's beleaguered hair-trigger sensitivity to "insulting" contamination (itself insulting) and its correlative (notional) transgressive sexuality, whether inward or outward, thus arouse the drama's "rough
music." At the same time, as Sir Epicure again suggests, such depictions
provide *and disguise* for the auditor a voyeuristic indulgence in *fantasy
luxury*, in the rich dual period sense of that term, conflating sexual and
material indulgence. (In a comparable way, honeymoon rituals both
castigate and envy.) Distanced by rank and excess (and of course as
Italian), the elite experience might be the more freely fantasized. Disguised and judged by the auditor's contempt, the excesses of such
superior luxury are there for the tasting. So the stage representations
perform two interlocking but dissonant functions (as has long been
observed regarding verse satire in this period). "Incest" then functions as
the privileged sexual metaphor for an exciting status vanity that arouses
its own pleasurable on-stage punishment. (The skimmington always had
a substantial festive component that rewarded its concerns with social
order.)

So Webster's investigation of the radicalized praxis of Ferdinand's
status incest begins in the dialectic relation between the spirals of elite
hauteur and aggressive upward mobility: the hunger triggered the fear,
which, felt as opportunity, fed the hunger. When Ferdinand narrows his
kind, his locus of self-identity, from status group to family, affirming it as
absolutely superior, ideally alienated from the infectious intercourse of
social life, it seems to me that Webster is measuring the felt threat, the
scale, of elite paranoia for us. It is *Webster* who has conflated incest and
endogamy, as a paranoid compression. The sexualization of the object
does not de-socialize it, as it were: indeed, it marks a massive libidinal
investment in social distinction. This overcoding, I suggest, is what the

incest is *for* in Webster's project. Ferdinand makes the duchess a symbol, flooded with affect, of his own defensively radicalized purity. In reaching for her he aspires to appropriate the old heroic tag *par sibi*, to be like only himself, excelling, transcendent, utterly other.[18] The gesture is criminal, pathological, but it is not only psychological; Webster is engaging a social pathology – compensatory status narcissism, gone mad. And Elizabethans *loved* to watch the mad.

Ferdinand's obsession with ontologizing social transcendence first appears in many small touches early in the play in which he carefully maintains an *alienation* from those below. Making small talk, Castruchio says the prince should not go to war in person, but rather "do it by a deputy." Ferdinand replies, "Why should he not as well sleep, or eat, by a deputy? This might take idle, offensive, and base office from him, whereas the other deprives him of honour" (1.1.99–102).[19] The hallowed pursuit of martial distinction warrants personal participation, but Ferdinand otherwise eschews participation, preferring to employ *prosthetic agents.* "He speaks with others' tongues, and hears men's suits / With others' ears ... dooms men to death by information, / Rewards by hearsay" (1.1.173–74, 176–77).[20] His courtiers are to be his creatures, without will or spontaneity: "Methinks you that are courtiers should be my touch-wood, take fire, when I give fire; that is, laugh when I laugh" (1.1.122–24). It is common to describe this behavior as usual for flatterers and ambitious men; Ferdinand appropriates the pathology, *requiring* it, publicly.[21] He also especially enjoys the distancing trick of *surprise*, the sudden revelation of difference: "He will seem to sleep o'th'bench/ Only to entrap offenders in their answers" (1.1.174–75).

His need for this effect is patent, but the habitual, even frenetic iteration of such demonstrations suggests the defense's instantaneous decay. The degradation of his auditors to mere instruments of reflection strips away their potency as human subjects who can ratify (as in Hegel's familiar asymmetrical dialectic of master and slave). At the same time, self-defeated Ferdinand also fails his political subjects (as we will see with Bosola below): instead of acting as the traditional fount of identity to them, he generates the loss of their identity, striving to become more himself by reducing others. His strategy of domination reduces them to tools, to things.

Ferdinand's strategic investment in his sister seeks the same end, of radical self-distinction, by several moments of logical force. What is below is always over-present to him, ever needing and rewarding the act of subjection. His initial leering assurances to his sister, that all of her most private thoughts and actions will come to light, duplicate his behavior as judge and spymaster: this is the invasive urge of the

authoritarian voyeur, seeking the positional pleasures of olympian specular control.[22] But the duchess is also, in regard to other men, the vessel
of Ferdinand's honor: both its bodily extension (a vulnerability) and an
ever-impending occasion for its self-defining defense (an opportunity).

The news of her liaison, a secret plucked out by his agent Bosola,
brings the swollen social focus of the threat clearly into view. For
Ferdinand instantly assumes massive disparagement of rank. He imagines "some strong thigh'd bargeman; / Or one o'th'wood-yard, that can
quoit the sledge, / Or toss the bar, or else some lovely squire / That
carries coals up to her privy lodgings" (2.5.42–45).[23] Such copesmates,
grotesquely rendered (as base laborers or effeminate youths), are the
formal correlatives of his own hubristic hysteria. In the instant of
recoiling conception his eye-rolling excess spirals them imperatively
apart, as social antipodes.[24] (Such degrading survives even when he
discovers Antonio's identity, as a gentleman: he describes him as "A
slave, that only smell'd of ink and counters, / And ne'er in's life look'd
like a gentleman, / But in the audit-time" [3.3.72–74].) For Ferdinand, to
think of invaders is to repel and degrade them: they need to be marked as
base, as mere laborers, defiled as such (as workers); yet by that very fact,
they are well-equipped with poles and bars, hot and potent threats of
defilement. By coupling with the duchess they couple with him and
contaminate him, taking his place.

His contrary desire is for exclusiveness, which he pursues not by
intercourse but by blockage. Mulryne is right, I think, to doubt the urge
to physical consummation: for Ferdinand the passion's fruit is in denial,
closed and whole in his preemptive possession. To use Firth's terms, the
point of Ferdinand's incestuous rage is not the achievement of sexual
relations, but the denial of institutional slippage *via* contaminating
relation. Just as the taboo is expressed as a denial but functions as a
positive pressure outward, so Ferdinand's infringing attitude looks like a
desire but functions as a hostile withdrawal inward. As James Nohrnberg
has suggested in another context, "incest has some claim to being a kind
of intentional chastity."[25]

This reversal deciphers another recalcitrant fact. Firth notes that "in
general the harmony of group interests is maintained" by the taboo; "the
'horror of incest' then falls into place as one of those supernatural
sanctions, the aura of which gives weight to so many useful social
attitudes." But in some cases the reverse is true: "Where [group interests]
demand it for the preservation of their privileges, the union permitted
between kin may be the closest possible" (340). Ferdinand's incestuous
impulse is determined by status paranoia; he feels a cognate but reversed
horror for the out-marriage which contravenes what he needs to believe

about social absolutes. Firth frames just this affective reversal in terms of racial rather than status out-marriage:

> The attitude toward incest has something in common with a popular, uninformed view about union of the sexes in the "colour problem." Here one meets with a comparable repugnance to the idea, the same tendency to put the objection on a "natural" or "instinctive" foundation. Close family sentiment is even invoked as the clinching argument in favor of the impossibility of the admission of such unions – in the well-known formula, "Would you like to see your sister marry . . . ." . . . Here, as in the case of the prohibition of the union of very close kin, is an irrational emotional attitude, developing from a set of powerful complex social institutions (341).

Hamlet is horrified that his own mother would "post with such dexterity to incestuous sheets." Ferdinand's horror is also aroused by posting and dexterity, but instead of incest the referent is the duchess's horrifying out-marriage.[26]

Her marriage threatens Ferdinand by showing that the supposedly ontological status boundaries are brittle, and can fall to the powers of flexible self-determination exhibited by the duchess and her base lover. This rewriting of the rules threatens to impose an awareness beyond his tolerance, of the human origin, and thus mutability, of the elevation upon which he rests himself. The suggestion is even more frightening in view of its source – one of his own kind, but changed, become heretic, apostate. His florid curative reaction (imprisonment, torture, execution) overflows with surplus motives.

His initial *imprisonment* of her certainly reisolates her, puts her in her place, restores the moat. But once imprisoned the duchess is subjected to a complex series of "cleansing" degradations which Ferdinand appropriates and adapts from the two ritual-purification practices of "churching" and the charivari, cross-related rituals governing the boundary fluidities of the menses, childbirth, and certain other erotic "impurities." The ceremony of churching derives from the purifications of Leviticus 12–16, twice revised, by Christian and Protestant editing. David Cressy has recently argued that the element of cleansing had become socially moribund in English churching rites, displaced by a specifically Protestant emphasis on thanksgiving and celebrating reentry to public life.[27] A great majority of women underwent the rite ("Purification" 125), and there is much evidence that their participation derived from "delight in the social and religious attention they received at their churching, rather than from male or clerical anxieties about unpurified women" (ibid. 119).

However, these are exactly *Ferdinand's* anxieties, and I suggest that a supposed purification after a contaminating fecund marriage is central to

Ferdinand's agenda. He fastens with weird activity on what he sees as his
sister's sexually corrupt physicality, and especially on bodily fluids. These
are supposed the ready referent of female sexual and genealogical
impurity, variably intermixing brother and sister and Ferdinand and
Antonio. "[T]hat body of hers, / While that my blood ran pure in it, was
more worth ... [than her] soul" (4.1.121–23), he cries. "Go to, mistress,"
he shrieks. "'Tis not your whore's milk that shall quench my wild-fire, /
But your whore's blood" (2.5.46–48). Surely we have here some of the
affect of the policed fluids of Leviticus 15, analogous to the invaded elder
Hamlet's "vile and loathsome crust," so reminiscent of the contiguous
defiling "scale diseases" of Leviticus 13–14. Shakespeare's patriarch
required purification by fire; Webster's deflects the "contamination"
back upon the woman he decries as its source. Not "leave her to
heaven," but a horrific scouring. Instead of King Hamlet's differential
judgment, Ferdinand calls in his first delirium for an ultimate punitive
co-mingling:

> ... I would have their bodies
> Burnt in a coal-pit, with the ventage stopp'd,
> That their curs'd smoke might not ascend to heaven:
> Or dip the sheets they lie in, in pitch or sulphur,
> Wrap them in't, and then light them like a match;
> Or else to boil their bastard to a cullis,
> And give 't his lecherous father, to renew
> The sin of his back.   (2.5.66–73)

Throughout such images we can see the repressed identification with the
criminal (the need to quench fire with fire) so familiar from the younger
Hamlet's delay. Perhaps we have too a glance at the churched wife's
return to sexual availability, as in both Leviticus and early modern
folklore.[28] However, Ferdinand's actual disposal, much less spontaneous
and more controlled, really pseudo-juridical, involves not these ironic
perversions of fruitful marriage-bed and board, but a different scene of
judgment, a different mixture of private and public, in the prison-house
of 4.1.

The basic condition of these torments is sheer literal *quarantine* (doing
the pseudo-public work of Othello's "Yet she must die, else she'll betray
more men" [5.2.6]). But their central project is rewriting the duchess's
ideological invention, by an endless cathartic brainwashing. Even the
iron-willed Bosola is wearied by these labors as the duke's remote
interrogator. He begs his master,

> Faith, end here:
> And go no farther in your cruelty –
> Send her a penitential garment to put on

Next to her delicate skin, and furnish her
With beads and prayer-books. (4.1.117–21)

Stimulated yet again by his sister's delicate skin, Ferdinand replies to this torturer's request for mercy with the night-piece of his famous and bizarre dance of the madmen. This much-discussed parody of wedding masque, anti-masque, and *memento mori* also seizes the excoriating energies of the *charivari* or skimmington.[29] The transformative disciplinary assault upon female hubris will not be the literal sulphurous ablutions of the coal-pit, but the humiliations of street justice, here stolen by the duke for his private purpose, yet operating by imposing a hateful and punishing *exposure* upon what Bosola sought as a final cloistered penitential retreat for his prisoner (something of Lear's "let's away to prison").

Ferdinand's extremely complex repositioning of private and public has certain collective roots. According to Ingram, this distinction is at the heart of the ritual: "charivaris ... demonstrated a contrast between the hidden and the manifest, the private and the public: destroyers of privacy, they asserted the validity of a system of collective values which were stronger than the vagaries of individuals" (99). And the responsibility for the discipline began at home. When such gender sinners were to be ridden on an ass, head to tail, the " 'next neighbour' was ordered to lead the animal, presumably to symbolize the duty of neighbourly surveillance. This motif was ... widely current in charivaris in early modern England" (93). According to the 1602 travel diary of the Duke of Stettin, who asked about a cucking-stool he saw,

> We were ... told that in England every citizen is bound by oath to keep a sharp eye at his neighbour's house, as to whether the married people live in harmony, for though in this realm much liberty is granted to the women, no licentiousness is allowed them.[30]

Though the "legal" element here is a fiction, the sense of permeable privacy and intimate surveillance fits very well with Ferdinand's self-constructing arrogation of a "collective" outrage, in fact quite private. And indeed (or perhaps "on the other hand"; Webster's paradoxes are now uncontrollable), such "purification" transforms the duchess from one untouchable status to another, "restoring" her to a private realm which only he may enter – though only in the dark, and by a deputy, having it all ways at once. For if her murder counts as a kind of rape, a consummate patriarchal appropriation, the duke typically employs an agent, a debased and dehumanized prosthesis used teasingly, like the dead man's hand.[31] The woman is now, after all, fallen; the damage is done, and he must distance himself from a new contamination. To destroy her is to destroy the necessarily potent source of doubt, to cauterize, to repress. And the process of destruction reconstitutes them both: she is now the felon, the outlaw; he, the transcendent judge and voice of the community.

These alienations characteristically allow his forbidden conduct while punishing hers. Once she is dead, a final recursion, blaming Bosola, allows him to deny his implication in them. Yet even the denial reveals his focus. He returns to the issue of disparity in rank when interrogating Bosola for what has now become an unauthorized murder: "Let me but examine well the cause: / What was the meanness of her match to me?" (4.2.281–82). Her marriage was an adulteration for him, which his own fantasy of possession was designed to occlude. Blaming Bosola, he now averts his eyes from his aversion, but he proves unable to afford a full repressive cleansing.

Such a usurping investment in denial can only be maintained by increasingly radical devotion to the task, a surgical practice degenerating toward ultimate alienation: the solipsism of insanity. Ferdinand had already long contracted his ground of being to the two of them. When he sees, gazing upon her corpse, that he has accomplished his revenge for her divisive betrayal, he utters the striking hidden fact that they were twins (4.2.267), restoring a lost unity between them even as her death makes him singular. The enormous condensation at work here may be partially untwisted with the aid of Pausanias's alternative version of the Narcissus fable. There Narcissus in fact had a beloved twin sister.

> Upon her death, he is said to have come to a fountain alone, and suffering from desire, gazed upon his own image there. But although that seemed somewhat of a solace, he at length perished with great desire, or as is more pleasing to others, threw himself into the fountain and perished.[32]

For Ferdinand the gaze of his dead sister's dazzling eyes is likewise intolerable, perhaps as reproachful witness, perhaps as vision of his own dead face, perhaps as witness to the limits of his power. Speaking of torture, Sartre argues that the sadist hyperbolizes the lover's desire to be the unique occasion, the total limit, of the beloved's capacity to choose, seeking to appropriate the other's freedom, to steal and own it: "this is why the moment of pleasure for the torturer is that in which the victim betrays or humiliates himself" (*Being and Nothingness* 523). However, Sartre argues, the victim always chooses the moment to yield, and so retains his freedom and denies it to the sadist (ibid. 523). When the duchess says, "Dispose my breath how please you" (4.2.228), perhaps she chooses her death, retaining some kind of freedom unbroken, blocking Ferdinand's ownership. The result, Sartre writes, is that "the sadist discovers his error when the victim *looks* at him; that is, when the sadist experiences the absolute alienation of his being in the Other's freedom ... The sadist discovers that it was *that freedom* which he wished to enslave, and at the same time he realizes the futility of his efforts" (ibid. 525–27). Maybe this is why Ferdinand says "Cover her face" (264).

After this, the circle shrinks relentlessly, becoming more and more isolate. When asked why he is so solitary, he replies that the noble eagle flies alone: "they are crows, daws, and starlings that flock together" (5.2.30–31).[33] Next he tries to divest himself of his shadow, attacking even this inherent multiplicity (5.2.31ff.). His lycanthropia, unitary wolf at last, brings him to his logical end in total isolation. Walled in alone, not in a secret garden but an inward hair shirt,[34] Ferdinand is finally *sui generis*, unique, a peerless class of one – a final entropic apotheosis of the superb Renaissance hero.

II

Like her brother, the duchess is also constructed by hypertrophy of will. Ferdinand, as we have seen, is pathologically endogamous, investing his energies much farther inward toward the nuclear core than is normatively fitting. His paranoia digs an ontological moat around itself. In contrast, the duchess is inordinately *exogamous*. Fettered in Ferdinand's enclosure, she also seizes self-definition, reaching out not only past the interdicted purity of her own family but beyond the frontiers of her own rank, to marry her admirable steward. What Ferdinand would hoard, she circulates. He fastens on the absolutes of ascriptive identity; the duchess, on the earnables of achieved character. And where Ferdinand's denials issue in unpolluted and ingrown sterility, the duchess's self-assertion is fecund, both biologically and ideologically.[35]

These opposed actions rest on the same base of will: the siblings share the compulsive focus of Marlowe's protagonists. If Ferdinand is an ingrown Tamburlaine (who, Puttenham tells us, was punished with childlessness for his presumption to absolute status),[36] the duchess is an exogamous family pioneer, ruthlessly seizing for herself a privatized domestic realm based on personal rather than Familial or status imperatives. This fetish of will allows a reading filtered through misogynist stereotypes for willful women: those, for instance, sometimes used to account for Cleopatra, Lady Macbeth, *Ado*'s Beatrice – temptress-whore, monster, shrew. The duchess is certainly radically willful, but Webster disrupts these damning constructions by two crucial means: (1) the claustrophobic stimulant of Ferdinand; and (2) the maternal motive (nuclear here, precisely *not* dynastic – Antonio provides a different center

– yet biologically and divinely sanctioned). Such pressures drive, even temporarily enable, the duchess to evade a reductive and instrumental-izing code by seizing strategies of self-determination hitherto typified in the masculine world of social action. But it is one of Webster's crucial points that the homology marks them fatally, as the very strategies of mobility which have activated Ferdinand's psychotic defenses.

This is to say, the duchess's enterprise is not simply private and romantic, nor is such an arena somehow the unquestionable natural home of women's matters, save in reductive constructions. Her appro-priation of masculine self-appropriation, here a refusal of the noble-woman's dynastic obligations in favor of personal marital autonomy (auto-*nomos*, self-rule, self-law), is itself one of the things that marks her unsentimentally as her brother's sibling, indifferent and reckless. Her seizure of her procreative self for private purposes does aim at a companionate center, but it is as familially obstreperous as Bel-imperia's. However, she aims not to deface, but to diverge, to devise an alternative, to invest in family over Family, as it were. This departure, like creative efforts at status mobility, tends to undermine the ontology of clear social distinctions, whether of status or gender identity. Yet, as we shall see, it is her capacitations as noblewoman that *enable* her ambiguous maneuv-ers. Such ambivalent complexity, like Ferdinand's incestuous bent, is irredeemably social.[37]

The duchess begins the play in the overdetermined placement of *widow*. As is well known, a husband's death signaled a relative liberation from male domination. T. E., author of *The Lawes Resolution of Womens Rights*, offers a convenient summary, asking widows why they grieve:

> Consider how long you have beene in subiection vnder the predominance of parents, of your husbands, now you be free in libertie, & free *proprii iuris* at your owne Law, you may see ... That maidens and wiues vowes made vpon their soules to the Lord himselfe of heaven and earth, were all disauowable and infringible, by their parents or husbands ... But the vow of a widow, or of a woman diuorced, no man had power to disallow of, for her estate was free from controlment.[38]

Such enlargement was, however, quite ambiguous. For T. E. the widow is both free and maimed: when widowed, "her head is cut off, her intellectual part is gone, the verie faculties of her soule are, I will not say, cleane taken away, but they are all benummed, dimmed, and dazled." Widows' independence was often excoriated, and indeed, the state was left with alacrity more often than we have thought, at least for many Elizabethan London widows: often under sheerly economic pressure, as Todd and Brodsky have shown, and also to regain the many benefits cited by Slater.[39] Yet the "remarrying widow" remained, contradictorily, a focus of similar censure, perhaps because she confronted every man with his finitude, with a picture of "the entry of another into his place" (Todd, "Remarrying Widow" 55), a kind of serial cuckoldry.[40] (Chapman's *The Widow's Tears* speaks of widows' remarriage as "but a kind of lawful adultery, like usury, permitted by the law, not approv'd ... to wed a second was no better than to cuckold the first" [2.2.26–28].) The remarriage of *young* widows especially was frequently described as sexually driven; and were they not, as sexually *knowing*, older than their years, a bit threatening to their possibly less experienced grooms?

This familiar construction tends to reduce and pathologize female self-determination as threatening lust. Pitt-Rivers notes generally that

> widows are commonly believed ... to be sexually predatory upon the young men ... A woman whose shame is not in the keeping of a man is sexually aggressive and dangerous. The association reaches its extreme representation in the figure of the witch, the unsubjected female who rides upon a broomstick to subvert the social order.[41]

Thomas Whythorne marks the masculine burden this way: "as he that wooeth a maid must be brave in apparel and outward show, so he that wooeth a widow must not carry quick eels in his codpiece but show some proof that he is stiff before."[42] And Ferdinand himself argues that "they are most luxurious / Will wed twice" (1.1.297–98).[43] General masculine hostility and insecurity combine here very naturally. Furthermore, such supposed widow's immorality was often materially linked to landholding. Writing of church-court charges of sexual crime, Ingram records that

> Quite often the woman accused of incontinence was a widow holding lands by manorial customs which specified that her rights lasted only so long as she remained "chaste and sole"; the accuser was usually someone who stood to benefit if the widow forfeited her holding.[44]

Such explanations tend to "stand on their feet" much of the supposed moral policing of delinquent women. Private interests frequently underlie public rights and rites, whether legal or informal. Certainly the weight of the "purifications" in *The Duchess of Malfi* is that the tortures are *Ferdinand's*: such ritual convicts not the married widow, but her barren brother – as can be seen when the madness slides from masque to master. The chaotic multiple murders of Act 5 make it clear that no ritual management of disorder has supervened here.

Such negating sexualization of female independence, widowed or otherwise, frequently involves tropes of radical gender "perversion." What Shakespeare's cross-dressed Jessica is shamed by, this trope maximizes. The whiff of anti-transvestite polemic boils into frightful satanic stench: see Pitt-Rivers's phallic broomstick and Shakespeare's bearded witches. But Webster's analysis splits the cultural trope, splits gender and sexuality, masculinizing the duchess while diverting specifically erotic heterodoxy onto other characters.

To accomplish this he first has the duchess commit herself to the conquest of Antonio in the unmistakably masculine voice of the Renaissance hero:[45]

> Shall this move me? If all my royal kindred
> Lay in my way unto this marriage,
> I'd make them my low footsteps: and even now,
> Even in this hate, as men in some great battles
> By apprehending danger, have achiev'd
> Almost impossible actions – I have heard soldiers say so –
> So I, through frights, and threat'nings, will assay
> This dangerous venture: let old wives report
> I wink'd and chose a husband.   (1.1.341–49)

The apostrophe, the amplification of the hostile odds, the abjection of the enemy, the martial comparison, the imperative call for historical (if female) witness – all are heroic topoi, Tamburlaine's trumpet vigorously displacing the impoverished trope of the "lustful widow." Instead, she seizes the role of cultural voyager: "I am going into a wilderness, / Where I shall find nor path, nor friendly clew / To be my guide" (1.1.359–61).[46] Going knowingly to colonize a new social realm of privacy, she arrogates to herself a defiance that here speaks essentially of gender, and only incidentally of sexuality. "As men ... so I."

This act of self-defining will can usefully be compared to the differently compliant postures of Cariola and Julia, whom Kenneth Burke would see as complementary "antinomies of definition" for the duchess. Cariola embodies selfless domestic service, Julia erotic subjugation, each of which the duchess frighteningly repudiates. Cariola, best of asexual servants, confirms the secret marriage and tends the duchess at childbed, selflessly joining other servants of daring ladies (Juliet, Portia, Desdemona, Beatrice-Joanna) in attesting to a female self-direction that acts within and yet refuses masculine categories of social control. For such women submission to the lady's lord is perfunctory, allegiance in the lady's rebellion automatic and simple. Compare Pedringano here. Cariola is dedicated but unambitious: a woman, for all her asexuality. Nor is she given the divided loyalties that would accompany the usual suitor of her own (though Delio was structurally obvious), nor the earthy sexual affect of Juliet's Nurse, Desdemona's Emilia, Beatrice-Joanna's Diaphanta. (She does seem to flirt with Antonio *on behalf of* the duchess, before her, in the boudoir scene: this is vicarious, but not precisely asexual.) In her minimal heterosexuality she seems happily to derive the whole of her identity from service dedication to her mistress, and so to exhibit for purposes of contrast one familiar form of domestic self-gift for the duchess to transcend. What she gives to her mistress, the duchess gives to no one, not Antonio nor Ferdinand nor patriarchy.

Such fulfilling and self-absenting vicarious investment in the life and purpose of the master may be compared to Kent's capacious but single-centered "Royal Lear, / Whom I have ever honored as my king, / Loved as my father, as my master followed, / As my great patron thought on in my prayers" (1.1.140–42), and likewise contrasted with the uncomfortable internal distantiation that defines Pedringano and his great servant-successors Iago, Oswald, Flamineo, Bosola, and DeFlores. Obviously closer to Kent here, Cariola seems to combine the old feudal mode of identity-in-service, with its expressly hierarchical origins, and some of an oppressed and collusive resistance in shared women's identity in patriarchal society. However, though Cariola unquestion-ingly aids the duchess's self-defining act, she also ends the scene with some of Emilia's realist choric doubt, here as to the potential for such female self-determination: "Whether the spirit of greatness, or of woman / Reign most in her, I know not, but it shows / A fearful madness" (1.1.504–6).

If Cariola enacts asexuality, Julia's erotic self-waste deflects the opposite charge of lasciviousness away from the duchess. Heady wife of old Castruchio and mistress of the cardinal, she personifies the willing and strategic sexual servant who is especially drawn to power, to men who can, by conferring erotic relation, make their women significant or safe. When Julia reaches out to the Cardinal and Bosola, she advertises in departure her husband's superannuated weakness and so caters to a model of woman as both yardstick of masculine worth and capable only of gender-derivative status. By breaking the ties of marriage she attests to the lover's power to draw a woman's heart even against double-standard patriarchal rigor. And in rejecting her decrepit husband she evinces ruthless erotic vigor, making herself especially alluring to such men.

But the result Julia achieves is finally self-wasting. She demonstrates not her own power of self-determination, but male power over her. Bosola merely employs her, and the cardinal wearies of her, and kills her. She thinks to achieve the powers of erotic alliance, but only tenders herself as a toy, and enables her own consumption and disposal. Ironically, the cardinal murders her for a final "hubristic" attempt to be a helpmate, to share in cerebral relation rather than merely physical. Julia's ultimate goals are partly congruent with the duchess's, since both seek personal security in a hostile masculine world, but Julia subjects herself to men who define her as pastime, as furlough from the business of *negotium* – the terms in which she offers herself to them.[47]

The duchess is forward in her wooing, but un-self-subjecting. She tempts Antonio's melancholy fantasy (wanting what he'll never get) with less and less oblique references to husband, will, and marriage. The thought of his children never born, a little wanton son riding a-cock-horse (here sex and parenting seem inseparable for him) brings him near tears.

> ... Fie, fie, what's all this?
> One of your eyes is blood-shot – use my ring to't,
> They say 'tis very sovereign – 'twas my wedding ring,
> And I did vow never to part with it,
> But to my second husband.   (1.1.403–7)

But when he looks through this ring, a lens offering *her* new view of them, what *he* sees is "a saucy and ambitious devil ... dancing in this circle" (412–13). "Remove him," she says; "There needs small conjuration, when your finger / May do it: thus – is it fit?" (413–15). "*He kneels,*" we are told, and she raises him, to his feet and her level.

She thus uses her forbidding social superiority to cancel itself, stripping herself of superiority to invent a parity for them to occupy together.[48] To this tempting magic trick Antonio responds with an instinctual warding-off:

> Ambition, madam, is a great man's madness,
> That is not kept in chains, and close-pent rooms,
> But in fair lightsome lodgings, and is girt
> With the wild noise of prattling visitants,
> Which makes it lunatic, beyond all cure –
> Conceive not I am so stupid but I aim
> Whereto your favors tend: but he's a fool
> That, being a-cold, would thrust his hands i'th'fire
> To warm them.   (420–28)

If Ferdinand's tortures in Act 4 appropriate the conservative social energies of the *charivari*, it is extremely striking to find exactly those energies here first, as *Antonio's* initial response to her wooing. To him this act is "great man's madness," she a saucy and ambitious devil, or the fire. Though Antonio is eventually positioned as utterly opposed to Ferdinand, here at the outset they are allied: the wooed husband-to-be is not just frightened, but *hostile*, resenting a dangerously forward woman. (The puns on "conceive" and "aim" are explicitly gendered, and belligerent.)

Since we now tend to perceive the duchess's goal as a marital norm, it may seem too domestic to count as explosive social mobility. But for a *female head of state* such companionate *marital* selection for express and state-exclusive domesticity, unequivocally across status and dynastic imperatives (Antonio's as much as Ferdinand's), was dizzying. Limited self-determination and mobility even for women were at least familiar cruxes, whether racily erotic on stage or as recruitment necessities, but the notion was only slowly naturalized. The scale and density of the duchess's careful and loving but matter-of-fact and (given Cariola's prepared ambush) dictatorial appropriation of her steward is hard to recover. Absolutist masculine appropriation from above is much more familiar. The range extends from the "quite lost" Duke Brachiano's criminal-dereliction wooing of Vittoria – "You shall to me at once / Be dukedom, health, wife, children, friends, and all" (*The White Devil* 1.2.273–74) – to Middleton's later Duke of Florence's extortionate wooing of his eventual wife – "I am not here in vain; have but the leisure / to think on that ... I should be sorry the least force should lay / An unkind touch upon thee" (*Women Beware Women* 2.2.334–35, 344–45). These comparable men do marry these women, but both wives begin with other husbands; marriage is not the men's initial goal, even if Brachiano does incline toward a companionate posture. To capture the Duchess of Malfi's particular *woman's* act, to grasp what Webster is trying to decriminalize here, we must see a combination of dissonant strategies. On the one hand, an ameliorative rewriting of Goneril and Oswald: marriage undoing disparity, a meeting of true minds. On the other, taming Petruchio: love liberated by domination. Webster's duchess does not just aim at marriage from the start; she is his way of imagining such an unthinkable goal, and *she* imagines it aristocratically, loving and forcing at once.

In the face of Antonio's masculine resistance, this work of imagination is laborious. The duchess flits back and forth between attack, intrigue, and renunciation. She criticizes high rank as hedging the will, forcing it into allegorical expression (as a tyrant fearfully equivocates, or as one dreams forbidden dreams), and calls on Antonio to awake. With coercive enticement she suggests what a wealthy mine she makes him lord of, and puts off vain ceremony with a flourish, to appear as a desiring and desirable young widow with only half a blush. Such double, not to say duplicitous, language is necessary (though not sufficient) to capture the wary steward, who has long made his peace with fantasies. The offer of her flesh and blood makes her nearly irresistible (though note the strands of power and desire intertwined in that term), but even in reluctant submission he can only swear dutifully to "remain the constant sanctuary / Of [her] good name" (460–61). Her kiss accepting his submission she calls his "*Quietus est*" (464), one of numerous references to death in this wooing. This is certainly a reluctant groom.

Sharpest of all, his will must finally be locked by the hidden spy. This conversion of spirit to letter is quite forcible. "Kneel," Webster has her command, and Cariola comes from behind the arras. "Hah?" he says. "Be not amaz'd, this woman's of my counsel," she replies (475–77), and they exchange vows. The witness was not, of course, essential: mutual declaration was sufficient. Cariola's presence is the coercive negative reinforcement, needed only for Antonio. Since he goes on to agree, he may be thought finally to submit freely (though *submission* is exactly the point). But since the law required no specific form of words, he may also be thought to feel he has already said (witnessed) words. Whatever Antonio's degree of freedom, the duchess's determination to have him, though clearly loving, is equally clearly "will he nill he." She repudiates both the hegemonic authority of her dynastic obligations, and the equally hegemonic authority of masculine independence: she invites his assumption of parity, and disables any right of refusal. His fears, not cowardly but conventional, help to justify the duchess's use of the rhetorical wiles of intrigue, for which she has been condemned – precisely, I think, for their masculine force; more "feminine" wiles would be more comfortable to many readers. Loving and forcing, she *combines* masculine and feminine modes here, the "spirit of greatness" *and* "of woman" (504), which Cariola can only see as a choice. However, her world proves just as hostile to the androgyne as to any other monster.

Once the marriage vows are uttered the duchess, a wife again, takes steps to accord Antonio such symbolic husbandly authority as she can. She has him lead her "blind" to the marriage bed, and will shroud her blushes (no longer half-blushes) in his bosom, "the treasury of all [her] secrets" (503).[49] So he remains her steward as well, here and after. Such ambivalence is general: the marital inversion, conceptually a liberated move outward into the wilderness, takes the ironic practical form of a secret unwilling withdrawal that grows more and more claustrophobic. This effective quarantine encloses her gesture of liberation, which sought to enact the ideal of reciprocity between unequals, so often imputed to the citizens of a supposedly organic hierarchy. Perhaps this ideal originates as an ideology of the nurturant family; in any case, in Jacobean society it serves mainly as an ideological pacifier. The duchess tries to reclaim it for familial privacy, with her forcible embrace: "All discord, without this circumference, / Is only to be pitied, and not fear'd" (1.1.469–70). She tries to banish old relations from the sphere of the new. But her power is limited, the marriage depressingly short-lived. Though three children are born, they arrive between acts (save for the first, who vanished behind the horoscope intrigue). Our sense of husband and wife living in peace together derives chiefly from the interrupted scene which ends that life (3.2). Their small talk before Ferdinand appears suggests just the sort of deep and fruitful ease so lacking elsewhere in the play. (We do not see the children here; our impression of the nuclear family comes largely from the duchess's lines about syrup for the son's cold.) But even their boudoir banter addresses (perhaps as usual?) the relationship's foundation in female power, and ironies abound. For instance, Antonio says he rises early after a night with his wife because he is glad his wearisome night's work is over. The affectionate inversion displaces the real reason for early rising: the oppressive need for secrecy, typical of adultery rather than marriage. Lightheartedness is simultaneously present and painfully absent.

When Ferdinand's eerie appearance disrupts the scene (and allows him a taste of substitution) the duchess enters a different isolation prefatory to tragedy. Her response to her brother's erect dagger takes a desperately agile variety of forms: she claims that she can die like a prince; she argues rationalistically that she did not set out to make "any new world, or custom" (3.2.111) in marrying; she claims that he is too strict, that her reputation is safe, that she has a right to a future unwidowed. But for Ferdinand all her claims are inert, mere self-justification. Her rational mode of interaction between peers is doomed here, for the urge to parity – with Antonio, with Ferdinand, with men – is the source of the general problem for Ferdinand. When she realizes this she flies without further question.

The tenure of her flight is as truncated in dramatic time as the marriage. But now as then, Webster has her pause to contemplate the larger significance of her actions. She envies the birds of the field, who may marry without restriction. This homely but revealing comparison reiterates Webster's patterned substitution of the duchess's out-marriage for Ferdinand's incest, as inverted object of horror. The terms of the juxtaposition are adapted from Myrrha's argument for the legitimacy of *incest* in Ovid's *Metamorphoses*: "Other animals mate as they will, nor is it thought base for a heifer to endure her sire, nor for his own offspring to be a horse's mate; the goat goes in among the flocks which he has fathered, and the very birds conceive from those whom they were conceived. Happy they who have such privilege!" (X.324–29). Webster's transvaluation of the trope to specify marital purity is very striking, and the vague allusion to the lilies of the field (Matthew 6:28) amplifies the effect of a relation beyond the corrupt limits of the social.[50]

She also wonders whether her brothers' tyranny is a form of God's will, considering that "nought made [her] e'er / Go right but heaven's scourge-stick" (3.5.80–81); she fears, yet hopes, that she is, like the salmon, higher in value nearer the fire. These metaphysical maneuvers are a psychic defense in the face of capture by Bosola: she strives to perceive, and thus absorb and process, her experience *sub specie aeternitatis*, placing her action in an intelligible cosmos less inhospitable than her social world. But these defenses also contain the kind of speculation familiar from Shakespearean tragedy, where the elevated are crushed as they inaugurate new conceptual options. I think Webster here moves distinctly beyond Shakespeare, whose women are insufficiently disillusioned to face the ultimate universal hostilities.

Once trapped, this woman recites a litany familiar from Shakespearean tragic experience. Ironically courtly to the last, she exhibits a "strange disdain" (4.1.12), refusing to grovel and reanimate the ideology she has left behind. She speaks of the thinness of daily life, feeling herself playing a part in tedious theater. She considers praying, but curses instead, moving from her brothers to a global Shakespearean call for original chaos;[51] like Job, she refuses to acknowledge sinfulness. Though stripped like the bare forked galley-slave, she insists on her founding *persona* of power, "Duchess of Malfi still" (4.2.142). But in reiterating her freedom's origin (in rank), she inevitably also reminds us of her deep inscription in that system, for she has no independent proper name. Webster insists that she is not Vittoria, not Livia, not Lucrezia or Cordelia, but one born to be trapped in rank, however she may struggle in the destructive element.

This defiant positioning is excruciating here, yet it foretells an ever more real appropriation. Some fifty years later the vigorously independent Margaret, Duchess of Newcastle exhibits a similar double consciousness, absolute firmness of identity *in relationality* – direct, whole, and limited, by turns and all at once. At the end of her 20-page life of herself, tailpiece to the 150-page life of her duke, she offers this apologia, her final words:

> ... I hope my readers will not think me vain for writing my life, since there have been many that have done the like, as Caesar, Ovid, and many more, both men and women, and I know no reason I may not do it as well as they: but I verily believe some censuring readers will scornfully say, why hath this Lady writ her own life? since none cares to know whose daughter she was or whose wife she is, or how she was bred, or what fortunes she had, or how she lived, or what humour or disposition she was of. I answer that it is true, that 'tis to no purpose to the readers, but it is to the authoress, because I write it for my own sake, not theirs. Neither did I intend this piece for to delight, but to divulge: not to please the fancy, but to tell the truth, lest after-ages should mistake, in not knowing I was daughter to one Master Lucas of St. Johns,

near Colchester, in Essex, second wife to the Lord Marquis of Newcastle; for my Lord having had two wives, I might easily have been mistaken, especially if I should die and my Lord marry again (178).

This duchess is one of two wives, Webster's has two husbands. Nevertheless, such a stunning mix of determined (dare one say, caesarian? ovidian?) self-identification and patriarchal relationality provides a strong and satisfying context for the fictional character's dual self-identification through her two husbands: Antonio, whom she chose, and the originary forebear duke by whom she became and remained to the end "Duchess of Malfi still."

However, the Duchess of Newcastle's encouraging post-civil-war future was not yet. Webster's duchess claims what she can, and departs defiant, her own deed's creature to the end. She sustains investment only in her children, the bodily fruits of the personal human love which motivated her original action. The only hierarchy she will acknowledge is a residual and absconded heavenly one, in this play utterly unrelated to any supposedly earthly representatives. Having detranscendentalized her social world, she sarcastically puts off her last merely feminine attribute, her tediousness (4.2.227), and bids Bosola tell her brothers they can feed in peace. This quiescence seems to some degree to be peace for her too, or at least resignation, and thus may slightly evacuate some of her labor of self-determination. Some would wish her to spit in her murderers' faces, like Vittoria. And indeed, as Rose observes, her death in Act 4 (somewhat like Antony's) shifts the play's energies past her, making her only "the bearer of meaning," not its maker (171). But this view seems to me to embody something of a fetish of the ending. Her project fails, but its work of imagining gets done, in detail and extremely memorably. It seems to me crucial and fruitful cultural labor.[52]

Webster leaves Cariola briefly behind as ironic coda, absent from felicity only to mark the limits of the female model her mistress has razed, by biting and scratching and shrieking a false and futile claim to the relational sanctuary of pregnancy by a young gentleman. "Why then, / Your credit's sav'd" (254–55), says Bosola, defender of the verities, and they strangle her.

III

With Antonio and Bosola we return to the site of Horatio and Pedringano, of upward mobility confusingly lived from below. These servants are members of the new class of instrumental men, functional descendants of fifteenth-century retainers who fought the Wars of the Roses for their masters. Under Henry VIII and Elizabeth some of these men came to major power, and many more served in lesser capacities, often as bureaucratic specialists but also as all-purpose henchmen. Wallace MacCaffrey notes that "the practice of the Elizabethan administration mingled confusedly the notion of a professional, paid public service with that of personal service to the monarch."[53] These roles interact in Antonio and Bosola – steward and spy, bureaucrat and hit-man. Each feels the new obscure insecurity later to be identified by reference to the cash nexus, the shift from role to job. Each feels it differently. Antonio certainly occupies a more assured position than Bosola, but they are seen to share the uncertain *a priori* situation, of opportunity and limit, of those whose achieved identity is insubstantial.

Antonio begins the play as a momentary choric voice, praising idealized courtly virtues and listing the *dramatis personae* for us in the reified generic terms of the seventeenth-century "character." But Webster at once undermines this spokesman's security by plunging Antonio into elevations. He loses his distanced footing in part through the very virtues which authorized his choric role, and is soon very ambivalently placed. We hear, for instance, of his victory in the joust, traditional peacetime arena for aristocratic character contests. (Antonio is no priggish Malvolio.) But such achievement begets only Ferdinand's condescension: "Our sister duchess' great master of her household? Give him the jewel: – When shall we leave this sportive action, and fall to action indeed?" (1.1.90–92). Such imaginary warfare "bores" the great duke, whose supposedly effortless possession of his own identity will not recognize Antonio's. Yet a moment later (1.1.224–30) the brothers, thinking to hire a spy, consider Antonio with Bosola: to noble eyes both are servants – men in the way of opportunity.

The different opportunity of the duchess's coercive self-gift also foregrounds a certain social insecurity. As steward Antonio occupies an achieved status of considerable power and security: the skilled estate manager was a Jacobean eminence. Antonio is satisfied to rest on this local pinnacle, in honorable service. Despite his erotic fantasies concerning his mistress, he must be coerced into further mobility. As we have seen, his horizon of mobility is securely circumscribed; beyond its limits he is ill at ease, unprepared for a society open to the top.[54]

Once he is carried into that turbulent realm he seems to become more confident and aggressive, more a man on the move. His sparring with Bosola, whose espionage he suspects from the start, takes the form of status insults. He sneers at him as an upstart, speaking from the rank he has secretly entered as the duchess's consort: "Saucy slave! I'll pull thee up by the roots" (2.3.36); "Are you scarce warm, and do you show your sting?" (2.3.39). In so doing he emphasizes his own capacity to make and break men, to establish or deny status; these sneers are combative and self-constructing at once.

Such utterances are, perhaps as usual, rooted in insecurity: "This mole does undermine me ... This fellow will undo me" (2.3.14, 29). But Webster isolates Antonio here: he neglects his wife and child in his fear. Barely able to cope with the storms of courtly intrigue to which the duchess has brought him, he is "lost in amazement" (2.1.173) when she goes into labor; of the cover story he mutters, "How do I play the fool with mine own danger" (2.2.69). When he hears the threats of Ferdinand's letters, he leaves his family as his wife directs him to, however grievingly, to face Ferdinand's murderous rage without him. Webster makes him fear for his own safety more than for theirs.

Antonio's insecurity also appears expressly in terms of gender roles. He submitted to his wife's coercive marriage proposal with the deference of the social subordinate he feels himself to be. Yet at one level of this enforced marriage he is miserable, as it subordinates him to a woman in that private context where both personal and gendered will are defining. When she reassures him that her brothers will not ultimately cause them harm, that "time will easily / Scatter the tempest" (1.1.471–72), he cannot endure the maternal address to his unmanliness. "These words should be mine," he says, "And all the parts you have spoke, if some part of it / Would not have savour'd flattery" (1.1.472–74). But he would never have spoken such words to her. It was not for him to dismiss her brothers as insignificant until she had done so; only then can he painfully claim, for his own sense of self, that he would have said so. The boudoir scene is wincingly similar. Antonio listens silently, in hiding, while Ferdinand threatens his wife. Having sworn not to seek out Antonio, the duke leaves; only then does Antonio dare to wish that "this terrible thing would come again, / That, standing on my guard, I might relate / My warrantable love" (3.2.147–49). But he was free just minutes earlier to defy Ferdinand. Exactly then, almost comically, Bosola knocks; Antonio cries in dread, "How now! who knocks? more earthquakes?" (3.2.155).

Antonio's secret marital elevation secures both his mistress's love and the gender subordination that comes with it. He reluctantly embraces the love, but continually struggles to compensate for the subjective loss of traditional masculine marital authority. Before Ferdinand's arrival he banters with slightly queasy but safe bedroom ease about his subordination, but only speaks defiance when it's safe. The cost to his gendered dignity wars with the cost to his life. Hitherto Antonio had filled a place where he felt secure and significant. When the duchess brings his erotic daydreams to life, they become social nightmares. He is not prepared for this life in the seismographic realm of noble intrigue. Antonio is a man of regularities, not an improviser (nor a killer) like Bosola. But for this very reason he is uncomfortable in his private relations with his wife, bound incoherently both to the traditional hierarchy of rank, which enjoins his submission, and to the traditional gender hierarchy, which enjoins him to superiority. His culture has not prepared him to be a subordinate husband, nor a princely consort continually at risk.

He is finally, I believe, a man who, being wrought, is perplexed and bewildered by a superior woman's ambitious love. His private disorientation is unceasing, but the text finally infects him with the centering energies of ambition. By the time the news of his child reaches Rome he seems so even to Delio, who fears "Antonio is betray'd. How fearfully / Shows his ambition now!" (2.4.80–81). As with Lorenzo's presumptions about Horatio's ambition, the masculine will seems an irresistible hypothesis. And at his death Antonio speaks of a "quest of greatness" now his own, retrospectively apparent by its present collapse. He would spare his son such false dreams, bidding him fly the courts of princes. (An ironic wish: the son's restoration at play's end bodes ill for him, whatever it may say for Amalfi.) The husband's final action, the desperately naive journey to the cardinal for reconciliation, freezes him for us, as one whose surprised elevation never brought much sense of how to navigate the webs of alliance and enmity.

IV

Like the other characters Bosola is haunted with governing the ground of his identity. As an *employee* he presents one of the most intricate examples of the Renaissance problematic of self-shaping. This complex representation is initially adumbrated through a blend of the predicates of counselor, malcontent, have-not, henchman, and aesthete, roles all marked by some kind of alienation.

Bosola enters on the heels of Antonio's normative set-piece on the French court, a figure of public service which gives the solipsistic vanities of the decorative gentleman a final cause in political service to the prince. In Bosola's intensified and privatized enactment of Castiglione's courtly counselor, Webster dissects the internal contractions of the life to which the nation's ambitious young men were drawn.

In swift succession Bosola annexes a variety of stances toward courtly reward and punishment. Antonio first labels him "the only court-gall" (1.1.23), a standoffish or outcast malcontent, yet at once complicates this estimate further:

... his railing
Is not for simple love of piety;
Indeed he rails at those things which he wants,
Would be as lecherous, covetous, or proud,
Bloody, or envious, as any man,
If he had means to be so .... (1.1.23–28)

The distanced moralist and the envious parasite coincide in uneasy
dissonance. Webster also evokes the unrewarded servant. When Bosola
demands belated reward from the cardinal for a suborned murder,
Webster links him to the social problem of the veteran soldier, vagrant
stranger in his own land. Bosola has not even the nominal fact of service
to his country to cushion his return to social life. He has been a more
private "soldier," and has taken the fall, serving silently in the horren-
dous galleys.[55] He will not rise in the pub, nor feast his friends on St.
Crispin's Day. (Indeed, unlike Pistol and even Black Will, he has no
friends.) He can only sneer bitterly at his employers for their depravity.
Yet Antonio has "heard / He's very valiant: this foul melancholy / Will
poison all his goodness." " 'Tis great pity/ He should be thus neglected"
(1.1.74–77). Some spoiled "goodness" in this envious professional killer
awaits Webster's plot. The author's arresting means for this development
derives the most complex of Bosola's ills not from neglect but from
employment.

For Bosola is preferred, to spy on the duchess. He is made a
henchman, an agent, an instrument, and so embodies the complex new
problems that arise from the status of employee. At this point in English
history service was in the process of the momentous shift from role to
job, and the ways it could ground a sense of self were changing. Hitherto
the prince had been seen as the sacramental source of identity. Puttenham captures this relation in a poem about Queen Elizabeth: "Out of her
breast as from an eye, / Issue the rayes incessantly / Of her justice,
bountie and might": these rays make "eche subject clearly see, / What
he is bounded for to be / To God his Prince and common wealth, / His
neighbour, kin[d]red and to himselfe" (100). In this view deferent service
was a mode of assent to the static fact of ascriptive rank, an "implicit
recognition of the legitimacy of the prevailing social order ... and a tacit
rejection of alternative definitions of the situation," as Wrightson might
have it (*English Society* 58). However, as Stone shows, King James's sale
of honors helped alienate the power to confer identity, from God's
representative to the money which bought him.[56] The human status, the
pliability, of such categories was gradually revealed. As ascriptive status
emerged as a commodity, the king's sacred role as fount of identity
began to decay, and the nature of identity itself began to change. It

became visible as *achieved*, a human product, contingent upon wealth, connection, and labor.

Later, when Marx described it, the notion could seem a conceptual liberation. As individuals express their life [i.e., as they "produce their means of subsistence"], so they are. What they are coincides with their production, with *what* they produce and with *how* they produce.[57] Here the human creates itself in the process of work. But in early modern England, when this insight began to be visible, it often seemed a loss rather than a liberation. The obligation to found identity on one's own actions seemed to sever the trans-individual bonds which bound the polity together, and left the individual on his own, save for the new power of cash, which could buy knighthoods, even titles. Marx specifies this historical passage as a demolition: the exchange relation of capitalism, he says, "has pitilessly torn asunder the motley feudal ties that bound man to his 'natural superiors,' and has left remaining no other nexus between man and man than naked self-interest, than callous 'cash payment.'"[58] For Bosola, an early transitional figure, such clear and retrospective formulation was unavailable. I believe it makes more sense to see him as one to whom this nexus seemed a lifeline, weaker perhaps than Elizabeth's nearly divine "rayes," but still somehow linked to the ontologically solid ground of the ruling aristocracy.[59] In examining Bosola's "neglect" Webster offers us a tragic figure whose isolation is formulated in terms of evacuating employment by another man.

This coincidence of loss and possibility first appears in Bosola's hostility toward his "miserable age, where only the reward / Of doing well is the doing of it" (1.1.31–32). Webster inverts the proverb (Tilley V81): virtue is *merely* its own, empty reward. What formerly derived absolute worth from a collective cultural judgment has now lost its savor, and is worthless unless vendible. Bosola is so far modern that he laments not the absence of the old mode, but its residual presence. Still, he gets what he seems to want almost at once, when Ferdinand says "There's gold" (1.1.246). The rest of the play assays (as Bosola dourly inquires) "what follows." For the post of intelligencer aggravates his discontent, though it frees him from the material want and shame which dominate his galley life. Such reward is mere hire and salary. He wants more, is miserable without it. It is senseless to read him as merely greedy for gain; we need to understand *what* more he wants.

Of course this "more" is some such totalizing self-realization as might be vouchsafed to Cariola and Kent. But the personal service through which Bosola seeks this ultimate goal in fact reduces and dehumanizes him. Kent's desires were deeply coincident with his master's ("What wouldst thou? – Service"), and even Jonson's repellent Macro sees force and value in reaching toward such coincidence:

> I will not aske, why CAESAR bids doe this:
> But ioy, that he bids me. It is the blisse
> Of courts, to be imploy'd; no matter, how:
> A princes power makes all his actions vertue.
> We, whom he workes by, are dumbe instruments,
> To doe, but not enquire: His great intents
> Are to be seru'd, not search'd. Yet, as that bow
> Is most in hand, whose owner best doth know
> T'affect his aymes, so let that states-man hope
> Most vse, most price, can hit his princes scope.   (*Sejanus* 3.714–23)

But Ferdinand's aims are explicitly withheld from Bosola ("Do not you ask the reason: but be satisfied" [1.1.257]), and so cannot be adopted as purposes.

Bosola is specifically alienated from the utility of the "intelligence" which is his labor's product, and so creates a reified commodity, and a reified self along with it. Marx formulates this action precisely:

> [Alienated] labor is *external* to the worker, it is merely a *means* to satisfy needs external to it ... the external character of labor for the worker appears in the fact that it is not his own, but someone else's, that it does not belong to him, that in it he belongs, not to himself, but to another ... [The worker's activity] ... is the loss of his self.[60]

Instead of founding his identity, Bosola expends it in his work. Hungry for ontological ratification, Bosola offers up to Ferdinand all he has. He expects this relationship, his service to his prince, to nourish and found him, with the life-giving social milk of rule and fealty which Puttenham described. But instead he merely spends himself, and gets paid. Then, of course, he works harder, presuming he has not yet earned his ontological paycheck; and the more he puts himself into his production, the more he loses it. This sense of Bosola's hunger explains what would otherwise seem his simply depraved ongoing decision to continue doing Ferdinand's dirty work, much in despite, he claims, of his own good nature. Compulsively seeking to be paid, recognized, acknowledged, identified, Bosola expends efforts that continually intensify his sense of need, and accomplish his exploitation. The cash payment is the full exchange-value to be gotten from this employer.

Bosola tries to obliterate this lack of ratification by means of a repressive device familiar on other grounds from the career of the English machiavel: the aestheticizing of intrigue. Noble machiavels may seek this stance in search of Ferdinand's *sui generis* alienation, but

Bosola's purpose is different. A clue to his practice can be found in Georges Sorel's suggestion that artistic creation anticipates the way perfected work will feel in the society of the future.[61] Such activity can confer the unity that alienated labor undercuts. Hence, it may be argued, an aestheticizing can restore a felt unity or wholeness to actions by *decontextualizing* them, separating them from the context which displays one's fragmentation.[62] In focusing on the aesthetic shape of, say, a suborned act of violence or betrayal, to the exclusion of awareness of the context that marks it *as* suborned, the alienated laborer can grasp a false sense of integrity by alienating himself from his alienation.[63] Seen in this light, Bosola's aestheticizing functions as a narcotic which lends a sense of totality while dulling awareness of its falsity. The part seems the whole, for he can devote his whole self (and so reconstitute it for the duration) to the means of the task while ignoring the opacity of its end.

The apricot incident exhibits this technique. Here Bosola observes the duchess's physical condition in considerable specialist detail (2.1.63–68) and applies a test for pregnancy – the typically alimentary Renaissance device of administering apricots (a laxative and thus labor stimulant). The trick is, he says to himself, "A pretty one" (2.1.70): Bosola watches not only the duchess but himself at work, taking pleasure in his professional prying, setting up private dramatic ironies and *sotto voce* gloating for his own entertainment (see 2.1.112, 117, 140, 145). Lukacs offers a theoretical frame. "The specialized 'virtuoso,' the vendor of his objectified and reified faculties does not just become the (passive) observer of society; he also lapses into a contemplative attitude *vis-a-vis* the workings of his own objectified and reified faculties" (*Reification* 100). Bosola is thoroughly engaged (and so unifyingly estranged) not only in the technicalities of his craft, but in appreciating his own stylistic flair.[64]

A similar bifurcation of consciousness can be seen in the interrogation scene (3.2), where Bosola discovers that Antonio is the duchess's husband. In order to unfold it properly we must first examine Bosola's youth, which was characterized by an ostentatiously aesthetic sense of his actions. For according to Delio, Bosola was

> a fantastical scholar, like such who study to know how many knots was in Hercules' club, of what colour Achilles' beard was, or whether Hector were not troubled with the toothache: he hath studied himself half blear-eyed, to know the true symmetry of Caesar's nose by a shoeing-horn; and this he did to gain the name of a speculative man.   (3.3.41–47)

Bosola has had the sort of university training that warped his predecessor Flamineo, gave him a sense of ambition and fitted him for little but mobility. The Lylyan dandy preceded, somehow gave birth to, the cardinal's thug (and the galleys). Delio's gossip shows that the exquisitely intellectual management of reputation is a familiar tool to Bosola, cognate with spying and thuggery; he has only retreated from its more precious manifestations.[65]

Under Bosola's interrogation, the duchess screens her relation to Antonio by accusing him of peculation. When Bosola defends him, she replies that he was basely descended. Bosola then replies with the contrast between ascription and achievement which is so central to the play: "Will you make yourself a mercenary herald, / Rather to examine men's pedigrees than virtues?" (3.2.259–60). This rebuke inspires her to reveal that Antonio is her husband, because it so clearly specifies the terms of her own rebellion in choosing him. Bosola's reply says as much about himself as about her.

> No question but many an unbenefic'd scholar
> Shall pray for you for this deed, and rejoice
> That some preferment in the world can yet
> Arise from merit. The virgins of your land
> That have no dowries, shall hope your example
> Will raise them to rich husbands: should you want
> Soldiers, 'twould make the very Turks and Moors
> Turn Christians, and serve you for this act.
> Last, the neglected poets of your time,
> In honour of this trophy of a man,
> Rais'd by that curious engine, your white hand,
> Shall thank you, in your grave for't; and make that
> More reverend than all the cabinets
> Of living princes. For Antonio,
> His fame shall likewise flow from many a pen,
> When heralds shall want coats to sell to men.[66]   (3.2.283–98)

She may not have set out to make any new world or custom, but her unequal marriage will legitimate deserving mobility of many kinds: the unemployed graduate will find preferment, the undowered virgin (Scarborrow's sister?) security with a rich husband. Alien Turks and Moors will flock like Othellos and Ithamores to her side in gratitude for this tolerance of heterodox origin. And this multifoliate action will be eternized by neglected poets happy to get the work. The duchess has ratified elevation by merit, and Bosola's applause betrays his own authentic experience of the dream – and of its attendant anomie, deprived of old securities, denied the new.[67]

Many readers accept Bosola's speech as "sincere"; others think it a ploy to loosen the duchess's tongue. I think it is both: his own authentic response, managed in pursuit of his employer's goal. This apparent contradiction is only a particular case of Lukacs' reified employee's general deformation: "His qualities and abilities are no longer an organic part of his personality, they are things which he can 'own' or 'dispose of like the various objects of the external world" (*Reification* 100). Bosola exchanges his authentic emotional stance for the information his master wants. But this self-commoditizing exchange manipulation is asymmetrical, for Bosola does not easily revert to the dispassionate stance of the intelligencer. Perhaps the plan for the false pilgrimage is a sarcasm enabling the difficult shift from intimacy to the spy-report by positing a ground for an intermediate stage of sneering distance. He can call her a politician, a soft quilted anvil and so forth, and return to his habitual malcontent mode. But even this self-manipulation (if that is what it is) is not fully anaesthetic, for when Bosola *returns* to his commoditized state (the force of the mediating pause of "What rests, but I reveal / All to my lord" [3.2.326–27]) it is with self-loathing: "O, this base quality / Of intelligencer!" (3.2.327–28). A further deflection is needed, a universal projection of the commodity model: "why, every quality i'th' world / Prefers but gain or commendation: / Now, for this act I am certain to be rais'd, / *And men that paint weeds to the life are prais'd*" (3.2.328–31). If the duchess's act was sordid, and his own no lower than any other, Bosola may sedate that portion of his response which sympathized with her action, at least long enough to file his report.

Of the well-known torture and murder scene, I will pause only to note how it combines the predilections of Ferdinand and his agent. The motive force is of course Ferdinand's (a fact often missed, owing to his apparent absence): Bosola remains an agent. Michael Warren (of the Nuffield Theatre) has suggested that his role in this scene might be made clear by "having Ferdinand on or above the stage, physically directing the action."[68] His *will* should indeed be manifest, but I would prefer to have the duke visible but still, frozen in his contemplative mode of alien voyeur. For his part, Bosola steeps himself in procedure, but is nonetheless touched by the insistent coherence of his fellow galley-slave. She does not reach for external legitimation as he has done, but rests in her identity as, like Middleton's Beatrice-Joanna, "the deed's creature," needing no DeFlores to tell her so. And as Bosola lives the parts he plays, his dismissal of earthly values besieges his increasingly stunted goals, even as he pursues ever more grimly the aesthetic anaesthesia of obsession with form. He is finally silent throughout the strangling, returning to life (that is, jerking away from reflection to active instrumentality) with the uncharacteristically brutal "Some other strangle the children" (4.2.239). He seems barely under control in the face of the violations he has caused, in less and less confident hope of what has now come to seem *re*payment from Ferdinand.

Instead, of course, Ferdinand rewrites the contract (repudiating debt as Jacobean nobles often did) by pardoning Bosola's *murders*, ironically restoring to his agent the fully humanizing capacity of the moral sense. (The "gift" inverts Lear's denial of Kent's loyal advice about Cordelia.)

> Why didst thou not pity her? what an excellent
> Honest man mightst thou have been
> If thou hadst borne her to some sanctuary!
> Or, bold in a good cause, oppos'd thyself
> With thy advanced sword above thy head,
> Between her innocence and my revenge! (4.2.273–78)

Action beyond the employer's instruction is available only to the independent human, not to the obedient tool that cannot think for itself. Ferdinand challenges Bosola's humanity to shift the blame, but he speaks his own heart too, called out of alienation too late, like Bosola's. But this castigation, meant to deflect his pain, only postpones it. In "pardoning" his henchman, he schizophrenically enacts revenge and forgiveness at once.

Though the reproach nourishes Bosola's developing rebellion against his reification, he cannot simply abandon his own project. He feverishly opposes legal, moral, rational, and courtly sanctions to Ferdinand's dismissal, demonstrating his service to be in all particulars deserving. This dismissal perverts justice, he says; you shall quake for it; let me know wherefore; "though I loath'd the evil, yet I lov'd / You that did counsel it; and rather sought / To appear a true servant, than an honest man" (4.2.331–33). The parallel with the duchess's defense in the boudoir is striking; here as there the arguments are incomprehensible to Ferdinand. And like the duchess, Bosola must face the ultimate failure of his project, for self-fashioning through employment:

> ... I stand like one
> That long hath ta'en a sweet and golden dream:
> I am angry with myself, now that I wake....
> ... off my painted honour:
> While with vain hopes our faculties we tire,
> We seem to sweat in ice and freeze in fire. (4.2.323–25, 336–38)

His dream of ultimate grounding at the hands of another stands revealed as a delusive petrarchan hope for an absolute beyond earthly grasp.

Faced with this failure, Bosola seeks his ontological grounding anew in a succession of actions which he sees as neither derived from another (as his service was) nor evasively contemplative: "somewhat I will speedily enact / Worth my dejection" (4.2.374–75). Personal vengeance will at least make him his own deed's creature. (This action conflates the dual

motives of compassion for the duchess and anger over his neglect:
Ferdinand causes both sufferings.) When we next see Bosola he is
accepting employment from the cardinal with ironic alacrity: "Give it me
in a breath, and let me fly to't: / They that think long, small expedition
win, / For musing much o'th'end, cannot begin" (5.2.118–20). Security
like virtue rests in the doing, in the subsuming process of direct and
unalienated action itself – in search of the vengeance which he desperately needs to be decisive, constitutive. As Bosola opens himself hope-
fully to the would-be sacramental powers of moral confidence to be
gotten from the act, he turns to a traditional self-sacrificial idiom: "O
penitence, let me truly taste thy cup, / That throws men down, only to
raise them up" (5.2.348–49). He still feels neglected and seeks advancement, but shifts his ground to the seemingly more reliable realm of a
transcendent moral order.

It can only be Webster's comment on this posture that Bosola's next
action (reminiscent of Cordelia's dead entry after Albany's "The gods
defend her!") is the unwitting murder of Antonio. This monstrous error
utterly disrupts his short-lived transcendental stance: "We are merely the
stars' tennis-balls, struck and banded / Which way please them"
(5.4.54–55). Self-substantiation through self-abnegation comes no more
readily than by hyperbolic service. Bosola now swears, "I will not imitate
things glorious, / No more than base: I'll be mine own example"
(5.4.81–82). He repudiates service to God and to Ferdinand alike as
falsely coherent, returning to a stance like the duchess's centering "I am
Duchess of Malfi still." If he cannot realize himself in any cosmic or
social terms, he may yet seek identity *par sibi*. He turns to seize a revenge
now sheerly his own.

In the play's final action Bosola begins firmly and purely enough,
killing the cardinal's innocent servant to secure the room. But mad
Ferdinand comes in as to the wars, finally falling to action in deed, and
deals death-wounds to all before Bosola kills him. Bosola breathes
longest, playing his own Horatio for the astounded witnesses:

> Revenge, for the Duchess of Malfi, murdered
> By th' Arragonian brethren; for Antonio,
> Slain by this hand; for lustful Julia,
> Poison'd by this man; and lastly, for myself
> That was an actor in the main of all
> Much 'gainst mine own good nature, yet i'th'end
> Neglected.   (5.5.81–87)

This book began with Kyd's Don Andrea dead and gloating. Bosola
provides a fitting chiasmus here: living, if only briefly, but neglected,
bereft – not of Andrea's erotic self-substantiation, but of the similarly

ontological rewards of feudal service. He casts himself finally and summarily as an agent, a vicarious servant of all the victims, not least for himself, murderer and murdered at once, haunted throughout by an always pending better self, now definitively neglected. The supposed restorative of revenge has littered the stage, but the body count, though lavish, is sterile. Bosola ends by fixing our eyes on this lack, this gulf, in his final line, about "another voyage" (105). For as Lear's undone button invokes nakedness and the heath, Bosola's departure is seaward, to the galleys, to the pathless wilderness from which he entered the play, a castaway looking for solid ground to call his own.

V

This is the burden felt by all, throughout these plays: the shaping of the social self in the abrasive zone between emergent and residual social formations. *The Duchess of Malfi* is what Kenneth Burke calls a magical chart, a cognitive decree which names a problematic situation and voices an attitude toward it.[69] Webster's chart reads the characters' urges and defining gestures as transformations of one another; they are fundamentally constituted by, "struck and banded which way please," a net of dimly understood and contradictory social forces; and that these forces shape and limit the kind of actions we habitually regard as individually authentic and chosen (and that carry the responsibilities we associate with tragedy and villainy). Webster provides a social world which constitutes what are by no means the transcendental subjects of traditional moral inquiry, yet which also lies continuously, if unevenly, open to their continuous intermanipulations and mutual constructions.

I believe this play was written, at least in significant part, to dissect the workings of the normative ideology set before us at its beginning. Far from providing criteria for the judgment of the heterodox characters (as criticism, seduced by power as order, has often presumed), this ideological frame and those who pose and endorse it are themselves interrogated. Moral judgments directed against the outcast duchess (as lustful, irresponsible, unwomanly, womanish) emanate from this ideological center; they are at one with high-minded humanist sneering at sycophantic servants whom the center in fact invents, summons up for service and ideological approbation. Webster strives to recover such stifled voices, to bare oppositional gestures usurpingly rewritten, both then and sometimes even now, as womanish eccentricity or baseminded-ness. He also sought, I think, to reclaim Ferdinand for comprehension (if not sympathy), by reading his motives as the absolutized and self-destructive core of a paranoid nobility's project for dominance. To the nominally transcendental grounding of homilies on the World Picture the play is addressed as a symbolic act, the reverse of Burkean Prayer – as an Imprecation.

Afterword

The rhetorical urge to placement that funds most conclusions faces an impasse here. My analyses constitute no linear argument, and produce no Conclusions or Results. For that matter, the endings to the plays I read do not always play a decisive role in my examinations. I have been much more immersed in quotidian flow or practice or conduct, the way that characters "go on with" the strategies of their lives. The goals of those strategies appear usually only in prospect, and are often evacuated in the event. Sometimes that evacuation is full, as with Walter Calverley's crushing muteness; sometimes merely conventional, as with Scarborrow's "all join hands"; sometimes an instant deflation, as with Black Will's "Now I can take you"; sometimes the point, as with Bosola, "i'th'end, neglected." So it is with my own closure, where it is clear that I have neglected much in these pages, despite their number: Shakespeare, Middleton, *The Witch of Edmonton*, *Eastward Ho*! And the scene broadens uncontrollably, to include a variety of depths left implicit, especially that of the many "historical" and "anthropological" texts that lie behind this book.

Such spreading responsibilities are, I think, the inevitable horizon of such analysis. They stretch beyond one's capacities, without any motionless boundary to relieve one of responsibility. Victorian scholars were perhaps more honest when they shared their "thoughts on" their subjects with us. We now feel, especially when Concluding, the most intense and opposite obligation, to frame and place and even seize our subjects, to master them (were the term still usable), to step back and hold them whole, to reveal them as decisively our own.

Writing this book has been largely different, some reversal of the familiar image of Hercules the rhetor, chaining his audience's ears to his tongue. I have felt my voice dragged along behind the texts, often overwhelmed, trying to keep up, never really equal to the obscure and distant fullness of these early modern imaginations and the overdetermined monuments they exchanged among themselves. The density of this overplus has of course been the constant stimulus to interpretation, something like the sonnet lady's refusals. (Nowhere has the reversing modesty of Watson's "small wedges" and "soft showers" seemed more just to me than in my reflections of, on, the work of these deeply thoughtful men 400 years dead.) This above all has been the exhilarating and wearying experience of writing this book: the experience of cultural thickness, blinding showering density everywhere. We are used to such provision with *King Lear*, but the otherness of such notably unsung texts as *The Miseries of Enforced Marriage* offers a similar but different, additional, accumulation of social traces of struggle, curiosity, fear, and relief.

These traces shadow forth an extensive interlocking human structure, its parts continually in motion, under advisement, both in the plays and in the playhouse. Over and over in these plays the intersecting discourses of status, gender, kinship, and service relations get used, by authors and characters, to amplify and conflict with and colonize one another, to seize the will. Now gender rebellion beckons, now kinship critique subsides in defeat; now servants rescue status referents, now they steal or buy them. Whether these gestures count as violations or constructions, as criminal or productive, is largely a matter of position, though by modern measure multiple oppressions are everywhere here. But the many subjections are not only that, only victimizations. The continuous resistances and appropriations these texts preserve constitute a cultural production second to no other function of the early modern theater. And these productions still serve us today, in quite varied and contradictory ways, in our own ideological and structural negotiations.

My aim has been to help make the willful interrogations and appropriations of structuration as visible, as conceptually provocative, and as concretely engaging or disturbing as the bitter triumphs, sweet accomplishments, or longed-for relief of betrothal, remarriage, sexual repudiation, murder, or revenge. For these ranges of practical thought and act are often, I think, one and the same – extensive and intensive, structural and embodied forms of the same gesture: mutually nourishing, mutually illuminating, mutually productive.

Notes

INTRODUCTION

1 For a precursor to this idea see Kaufmann's notion of "autointoxication," in "Ford's Tragic Perspective" 536.

2 See Williams, *Marxism and Literature* 115–16. For a rich recent query into such matters see Strier's essay on Tradition in *Resistant Structures*.

3 Giddens, *Constitution of Society* xvi. Giddens's introduction outlines these various streams *inter alia*. Here it suffices to say that among the groups to which he acknowledges this kind of relation are phenomenology, the Frankfurt School, hermeneutics, ordinary language philosophy, and ethnomethodology.

4 Giddens, *Constitution of Society* xvii–xviii. Cf. studies by Geertz, Christian, Cain, and Scott.

5 Giddens, *Modernity and Self-Identity* 2.

6 In *Modernity and Self-Identity* Giddens generally argues for the fundamental *discontinuity* between pre-modern or traditional societies and those of modernity. "Modern institutions differ from all preceding forms of social order in respect of their dynamism, the degree to which they undercut traditional habits and customs, and their global impact. However, these are not only extensional transformations: modernity radically alters the nature of day-to-day social life and affects the most personal aspects of our experience" (1). In arguing for this particular strand of developmental *continuity*, I propose to read as active our label for the late sixteenth and early seventeenth centuries as "early modern England." This is not to ignore historical *distances*, but to assert historically specific *relations*.

7 Therbörn, *The Ideology of Power* 17.

8 Bacon, "Of Vain-Glory," in *Essays* 158; "Of Honour and Reputation" 160.

9 In the BBC production of *Othello*, when Bob Hoskins's brilliant Iago is hauled before the bed he has loaded, he *giggles*. This emission stands with Othello's foam as an example of the kinds of emotional spasms with which I shall be concerned. (For the Burkean scene, see Burke, *A Grammar of Motives* xv–20.)

10 For a stunning analysis of Lear's "donations," see Berger, "What Did the King Know and When Did He Know It?"

11 *Doctor Faustus* 1.1.6.

12 For an erotic period specimen of this trope, see Middleton and Rowley, *The*

Changeling (1622), where DeFlores thus imagines his conquest of Beatrice: "BEATRICE Thy reward shall be precious. DEFLORES That I have thought on; I have assured myself of that beforehand, And know it will be precious; the thought ravishes" (2.2.130–32).

13 For this possibility see Freud, *Civilization and its Discontents* 724–25. For Marlowe, see Barber's remarkable essay "The forme of Faustus fortunes good or bad."

14 Auden, "The Joker in the Pack" 256. I take pleasure in acknowledging the great influence of Auden's essay on my sense of the issues in this book.

15 See *Outline* 164–71.

16 Consider the intersection of Stone, *The Crisis of the Aristocracy*, Burke on identification in *Rhetoric* 19–23, and Whigham, *Ambition and Privilege passim*.

17 See Sartre, "Concrete Relations with Others: Love, Masochism, Sadism" 471–558.

18 This is Poster's useful summary of Kojeve's presentation of Hegel, in *Existential Marxism in Postwar France* 13; for Hegel's argument see *Phenomenology of Spirit* 111–19 (Miller translates the terms as "lordship" and "bondage"). See also Sartre's discussion of the Look in *Being and Nothingness* 340–400.

19 Kyd, *The Spanish Tragedy*, ed. Edwards.

20 For a related but independent notion of abjection see Kristeva, *Powers of Horror*.

21 See Whigham, *Ambition and Privilege passim*.

22 Wrightson, "The Social Order of Early Modern England" 199.

23 For cross-dressing in terms of social rank, see Harte, "State Control of Dress and Social Change in Pre-Industrial England"; Jardine, "'Make thy doublet of changeable taffeta,'" *Still Harping on Daughters* 141–68; and Whigham, *Ambition and Privilege* 155–69.

24 See Maclean, *The Renaissance Notion of Women*; Henderson and McManus, *Half Humankind*; Woodbridge, *Women and the English Renaissance*; Davis, "Women on Top."

25 See, for suggestive explorations, Jardine, *Still Harping on Daughters*; Laqueur, *Making Sex*; Dollimore, "Subjectivity, Sexuality, and Transgression"; Traub, *Desire and Anxiety*. For a fascinating treatment from the perspective of object-relations psychoanalysis, see Adelman, *Suffocating Mothers*. See also, for a general theoretical inquiry of great suggestiveness for Renaissance studies, Valverde, "Beyond Gender Dangers and Private Pleasures."

26 The English Renaissance transvestite theater and its larger correlative, cross-dressing, have received suggestive attention lately: see, for instance, Jardine, "'As boys and women are for the most part cattle of this colour,'" in *Still Harping on Daughters* 9–36; Sandra Clark, "*Hic Mulier, Haec Vir*, and the Controversy over Masculine Women"; Levine, *Men in Women's Clothing*; Rackin, "Androgyny, Mimesis, and the Marriage of the Boy Heroine"; Jean Howard, "Crossdressing, The Theatre, and Gender Struggle"; Garber, *Vested Interests*; and Orgel, *Impersonations*.

For extraordinarily provocative discussions of general theoretical reconfigurations that can result from meditation upon the conceptual problematic of the homoerotic, see Sedgwick, *Between Men*, and the same author's *Epistemology of the Closet*. For related materials, see Person, "Sexuality as the Mainstay of Identity"; Dollimore, "Shakespeare, Cultural Materialism, Feminism and Marxist Humanism"; and the same author's *Sexual Dissidence*.

27　The literature on Queen Elizabeth and gender has become enormous. For excellent representative samples, see Marcus, "Shakespeare's Comic Heroines, Elizabeth I, and the Political Uses of Androgyny," and several studies by Montrose: "Gifts and Reasons: The Contexts of Peele's *Araygnement of Paris*"; "'Eliza, Queen of Shepheardes' and the Pastoral of Power"; "'Shaping Fantasies': Figurations of Gender and Power in Elizabethan Culture"; and "The Work of Gender in the Discourse of Discovery."

28　See Cressy, "Kinship" 38–44 for these citations and a summary of the current orthodoxy.

29　See Bourdieu, *Outline* 31 and *passim*.

30　Wagner, *English Genealogy* 358. For related materials see Whigham, "Elizabethan Aristocratic Insignia."

31　See Kelly, *The Matrimonial Trials of Henry VIII*; Warnicke, *The Rise and Fall of Anne Boleyn*; Boehrer, *Monarchy and Incest*.

32　See Goody, *Development* 172.

33　Ibid., 172–73; see also Ingram, *Church Courts, Sex, and Marriage*, and Amussen, *An Ordered Society*.

34　Quoted in Goody, *Development* 175.

35　See ibid., 178ff.

36　See Hurstfield's excellent *The Queen's Wards*, and Blayney, "Wardship in English Drama."

37　See Marx, *The Communist Manifesto*.

38　For a recent general treatment, see Braunmuller, "'Second Means,'" and also Strier's striking essay on *King Lear*, "Faithful Servants."

39　See Leinwand, "Negotiation and New Historicism."

40　Burke, *A Rhetoric of Motives* 115, 279.

41　Jardine, *Still Harping on Daughters* 92.

42　Godelier, "The Origins of Male Domination" 7.

43　Churchill, *Vinegar Tom* 136 (scene 1).

44　Our collective sense of how to operate the interpretive tools for social space has been developing at least since the 1970s. My own early work on courtly status now seems too one-dimensional to me, as Malcolmson suggests, criticizing an early version of Ch. 4 as "tend[ing] to collapse" gender issues into status issues. She observes generally, "If feminist writers in the 1970s ignored problems of class … then new historicists and cultural materialists in the 1980s often reduced gender concerns into a symbolic means of articulating what is 'the real subject': status, or issues of power in general" ("'What You Will'" 52–53). Having learned from both patterns, we now assume the need for attention to multiple determinations and interpellations. Determining how best to attend is the work of a large collective project, under construction, to which I hope here to contribute. (In this light, the more recent habit of unpacking the subjected pole of a power relationship as "positionally feminized" offers a ready way to reread, for instance, *Ambition and Privilege* productively for gender relations.)

45 I thus, as will become clear, use the much-debated and many-faceted term "literary" with the following moments of force. (1) To embrace as full of historicity the category of "fictions," so often held suspect by historians; that is, to embrace its evidentiary or monumental capacity (as Foucault might say), *contra* a dismissive concern with the "realities" of "fact." (2) *Not* to inscribe a hierarchy of value among kinds of early modern writing, as is common in modern humanist literary interpretation. (3) Without judgmental reference to the thorny question (here deferred) as to the early modern value judgment of the status, "literary" or not, of dramatic texts. (4) To identify my principal relation to early modern dramatic writings not centrally as scripts for performance (that is, as aids to recovery of playhouse events), though this is of great interest, but more as linguistic stuff, whether heard or read. (5) Finally, and hypothetically, to mark a kind of writing – here, dramatic texts – that voices and preserves the contours of the practical consciousness (complete with implicit social and interpretive competences) of the characters it constructs.

46 "Every confrontation between agents in fact brings together, in an *interaction* defined by the *objective structure* of the relations between the groups they belong to (e.g. a boss giving orders to a subordinate, colleagues discussing their pupils, academics taking part in a symposium), systems of dispositions (carried by 'natural persons') such as a linguistic competence and a cultural competence and, through these habitus, all the objective structures of which they are the product, structures which are active only when *embodied* in a competence acquired in the course of a particular history (with the different types of bilingualism or pronunciation, for example, stemming from different modes of acquisition)." (See *Outline* 81.) Burke prefigures such a view in his discussion of the "inferiority complex": "It is not merely an implied comparison between the self and another; it is a comparison between what I think I stand for and what I think the other stands for, in the terms of some *social* judgment" (*Rhetoric* 282).

47 *Outline* 2.

48 Giddens, *Constitution of Society* xxii–xxiii.

49 For a suggestive treatment of such activity in specific relation to *reading*, see Wadlington, *Reading Faulknerian Tragedy* 26–49.

50 See Bourdieu, *Outline* 81, cited above in note 32. Such a claim is convergent with Foucault's proposition that such traces of the past are not documents but monuments. Compare *Archaeology of Knowledge* 6–11.

51 *Constitution of Society* xxx.

52 Whigham, *Ambition and Privilege* 27–29.

53 Giddens, *Constitution of Society* xxviii. Wrightson's sense of local historicity is relevant: "If we are to explore further the social order of early modern England, then it seems to me that it is best explored at the vitally important local level. We need to know more about the range of variation in both local structures of stratification and local perceptions of the social order, about varying patterns of social relations and the conditions of their historical development in distinctive contexts. ... This is not just to advocate local

study for its own sake. The accumulation of detail can never be an end in itself. The thick context of local study, however, can do much to make concrete and accessible the abstractions and generalizations of historical interpretation if it is combined with a readiness to think anew in a manner which is theoretically informed without being imaginatively dependent." ("The Social Order of Early Modern England" 201–2.)

54 Montrose, *The Purpose of Playing: Shakespeare and the Cultural Politics of the Elizabethan Theater* (in press, University of Chicago Press).

55 For highly institutional examples of both such energies and the losses attendant upon their occlusion one ought to cite *The Norton Anthology of English Literature: Major Authors*. Marginal notes gloss *queinte* as "pudendum" (in *The Wife of Bath's Prologue*) and coilons as "testicles" (in *The Pardoner's Epilogue*).

56 I set aside the indeterminate possibility that Shakespeare wrote *Arden of Faversham* or *A Yorkshire Tragedy*, the latter published under his name (an attribution widely viewed as apocryphal).

1. FORCING DIVORCE IN *THE SPANISH TRAGEDY*

1 Two kinds of repetition mark this: the play's enormous recurrent popularity (in terms of editions, revivals, quotations, and caricatures), and its elaborate relation as analogue to so many later central works. The play was first performed in early 1592, twenty times that season (for the play and/or its putative first part), and revived in 1592–93, 1596–97; Jonson was paid for his additions in 1601 and 1602, and (as "Horace") was mocked by Dekker in *Satiromastix* for playing Hieronymo in a touring company; Edwards infers continued performance through 1615; there are ten early editions (1592, 1594, 1599, 1602, 1603, 1610, 1615, 1618, 1623, and 1633). (See Edwards edition lxvi–lxviii.) Boas lists numerous quotations, straight and comic: see Kyd, *Works* lxxviii–ciii.

2 See, for instance, its founding role in Bowers's *Elizabethan Revenge Tragedy*.

3 Edwards edition lii–liii. (This edition is cited throughout).

4 The shift from a Platonic to an Aristotelian view is especially striking on the tongue of a visitor from the afterlife. Also, for a different view see Barish, "*The Spanish Tragedy*, or The Pleasures and Perils of Rhetoric" 67.

5 The elder Hamlet has it both ways (he recalls his body lovingly too, almost narcissistically), but Kyd makes a choice here, in keeping with a generally critical posture of the play toward received pieties.

6 Wayne Rebhorn suggests to me privately that the martial associations of this highly figural name encode the double placement of Bel-imperia in the text, signaling her desire to rule herself by ruling others, as well as others' treatment of her as property. David Riggs comments further in a private communication that Bel-imperia, both as an empire in herself and the means to dynastic solidification of one, could not be possessed "in secret," as Andrea thinks; indeed, that it is he (and his double Horatio) who must undergo erasure from formal state knowledge, as impediments to the political and dynastic text that Bel-imperia and Balthazar are to write. The return of both men from the dead (Andrea at the outset as ghost, Horatio at

the close as unveiled corpse) is then an enclosing explosive return of the politically repressed.

7 Compare Webster's more detailed exploration of the transgressive wooing in *The Duchess of Malfi*. There we find similar fantasies, and a similar dangerous noble stoop; the necessary women's initiative; and similar gentlemen's discomforts, deriving from the tension between gender superiority and status inferiority. See Ch. 4 below.

8 For such problematizing discussions of *King Lear*, see Elliott, "The Initial Contrast in *Lear*"; Jaffa, "The Limits of Politics: *King Lear*, Act 1, Scene 1"; and most recently Strier, "Faithful Servants." Shapiro explores a related development, examining how the spectacle of *The Spanish Tragedy* came later, in a Caroline context, to figure a woman's ideological rebellion against cultural norms. He is concerned, however, with an identification between a Caroline woman and some of *Hieronymo's* actions; I will be focusing on effects having mainly to do with Bel-imperia. See "'Tragedies Naturally Performed'" 108–10.

9 Texts cited from *Statutes* (modernized throughout).

10 Lorenzo's status as heir apparent might have seemed too empowering if he were the king's son and direct heir. Maybe Kyd felt that the status insecurities Lorenzo feels regarding Andrea and Horatio would have been partially blocked, and so displaced Lorenzo's parentage laterally, inventing Castile, to weaken the pressure.

11 Bel-imperia might also be captured in eventual relation to Balthazar, via 33 Henry VIII c. 21 c. viii: if the king

> should take a fancy to any woman, of what estate, degree or condition soever she be, either subject or resident within his Dominions or Realms in way of Marriage, thinking and esteeming her a pure and clean maid, when in deed the proof may or after shall appear contrary ... and yet she nevertheless willingly do couple her self with her Sovereign Lord and King in marriage, without plain declaration before of her unchaste life unto his Majesty, ... then every such offense shall be deemed and adjudged High Treason.

This treason would probably be seen to occur with Bel-imperia's actual marriage to Balthazar, perhaps in reference to him as heir apparent of Portugal, certainly in respect of the king of Spain, who offers his blood, and guarantees it in and through her. The issue of guilty knowledge goes further. Anyone else with such knowledge, "hearing say by honest report ... that such a Woman being not chaste shall marry with her Sovereign Lord and King of this Realm, to the danger of his most Royal person and of his Succession," and not reporting it, "Such offense shall be taken and deemed misprision of high treason" (33 Henry VIII c. 21 c. ix).

12 I do not mean to suggest that the dynastic issue is not central. In 2.3 the King calls on Castile to manage Bel-imperia's resistance to Balthazar, lest the political match come to naught; and such resistance, though presented as personal, could never be solely that for one of Bel-imperia's rank. Indeed, Bel-imperia's rebellion is the more potent *given* her dynastic destiny: she means to disrupt both familial and political subjection. Nonetheless, the explicit *legal* discourse of treason, which would be so essentializing, criminalizing, for the audience, is not used.

Such hubris is recognized quite explicitly as treason in *The Broken Heart.* Ithocles pursues Calantha, "the princess, the king's daughter, / Sole heir of Sparta." When he injures his sister Penthea, he calls upon her in self-reproach (in typical Ford accents) to "revenge [herself] with bravery, and gossip / [His] treasons to the king's ears" (3.2.100–04).

13 The main statute on this crime is 25 Edward III st. 5 c. 2 (1352), the founding specification for all kinds of treason: "there is another manner of Treason, that is to say, when a Servant slayeth his Master, or a Wife her Husband, or when a Man secular or Religious slayeth his Prelate, to whom he oweth Faith and Obedience" (*Statutes*). The final phrase marks the defining status of the issue of authority. For a highly useful exploration of the crime see Dolan, "The Subordinate('s) Plot." Compare also the more literally murderous petty treason in *Arden of Faversham* below.

14 For a related examination of ideological rebellion, see Dolan, "Gender, Moral Agency, and Dramatic Form in *A Warning for Fair Women.*" Dolan grapples usefully with the uncertain status as petty treason of non-murderous acts (in this case, Anne Sanders's degree of guilt as an *accessory* to the murder of her husband). See esp. 210, 213.

15 *Outline* 35–36.

16 Slater, *Family Life* 60.

17 Harris, "Power, Profit, and Passion" 60–61. For a similar definition see Houlbrooke, *The English Family 1450–1700*: "A suitable marriage, especially among the propertied classes, was one which gave the individual and those closest to him potentially useful new kinsmen, and increased the number of people through whom favours might be sought and advancement achieved" (73–74). "In practice," Houlbrooke judges, "matches ranged across a wide spectrum which ran from the arranged at one end to the completely free at the other. The degree of freedom allowed the individual depended among other things upon his or her sex, prospects of inheritance and social rank" (69). Bel-imperia is, by all three of these measures, maximally restricted in her actions.

18 Lévi-Strauss, *The Elementary Structures of Kinship*; Rubin, "The Traffic in Women." See also Sedgwick, *Between Men.*

19 *Women Beware Women* 4.1.32. Middleton's Bianca suggests that such thoughts are begotten by the very restraint meant to guard against them. For a fascinating discussion of how wandering and error get gendered, see Parker, "The Metaphorical Plot," in *Literary Fat Ladies* 36–53.

20 See Therbörn, *The Ideology of Power* 17. As has often been noted, oppressed roles have their own quite genuine and effective satisfactions, even as those satisfactions function to pacify incipient resistances. Shirley Ardener observes, for instance, in her influential study "The Nature of Women in Society," that members of what she calls muted groups

> may . . . come to an accommodation with the social structure in which they are placed, and find their own satisfactions in its interstices. Their alternative systems of value, which may be rich and complex, should be respected, and should receive greater attention than they sometimes do. . . . [I]nstead of ignoring the dominant group, or of merely tolerating its demands, [they] may go even further and accept the

burden of maintaining or 'policing' a system which to onlookers appears to disadvantage them....

Rewards for such rule enforcement often result, both abstract and tangible. (See Ardener's introduction to *Defining Females* 28.)

21 Slater, *Family Life* 142–43.

22 Rehearsing various tales of parental authority, marital selection, and changing rationales, Stone describes the veto as "a concession which by then [in the case at hand, ca. 1639] had been generally made by most parents." His series of examples is meant to illustrate "the transitional pattern of marriage among the early seventeenth-century English landed classes as they moved uneasily between one set of values based on kin interest and marriage arranged by others with a view to financial advantage, and another set based on allowing children a right of veto in order to provide a better chance of marital harmony." Under the influence of Protestant notions of the moral force of personal choice in holy matrimony, Stone argues,

> ... it was therefore thought necessary to concede to the children the right of veto, the right to reject a spouse chosen by the parents on the grounds that the antipathy aroused by a single interview was too great to permit the possibility of the future development of affection. This right of veto could only be used with caution and probably only once, or at most twice, while for women there was always the risk that its exercise might condemn them to spinsterhood, if their parents failed to provide another suitor.

(See *The Family, Sex and Marriage* 187, 189, 190.)

23 See Dekker, Ford, and Rowley, *The Witch of Edmonton* 2.2.56–58.

24 Compare Slater's discussion of Mary, Lady Verney, wife to Sir Ralph, as one wife who appears to have so invested herself (*Family Life* 64–73).

25 As a condition of submitting to her brother's dynastic plan to marry her to the old and ailing Louis XII of France, Mary extorted from Henry the right to choose a second husband on her own, without interference, when her first should die. The terms of this agreement lead Harris to conclude that "Mary's bargain with her brother shows that she rejected the definition of marriage that dominated discourse and practice at the top of the social and political hierarchy and that she resented being used as an asset to advance the interests of the Tudor dynasty" ("Power, Profit, and Passion" 64).

26 For similar explorations of brotherly authority over sisters' marriages, compare the Ithocles–Penthea and Orgilus–Euphrania relations in Ford's *Broken Heart*.

27 Stone, "Social Mobility in England, 1500–1700" 17–21. Kyd's own placement (similar to Horatio's) as the son of a scrivener is also relevant.

  Consider also the ballad of 1599 derived from *The Spanish Tragedy*: in this song, sung in first person by Hieronymo, we learn that he "wonne great honour in the fielde" (14). Here Hieronymo too has been a star soldier; Horatio is a second-generation gentleman warrior who might well have followed his father's later career in law enforcement and state service. Though the ballad is presumably by another hand, the fact that its author thought this an appropriate elaboration of Hieronymo's career speaks to contemporary perceptions of his social character. (The ballad first appeared in 1599; there were seven printings by 1638. See "*The Spanish Tragedy*:

Containing the Lamentable Murders of Horatio and Bellimperia with the Pittiful Death of Old Hieronimo," in Kyd, *Works* 343–47; see also xcvii.)

28 See Mulryne's note to 2.1.11–18.

29 Quoted by Hurstfield, in *The Queen's Wards* 257, from Peck's *Desiderata Curiosa*, i, 64–65. Hurstfield also cites an alternative version: "marry thy children in haste lest they marry themselves" (143). If "children" is less gender-specific than "daughters," "haste" is more anxious than "time."

30 These proverbs clearly exhibit the dual project of social and marital control that strives both to *compel* and to *contain* children's love, toward and away from various objects. (That is to say, Balthazar and Andrea/Horatio are *linguistically institutionalized* loci of concern.) Wielded by children, these proverbs can defy parental control. On a parent's lips, they can help render tolerable those children's frustrations of parental desire. (These among other uses, no doubt, in accordance with Kenneth Burke's understanding of the form in "Literature as Equipment for Living.")

31 Such controlling could also, of course, infuriate males subjected to it, and drive them to rage and rebellion, as we shall see below: this action is the core of *The Miseries of Enforced Marriage*.

32 Younger brothers were much less likely to experience coming of age as a liberation of will, since it often signaled not a departure from familial dependency but an embarkation upon unsponsored and penurious adulthood.

Certain aspects of my treatment of Bel-imperia have been anticipated generally by Spriet, "Antisocial Behavior and the Code of Love in Kyd's *Spanish Tragedy*." He sees her love as a rebellion against family and state (4).

33 See Barish's appreciation in "*The Spanish Tragedy*, or The Pleasures and Perils of Rhetoric" 66.

34 It is true, of course, as Richard Strier reminds me in a personal communication, that the famous sequences of Petrarch and Sidney end in male failure. But I refer here to the sonnet discourse's indefatigable self-renewal, to sonneteers' happy incapacity to take their rejections seriously. This is to focus on sonnet process rather than on any sequence resolution, itself a rare quantity, if present at all. (Indeed, Sidney's sonnets 70 and following explore the insufficiency of experiences of resolution.) I would argue that the principal attribute of the form is undeterred repetition, that endlessly achieves confident satisfaction in devouring resistance as unserious, even merely formal. This is the confidence I hear in Lorenzo's use of Watson, perhaps more typical of petrarchan rather than Petrarch's sonnets, the form by the 1590s more English and less transcendental than the Italian original. For a related view see Jones and Stallybrass, "The Politics of *Astrophil and Stella*": "although the lover depicts himself as humble suitor to a dominating lady, he actually performs an act of public mastery, demonstrating his virtuosity in the practice of a masculine convention" (54).

35 The expressions were of course common. For a list of analogies see Forsyth, "Notes on *The Spanish Tragedy*" 78–84.

36 See Lewis, *The Allegory of Love* Appendix II, 364–66, for a discussion of the history of this complex word's erotic context.

37 In *Much Ado about Nothing* (at 1.1.250) Don Pedro repeats the line to
   predict that Benedick will eventually love, aligning gender in the traditional
   way, between bull and human male. Benedick denies it, as precisely
   constituting cuckoldry, the alternative form of subjection to women.
38 See, for instance, *The Faerie Queene* 2.8.42, 6.5.19, 6.6.27, 6.7.47. (Bel-
   imperia certainly feels herself to be surrounded.) In a related instance, Furor,
   a frantic mighty man without self-governance, is compared to "a blindfold
   Bull [who] at randon fares, / And where he hits, nought knowes, and whom
   he hurts, nought cares" (2.4.7.8–9). There may also be a link to Jove's rape
   of Europa.
39 In *The Woman's Prize, or The Tamer Tamed* (his sequel to *The Taming of
   the Shrew*, which Chambers dates 1604), Fletcher writes thus of Maria,
   Petruchio's second wife: "The free Haggard / (Which is that woman that
   hath wing, and knowes it, / Spirit and plume)" (1.2.149–51); cited from
   Bowers edition, vol. 4.
40 Tilley notes proverbial versions of these metaphors of bull (T303), hawk
   (T298), and oak (T304), all speaking of eventual submission of the will. For
   a congruent dialogue regarding such double reference, about "wild" and
   "tame" in Wyatt's "Whoso List to Hunt" and "They Flee from Me," see
   Stephen Greenblatt, *Renaissance Self-Fashioning* 150–53, and Fowler's resistant review, "Power to the Self."
41 Compare Auden's paraphrase of the practical joker's fantasy utterance:
   " 'You thought you were all-powerful and untouchable and could injure me
   with impunity. Now you see that you were wrong. Perhaps you have
   forgotten what you did; let me have the pleasure of reminding you' " ("The
   Joker in the Pack" 250).
42 One might also adduce Chaucer's equally sexual but softer image of April's
   "showres soote [sweet]" piercing the drought of March to the root and
   beginning *The Canterbury Tales*; Chaucer's engendering is also much
   stronger than the Watson image. Chaucer and Spenser are writing of
   beginnings, while Watson dreams of a success at long last, which might
   justify enervation. It is, in any case, Kyd's highly programmatic choice to
   position pugnacity and flaccidity as he does.
43 Watson, *The Hecatompathia or Passionate Century of Love* 83. Watson's
   sequence, like *The Shepheardes Calender*, is elaborately annotated, its
   relations to continental forebears indexed; though Spenser's inferior,
   Watson still seems to me more interesting than has been thought.
44 It is interesting to wonder whether yokes are for (stiff-necked? stiff?) males,
   bridles (being oral?) for females. Interesting work has been done on such
   bridling of late: see Wayne's study of the silencing bridle for women (the
   "brank"), in "Refashioning the Shrew"; Underdown, "The Taming of the
   Scold"; Fraser, *The Weaker Vessel* 103–4 and the illustration following 112;
   Parker, *Literary Fat Ladies* 26–31; and Boose, "Scolding Brides and Bridling
   Scolds."
45 Joseph Hall, *Virgidemiarum*, 1.3.9–12, in *Poems* 14.
46 See Burke, *Grammar* 21–58.
47 For a related metaphor of vegetable and sexual rising see *The First Part of
   Hieronymo* i.75–77. When Andrea departs to Portugal as ambassador,

Horatio comforts Bel-imperia with this piece of advice: "Madam, in this circle / Let your heart move; / Honor'd promotion is the sap of love." One sort of rising begets another. Likewise, one kind of dying begets another. The most potent replay of this familiar trope occurs when Horatio dies in 2.4, discussed below.

48 John Rumrich fascinatingly suggests to me a strong intertextuality linking this motif in Kyd, the May–January match in Chaucer's *Merchant's Tale*, and Pluto and Proserpine, who preside over both texts. Both May and Proserpine (to use Kyd's spelling) are types of enforced and inappropriate marriage, though coded in terms of age rather than rank, and with their mates of course also figure winter and spring, barren miserliness and fertility. The eventual exposure of May to January in the garden, having sex in a tree with a young squire while her husband watches from below, strikingly prefigures the different arrangement of the same details in Hieronymo's garden in 2.4, where Bel-imperia and Horatio have sex while watched from above by her brother and Balthazar, who then hang and stab Horatio in a tree. January is initially blind, but is given his sight for this event by a sympathetic Pluto; an equally sympathetic Proserpine gives May a magic power of denial, with which to hide in plain sight. Such supervisions certainly seem to raise issues linked to Kyd's.

49 Regarding which interrogations, we would do well to recall that Kyd was Marlowe's roommate (or office-mate), perhaps well acquainted on his own with corrosive interrogations of piety. For a thoughtful general discussion regarding Kyd's interest in causations, see Edwards, *Thomas Kyd and Early Elizabethan Tragedy* 27–28.

50 In 1956 Empson proposed that Lorenzo and Balthazar arranged Don Andrea's *murder* on the battlefield. His argument has not found favor: the obliqueness of the evidence necessitates a Bradley-esque intricacy of supposition. But many of the play's characters behave as if Lorenzo and Balthazar murdered Don Andrea, and the idea gives additional force both to the general parallel between Bel-imperia's lovers and their entitlements to revenge. It is an attractive hypothesis.

51 This desire is perhaps to be distinguished from the similar desire to flout or defy, a posture fundamentally public and confrontational. More will be said below about pleasures and powers attendant upon secret knowledge; here we may briefly imagine a secret defiance that derives an additional sadistic piquancy from calmly and smilingly duping one's "guardians."

52 See Ridley, *Statesman and Saint* 283–84. I have recently been told, however, that for at least sixty or so years my family kept the razor with which my great-grandfather killed himself. Relics of the body seem still to have enormous powers.

53 *OED* specifies as follows: sb. 7a: "Something given as a mark of favour; *esp.* a gift such as a knot of ribbons, a glove, etc., given to a lover, or in medieval chivalry by a lady to her knight, to be worn conspicuously as a token of affection," and sb. 7b: "A ribbon, cockade, or the like, worn at a ceremony, e.g. *a bride's, coronation, wedding favour*, in evidence of goodwill; also, a similar decoration worn as a party-badge."

For girdles compare *Sir Gawain and the Green Knight* (and Friedman and

Osberg, "Gawain's Girdle as Traditional Symbol"), and, more recently, the talismanic garter belt in the film *Bull Durham*, which conferred athletic potency on its male wearer. For gloves see Horatio below (1.4.99sd), and the famous incident with DeFlores in *The Changeling* at 1.1.228–40. For handkerchiefs see Boose, "Othello's Handkerchief." Also consider the favor as an individual version of the livery badge of allegiance and identity; see Whigham, "Elizabethan Aristocratic Insignia" 352–53.

54 This anonymous play from 1605 presents the events that led up to those of Kyd's text. Its modern editor, ascribing it to Kyd, argues that it is a "memorial reconstruction" of a lost "Spanish Comedy" mentioned by Henslowe, supposedly the first half of a two-part Kyd play that closes with *The Spanish Tragedy* (Cairncross xii–xxi).

55 See Jensen, "Kyd's *Spanish Tragedy*: The Play Explains Itself" 13–14. In a related extension, Herbert Coursen, one of few readers to respond to Empson, speculates that the scarf might have made Andrea a marked man on the battlefield; see "The Unity of *The Spanish Tragedy*" 772. For a more distant, historical parallel consider the relics of catholic martyrs: John Bellamy notes that "in the later years of Elizabeth, with the execution of many catholic priests, there arose a desire among co-religionists to have some memento of the victims, a feature of execution not noticeable previously, although bystanders were reputed to have dipped their hand-kerchiefs in Sir Thomas Wyatt's blood." Bellamy then cites various examples of witnesses taking (or being prevented from taking, by the authorities) articles of blood-stained clothing from the dead bodies of such victims. See *Tudor Law of Treason* 208.

56 Note to 60–68 in Mulryne's edition.

57 Even if Don Andrea was not murdered, their intervention in some form (some meaning of "thrust him forth my father's way" at 3.10.59) is a narrative fact of the play.

58 For a related treatment of revenge, see the fine essay by Sacks, who suggests that "revenge is a crucial marshaling of anger . . . an action in which the survivor assumes *for himself* the power that has bereaved him" ("When Words Prevail Not" 579). Three situations of pause or blockage seem relevant here: (1) "But how can love find harbour in my breast," Bel-imperia says, "Till I revenge the death of my beloved?" (1.2.64–65); (2) Andrea's inability to cross the stream of Acheron until his funeral rites are done (1.1.20ff.); and (3) Hieronymo's inability to rest until he has avenged Horatio's death (2.5.51ff.). In each of these cases an act of homage to another enables the completion of the work of mourning and allows one party to secure for the self some power derived from the loved one. Perhaps there is also a vicarious link with the self-conceiving mechanism of *nemo me impune lacessit*: "no one harms my loved one with impunity," as it were. Thus events that require revenge may be defined as challenges to one's own core identity, a formulation that allows us to see Lorenzo's actions as likewise avenging. Revenge is conceivable not only as sweet, but as purifying and self-restoring.

59 Harris, "Power, Profit, and Passion" 77.

60 Meaning, as is the standard early modern usage, "that group of influential

advisors who usually included most of the senior members of the kin." See Stone, *The Family, Sex and Marriage* 5. The king uses the term thus at 2.3.43.

61 Can Bel-imperia also be alluding to her brother, entering with Balthazar, as murderer here?

62 The referent of this unredeemability may also be seen in Mary Tudor's story. Once her aged husband Louis XII died, Mary again became a commodity on the European marriage market. Harris notes that her attraction was much enhanced "because rumors were circulating that she was still a virgin" (72). That such a "condition" counted as a natural repository for continent-wide fascination and desire marks the preciousness of what Bel-imperia consciously destroys.

63 See Deuteronomy 25.5–6: "If brethren dwell together, and one of them die, and have no child, the wife of the dead shall not marry without unto a stranger: her husband's brother shall go in to her, and take her to him to wife, and perform the duty of an husband's brother unto her. And it shall be, that the first-born which she beareth shall succeed in the name of his brother which is dead, that his name be not put out of Israel." Such a construction of erotic filial duty certainly resembles the analogous case of Andrea and Horatio, marked by similar elements of bonding, loving obligation, and female identification. Further specificity is possible: according to Alan Unterman, "the Kabbalists saw a child born from a levirate marriage as a reincarnation of the dead brother, thus providing a *tikkun* [rectification] for his restless soul . . . ." (See Unterman 120.) Horatio's survivor duties toward his friend may extend past rescue and burial of the corpse to erotic substitution. Bel-imperia may further absorb some of this dutiful energy by affiliation, though whether by contiguity or substitution is not altogether clear: cf. "But how can love find harbour in my breast, / Till I revenge the death of my beloved" (1.4.64–65). See the discussion of this soliloquy below. (Thanks to John Rumrich for the Kabbala link.)

64 For detailed treatment see Scarisbrick, *Henry VIII*, ch. 7. For a more general historical summary of such matters see Wolfram, *In-Laws and Outlaws*, ch. 2.

65 Perhaps it is relevant that *The First Part of Hieronymo* specifies such an age-relationship between the two young men: when Hieronymo nominates Andrea as ambassador to Portugal, the king approves the choice but adds, "I'd rather choose Horatio were he not so young" (i.61).

66 Compare also Mallin's discussion of Aeneas' challenge to the Trojans in "Emulous Factions and the Collapse of Chivalry" 158–65.

67 See, for instance, Mehl, *The Elizabethan Dumb Show* 65.

68 One measure of Bel-imperia's double bind is that Mulryne condemns her for calculation, Lorenzo for being swept away: either way her will is corrupted.

For a thoughtful reading of this speech in rhetorical terms, as a failure, see Barish, "*The Spanish Tragedy*, or The Pleasures and Perils of Rhetoric" 74–75.

69 See Stone, "Social Mobility" 34–35. The phrase "Don Horatio, our Knight Marshal's son" takes on something of the feel of a Homeric formula, being used repeatedly *verbatim*. (See 1.1.25, 1.2.76, especially 2.1.79, and 2.3.36.)

The specification of both father (genealogy) and father's occupation (achieved, not ascribed status) is quite an appropriate way to mark Horatio thematically.

70 The stage direction after 2.2.6 is obscure: "Pedringano showeth all to the Prince and Lorenzo, placing them in secret." Are the viewers present from the beginning of the scene (are they shown "all"), or do they enter here, and miss the first six lines?

71 See Allen, "On *Venus and Adonis*," on the hard and soft hunts.

72 Andrea's mistake was first noted as such, so far as I know, by Edwards, in *Thomas Kyd and Early Elizabethan Tragedy* 27–28.

73 This scene provides an antidote to Martin Wiggins's assumption that Lorenzo "lacks overtly political motivation" for his actions (*Journeymen In Murder* 53). The royal family is explicitly concerned throughout with Bel-imperia's dynastic political utility.

74 Quoted from *The Shorter Poems of Edmund Spenser* 674–75: ll. 315, 319–22.

75 Is it considering too curiously to hear behind Pedringano's word "match" (13) the more usual locus of marriage, reminding us by this implicit contrast of precisely what Bel-imperia is *not* doing? Compare Fish, *Surprised by Sin* 93–94.

76 I owe this astute observation to Eric Mallin.

77 Perhaps Horatio's mystified shock can be read back from Shakespeare's possible quotation of it in *The Comedy of Errors*: captured as a madman by servants acting at Adriana's request and Pinch's advice, Antipholus of Ephesus likewise cries, "What, will you murder me?" (4.4.109).

78 For debate regarding the order of the hanging and stabbing (in performance), see the exchange between Schaar and James Smith in *ES*.

79 Or should we say he *accepts* her from her brother, whose first words are, "My lord, away with her, take her aside" (2.4.51)? Is this, coupled with the initial erotic expectation of the spectacle, and the closing "Stop her mouth" (2.4.63), perhaps evidence for a parody of a wedding ceremony here?

80 I take pleasure in acknowledging the influence here of a fine unpublished essay from 1983 by Christopher Highley, on Lorenzo's habits of self-isolation.

81 Burke, *Rhetoric* 284. Burke is concerned here with the articulation of his fascinating concept of "pure persuasion," but he quite actively does not replace the sexual or political with the formal: see, for instance, 285:

> Both psychoanalytic and institutional accounts [of erotic aberration] indicate important sources of pressure for the *animus* behind a given expression. Resources of classification, of abstraction, of comparison and contrast, of merger and division, of derivation, and the like, may characterize the thinking of man *generically*, over and above the nature of his social or personal problems. But his social and personal problems provide the incentive for the particular emphases of his expressions. You are not finished when you have analyzed the formal or dialectical devices implicit, say, in a doctrine of "white supremacy." The "pure persuasion" of the form is frail indeed, as compared with its localized rhetorical application. Psychoanalytic and institutional criticism is needed, to reveal the doctrine's nature as a "scapegoat mechanism" for flattering a sick psyche by proclaiming the categorical superiority of one's "kind," and by organizing modes

of injustice that are morbidly considered advantageous to the conspirators as a class.

82 Are similar substitutions at work in King Harry's iron-age approbation of Bardolph's later hanging? "We would have all such offenders so cut off" (*Henry V* 3.6.107)? (Bardolph's desires of course figure Falstaff's.)

83 For evidence that marionettes (stringed puppets, sometimes also called *fantoccini*) were known in early modern England, and thus that Lorenzo could originally and, as it were, "literally" have been seen here in 2.4 as a puppeteer (pulling strings), see the chapter on puppets in England in "Yorick" (pseudonym of P. C. Ferrigni), *La Storia dei Burattini* 287–310 (esp. 287–97 for Elizabethan and Jacobean materials). For the history of marionettes in early modern Europe generally, see Magnin, *Histoire des Marionettes en Europe*, Chesnais, *Histoire Générale des Marionettes*. For an early reference see Girolamo Cardano's account of seeing them, in ch. 63 of *De Varietate Rerum* (1557), quoted and discussed in Yorick, *La Storia dei Burattini* 104–7. I owe special thanks to Jackson I. Cope for these references.

84 The idiom of masters calling servants masters is itself noteworthy. Perhaps ironic in Lorenzo's mouth, the expression might also, perhaps more generally, function as a *noblesse oblige* lubricant. Consider also the practice of calling small boys "master" instead of "mister." A complex range of tones was no doubt possible.

85 For a repetition of the joke, see Marston's *The Malcontent*: "MENDOZA I'll hoist ye, ye shall mount. / MALEVOLE To the gallows, say ye?" (4.3.81–82).

86 For another correlation of sexual arousal with elevation, see Spenser, *The Faerie Queene* 3.10.48 (the culmination of the tale of Malbecco, Hellenore, and the Satyres):

> At night, when all they went to sleepe, he vewd,
> Whereas his louely wife emongst them lay,
> Embraced of a *Satyre* rough and rude,
> Who all the night did mind his ioyous play:
> Nine times he heard him come aloft ere day . . .

87 David Willbern has partially anticipated the sexual aspect of my reading here, in "Thomas Kyd's *The Spanish Tragedy*." There he reads Lorenzo's sarcasm as a reference to the hanged man's literal (penile) erection, both "high" and "dead" (251), and furthermore suggests later that the professional Hangman's topping of Pedringano's overtly upreared defiant humor is a figurative castration (258).

88 Once again Mary Tudor provides a parallel. After forcing her marriage upon Suffolk by threats, she strives to protect him from her brother's legendary wrath by taking the responsibility herself. Suffolk's own self-abnegation to Henry took the most abject forms; Mary took another tack:

> Unlike Suffolk, she tried to justify their action by explaining the fears and rumors that had motivated them. She was particularly concerned to exculpate her husband, who was in far greater danger than she, and assumed responsibility through a detailed account of her ultimatum. Although she referred to herself as "your most sorrowful sister," she "humbly required" rather than "begged for" compassion, a choice of words that explicitly avoided the abject and desperate quality of Suffolk's pleas to the king (Harris, "Power, Profit and Passion" 81).

Also like Bel-imperia, Mary was unsuccessful. Wolsey wrote another letter for her to sign, containing "her undertaking to give Henry her whole dowry and trousseau, the plate and jewels she had from Louis, and as much of her dower as he wanted. Throughout, Mary 'beseeched' rather than 'required'" (ibid. 82). This time it worked.

89 For another view of Kent, see Strier, "Faithful Servants."

90 See Stone, "Social Mobility": "The most fundamental dichotomy within the society was between the gentleman and the non-gentleman, a division that was based essentially upon the distinction between those who did, and those who did not, have to work with their hands" (17); see also Stone, *The Crisis of the Aristocracy*, for a full account; for a brief summary of some relevant links between the dissolution and increased social mobility into the ruling elite, see Whigham, *Ambition and Privilege* 6–18. Note that this amounts to arousing and using Pedringano's class fantasy as a means to block Horatio's.

91 The enclosed, retentive logic of Lorenzo's position is familiar as the machiavel's norm; its other, outward face, equally machiavellian, is intrusiveness. We can see the interanimating dialectic simply put in the tones used by Avarice to Homicide in Yarrington's *Two Lamentable Tragedies* (1601): "Thou seemes to be a bold audatious knave, / I doe not like intruding companie, / That seeke to undermine my secrecie" (sig. A2v). The presuppositions of this dialectic (on which Lorenzo's manipulation of Pedringano here is founded) have been studied by Goffman: "Although one social relationship requires keeping away from a particular personal preserve, another relation will license and even oblige its penetration. All of these penetrative acts through which some persons are shown support are acts, which, if performed to other persons, would violate them" (*Relations in Public* 64). For a suggestive example from della Casa's Galateo, see Whigham, *Ambition and Privilege* 183.

92 Cf. the frequent criterial label of a worthy but ungentle man being seen as "a Gentlemans companion, of good reputation and calling" (see Taylor, "The Unnatural Father" 137).

93 Iago behaves likewise with Roderigo, but does not have the trope of the superior's self-gift to work with, that Lorenzo makes so much of.

94 Michael Levin offers a general psychologistic account of Lorenzo's posture without placing him in relation to the specifics of Elizabethan social divisions: he has "a colossal vanity which demands continual proof of his superiority to mankind as a whole" ("'Vindicta mihi!'" 314).
    For the young George Herbert's deployment of this trope, compare Strier, "Sanctifying the Aristocracy" 55–56.

95 Compare *Macbeth* 1.7.46.

96 Compare *Macbeth* 3.6.5, 7.

97 Those, anyway, of those he would exploit: Balthazar's supposed ecstasies in 2.1 irritated him in the extreme, presumably because they occurred on Lorenzo's side of the equation, in an ally.

98 Compare, on this issue of self-isolation, Braden's fascinating examination of the logic of stoic thinking (especially regarding the refusal of vulnerability) as it appears in Elizabethan tragedies (including this one), in *Renaissance Tragedy and the Senecan Tradition*.

99 Is this enjoined combination of secrecy and knowing boldness a forerunner of the "ambiguous giving out," which Hamlet proscribes for his partly-informed mates on the battlements at 1.5.187?

100 Auden, "The Joker in the Pack" 255. Compare the related question as to whether the Duke Ferdinand observes his sister's tortures at the hands of his agent Bosola in *The Duchess of Malfi*. See Ch. 4 below.

101 For a contemporary analogue to this aestheticized action see Thomas Rogers, *Leicester's Ghost* (1602–04), in which the dead earl comes from the grave to tell his story:

> My servant Gates did speed as ill or worse,
> To whome I did my close intents impart
> And at his neede, with mony stuft his purse
> And will'd him still take curradge to his harte:
> Yet in the end he felt the deadly smarte . . .

> Of pardon I did put him still in hope
> When he of fellony was guiltie found,
> And doe condemn'd, till his last freind, the rope,
> Did him vphold from falling to the ground. . . .

> . . . all future mischeife to preuent,
> I let him slipp away with my consent:
>   For his repriuall, like a crafty fox,
>   I sent noe pardon, but an emptie box.   (778–82, 785–88, 795–98)

Fredson Bowers reasonably identifies Rogers's presentation as a direct recollection of Pedringano's death-scene. Rogers altered the narrative from that in the presumed source, the so-called *Leicester's Commonwealth* (1584), by adding the detail of the empty box. The link may also work in the opposite direction, for according to the earlier text the "Privado" Gates (as the *Commonwealth* terms him) made a relation of Leicester's evil deeds, which its current holder, one "H," will release "when so ever it shall please God so to dispose of her Majesties heart, as to lend an indifferent eare, as well to [Leicester's] accusers, as to himselfe, in judgement." If Kyd gave Rogers the detail of the box, the *Commonwealth* might have offered Kyd the detail of Pedringano's posthumous letter of discovery. For Bowers see "Kyd's Pedringano" 248–49. Rogers is cited from Franklin B. Williams, Jr.'s edition, *Leicester's Commonwealth* from Burgoyne's edition (71, 74).

Wiggins usefully notes (*Journeymen in Murder* 106) another piece of evidence that the Pedringano death-trick became a trope: in 1610 Robert Daborne referred to *The Spanish Tragedy* as "the play of *Pedringano*," in A *Christian Turned Turk*. Ending a long line of intrigue, one character subjugates another thus:

> RABSHAKE . . . Do you not laugh? Have you not gulled the world fairly?
> JEW Thou hast mistaken me; know thou art all my care.
> RABSHAKE And you would be rid of me, I conceive you sir, though I am no politician: I have seen the play of Pedringano sir, of Pedringano sir.   (2070–75)

102 For a meditation on Pedringano's execution, Hieronymo's play, and the dramatistic interpenetrations of theatrical and state executions, see Shapiro, " 'Tragedies Naturally Performed' " 99–113.

103 Mehl notes that Hieronymo is well situated for this particular option, since he has throughout played something of the role of Master of Revels to the Spanish court; see *The Elizabethan Dumb Show* 67.
104 Given the coincidence of the arrival of the Portuguese Viceroy at 3.14 and the announcement of the betrothal of Bel-imperia and Balthazar at 3.14.14–16, Hieronymo's play, "the first night's sport" (4.1.64) for the embassy, is in effect meant to celebrate the betrothal. Compare Willbern, "Thomas Kyd's *The Spanish Tragedy*" 261.
105 This is the second book Hieronymo is seen with; the first is (widely assumed to be) his Seneca in 3.13. Given Erasmus' famous punning usage of *enchiridion* (hand-tool, hand-weapon) to entitle his pocket-sized *Handbook of the Christian Soldier*, one may wonder if Hieronymo's student play from Toledo, a weapon conveniently ready to hand, lies somewhere behind Othello's unseen hidden sword, of "the ice-brook's temper" (5.2.262). Toledo was world-famous for swords, tempered in snow-broth mountain brooks.
106 Again, a female winter nips blossoms. One might also explore a reading of Isabella's suicide in dual terms, of the existential notion of suicide as an assertion of being, and of the common Renaissance view that suicide was the appropriate response for women to sexual invasion and the loss of some version of official reason for being. (Can the murder of a child function for mothers as rape does for maids?) In cases like Lucrece's the act counts as a kind of oath; here it is close to that, a curse. Both as curse and as violent "I am," Isabella's act parallels Bel-imperia's to some degree, though directed self-containingly at herself, as is common with such protocols.
107 Barish, "*The Spanish Tragedy*, or The Pleasures and Perils of Rhetoric" 82.
108 As a practical joke we might compare the page's empty box to Hieronymo's empty mouth: no pardon or other relief is forthcoming.
109 For a reading of Hieronymo's silence in terms of the repressed reference of emergent essentialist humanism, see Belsey, *The Subject of Tragedy* 75–78.
110 Edwards, "Shakespeare and Kyd" 152. For a related reading of interest, see Aggeler, "The Eschatological Crux in *The Spanish Tragedy*."
111 Hunter, "Ironies of Justice" 93.
112 See the letter of dedication to Kyd's *Cornelia*, addressed to the Countess of Sussex (Kyd, *Works* 102).

2. HUNGER AND PAIN IN *ARDEN OF FAVERSHAM*

1 Martin Wiggins provides a quantitative measure of this emphasis, noting that Black Will speaks 270 lines, fewer only than the three principals Arden, Alice, and Mosby. By comparison, Pedringano has only 95 lines, Lorenzo indeed only 330. See *Journeymen In Murder* 62.
2 Dolan discusses a related usage of "shifting" to denote women's maneuvering within the confines of subsumptive marriage, taken from T. E.'s encyclopedia *The Lawes Resolutions of Womens Rights* (1632). See "Home-Rebels and House-Traitors" 1–31; for shifting see 6.
3 I cite throughout from Martin White's edition.
4 Stone's *The Family, Sex, and Marriage* triggered the debate, arguing that

social and demographic matters tended to create families in which individual emotional bonding was much attenuated, compared to modern norms. Miriam Slater's *Family Life* elaborated Stone's arguments. For the opposite point of view see important reviews of Stone by E. P. Thompson (*New Society* 8 [1977]: 499–501), and Alan Macfarlane (*History and Theory* 18 [1979]: 103–26) and the debate between Slater and Sara Heller Mendelson in *P&P* 85 (1979): 126–40.

In a related critical gesture, given another sense of "suffering," Dolan sees Arden as a "suffering" recipient, an object of action rather than an agent: "While Holinshed gives Arden his own agenda, a master's plot driven by acquisitiveness and ambition, the play suppresses that possible plot and the agency it would confer on Arden and instead plays out the multiple plots of the multiple subordinates." This view reads Arden as structurally (rather than emotionally) evacuated, a figure who simply "holds the place that stands for privilege and power, the place for which his subordinates compete." I read the passivity, at least in part, as *full, exhibiting suffering*, rather than as *empty because passive*. Dolan wonders why Arden "tolerates an adultery he suspects"; I think such "tolerance" is problematic only if defined dialectically with the enraged self-projection supposedly obligatory for early modern English husbands. I think Arden suffers rather than tolerates his wife's infidelity. Part of the author's experiment here is the exploration of this privatized response. See Dolan, "The Subordinate('s) Plot" 317–40; passages cited from 330.

Elsewhere Dolan argues richly for an "economy of marital subjectivity" for agency-filled *wives* (in the cases she examines, murderous, petty-treasonous ones) in early modern England. This capacity was only barely imaginable, under two preconditions: first, that the wife be seen in violence (resisting husbandly subsumption), and second, that her agency was necessarily, dialectically, coextensive with an evacuation of the husband's agency, in zero-sum-game fashion. Such a view provides yet another way to understand Arden's relative recession in his own play. For this argument see "Home-Rebels and House-Traitors" 10–15.

I wish here to acknowledge a general debt to Dolan's thoughtful analyses, in these essays and in "Gender, Moral Agency, and Dramatic Form in *A Warning for Fair Women*."

5 *OED* presents three meanings of *botcher*: (1) a mender, repairer, or patcher; (2) a cobbler; (3) one who does a thing bunglingly. The condescending sense here probably emphasizes the poorer end of the spectrum. White cites Johnson's *Dictionary*: "A mender of old clothes; the same to a tailor as a cobbler to a shoemaker."

6 For evidence that this public interest continued as late as 1633, see *Arden of Faversham*, ed. Wine xlvi. References to the supplementary materials in this edition (hereafter Wine) appear in the text.

7 See Stone, "Social Mobility in England," and *The Crisis of the Aristocracy passim*.

8 For detailed studies see, for instance, Warnicke, *The Rise and Fall of Anne Boleyn*; and Harris, "Power, Profit, and Passion."

9 For more on the relation between play and sources, see Lieblein, "The

Context of Murder" 183–86, and Orlin, "Man's House" (an especially rich exploration).

10 This critical explanation for the invention of "Clifford" was first offered in modern times by Lionel Cust, C.V.O., Litt.D., F.S.A., in "Arden of Feversham" 114. However, the ballad of 1633 (seemingly based on the play) puts the general attitude in Alice's own mouth: "to my friends and kindred all a shame, / Blotting their blood by my unhappy name" (Wine 164).

11 Frances Bushby, *Three Men of the Tudor Time*: for Roger see 121–23, 124–45; for Thomas see 190–91; for death dates see 168–69, 191.

12 Cust, "Arden of Feversham" 102.

13 Holinshed's *Chronicles of England, Scotland, and Ireland* (1587), quoted in Wine 148–49.

14 Harley MSS. 542, ff. 34–37B: "The history of a most horible murder comytyd at ffevershame in Kent." See Wine xli–xliii, and footnotes in his Appendix II.

15 Perhaps such behavior is cognate with the increase in financially motivated aristocratic marriage downward into the mercantile classes. The difference between selling wives and selling children is important but not utterly distinguishing. See Stone, "Social Mobility" 53–55 and *Crisis* 627–32. Stone's main emphasis in this section of *Crisis* is on noble, as opposed to gentry, intermarriage with the merchant class, statistically infrequent; the gentry were less proud, and such intermarriages were far more common. The gentry population was itself, of course, distinctly larger, and growing; such intermarriages were thus absolutely as well as relatively more frequent, and more visible.

16 For a theoretical treatment of this maneuver as it appears in the zone of courtesy theory, see Whigham, *Ambition and Privilege* 169–83. For the frequency of this practice see Stone's chapter epigraph for "The Inflation of Honours": "It pityethe me to se all the partes of this kingdom almost in Flames of Fyrie quarelles, only for goinge before, and no man more contentious for it then suche as wear wonte to go behynde" (memorandum by a herald in 1604: Bodl Wood MSS. F 21, f. 22; *Crisis* 65).

17 Greene's resentment and language are doubled at a lower status level by Reede, a poorer tenant also displaced by Arden's acquisition of the abbey lands. He pleads with Arden for relief for his family (xiii.11–17), and curses "the carl" (xiii.9) when Arden replies with legalist denial. The Epilogue returns emblematically to this ungentle behavior: Arden's body, we are told, "lay murdered in that plot of ground / Which he by force and violence held from Reede; / And in the grass his body's print was seen / Two years and more after the deed was done" (Epilogue 10–13). For treatment of land-ownership in *Arden of Faversham* see the excellent essays by Orlin and Sullivan; both provide helpful bibliography.

18 For another reading see Orlin, "Man's House" 71ff.

19 This tradition is taken "from manuscript notes, apparently by a Mr Burton, found in a lumber-room at the Dolphin Inn in Faversham, and recorded in *The Monthly Journal of the Faversham Institute* (August, 1881). The writing seems to be in an eighteenth-century hand, and the writer claims to have travelled throughout Kent and the Isle of Sheppey to gather information

from the 'auncientist people' about the principals involved in the Arden story. To what extent the oral tradition can be trusted it is not possible to determine; the play itself may have guided it" (Wine xxxvii). Perhaps the exactly doubled ages (28 and 56) suggest a literary, folktale quality rather than that of historical evidence, as Richard Strier has suggested to me. However, Orlin has discovered an undated chapbook (perhaps early eighteenth century) that also specifies Arden's age as fifty-six when he came to Faversham, which perhaps corroborates Mr. Burton's tale (see Orlin, "Man's House" 86).

20 Miriam Slater, *Family Life* 79 (the bracketed insertions are Slater's).

21 Consider also the possible conceptual force of Alice's status as *step*-daughter. Given the comparative frequency of remarriage during this time, the affinal or acquired version of parent–child relation was probably less secondary or alien than our bald term "step" might suggest. Certainly marital linkage was often felt to generate a "one flesh" coincidence in which affinal and agnatic distinctions ceased to apply: Hamlet feels his mother has married her brother; later in *Arden of Faversham* Clarke calls Mosby "brother" (looking forward to marrying Susan); Macfarlane elsewhere documents the use of "son" for "son-in-law" and "mother" for "mother-in-law" (see *The Family Life of Ralph Josselin* 114, 141). At the other extreme, however, might reside Gloucester's resentful feelings toward his bastard son Edmund. Perhaps Alice's marriage to Arden (probably at least "arranged," if not "enforced") had some flavor of "away she shall," of removing an ill-contented and unwanted burden likely to cause trouble. Something of this attitude colors marrying of daughters and sisters generally, as we have seen with Lord Burghley's advice about marrying daughters. Wandering to-be-dowered daughters were even less welcome than wayward sons. Alice's "step" status and possible misbehavior with Mosby would perhaps just amplify some normal concerns. For frequency of second marriage see Brodsky, "Widows in Late Elizabethan London."

22 Compare Harold Jenkins's observation that Hamlet is both subject (revenger) and object of a revenge mission. See his edition of *Hamlet* 143–44.

23 Perhaps *The Spanish Tragedy* similarly created a need for *The First Part of Hieronymo*.

24 The culture's defiant recuperative punishment took many forms, often including such gestures seizing the criminal's acknowledgment. Perhaps this was likewise the case with the ceremonial severing and casting out of another criminal privity, the genitals, similar sign of erected wit and infected will. Were they too held up, offered to view as a trophy of justice? Similarly, in a report of the execution of Balthazar Gerard, murderer of the prince of Orange, we learn that "his heart was pluckt out and cast at the villaine's face (yet in some life)." See *A true Discourse Historicall of the succeeding Governors in the Netherlands, and the Civil Warres there begun in the yeere 1565* (1602): 51; cited in *The Works of Beaumont and Fletcher*, ed. Alexander Dyce (1844): 7.133 (note to a topical reference to Gerard in *The Woman's Prize, or The Tamer Tamed* 2.2).

25 For an interesting opposite passage of transgressive fantasy we might turn to *A Warning for Fair Women*, where an old poor man admits to having

(literally) dreamed of marrying a young gentlewoman, Anne Sanders (the female lead).

> [OLD JOHN] ... dreames are but fancies: I dreamed my self last night, that I heard the bels of barking as plaine to our towne of Wolwich, as if I had line in the steeple. And that I should be married, and to whom trowest thou? but to the fine gentlwoman [sic] of London that was at your masters the last summer?
> [BEANE] Who? Mistres Sanders? I shall see her anon, for I have an errand to her husband: shal I tell her ye dreamed of her?
> [OLD JOHN] Gods forbod, no: sheele laugh at me, and call me an old foole.

(Cited from Cannon edition 1040–52.) Cross-class desire (though tamingly cross-generation too) seems in this case a matter for mild amusement, perhaps even flattery; Mrs. Sanders is imagined as quite unthreatened (though she falls for a young gentleman herself in due course of the main plot, as the tragedy unfolds).

26 Surely this physical fantasy contains some of the same symbolic capital as Lorenzo's "yet is he at the highest" "elevation" of Horatio. In each case the ambitious body is made to exhibit by negation the moral truth the violator imposes on and extracts from it.

27 This prohibition appears to derive from the famous sumptuary statute of 37 Edward III, c. 9 (1363), which forbad "People of Handicraft, and Yeomen" to wear "Stone, nor Cloth of Silk nor of Silver, nor Girdle, [Knife, Button,] Ring, Garter, nor Brooch, Ribbon, Chains, nor no such other Things of Gold nor of Silver," along with much else (brackets in original). There is no direct reference to swords. (Cited from *Statutes of the Realm*.) For analysis of such legislation and its changing afterlife in royal proclamations during the Tudor period, see Whigham, *Ambition and Privilege* 155–69.

28 See *Outline* 1–2 and *passim*.

29 I see no obvious relevance of the classical episode where the poet Arion is saved by dolphins, save inversion of its effects here. Faustus' treacherous hay-horse of desire – and even Bottom's bottle of hay, perhaps – seem more relevant, in terms of religio-magical invasions of superior preserves of pleasure and power. The driving oral erotics of sweetness is at work here too, though perhaps not with the tinge of regression so central in *Faustus*; see Barber's wonderful essay " 'The form of Faustus' fortunes good or bad.' "

30 *The Subject of Tragedy* 130. Belsey's excellent discussion here, which traces much of the early modern debate over marital control, divorce, and the like (see 138–44), inaugurates the much increased interest in *Arden* in recent years. Some of its judgments have been extended (and others disputed) in a fine essay by Attwell, "Property, Status, and the Subject." I am greatly indebted to these fine analyses.

31 Compare Attwell, "Property, Status, and the Subject" 341:

> Confined to a bourgeois marriage, [Alice] flagrantly breaks out of its restrictions with increasing risk of discovery, and by so doing comes to represent, paradoxically, the assertiveness and self-seeking in terms of which the emergent society was being viewed. (What this shows, from a methodological point of view, is the importance of paying attention to the potentially contradictory nature of a work's

relation to historical transitions: that Alice should rebel partly as an aristocrat resisting the narrowed social range of a bourgeois marriage, and partly as a representative of the appetitive self which is newly thrust into the culture, is both a telling instance of such contradiction and a reminder of the potential dangers of stabilizing dramatic characters in terms of a unified psychology or fixed potential.

32 This move can be paralleled, perhaps significantly, in Marlowe, in *The Massacre at Paris*: "Sweet Mugeroune, tis he that hath my heart, / And Guise vsurpes it, cause I am his wife." (xv.3–4). Certainly the verb *usurp* suits the pugnacious will so typical of Marlowe's work.

33 For the classic statement see Haller and Haller, "The Puritan Art of Love."

34 "An indissoluble union could be created solely by the consent of the two parties expressed in words of the present tense – a contract of marriage or spousals *per verba de praesenti*. ... Neither solemnization in church, nor the use of specially prescribed phrases, nor even the presence of witnesses, was essential to an act of marrriage" (Ingram, *Church Courts, Sex, and Marriage in England* 132). Given the anti-social energies of this particular relationship, I presume the privacy to be not limiting (often church solemnization was put forward as offering full ratification) but enabling.

For discussions of this institution as treated in the drama of the time, see Harding, "Elizabethan Betrothals and *Measure for Measure*"; Schanzer, "The Marriage-Contracts in *Measure for Measure*"; and Wentersdorf, "The Marriage Contracts in 'Measure for Measure.'" The principal period source for law and logic is Henry Swinburne, *A Treatise of Spousals*. This work, published in 1686, was written, in Ingram's judgment, in the closing years of Elizabeth's reign (42). For more on Swinburne see Derrett, *Henry Swinburne*.

35 Nashe, *The Unfortunate Traveller*, in *Works* II, 293.

36 The basic statute for these crimes is 25 Edward III, st. 5, c. 2 (1352), the founding specification for all kinds of treason: "there is another manner of Treason, that is to say, when a Servant slayeth his Master, or a Wife her Husband, or when a Man secular or Religious slayeth his Prelate, to whom he oweth Faith and Obedience." The final phrase marks the defining status of the issue of authority. (Texts cited from *Statutes*.)

For a highly useful examination of petty treason see Dolan, "The Subordinate('s) Plot." For a fascinating discussion of the related servant disobediences of Gloucester and Cornwall's anonymous Servant in Act III of *King Lear*, see Strier, "Faithful Servants" esp. 118–20.

37 Dolan draws attention to the collapse of the categories of high and petty treason in women's experience. Men guilty of high treason and petty treason received different, if related, punishments; women guilty of treason high or petty were burnt at the stake. Such coinciding suggests that for women, "high and petty treason were not only analogous crimes, but that they were virtually indistinguishable" (Dolan, "Home-Rebels and House-Traitors" 4). This is to say, husband and king wielded nearly identical authority over them.

38 For Henry and Anne see Warnicke, *The Rise and Fall of Anne Boleyn* 197. For witchcraft as a social praxis of the accusers, see Macfarlane, *Witchcraft in Tudor and Stuart England*.

39 For an exploration of the origins and operations of this summons to apocalypse, see Braden, "Senecan Tragedy and the Renaissance."

40 It is an apt pun that within this "resolute" pledge lies *resolve* in Hamlet's opposed sense of *dissolve*, as in "melt, thaw, and resolve itself into a dew" (*Hamlet* 1.2.129–30). Thanks to Karen Cunningham for calling my attention to this doubleness, via McAlindon's "The Ironic Vision: Diction and Theme in Marlowe's *Doctor Faustus*."

41 Twice in *Two Lamentable Tragedies* (a play with two completely unrelated plots) a like motive is specified. In one plot, Fallerio seeks to kill the orphan whose guardian he is, in order to advance his son: "And then my sonne shalbe his fathers heire, / And mount aloft to honors happy chair" (B3r; they two are inheritors of all the goods if the ward die). Similarly, in the other plot the murderous First Ruffian says of a good prospect, "Swones her[e]'s rewards would make one kill himselfe, / To leave his progenie so rich a prize" (D1v).

42 Such a domestic structuring of desire in many ways resembles Black Will's, discussed below. Will is, however, much more defined by exclusion and homelessness.

43 The author also includes various references to *meals*, another familiar trope of domesticity. When Arden and Franklin prepare to depart for London, aiming to give Alice room to work off her unhappiness, Arden bids "gentle Alice" prepare their breakfast (i.91), and repeats the instruction later (i.299) before Mosby. He laments that the adultery is the "common table-talk" of Kent (i.344). When she does prepare the breakfast, the broth is poisoned (i.365–66). In London, he and Franklin make plans to dine at the ordinary (vi.42). On their way home after, as they unwittingly approach Black Will and Shakebag's ambush, a qualm of heart assails Franklin; Arden attributes it perhaps to the dinner meat (ix.69–70). When they meet Lord Cheiny, he asks them to eat with him, first supper (on the spot; they cannot) and then dinner the next day (ix.107, 112). When they leave the next day for this date, they assure Alice that they'll return soon: "we mind to sup with thee" (x.34). The final meal is the scene of the murder. Franklin is to be detained elsewhere till suppertime (xiv.97); Arden brings Mosby home with him, to Alice's pretended annoyance, though she says aside "You have given me my supper with his sight" (xiv.176). (Wine believes this phrase means "the mere sight of Mosby takes my appetite away"; see his note on xiv.176.) Arden serves Mosby wine while they play at tables and await supper (xiv.221), just before the murder.

The force of these domestic references is variable, foregrounding by turns a carefully civil but authoritarian husbandly status; a setting for private discussion of others' privacy; the substitution (as if unpained) of the restaurant meal (complete with indigestion) for the lost happy home; the lord's hospitality (felt as a command); the apologetic promise to be home early afterward, to sup with the wife at home; and the final convivial scene of reparative invitation and reparative murder. The repeated "broken feast" motif of the poisoned breakfast and the final murder before supper presumably implies the prior element of secure and securing domesticity. Arden's meals as narrative function oscillate among husbandly authoritarianism, a besieged nostalgia for untroubled family privacy, and a horrific hot-and-cold inversion of "feminine" nurturance and domestic safety. Perhaps too there is a glancing opposition to the motif of the hunger of the poor murderers. All of these items tend to keep in present memory a fragile scene of domestic peace and the conflicting needs and wishes that constitute and sustain it in its instability.

44 For a discussion of the explicit period use of rings as figures for the vagina, see Williamson, "The Ring Episode in *The Merchant of Venice*," and her additional thoughts in *The Patriarchy of Shakespeare's Comedies* 49–53. She reports the period use of the figure by Rabelais, Erasmus, and Poggio, and traces it to the folk-motif of Hans Carvel's Ring. "A version of it appears in *Mery Tales and Quicke Answeres* in *Shakespeare Jest Books*, ed. Hazlitt, 1:28: 'A man that was right jealous on his wife, dreamed on a night as he laid abed with her and slept, that the devil appeared unto him and said: wouldst thou not be glad that I should put thee in surety of thy wife? Yes, said he. Hold, said the devil, as long as thou has this ring upon thy finger, no man shall make thee cuckold. The man was glad thereof, and when he awaked, he found his finger in ***' [sic]" (cited in *Patriarchy* 189, n. 60). For further discussion, see Willbern, "Shakespeare's Nothing," and Kahn, "The Cuckoo's Note."

45 Richard Strier reminds me that the use of wedding rings was actively contested by Puritans, who thought it a remnant of popery. See, for instance, *An Admonition to the Parliament* (1571):

> As for matrimonie, that also hathe corruptions to many. It was wonte to be compted a sacramente, and therfore they use yet a sacramental signe, to which they attribute the vertue of wedlocke. I meane the wedding ring, which they fowly abuse & dally with all, in taking it up, and laying it downe: In putting it on, they abuse the name of the Trinitie, they make the newe marryed man, according to the Popish forme, to make an idol of his wife, saying: with this ring I thee wedde, with my body I thee worshippe, etc.

Cited from the subsection entitled "A View of Popish Abuses," Article 1, paragraph 9; text taken from *Puritan Manifestoes* 27.

46 "It is notorious in anthropological literature that in many societies a marriage creates, not as in England a union of two persons in which they become as one, but an alliance between two groups of blood relations. So much have anthropologists been impressed by this type of view that Leach, who once studied such a society, at one time defined marriage as 'an alliance between two groups,' apparently oblivious of the quite different concept of marriage in his own society, England. In England, a marriage creates no relationship (or alliance) between the kin of the spouses. The blood relations of a husband and wife are in no way related. Relationship exists only between the married couple and the kin in each side." Wolfram, *In-Laws and Outlaws* 16–17. There does seem to be a shadow of such extended affinal relations in England, in the form of step-relations (Alice was step-daughter to North), but it seems to apply only in the newly formed nuclear family.

Wolfram's distinction does not deny the presence of political and social alliance between the two families, but rather asserts the absence of relations *as if by blood* between kin of the spouses. The *spouses* do acquire such relation to each other's kin in the marriage, as Hamlet's sense of his mother's remarriage as incestuous shows. Wolfram's point is that such linkage is acquired by the spouses alone.

47 For a related example of such seizure cf. Cressy's report of a striking case from 1617 in which a woman denied official churching after childbirth "did take the Book of Common Prayer and read the thanksgiving herself openly in the church." See "Purification, Thanksgiving and the Churching of Women" 130.

48 See, for instance, Goody, *The Development of the Family and Marriage in Europe* 147–51; Ingram, *Church Courts, Sex and Marriage in England* 134.

49 See, for instance, the letter attributed to Babington, supposedly addressed to Mary, Queen of Scots: "I vow and protest before the face of Almighty God (Who miraculously hath long preserved your sacred person, no doubt to some universal good end) that what I have said shall be performed, or all our lives happily lost in the execution thereof; which vow all the chief actors herein have taken most solemnly, and are, upon assurance of your Majesty's letters unto me, to receive the Blessed Sacrament thereupon, either to prevail in the Church's behalf and your Majesty's, or fortunately to die for that honourable cause." (See Alan Gordon Smith, *The Babington Plot* 35.) Similar swearings were sworn in the Gunpowder Plot: see Gardiner, *What Gunpowder Plot Was* 33–34, 62. For dramatic examples see, for instance, *Richard II*: "A dozen of them here have ta'en the Sacrament, / And interchangeably set down their hands, / To kill the King at Oxford" (5.2.97); and Webster's *The White Devil*: "You have ta'en the sacrament to prosecute / Th'intended murder" (4.3.72–73). The nobles dominate Edward II and his favorite Gaveston with this device, in Drayton's *Piers Gaveston* (1593): "They forced mee for to abjure the Land. / Forcing the King to further this intent, / By solemne oth upon the Sacrament" (ll. 1294–96, cited from Drayton, *Works* 1:194).

For information on this subject I thank Professor Karen Cunningham, who suggests that "'sanctifying' assassination turns the sacrament upside down – or rather, dramatizes the fact that the sacrament itself is undergoing change as a contested ritual, the object of a contest among rulers and 'usurpers' (to pick up the diction of officialdom)" (private communication). Such a contestatory gesture bears a distinct structural resemblance to Alice and Mosby's London venture.

50 Compare the dual motives, discussed below in section III, of Clarke's service to Mosby, to establish clientage and kinship with Mosby through murdering Arden and marrying Susan: which is means, which end?

51 See, for instance, Montrose, "The Purposes of Playing." For a famous treatment of how stage plays appropriate the sabbath, and thus compete with the church, see Philip Stubbes, *The Anatomie of Abuses* sig. L5r–M2v.

52 For a discussion of such vicarious self-depiction, a common phenomenon in this form among the unlettered, see Whigham, *Ambition and Privilege* 54–60.

53 For a powerful analysis of the conflicting notions of obedience and authority in such cases see Strier, "Faithful Servants."

54 Kussmaul, *Servants in Husbandry* 4. The agrarian servant-laborer and the domestic servant, "hired to establish and maintain the status of the family

and to attend to its personal needs" (4) are distinct groups for Kussmaul, who focuses on the former. As domestic servant and envious younger brother of a rural freeholding heir Michael complexly spans both categories.

55 Sir Robert Filmer, deriving royal authority from the familial matrix of patriarchy, cites scriptural precedents (Cain and Abel, Jacob and Isaac) to specify heirs as having patriarchal (and thus quasi-royal) authority over their brothers. "All kings," he says, "be not the natural parents of their subjects, yet they all either are, or are to be reputed as the next heirs to those progenitors who were at first the natural parents of the whole people, and in their right succeed to the exercise of supreme jurisdiction. And such heirs are not only lords of their own children, but also of their brethren, and all others that were subject to their fathers." (Cited from Filmer, *Patriarcha and Other Writings* 10.) By similar analogy, Michael's fratricidal impulses are also petty-treasonous (compare similar analogies in note 79 below).

56 There is a fortuitous link between the Arden story and direct ideological address to murdering elder brothers. Lionel Cust informs us that Arden's lands were eventually acquired by Sir George Sondes (with whose family they still lay when Cust wrote in 1920; see "Arden of Feversham" 101, 103–04). In 1655 Sir George's younger son Freeman (shades of Franklin!) murdered his elder brother George, the heir, arousing a flurry of public discussion in "rumours and flysheets." According to Joan Thirsk, "the public leapt to the conclusion that Freeman was a deprived younger son, ill-treated by his father, despised and rejected by his elder brother. The rumours were so wild that Sir George Sondes, the unhappy father, was stung into writing a circumstantial account of the upbringing of the two sons," making it clear that "the elder was of a gentle, amiable disposition, the younger ... envious and quarrelsome." Whatever else may be true of this father's explanatory gesture, it denies a supposedly excessive and destructive respect for primogeniture, for "both boys had been equally cherished." However, such blame had become common in contemporary reflections on the causes of the Civil War. According to Thirsk, William Sprigge, author of *The Modest Plea for an Equal Commonwealth* (1659), "hinted darkly" that the English system of inheritance "was the cause of many shakings and convulsions of these later ages. Who could blame younger sons if, in their valiant efforts to build up their own fortunes, they purchased the ruin of the commonwealth's peace and government?" (Thirsk's summary). Sprigge may have spoken from experience, being a younger son himself (see *DNB*). See Thirsk, "Younger Sons in the Seventeenth Century" 372–73. Such reflections depart from the petty-treason overtones of Michael's lust for his brother's farm. Thirsk's general conclusion is that the perceived abusive force of the primogeniture system was generally restricted to the aristocracy (see 364, 370, and *passim*). Michael's case (or perhaps the *Arden* author's case) provides a counter-example that expands the ideological threat from below.

57 Compare the related critical argument about Jacob's manipulation of Laban's sheep in *The Merchant of Venice*. Antonio insists that taking interest is unjustified by the Old-Testament folktale: "This was a venture, sir, that Jacob served for, / A thing not in his power to bring to pass, / But swayed and fashioned by the hand of heaven" (1.3.89–91). Antonio's objection is

often extended from Laban's sheep to Antonio's venturesome shipping, presented as risky, in moral contrast to Shylock's taking of interest, presented as non-risky, and so low or immoral. Indeed, Lewalski extends the matter to the full range of "Christian love," in "Biblical Allusion and Allegory in *The Merchant of Venice*." In both plays the foregrounding of active and passive modes enables associations of brave manliness to rise and posture. In Arden the contrast further embraces that between various blows, right-down and otherwise, and Arden's new-man management of the legal code. Greene and Reede might well argue that, as in *The Merchant of Venice*, the contrast keeps collapsing into identity. As Belsey notes, we can see both Arden and Alice as business-oriented, negotiating contractually to get what they want (132).

58 Wolfram, *In-Laws and Outlaws* 118.

59 Susan's aptness as a conduit of relation was presumably to be emphasized by another editing of the source materials: Wine observes (xxxix) that in Susan the author combines two separate source characters: Mosby's sister and Alice's maid.

60 For venturing see note 57 above; for romanticizing commerce see Sklar, "Bassanio's Golden Fleece" 502–3; and Whigham, "Ideology and Class Conduct in *The Merchant of Venice*."

61 Such also are the anxieties of shifting Pedringano: his "loyalty" to Lorenzo begins in extortion, and his loyalty to Serberine survives long enough to mount a struggle, though not to win it. For the poles between which such struggles oscillate and sometimes (as with Michael) attempt to mediate, see Strier, "Faithful Servants."

62 Recall Shylock's related demystification of the glories of Christian commerce in *The Merchant of Venice* 1.3. Compare also various proverbs on the notion that "words are but wind': see Tilley, *Dictionary of Proverbs* W833, W412, W439.

63 For another discussion of comic assassins, see Wiggins, *Journeymen in Murder* 78–81.

64 The now-standard work is Heal, *Hospitality in Early Modern England*.

65 The coinciding hungers for beef and recognition help to construe the oddly detailed description of one Jack Fitten, a thief, of whom Bradshaw seeks news from Black Will. Fitten is "A lean-faced, writhen knave, / Hawk-nosed and very hollow-eyed, / With mighty furrows in his stormy brows" (ii.47–49). We can compare these lines with other examples: DeFlores's description of loathsome men not unlike himself, who have "wrinkles like troughs, where swine-deformity swills / The tears of perjury that lie there like wash / Fallen from the slimy and dishonest eye" (Middleton and Rowley, *The Changeling* 2.1.43–45); the mountebank Pinch in *The Comedy of Errors*; the lean Ithamore in Marlowe's *The Jew of Malta* (see 2.3.128–29); the "hollow discontented looke" of the assassin in Yarrington's *Two Lamentable Tragedies* (sig. E1r); and the famous look of Cassius. Wrinkles seem to figure a literal hunger, perhaps underclass hunger, and fit with both malcontent and prodigal as they appear in the imagery. Compare Wiggins, *Journeymen in Murder* 150–51.

66 Wine notes (xlvi) the presence of another Black Will in *The True Tragedy of*

Richard III (one of the murderers of the princes in the tower). Wiggins suggests that "the appearance of two distinct Black Wills in two separate bodies of source material . . . suggests a type-name" (*Journeymen in Murder* 66.)

67 The issue of hunger in particular has a different, collective, form, from which Black Will and Shakebag are isolated, in yet another denial of the community they so desire. Scarcity generally fell harder upon the poor than their betters, and disorder (and arrests for theft) rose disproportionately among the deprived. The authorities commonly resorted to a metaphysical explanation of dearth, as God's judgment upon an erring populace, and stepped up the conspicuous policing of such nodes of potentially sinful energy as alehouses. At the same time, "grasping" middlemen were blamed for greed and hoarding, and often forced to sell their stores to the poor at minimal rates. Such disciplining was often triggered by popular grain riots, of the "deserving" poor. These accounts thus enabled both explanation and the experience of effectual remedial action, and seemed to exhibit the responsiveness of the dominant to the sufferings of the poor. Walter and Wrightson thus conclude in a famous essay that "while [dearth] could undoubtedly contribute to social disorder, there is evidence that the awareness of dearth, the memory of its past and the fear of its future occurrence, could serve as an active element in the maintenance of social stability." See their "Dearth and the Social Order" 22–42; citation from 22. Black Will and Shakebag seem to provide a view of the failure of such negotiation, issuing in vengefulness and social disruption.

68 Alice also tries to poison Arden with broth (i), producing the usual count of six. Dolan, including other hypothetical plans, counts eight; see "The Subordinate('s) Plot" 332.

69 Ibid.

70 Brown, " 'This thing of darkness I acknowledge mine' " 63.

71 Relentlessness is the force of the phrase in the Bible. In 1 Samuel David speaks of God's vengeance against his servant's enemies: ". . . he hathe requited me euil for good. So and more also do God vnto the enemies of Dauid: for surely I wil not leaue of all that he hathe, by the dawning of the day, and that pisseth against the wall" (*Geneva Bible* 25: 21–22). The gloss reads, "Meaning by this prouerbe, that he wolde destroye bothe smale & great." Similarly, in 1 Kings God's prophet Ahijah tells the wife of Jeroboam that the lord will "bring euil vpon the house of Ieroboam, and wil cut of from Ieroboam him that pisseth against the wall" (14: 10); the gloss reads, "Euery male euen to the dogs." (Cited from *The Geneva Bible*.) With this image Will seems to situate himself as a wrathful Yahweh. One might less apocalyptically suggest that Will's fantasy of murdering those who piss against walls glosses both defiant social mobility and its punishment *in flagrante delicto*. He can easily be seen to occupy both poles, at least in fantasy. A related fantasy of public urination certainly enacts such energy in *The Miseries of Enforced Marriage* (1497–99, discussed below).

Gail Kern Paster suggests further to me that Will's threat amounts also to "a comic version of killing a sleeping man – killing a man while he's doing that which a man has a right to do in security, in any rightly constituted social order, with his back turned or his eyes closed, fulfilling nature's command"; she compares "Macbeth does murder sleep" (private communication).

72 For one look at the world I imagine Will to have left behind, consider Hodge's plea to Diccon for help in *Gammer Gurton's Needle*.

> Chill run, chill ride, chill dig, chill delve, chill toil, chill trudge, shalt see;
> Chill hold, chill draw, chill pull, chill pinch, chill kneel on my bare knee;
> Chill scrape, chill scratch, chill sift, chill seek, chill bow, chill bend, chill sweat,
> Chill stoop, chill stir, chill cap, chill kneel, chill creep on hands and feet,
> Chill be thy bondman, Diccon, ich swear by sun and moon.   (2.1.55–59)

This pledge of service lists what Hodge has to work with, to engage Diccon's aid: the lexicon of rural physical labor, here proffered as willing servitude. For a reading of this moment as "a structural crisis with implications for the whole community," see Paster, *The Body Embarrassed* 119–21.

73 Gary Taylor's hypothesis as to the on-stage killing of the French prisoners gives special point to the parallel, emphasizing Pistol's "moment of greatness" as he kills the prisoner whose ransom would make him "a made man," without which he returns to England as he left it, a destitute bloodsucker bawd and cutpurse. See Taylor's edition of *Henry V* 4.6.39 and Introduction 65–66.

74 Will's echo of Arden's revenge-fantasy against Mosby (i.37–43) triggers an odd linkage between the highest and lowest (main) characters in this play, both excluded, furious, starving, pathetic. Arden, however, speaks only in specular terms, stopping well short of identifying himself with the hands-on practitioner, as Will does.

75 The term was also applied to Jews and gypsies, and to a whole set of occupations which were often combined with that of executioner: "The hangman regularly had to supervise the prostitutes, or acted as a brothel keeper himself. Sometimes he had to catch dogs, clean the streets and the public latrines, or, in the early modern period, take care of syphilis patients. Worst of all, he could be a skinner." (Why this last occupation is so horrible is unclear.) Spierenberg judges that "first the hangman was infamous and, because of that, he was a convenient candidate for other low tasks." See Spierenberg, *The Spectacle of Suffering* 21. (For Jews and gypsies see 17, 169–75. Further references to Spierenberg will appear in the text.) Shakespeare's Pompey shows that recruitment might flow in the opposite direction, from bawd to hangman.

76 Cited from the Bowers edition, vol. 4.

77 Given this litany, one might wonder why even Will would identify himself with such a one. Aside from the author's need for a sufficiently intense irony to measure Will's marginality, Spierenberg offers one other option. Hangmen were at least sometimes very well paid, so much so as to arouse envy, and some of the emotions Arden felt for Mosby.

> Around 1500 we first hear of prohibitions directed against their too luxurious way of living. Thus the hangman of Kampen was warned in 1475 not to "walk around like a nobleman or merchant." Financially he could apparently afford to play the gentleman. Similarly, the hangman of Augsburg was not allowed to "dress as a cavalier or play the big man." This sort of prohibition was very common in sixteenth-century Germany. Charles V prescribed a grey costume for the execution-

er, while variations with red were the rule elsewhere. The executioners remained well dressed and rich nevertheless, such as those of Frankfurt and Hamburg (35).

The unevenness of preserved records often forces Spierenberg to work laterally, moving back and forth across Europe for his data. Still, he argues at the outset that "the available literature on crime and justice in early modern England suggests that a system of prosecution of serious crimes, physical punishment and exemplary repression prevailed there, which was basically similar to that on the Continent" (10). Given that "the office [of hangman] was only fully developed and institutionalized in the first half of the sixteenth [century]" (25), the direct relevance of this material to *Arden of Faversham* seems clear. The rise of the nation-state appears to have produced similar patterns in this matter as in so many others. The executioner, like the steward, might achieve by his own efforts the capacity to swagger – and be hated for it.

78 Shakespeare uses (or uses again) a closely related image in *As You Like It* (4.3.114–19), upon which Montrose comments suggestively: see " 'The Place of a Brother' " 44 and esp. 50–51.

79 Killing his master would be direct petty treason (specified in 25 Edward III st. 5 c. 2). Aiding Mosby to Alice's bed is for Michael a highly related act, closely resembling acts of statutory high treason. 33 Henry VIII c. 21, x (an Anne Boleyn statute) specifies that "if the Queen or Wife of the Prince move procure or stir any person by any Writing or Message word or tokens or otherwise for that purpose to use or to have carnal knowledge with them, or if any person do move procure or make means to the Queen or Wife of the Prince to use or have carnal knowledge of them or any of them," then all of them "and their aiders Counselors and abettors" shall be deemed high traitors. To work by analogy from king to master, Michael is guilty of something very like petty treason here too. (For a related analogy see note 55 above.) For practical detail on the workings of the Henrician statute, see Warnicke, *The Rise and Fall of Anne Boleyn* 203–04, 216.

The central object of protection is obviously the royal bloodline. An earlier statute, 28 Henry VIII c. 24 (the Thomas Howard attainder), addresses the same concern: it forbad anyone to "espouse marry or take to his wife any of the King's children [being lawfully born or otherwise commonly reputed or taken for his children,] or any of the King's Sisters or Aunts of the part of the Father, [or any the lawful children] of the King's Brethren or Sisters [not being married,] or contract marriage with any of them, without the special license assent consent and agreement first therunto had and obtained of the King's Highness in writing under his great seal, [or defile or deflower any of them not being maried]." This statute, to work by a related analogy, of usurpation, would similarly capture Mosby as a traitor. (Texts cited from *Statutes*.) Compare also the analogy with Michael and his brother; see note 55 above.

80 As Richard Strier points out to me, a lovely ironic pun, worthy of comparison with the aid Faustus buys of Mephistopheles.

81 In many Renaissance texts a hero (or one who deserves to be so thought of) is, by means of this phrase, said to achieve fullness of identity by approximating an ideal version of himself. See, for instance, "Then should the

warlike Harry, like himself, / Assume the port of Mars" (*Henry V* Prologue 5–6). For other examples (including negative ones), see Hereward T. Price, "Like Himself."

82 Regarding such dreams of autonomy, compare Donne's distinction between being vicar and being hangman to Fate, in *Satire III*: 90. He speaks of kings, of course.

83 *OED*'s first citation for the unusual term "hunger-bitten" is from Cheke's *The hurt of sedicion howe greuous it is to a communewelth* (1549): "When every man for lack is hungerbitten" (34); "hunger-bit" first appears in Sternhold and Hopkins' *The whole boke of psalms* (1549–62): "The Lions shall be hungerbit, and pinde with famine much" (34: 10). These earliest usages together embrace just the territory Black Will inhabits, linking social injustice and retributive danger.

Wine adduces another use of "hunger-bitten," from the roughly contemporary *Locrine*: "The hunger-bitten dogs of Acheron" (4.2.67). The entire passage is a striking permutation of concerns here. Humber, King of the Scythians, has come from battle wounded to a desert forest, where he fears to starve; the clown Strumbo watches, eating his picnic breakfast while Humber expostulates.

> Was euer land so fruitlesse as this land?
> Was ever soyle so barrein as this soyle?
> Oh no: the land where hungry *Fames* dwelt
> May no wise aequalize this cursed land;
> No, euen the climat of the torrid zone
> Brings forth more fruit then this accursed groue.
> Nere came sweet *Ceres*, nere came *Venus* here;
> *Triptolemus*, the god of husbandmen,
> Nere sowd his seed in this foule wildernesse.
> The hunger-bitten dogs of *Acheron*,
> Chast from the ninefold *Puriflegiton*,
> Haue set their footesteps in this damned ground.   (4.2.57–68)

84 *Arden of Faversham* has long been thought perhaps to echo *The Spanish Tragedy*. Boas regarded the author of *Arden* as "the first among [playwrights great and small] to show incontestable evidence of [Kyd's] influence." He cites the resemblance between *Arden* and *The Murder of John Brewen* "and the similarity of certain lines and phrases in the play and in *The Spanish Tragedy*" as evidence for the conjecture that Kyd wrote *Arden*. Boas rejects this view, but allows, "Yet in the cadence and diction of many passages, and in the combination of lyrically elaborate verse-structure with colloquial directness of speech, *Arden of Faversham* recalls the manner of Kyd far more nearly than that of Shakespeare, to whom it has often been groundlessly attributed." He goes on to argue at least for direct linkage between *The Spanish Tragedy* 2.5 (Hieronymo's "naked bed" speech) and *Arden* iv.87 ("What dismal outcry calls me from my rest?"). In the light of this received example, Mosby's fear of "nipping" may be another echo. (Kyd was probably not the author of *John Brewen*: see Gorrell, "John Payne Collier.")

85 That is, as bees are smoked out of their hives before the wax and honey are taken; see White's note in his edition.

86 Compare Shakebag's use of the starven lioness image at iii.103–6; Mosby's version of the language of Nature stresses combative rivalry rather than justified savagery on behalf of starving children.

87 Perhaps thus comparable to those helpless ones who will die while pissing against a wall? See Paster's comment, note 71.

88 Should we hear *gate* as vaginal here? On at least two occasions Shakespeare invites such a reading, in the scenes in *Henry V* and *Coriolanus* where cities are beseiged. The latter is more noted, wherein Volumnia describes her son's invasion of Rome by saying "Thou shalt ... tread ... on thy mother's womb" (*Coriolanus* 5.3.123–24). In the former case Henry threatens the citizens of Harfleur with literal and figurative rape. When the governor of the city finally capitulates, he jussively transforms Henry's imagery to that of sympathetic marriage: "We yield our town and lives to thy soft mercy. / Enter our gates, dispose of us and ours" (*Henry V* 3.3.48–49). After the repeated references to hardness in Henry's threats, "soft" has detumescent force, and "dispose" the tone of marriage settlements, soon directly enacted regarding Katherine and France generally. Donne uses the same figure in Holy Sonnet 14 ("Batter my heart"). Perhaps Mosby's fears of "danger's gate" and the "gates of death" unpack Alice's body as well as his own future, once again suggesting sexuality as opportunity, here going bad.

89 This striking confluence of erect phallic pillars, the cement/semen of in/ constant love, pride, falling, and dust prefigures George Herbert's lines in "Church Monuments":

> Deare flesh, while I do pray, learn here thy stemme
> And true descent; that when thou shalt grow fat,
> And wanton in thy cravings, thou mayst know
> That flesh is but the glasse, which holds the dust
> That measures all our time; which also shall
> Be crumbled into dust. Mark here below
> How tame these ashes are, how free from lust,
> That thou mayst fit thy self against thy fall.

(Cited from Hutchinson edition 65.)

90 Alas, the frontispiece woodcut from the 1633 quarto (White edition xxix) does not show Mosby with either iron or dagger; he sits behind the gaming-table, waist out of sight, while the others stab Arden. The woodcut otherwise departs from the play, because Alice, Susan, and Michael all bear daggers.

91 If we prefer Holinshed's stabbing with the knife, rather than the pressing-iron, it becomes appropriate to note Wine's report of the 1970 La Mama Experimental Theatre Club performance, in which Alice castrates Arden after the murder, presumably in harmony with the various metaphorical castrations throughout the play. See Wine lv–lvi.

3. THE IDEOLOGY OF PRODIGALITY IN *THE MISERIES OF ENFORCED MARRIAGE* AND *A YORKSHIRE TRAGEDY*

1 Citations are taken from *A Yorkshire Tragedy*; *Two Most Unnaturall and Bloodie Murthers*, rpt. in Cawley and Gaines edition, 94–110 (passages identified by the editors' continuous line numeration); and Wilkins, *The*

Miseries of Enforced Marriage. I have modernized the Wilkins play's unruly spelling; furthermore, owing to its general unfamiliarity, I have quoted liberally rather than sparingly.

2 Initially the change is perhaps no more than "the substitution of the family name Scarborow [*sic*] for that of Calverley; that is, the substitution of the name of one old Yorkshire town for that of another" (Maxwell, "*A Yorkshire Tragedy*" 169). Both syllables take on richer meaning as the play progresses.

3 Scarborrow lacks only a mother, the usual omission. For theorizing attention to this absence see Rose, "Where Are the Mothers in Shakespeare?" and Adelman, *Suffocating Mothers.*

4 *English Society* 74. Wrightson thoughtfully reviews and updates the debate over affective marriage and family formation (66–88).

5 See *The Lady Falkland her Life,* in Cary, *The Tragedy of Mariam* 217.

6 For the veto see Stone, *The Family, Sex and Marriage* 187, 189, 190 (cited fully above, Ch. 1, note 22).

7 *The Scholemaster,* in *English Works,* 204.

8 Houlbrooke, *English Family* 179; Macfarlane, *Josselin* 117–18.

9 *The Queen's Wards.*

10 The long dash is taken from Blayney's Malone Society text. It may register the ostentatious pauses of sarcastic narrative rehearsal, or perhaps mark various muggings.

11 *Two Most Unnatural and Bloodie Murthers* 12–20.

12 In *A New Way to Pay Old Debts* this fantasy is Massinger's. Consider Sir Giles Overreach's explicit plan for marrying his daughter Margaret to Lord Lovell (Edwards and Gibson edition, 3.2.112–18, 123–26, 145–53):

> MARGARET You'll have me Sir, preserve the distance, that
> Confines a virgin?
> OVERREACH Virgin me no virgins.
> I must have you lose that name, or you lose me.
> I will have you private, start not, I say private;
> If thou are my true daughter, not a bastard,
> Thou wilt venture alone with one man, though he came
> Like Jupiter to Semele, and come off too.
> And therefore when he kisses you, kiss close. . . .
> Or if his blood grow hot, suppose he offer
> Beyond this, do not you stay till it cool,
> But meet his ardor, if a couch be near,
> Sit down on't, and invite him. . . .
> Forsake thee when the thing is done? He dares not.
> Give me but proof, he has enjoyed thy person,
> Though all his captains, echoes to his will,
> Stood arm'd by his side to justify the wrong . . .
> . . . I will make him render
> A bloody and a strict account, and force him
> By marrying thee, to cure thy wounded honor.

13 Ingram, *Church Courts, Sex, and Marriage* 132.

14 Whytford cited by Harding in "Elizabethan Betrothals and *Measure for*

Measure" (145), from G. E. Howard, *A History of Matrimonial Institutions* (1904), 1, 350.

15 Furnivall, *Child Marriages* (1897): xliii; cited by Harding (145).

16 See Rubin, "The Traffic in Women," and Sedgwick, *Between Men*. Overreach's social aspirations for his daughter's upward marriage are homosocial in purpose, even if achievement rather than ascriptively oriented; his daughter's resistance obviously marks her subjection and shame.

17 In doing so I take up a hint from Richard Helgerson. Speaking of how English prodigal prose fictions depart from traditional European iconographic and interpretive traditions, he observes: "Particularly conspicuous is the lack of any repeated attention to the merciful resolution: the joyful reception by the father of his erring son, the killing of the fatted calf, the bestowal of the best robe, and the placing of a ring on the prodigal's hand and shoes on his feet. ... Not the parable of the Prodigal Son, with its benign vision of paternal forgiveness, but rather the paradigm of prodigal rebellion interested the Elizabethans." (See *The Elizabethan Prodigals* 3.)

18 An idiom that proverbially combines defilement with stickiness, thus inviting association with the misogynist lexicon here examined.

19 From another angle early modern men often experienced (coded, constituted) the whore as quite threatening: as a predatory parasite of great potency. For instance, in Middleton's *A Trick to Catch the Old One* Witgood greets his partner Courtesan with these words:

> "My loathing! [a vocative, responding to her words "my love"] hast thou been the secret consumption of my purse? and now com'st to undo my last means, my wits? wilt thou leave no virtue in me, and yet thou never the better?
>
> Hence, courtesan, round-webbed tarantula,
> That dryest the roses in the cheeks of youth!"   (1.1.28–32)

It is part of Middleton's remarkable independence of mind that this view is precisely deconstructed (and in terms of agency) in this play. Courtesan repudiates this speech, and Witgood recants: "I do thee wrong, / To make thee sin and then to chide thee for't" (1.1.38–39). Elsewhere, however, the stereotype stands, usually a convenient displacement. Marston's Dutch courtesan Franceschina, for instance, is praised, as "none of your ramping cannibals that devour man's flesh" (1.2.96–97), though she eventually proves a "comely damnation" (5.3.48). In Wilkins's different agenda here the gallants resort to figurations of the whore precisely to seize agency, over against the *subjections* of marriage.

20 Douglas "Standard Social Uses of Food" 30.

21 Douglas "A Distinctive Anthropological Perspective" 8.

22 Douglas, "Standard Social Uses of Food" 33.

23 This is Douglas's useful summary of Gusfield's point, in "A Distinctive Anthropological Perspective" 8; see Gusfield, "Passage to Play." Gusfield's concern with post-traditional work and leisure time may be recuperable to some degree, as another binary to pair with female and male, family and prodigals, Yorkshire and London, subjection and freedom. Prince Hal and Falstaff come to mind as well. Like Shakespeare, Wilkins is interested in the manifest instabilities in this structural array, as the play gradually reveals.

24 In the US a "bus-boy" is the menial laborer – usually a young male – who

clears the table in a restaurant after the meal, taking away the dirty dishes in his "bus tub." "Bus-boy" is itself a notable usage. The institutional site of the *restaurant*, of public feeding (both subjective and objective), is extremely rich in the categorical and boundary significations that mark power-relationships for our culture. Not only are bus-boys demoted by both gender and age (a boy is neither a man nor an adult), but they are also often aliens, and (is this redundant?) illegal, perhaps insufficiently individual (sharing one green card) and often unintelligible (speaking little English), save to each other – thus perhaps similar to Prince Hal's scorned, mocked, aped, languageless, and loving Francis the drawer. Consider also the asymmetrical categories of waitress and waiter, for instance, usually also dispersed (like host and hostess) by class (of server and of customer both), and dressed in one or another range of (sometimes hidden, often gender-emphasizing)) uniform. Or ask why most cooks are men, and the most powerful figures – and the most likely to be *prima donnas*, as we complexly say – in the restaurant. Why not say "cooker" and "cookette"? (Coquette? Croquette?) Why did "waitperson" need to be coined at all? Why must some waitpersons, according to corporate logic, tell us their names, or wear nametags? Some customers use these names, some do not: which ones, and why? Which ones allow, or seize upon, or confer, or use, the waitperson's (gendered) personhood? (Homophobic joking arises with some frequency in this setting.) For some revealing assimilations of these questions about food to more general matters, see Ortner, "Is Female to Male as Nature Is to Culture?" 80.

25 There are other strange food images in *Hamlet* that invert or recurse feeding: think of Pyrrhus in burning Troy on his way to mince Priam's limbs, the blood of his victims "bak'd and impasted" [2.2.459] on him like a crust. Perhaps this slant-rhymes the hunger-bitten lioness of *Arden of Faversham* and *As You Like It*? Compare too Iachimo's discussion of vomiting desire (*Cymbeline* 1.6.43–46); interestingly, he also tropes "the cloyed will – / That satiate yet unsatisfied desire," as a "tub both filled and running" (47–49).

Regarding female vessels cf. Numbers 19:15: "And every open vessel, which hath no covering bound upon it, is unclean."

26 Ilford has already claimed that cuckoldry is by definition monstrous and disparaging: "a man is made a Beast by being married. Take but example thy self from the Moon, as soon as she is delivered of her great belly, doth she not point at the world with a pair of horns, as who should say, married men, some of ye are Cuckolds" (136–40). The degrading announcement follows hard upon a foregrounding of the ultimate female physicality, fecundity – some would say the most threatening to men. (For a remarkable exploration of such matters see Adelman, *Suffocating Mothers*.)

27 See Slater, *Family Life* 12.

28 There seems to be something of a submerged discourse here, on drinking and the sexual power-balance: the link appears elsewhere. See, for instance, Marston's *The Fawn*, where Sir Amoroso Debile-Dosso, a worn-out and presumably syphilitic lecher, is "grown the very dregs of the drabs' cup" (1.1.74). In *The Merry Wives of Windsor*, however, earls and even pensioners have proved unable to corrupt Mistress Ford, says Quickly: "they could never get her so much as sip on a cup with the proudest of them all" (2.2.71–72).

29 *The Faerie Queene* 2.12.87.

30 Falstaff's career establishes this rich vein, but such recursive images recur familiarly thereafter in *Hamlet*, and especially sharply in *Troilus and Cressida*: think of Thersites' sniggering observation, "How the devil Luxury, with his fat rump and potato finger, tickles these together. Fry, lechery, fry" (5.2.56–58).

31 The obvious links here connect with Goneril and Regan, but Cordelia's initiating "nothing" certainly threatens her father's libidinal investment in her, and Lear threatens all of his daughters' sexualities in return. (*King Lear* was first staged, at the latest, at court on December 26, 1606; probably earlier, at the Globe, in 1605.)

32 Stallybrass, "Patriarchal Territories."

33 We should not mistake the daughter's "right of refusal" as anything much like modern freedom of choice. Her horizon was really twice limited: the field of view would only hold one candidate at a time, and the right of refusal was finite. (Stone imagines two iterations at most: see *The Family, Sex, and Marriage* 190.) No general comparison of suitors was possible (except retrospectively).

34 For the tortured victim's freedom see Sartre, *Being and Nothingness* 523–24. For the torturer's nice discrimination see Kasper Gutman's address to Sam Spade in Huston's *The Maltese Falcon*: Bogart claims that torture cannot make him talk because it must carry the threat of death behind it, and they cannot afford to kill him, since he alone knows where the bird is. Such confidence, Sidney Greenstreet suggests, rests on a delicate balance. So does Clare's: we would now regard her situation as tormented, but I believe she takes it as an opportunity. In any case, with Scarborrow she occupies both poles, subjected and subjecting at once.

35 We are used to presuming that *The Miseries of Enforced Marriage* is, like *A Yorkshire Tragedy*, an explicit dramatization of the Calverley story, but according to Blayney the first mention of this identification dates from 1879. P. A. Daniel says that "it has hitherto completely escaped notice that [*The Miseries of Enforced Marriage*] is founded on the narrative of the Calverley murder, published in 1605, which was the source of the 'Yorkshire Tragedy'" (cited from Daniel's "Shakspeare's[?] 'Yorkshire Tragedy,' 1608," 432, by Blayney in "Wilkins's Revisions" 23). Given the fictitious names and substantial plot alterations of *Miseries*, not to mention the generally frequent departure from "historical record" so common in plays said to be so based, some among the first audiences might have entertained no such detailed presupposition. The title would have suggested only the possibility.

36 For development beyond the formulations of Althusser (in "Ideology and Ideological State Apparatuses") and Therbörn (in *The Ideology of Power*), see Giddens, *Modernity and Self-Identity*. Giddens argues for an increasing role for conscious action in this regard from the early modern period onward, and sees this pattern as definitive of modernity.

37 Note how elopement is *gendered*. The normal usage rests on defining the bride as stolen daughter, that is, on paternal authority over *her*. Sons seem to participate in eloping only as bridegroom-thieves, relationally to the female; they do not elope from their own parents. The notion of elopement

depends on, is defined against, the more severe control that attaches to daughters. But wardship appears to provide this obstacle for the son. Wardship feminizes the son in yet another way: a ward must (that is, *can*) elope, a move otherwise specific to the more oppressed and controlled category of daughters. Or is this extreme? Perhaps a strong form involves eloping from the daughter's parents, a weak form from the sons' (or from both, from the parental generation as a whole), *except* here, where wardship strengthens the weak form into equivalence with the strong? In any case, Lord Faulconbridge experiences Scarborrow's self-betrothal much as a jealous father like Brabantio might experience his daughter's act (as rebellion or desertion, even theft of self).

38 Hurstfield, *Queen's Wards* 143.

39 Compare the conservation of female symbolic capital in Alice's possibly enforced marriage in *Arden of Faversham*.

40 Carter, speaking to his intended son-in-law, says, "Take her to thee. Get me a brace of boys at a burden, Frank; the nursing shall not stand thee in a pennyworth of milk. Reach her home and spare not" (1.2.211–15).

41 Compare the frequent resort to this move by women resisting marriage, as in *The Changeling*.

42 This troping of whoredom, so different from Ilford's, prefigures Clare's same experience when the news of his enforced marriage reaches her at 816ff.

43 See Slater, *Family Life* 78–80, 101–2, and 187 note 140.

44 This fossil speech-prefix for Lord Faulconbridge (at 324 and 453) perhaps suggests Wilkins's extrapolation from *Two Most Unnatural and Bloodie Murthers* as to the actual identity of Scarborrow's guardian: see Blayney, "G. Wilkins," and "Wilkins's Revisions" 23.

45 See Hurstfield, *Queen's Wards* 139–41.

46 In line 514 I retain "pergest," which I prefer to the tamer "percist," i.e., "persist"; see Blayney, "Variants" 178–79.

47 Compare the young men in Chaucer's *Pardoner's Tale*.

48 Is it coincidental that ten lines later Hal alludes to Doll's kinship with Falstaff as "even such kin as the parish heifers are to the town bull" (2.2.149–50)?

49 There is further continuity with the ironic reference to keeping lean and taking physic later in the passage; fattening, and thus fattening on, such calves as Scarborrow is precisely Ilford's practice.

50 For discussion see Bray, *Homosexuality in Renaissance England*; Bruce Smith, *Homosexual Desire in Shakespeare's England*; and Orgel, *Impersonations*. For the emergence of the modern homosexual subject-position see Traub's useful bibliographical summary in *Desire and Anxiety* 166–67.

Perhaps the textual history implies the erased presence of homoerotic energy here: one version of Q1, possibly expurgated, omits the phrase "keep a Catamite" altogether. Maybe this textual moment captures a transition from prehistory to history. See Blayney, "Variants" 178–79. It is unclear which version of Q1 is corrected and which not (if correction is indeed the issue): perhaps the reference is instead a late authorial addition.

51 A related textual alienation occurs in the anonymous *A Warning for Fair Women* (1599), another play about a kind of enforced marriage. There one

Browne woos happily married Anne Sanders, aided by a Mrs. Drurie, who reads Anne's palm and prophesies a second husband for her. Anne wishes God's will to be done, but recoils from any wish for a second marriage. Then a dumb show depicts her conversion to active participation in the murder plot: "the Furies fill wine, Lust drinckes to Browne, he to Mistres Sanders, she pledgeth him: Lust embraceth her, she thrusteth Chastity from her, Chastity wringes her hands, and departs" (810–13). As in *Miseries*, the playwright omits any psychologistic confrontation with the crucial moment of willed conversion. The contrast with the detailed investigations of Faustus and Macbeth is strong. *The Miseries of Enforced Marriage* of course goes even further, into full invisibility. Wilkins's will seems clear, though not his purpose.

52 See *Being and Nothingness* 509 (and 506–10).

53 Compare Mallin's discussion of competitive male bonding in the group kissing scene in *Troilus and Cressida*, in "Emulous Factions" 161–62. The interlacing of hetero- and homoerotic relations link strongly to the prodigal ideology here. Compare too how modern parents can instrumentalize children as relational tools, as in "Go give your aunt a kiss."

54 See Boose, "The Father and the Bride in Shakespeare."

55 See Slater, *Family Life* 27–31, and consider the expressly familial depredations of Pecunius Lucre in Middleton's *A Trick to Catch the Old One*.

56 For reproductions see Goody, *The Development of the Family and Marriage in Europe* 134–46.

57 When Harcop confronts his daughter's death and chooses perjured Scarborrow as the vessel of responsibility, he returns to the same language: "he deceived thee in a Mother's hopes, / Posterity, the bliss of marriage" (912). The dream, if differently held, is both his and hers – a final reaffirmation of the commitment to such familial production and reproduction.

58 One can, of course, read Clare's investment simply as internalized oppression, but this seems something of a Freudian loop. Internalized oppression existed, and was widespread, but Clare's honed interrogation of Scarborrow ought to earn for her the right to be taken seriously, like Rosalind or Portia, as a representation of an intelligent and thoughtful, i.e. unbenighted, early modern Englishwoman. If all such women "must have been" embracing their own simple oppression, if the only legitimacy lay in striving to be Moll Cutpurse, then we indulge, I think, in a great anachronism – or a great condescension.

59 For a related (and chilling) idea from absolute-monarchy theory, see Somerville, *Politics and Ideology in England, 1603–1640* 25: "In matrimony the power of the husband sprang not from any transference of power by the wife, but from God. The wife's consent made the man her husband, but did not give him power, for husbandly power was natural, and had been imprinted by God in man's nature at the creation." This analogy, taken from Marc'Antonio De Dominis, *De republica eccesiastica pars secunda* (919), is used to explain that kings might be chosen by the people without that fact implying that the people had any inherent capacity for political power themselves. Similarly, the loci of origin of married status and of gender-political subjection are split apart on this account, denying the

woman any prior capacity as an independent reservoir of self-determination which might then be transferred by will. Clare is likewise degraded, regardless of her will.

60 The *tester* is the canopy over the bed.

61 The mirror-reversal of Ilford's fantasy of predatory daughters and fathers perhaps amounts to standing patriarchy on its feet, to adapt Marx's critique of Hegel. Yet such a view may obscure other important aspects of this social knot, imperfectly visible within the analytic dimension of gender, only locally singled out at present.

62 For a link between bloody cloth and enforced marriage (and the bloody handkerchief in *The Spanish Tragedy*), see Blayney, "Field's Parody."

63 Compare the situation in *Timon* 1.1, where an Old Athenian is angered when his daughter is wooed by one of Timon's servants; the father has been "inclined to thrift" all his life, and says, "My estate deserves an heir more raised / Than one which holds a trencher" (125–26). Sonless old men did sometimes invest essentially dynastic desires in their daughters.

64 Are there status differences between Harcop's prospective enforcement and Lord Faulconbridge's? Perhaps Harcop would only bargain his way into controlling Clare: compare the successful pleadings of Old Thorney with Frank in *The Witch of Edmonton*. Lord Faulconbridge delivered Scarborrow an ultimatum, but he began slowly, only becoming enraged when Scarborrow flouted his will. Indeed, Harcop reproaches Scarborrow precisely for betraying an unenforced obligation, freely entered into:

> ... villain, to betroth thyself
> To this good creature, harmless, harmless child,
> This kernel hope, and comfort of my house,
> Without Enforcement, of thine own accord,
> Draw all her soul its compass of an oath,
> Take that oath from her, make her for none but thee,
> And then betray her?   (974–80)

Harcop denies any part in the betrothal (though his own silence at the end regarding the guardian might easily be seen as culpable; hence perhaps the denial), the more to convict Scarborrow. Clare, however, feels her father's enforcement always looming, a clear limit to her fate (whether to choose someone or no one). Each deals with Lord Faulconbridge's enforcement and its effects by making personal use of the same concept. Wilkins's mastertrope permeates his entire discourse of marital determination.

65 Several kinds of logic construct such a denial. (1) An inversion of the logic of "condoning adultery." In such case, "if there was sexual intercourse between [husband and wife] after adultery by either was known to the other, the adultery was considered to have been condoned, and was no longer grounds for divorce, unless fresh acts of adultery were committed" (Wolfram, *In-Laws and Outlaws* 118.) (2) The rape victim's supposed obligation to suicide. This configuration is closest to Clare's case, since both deal in suicide. Clare and Scarborrow share the gesture structurally, though suicide and sexual abstention are so incommensurate in scale as to seem an opposition. The shared sense of sexual violation is strong, however. (3) As with Angelo and Mariana in *Measure for Measure*, the fact that a broken betrothal *per verba*

de futuro would be reactivated and made a marriage by sexual intercourse. (See Pollock and Maitland, *The History of English Law* 2.368.) (4) That in thus banishing marital sex Scarborrow perhaps echoes Clare's own momentary wish for a regressed virgin life free of parental marital dominion.

66 The reference is doubly ironic, really, since Pharaoh's kine remained lean, as will the gallants outside Family.

67 Hence perhaps the Prodigals' focus on the riches got by marriage rather than on Scarborrow's relation to his own family name, which of course has its own financial portion attached (released to him upon marriage). Scarborrow himself tends in his hostility to conflate his traditional obligations to both sides of his family, blood and affiance, Scarborrow siblings and his Faulconbridge wife.

68 Such sentiments resemble Posthumus's bitter "we are all bastards" (*Cymbeline* 2.5.2). His cuckolding "full-acorned boar," that "cried 'O!' and mounted" (16–17), chimes fascinatingly with the Prodigal discourse, especially in linking swine and power.

69 We might also remark an etymological fact. *OED* defines *bully* as "a term of endearment and familiarity, orig. applied to either sex: sweetheart, darling." ... "Later applied to men only, implying friendly admiration: good friend, fine fellow, 'gallant.'" (sb.I.1). These terms perhaps overlap in a certain libidinal fashion, describing the gray-area embrace of community that Wentloe extends to Scarborrow. It seems also likely that Wilkins means *bully* to echo the calf imagery, here inflated to bull status in congratulation, a breath later (at 1205) repositioned as bovine/prodigal cannibalism.

70 For a sense of the totalized normative ground that Wentloe and Bartley seek to pull out from under marriage, like a rug, see these lines from Middleton's *The Phoenix* (1607):

> Reverend and honorable Matrimony,
> Mother of lawful sweets, unshamed mornings,
> Dangerless pleasures! thou that mak'st the bed
> Both pleasant and legitimately fruitful!
> Without thee,
> All the whole world were soiled bastardy.
> Thou are the only and the greatest form
> That put'st a difference between our desires
> And the disorder'd appetites of beasts,
> Making their mates those that stand next their lusts.   (2.2.161–70)

Middleton's highly moral Phoenix, a self-conscious duke's heir, appears almost to see bastardy as a universal precondition, deflected by marriage, rather than as a negative logical product of the system. Similarly, Scarborrow's companions see it as a universal that marriage simply disguises.

71 I owe special thanks to Dorothy Stephens for striking comments throughout on the matter of Egypt.

72 For an unsentimental analysis of this transition, see Giddens, *The Consequences of Modernity* 100–11, and esp. the chart at 102.

73 For a rich introduction to the early modern protest on behalf of neglected younger brothers see Thirsk, "Younger Sons."

74 For a bricoleur's parallel compare *King Lear* 3.4.14–16: "Filial ingratitude! /
Is it not as this mouth should tear this hand / For lifting food to it?"

75 Given Wilkins's emphasis on drink as a marker of selective identification, it
is interesting to note the general absence of the "hem, boys" pledging
discourse so well known from Prince Hal's below-stairs sojourn with Francis
the drawer. There a privatized sub-society at potential odds with traditional
authority is at least partly visible to Hal, who fishes ambivalently for it, and
drinks at least partly with and to it. Why "hemming" should not serve here
in opposition to the traditional authority of the family is not clear. Certainly
Harcop's imitative or pleading hemming (171) presupposes such an oppositional bond, by its hearty envious self-insinuation. Perhaps hemming is too
associated with holiday escapist time, too hard to recast as a full alternative
way of life, which is what Wilkins seeks to oppose to kinship ideology.

It is likewise surprising to find so little troping of *vomiting* in the play. The
figure of vomiting at 1347 nicely captures the idea of Ilford living off
Scarborrow's own substance, lost in dissipation. Prodigal vomiting would
perfectly oppose ingesting familial nourishment, as organic *spilling* – as if
wine makes one vomit one's food (perhaps even "vomit it to" others). For
analogous troping see Middleton's *Michaelmas Term* (Levin edition
1.1.184–94), where some gallants discuss where to eat venison:

> SALEWOOD The Horn were a fit place.
> LETHE For venison fit,
> The horn having chas'd it,
> At the Horn we'll –
> Rhyme to that?
> COCKSTONE Taste it.
> SALEWOOD Waste it.
> REARAGE Cast it.
> LETHE That's the true rhyme, indeed.
> We hunt our venison twice, I tell you,
> First out o'th'park, next out o'th'belly.
> COCKSTONE First dogs take pains to make it fit for men,
> Then men take pain to make it fit for dogs.

Perhaps Wilkins's silence here also derives from a preemptive prior coding:
the benign utility of vomiting in Renaissance medicine. (See Paster, *The
Body Embarrassed*). Can it be relevant that vomiting is, as it were, as solid to
gaseous hemming? Can the omissions be cognate?

76 For the coincidence of barmaids, alehouses, and sexual sale, see Quaife,
Wanton *Wenches and Wayward Wives* 146–49. For road as whore, see *Henry
IV, Part Two* 2.2.158.

77 For rich treatment of sibling rivalry in this play see Montrose, " 'The Place
of a Brother.' "

78 Perhaps there is also some association through *pollack* with the wide variety
of tropes in which fish figure (sexual) women.

79 For these frightening details see Boose, "Scolding Brides and Bridling
Scolds."

80 Another sense of the same effect is that pissing is not phallic but leaky and
vulnerable, in the mode Stallybrass has marked in "The Body Enclosed":

maybe Scarborrow's pathetic attempt at masculinity displays him as feminized. Compare Paster, *The Body Embarrassed* 23–63.

81 This transformation from passive to active (the shift from such homelessness as Shakebag fears to brave outlawry; see also *As You Like It* 2.3.31–33) raises a comparative question regarding women and whoredom. What is the strong term for women? If an abandoned daughter or sister must turn punk, as everyone assumes, the role seems to figure an ultimate loss whose structural core is passivity. (That's why Prodigals like them.) They have lost even the fictional empowerment conferred on maids by courteous wooing. Are the grasping whores so feared and mocked and spurned and castrated by misogynist thinking really then the strong pole? Scorned but also feared, as would-be agents, whose hunger for agency is especially intense and fearful by view of their totalized subjection? The rage of Scarborrow's self-destruction and his characterization of himself as weak as a punk (1472) seem to fit this view.

82 This odd image may derive from Marston's *Fawn*: "NYMPHADORO How dost thou feel thyself now, Fawn [having been promoted]? HERCULES Very womanly, with my fingers: I protest I think I shall love you. Are you married?" (*The Fawn* 2.1.46–48). The link between promotion and eroticism is striking, and both plays concern resistance to Family.

83 Ilford's irritation at Bartley's query about filial feeling may be a Scarborrow-esque denial out of injury, shadowing his origins. The gesture resembles Antonio's denial of love in *The Merchant of Venice* when his feelings of loss are interrogated ("Fie fie!" – 1.1.46).

Note also the presumption that inheritance requires marriage. Ilford claims emotional indifference to his father's death, but moves to provide for an heir at once. Perhaps wiving secures thriving, as Petruchio's rhyme suggests. Both he and Ilford have "goods at home," but set off at once "to wive it wealthily" (*Shrew* 1.2.55, 56, 74).

84 For a link between this speech and the cattle discourse, here and in Marston's *The Fawn*, see Richard Levin, "A Marston–Wilkins Borrowing."

85 Wentloe later imagines that Scarborrow has arranged the trick marriage of Sister to Ilford, with a view "to be rid of her himself" (2182–83).

86 See Bourdieu's emphasis on the generally dual status of brotherhood in this regard: "the closest genealogical relationship, that between brothers, is also the point of greatest tension, and only incessant work can maintain the community of interests" (*Outline* 39).

87 As Dorothy Stephens reminds me, the term *puppet* proliferates the notion of seizure here: originally a diminutive endearment (as *OED poppet* sb.1); then generally contemptuous (puppet sb.1); also a mere figure of a human being (sb.2); also "contemptuously applied to an image or other material object which is worshipped" (sb.2b); also "a person ... whose acts, while ostensibly his own, are suggested and controlled by another" (sb.3b). Poppet also can refer to "a small human figure, used for purposes of sorcery or witchcraft" (sb.2b).

88 See Bourdieu, *Outline* 11–12.

89 Regarding such obsessive repetitions (see also "their soules" at 2638), compare Wojciehowski, "For the Love of the Father."

90 There is a series of arguments among earlier readers about the relation between the authors and texts of *The Miseries of Enforced Marriage* and *A Yorkshire Tragedy*, energized by the possibility of Shakespeare's involvement, by the *Tragedy*'s self-description as "one of the four Plays in one," and by the general concerns with textual disintegration in the first half of the century. These arguments explore versions of the idea that the *Tragedy* was an alternative ending for *Miseries*. I am interested rather in the effects of the various endings than their ascription history. However, for convenience I list some significant contributions to this discussion: Fleay, *A Biographical Chronicle* II: 206–8; Sykes, *Sidelights on Shakespeare* 77–98; A. M. Clark, *Thomas Heywood* 301–28; Friedlander, "Some Problems of *A Yorkshire Tragedy*"; Maxwell, "*A Yorkshire Tragedy*" 138–96; Blayney, "Wilkins's Revisions."

91 Indeed, Cawley and Gaines present evidence that Calverley turned down a larger dowry (£1500, compared to £1000) attached to his guardian's choice, in order to gain what thus looks like a love-match. "Walter thus seems to have married the woman of his choice, the one that [her mother, Anne Lady Cobham, said in a letter of 1599 to Sir Robert Cecil that] he took 'some likinge of' " (Introduction 9).

92 Some think this scene was added to allow this play to flow from the narrative of *The Miseries of Enforced Marriage*: see Cawley and Gaines edition 13–15.

93 The role of the pamphlet's Harcop figure (invisible in *A Yorkshire Tragedy*) also differs somewhat from Harcop's in *Miseries* (where it was associated with one version of enforcement). Calverley was invited in direct hope of landing him for the daughter (see *Murthers* 15–19), but the young people "fall in love" privately, and when he learns of it the father plays an overtly hands-off role. The news "came to the fathers knowledge, who with a natural joy, was contented with the contract; yet in regard Maister Caverleys yeeres could not discharge the charge his honourable guardian had over him: the father thought it meete, (though the lovers could have wished it otherwaies,) to lengthen their desired haste, till time should finish a fit howre to solemnize their happy wedlocke" (*Murthers* 26–32). The father makes no move to notify the guardian, but also acknowledges his authority, and though he wants the ward for "Clare," does not act to steal him, letting time do the work.

94 Cawley and Gaines 1–2.

95 For related emphases see the heir Matthew Flowerdale's endlessly asserted rage in *The London Prodigal*.

96 See Goffman, "Where the Action Is" 149; Goffman attributes the line "to Karl Wallenda, on going back up to the high wire after his troupe's fatal Detroit accident."

97 The comparison with Scarborrow is instructive. Scarborrow feels betrayed as a gentleman when he is forced to falsify his oath to Clare (see *Miseries* 469–71); this besmirches his honor. He hates being revealed as *weak*. But it does not elevate Lord Faulconbridge improperly above him. Lord Faulconbridge is, after all, his superior in rank; no one questions that fact, only the hateful power that goes with it.

98 This solution was not restricted to the Calverley discourse (cf. Scarborrow's

similar words at 2387). John Taylor the Water Poet retold the tale of the murderous fishmonger John Rowse, "a Gentlemans companion, of good reputation and calling," who strove (with similar partial success) to kill his children to save them from the shame and grief of begging their livings. See "The Unnatural Father" 137. (Taylor cites the similar case of *Arden of Faversham* for a moral explanation via lust; see 140).

99 See *Miseries* 915. The Husband's multiple stabbings have much of the affect of modern psychotic murder, but such cumulative horror is evident in other early modern plays. Not only *Macbeth*, but also, closer to home here, in *Two Lamentable Tragedies*, where the murder of Master Beech the chandler is stage-directed precisely thus: "*Then being in the vpper room* Merry *strickes him in the head fifteene times*" (sig. B4r).

100 See Maxwell, "*A Yorkshire Tragedy*" 177.

101 Cawley and Gaines, Introduction, 11. Maxwell in fact suggests that these two strands may have been causally related: "It may well have been that the report concerning his brother [regarding his imprisonment] decided him to put into execution at once the thought which he had entertained 'for the whole space of two years' of killing the children, whose legitimacy he questioned, and so make his imprisoned brother his heir" ("*A Yorkshire Tragedy*" 166). Killing ("one's") children (even if bastards) to endow a brother as heir would indeed instantiate familial contradiction.

102 The play begins with Roderigo's wounded complaint about Iago's concealment of the elopement.

103 Dated 3 July and 24 August 1605, respectively; see Cawley and Gaines, edition 11, and notes 50 and 51, citing Arber's Stationer's *Register*, III, 295, 299.

4. SEXUAL AND SOCIAL MOBILITY IN
THE DUCHESS OF MALFI

1 For a summary of the debate see Aberle *et al.*, "The Incest Taboo."

2 Goody, "Incest and Adultery" 32, 35–42, 46.

3 Burke, *Rhetoric* 279–80. However, compare Marotti, "Countertransference," esp. 486.

4 Parsons, "The Incest Taboo" 19. As has often been observed, this account slurs the distinction between the incest taboo (on sexual relations within the group) and the injunction to exogamy (prohibiting marriage within the group). For the purposes of this study the gap may be collapsed, given the link between prohibitions of sex and of marriage within a descent group. "If therefore the rule of exogamy is to be related to the external value of the marriage alliance ... then the intra-group prohibition on intercourse cannot be dissociated from it. The rejection of temporary sexuality within the group is in part a reflection of the rejection of permanent sexuality, and the latter is related to the importance of establishing inter-group relations by the exchange of rights in women" (Goody, "Incest and Adultery" 44). In the case of incest with blood relatives (as in Webster) the explanations of the incest taboo and exogamy thus tend to be congruent. It should also be observed that Parsons's attention (and mine) begins with consensual incest,

as a structural phenomenon; incest as child abuse, perhaps our most familar modern form, requires a different historical specificity, and will be bracketed here.

5 Firth, *We the Tikopia* 340.

6 It is no surprise to find this open formulation in a pioneering study of Polynesia, a region famous (among anthropologists, anyway) for incest. Russell Middleton quotes this passage by way of conclusion in arguing for the non-universality of the incest taboo by reference to Egyptian exceptions, especially in the middle class. See "A Deviant Case." Bourdieu's analysis of parallel-cousin marriage, "a sort of quasi-incest" strategically deployed (*Outline* 40), offers an extended test of this kind of thinking (see 307–71).

7 *The Complete Works of John Webster* II.23–24.

8 Leech, *John Webster: A Critical Study* 100ff.

9 Mulryne, "*The White Devil* and *The Duchess of Malfi*" 223.

10 Leech, *Webster: The Duchess of Malfi* 57. The issues of restraint seem to be adapted from Ernest Jones's famous account of Hamlet's delay. See *Hamlet and Oedipus*.

11 *John Webster* 144.

12 Rose faults my "complete rejection" of "an analytic focus on the erotic" (*The Expense of Spirit* 162). And Malcolmson, writing of gender and status, remarks upon the Burke epigraph's displacement of the sexual by the social ("'What You Will'" 52–53). McCabe concurs, and judges further, "Whigham's interpretation suffers from confusing incest with endogamy, related concepts certainly but hardly identical," dismisses my concern with a reductive eroticizing of the Duchess's actions, and asserts that "Ferdinand's overtly canvassed pride is at best a *sexual posture*" (*Incest, Drama, and Nature's Law* 251–52).

So far as neglect of the erotic goes, to some degree the problem inscribes a critical-historical transition, having to do with varied and shifting definitions and positionings of the erotic (the sheerly personal? the private? lust? the "feminine"? procreation? parturition?) and the social (the political? the status-specific? the "public"?). I was originally differing with an earlier interpretive tradition (of the 1960s and 1970s), then still powerful, that seemed to me moralistically and sometimes misogynistically reductive, treating the Duchess as limited to and defined by a reduced and negative notion of the erotic (see Leech; Calderwood, "*The Duchess of Malfi*"; Peterson *Curs'd Example*). In proposing a sense of women's identity that transcended the "merely" erotic I hardly meant to deny women a significant erotic identity; it seemed crucial to insist on the *social* – as a claim to, not a denial of, the Duchess's substantiality. Hitherto her social identity had generally been reduced to her status as duchess, and acknowledged only as her failure to live up to it. Insofar as my insistence displaced appropriate attention to a rich sense of the erotic, I erred, and accept my reproof. The Duchess's sexuality is patently central to the play. With respect, however, I wish to claim an error of letter, not spirit. I persist in thinking her sexuality to be inescapably social, which for me embraces the private and public, conferring upon them, as Rose nicely puts it, "equal distinction" (162).

13 *Grammar* 24–25; see 21–58 generally.

14 McCabe argues that "an aristocratic endogamist" would be anxious to provide issue, and cites D'Amville's action in *The Atheist's Tragedy* (*Incest, Drama, and Nature's Law* 252; cf. 218–22); thus Ferdinand's incest supposedly cannot have this force. But if reproduction entails contact, and all contact is felt as degrading, then Ferdinand can easily, if illogically, be so endogamous as to be both incestuous and completely withholding. His is not, after all, rational behavior. (Ferdinand does, of course, speak of a candidate, the Count Malateste [3.1.41], but the character does not appear; Lorenzo's Balthazar is not here at all.)

15 "Honour and Social Status" 31.

16 See *Church Courts* 245–49.

17 Some of this critique's energy probably also derived from native English resentment of what was widely perceived as *Scots* favoritism in the first years of the new king's reign: a sort of irresponsible *nationalist* incest.

18 On *par sibi* see Hereward T. Price, "Like Himself." On the general issue of "degree" compare Selzer, "Merit and Degree in Webster's *The Duchess of Malfi*," which overlaps my analysis here, but works with a reified moral sense of "degree" and does not address ideological concerns. He does, however, directly link the incest motif to social segregation, observing that Ferdinand's "tendency toward incest" is "rooted in an obsession with rank" (74).

In "Mine Eyes Dazzle" Empson argued, more specifically historically, that "Elizabethans believed that Lucrezia Borgia went to bed with her brothers because, owing to her intense family pride, which was like that of the Pharaohs, she could find no fit mate elsewhere" (85). Much later he wrote to me that he could not recall the documentary source for this claim, though there was one. Tales of incest with her father, Pope Alexander VI, seem to have begun when he dissolved her marriage to Giovanni Pesaro, who charged that Alexander wanted her for himself; public opinion soon extended the idea to her brothers (Erlanger, *Lucrezia Borgia* 100). England gloated accordingly. *The Pageant of the Popes* (1574, attributed to John Bale), for instance, reports various epitaphs for Alexander and Lucrezia: "Defying lawes of earth and heaven and God himselfe erewhile, / So that the sinful father did the daughters bed defile" (sig. Y4r), and "Here lyes Lucretia chast by name, but Thais lewd by lyfe, / Who was to Alexander Pope [sic] both doughter and his wyfe" (sig. Y5v; translating a Latin epitaph by Giovanni Pontano; see Erlanger 327). I have not, however, found Elizabethan texts expressing Empson's exact view. (See Mallett, *The Borgias*; Fusero, *The Borgias*; and Erlanger, *Lucrezia Borgia*.)

The constructive (as opposed to distinctive) version of such investment is easier to find. Ovid's Myrrha laments her subjection to the incest taboo, and envies those "tribes among whom mother with son, daughter with father mates, so that natural love is increased by the double bond" (*ut pietas geminato crescat amore*) (*Metamorphoses* X.331–33).

19 Citations are taken from Brown's edition.

20 The prosthetic metaphor was used expressly at the time. "One French writer, discussing Henry IV's murderer, [observed] that, just as the knife was 'but the instrument of Ravailac,' so Ravaillac [sic] was just the

instrument of his Jesuit masters." Cited from W. Crashaw (translator), *A Discourse to the Lords of Parliament* (1611), A2v (by Wiggins, *Journeymen in Murder* 63).

21 For the norm, cf. another tyrannical ruler, who dismisses an impudent courtier with these words: "Away with him, Ile teach him know his place; / To frown when we frown, smile on whom we grace." The ruler is Mary Tudor, the impudent servant a spokesman for the young Princess Elizabeth, in Heywood's *If You Know Not Me, You Know Nobody* [1605] (cited from *Dramatic Works of Thomas Heywood* I:197). Cf. also Wyatt, "Mine own John Poyntz" 53–54: "Grin when he laugheth that beareth all the sway, / Frown when he frowneth and groan when he is pale . . . ."

22 Hunter observes of the related "disguised prince" motif that one usually finds both "the desire to participate" and "the desire to condemn and withdraw." (See "English Folly and Italian Vice" 101; cf. Auden, "The Joker in the Pack.")

23 Bargemen's thighs were independently noteworthy. In a poem on the removal of Queen Elizabeth's corpse to Whitehall by water, William Camden writes, "I thinke the Barge-men might with easier thighes / Have rowed her thither in her peoples eyes." (See *Poems* 112.)

24 That we still respond to such shocks, though perhaps along different axes, may be seen by reference to Billy Wilder's *Sunset Boulevard* (1950), where we shudder at the news that Erich von Stroheim, Gloria Swanson's butler, is her former husband. Then as now these are categories difficult to mix.

25 Nohrnberg, *The Analogy of 'The Faerie Queene'* 432.

26 This argument also appropriates Brennan's formulation (to which I am indebted) that Ferdinand responds as a cuckold rather than a wounded brother ("The Relationship between Brother and Sister" 493). The audience of *The Duchess of Malfi*, like Hamlet, might be "horrified" by incest as "too far in"; the cuckold, like the incestuous Ferdinand, is enraged by sexual activity "too far out." Hamlet perhaps bridges the categories, horrified by the incest and envying its beneficiary.

27 See "Purification, Thanksgiving, and the Churching of Women." Regarding the element of "reentry," cf. Philip Slater's suggestion that "the advent of the first child in itself tends to weaken the exclusive intimacy of the dyad, first by providing an important alternative (and narcissistic) object of cathexis for each member, and second, by creating responsibilities and obligations which are partly societal in nature, and through which bonds between the dyad and the community are thereby generated" ("Social Limitations on Libidinal Withdrawal"127). Perhaps the ritual of churching was also a kind of summons from the seductive dyadic withdrawal of mother and child, famous for this capacity to disrupt (and replicate) the mutual absorption of husband and wife.

28 See Leviticus 12:1–7, usually interpreted as specifying two waiting periods: seven days before sexual relations, 33 before the resort to the sanctuary (or 14 and 66 with a supposedly more polluting female child) (see *The Anchor Bible*, Leviticus 1–16: 763–1009); "The Churching of Women" 115–16; and Crawford, "Attitudes to Menstruation" 60–63.

29 See Ekeblad, "The 'Impure Art' of John Webster," and Wadsworth,

" 'Rough Music.' " See also Pitt-Rivers, "Honour and Social Shame" 47ff.; Thomas, "The Place of Laughter" 77; Ingram, "Rough Music"; and Davis, "Women on Top."

30 Cited by J. W. Spargo in *Juridical Folklore* 9–10.

31 For fascinating discussion of the erotic force of the prosthesis see Randall, "Rank and Earthy Background."

32 I cite Nohrnberg's translation of Comes' Renaissance version from the *Mythologiae*, which details the death (see *The Analogy of 'The Faerie Queene'* 433n); for Pausanias see *Description of Greece*, IX, 31.78.

33 Ferdinand is troubled by the birds of the field, to whom the duchess looks with envy, as we shall see.

34 For this striking and convincingly authorial view of Ferdinand's internal wolvish hair see Susan C. Baker, "The Static Protagonist in *The Duchess of Malfi*" 350.

35 Allison observed a version of this balanced contrast some thirty years ago. Speaking of the "self-will and erotic bent" that Ferdinand and the Duchess share, he says that "obverse aspects of the same temperamental excess have brought brother and sister to catastrophe" ("Ethical Themes" 266.)

36 Puttenham, *The Arte of English Poesie* 106.

37 Despite documentary arguments against remarrying widows and for the obligations of state service, I think it unlikely that auditors are supposed to find the Duchess's action immoral, anti-social, hubristic, and licentious, as some readers believe (e.g., Leech, *Webster*; Calderwood, "Styles of Ceremony"; Peterson, *Curs'd Example*). Certainly the Duchess's plight is pathetic, but the chief objection to seeing her as deservedly punished is that it is precisely the ideology that grounds such a judgment – Ferdinand's ideology – that the play puts most deeply in question. And anyway, any reader of Boklund's source study can see how far Webster went to problematize moral judgments that were easy for William Painter. Empson's irascible retort to Leech is essential reading on this point: "the play has a popular Dickensian moral, against the wicked rich; whereas our critical attempt to recover the ethics of a nobler age has been limited to recovering subservient or bootlicking morals" (" 'Mine Eyes Dazzle' " 85). Steen rehearses a quite varied range of contemporary reactions to the similarly transgressive marriage of Arbella Stuart ("The Crime of Marriage").

38 *The Lawes Resolution* 232.

39 See Brodsky, "Widows in Late Elizabethan London"; Todd, "The Remarrying Widow"; and Slater, *Family Life* 142–43 (quoted above, pp. 28–29). Slater recounts mixed effects, in which widows had more freedom in spousal choice for the next marriage, since the widow's jointure served as a dowry at her own disposal, but concludes that few gentlewomen were "willing to remain in that condition permanently. As one widow who spoke from experience put it, widowhood was a 'desolate, discontented, estate' " (*Family Life* 105–6).

40 In "Catholic and Protestant Widows" Mikesell reads these options as religiously coded.

41 "Honor and Social Status" 69–70.

42 *Autobiography* 33; see also 156.

43 See Stone, *Family, Sex, and Marriage* 281–82; Todd convincingly disputes the empirical credibility of widows' supposed lustfulness ("The Remarrying Widow" 77).

44 Ingram, *Church Courts* 245. For a different argument linking punishment of the Duchess with landholding and inheritance, see Jardine, "A Case Study."

45 Marlowe is adduced here by Berggren ("Womanish Mankind" 353). The echo of Tamburlaine's royal human footstools is striking, but the link is not sheerly Webster's intensive metaphor. Elizabeth Cary, author of *The Tragedy of Mariam*, also wrote in youth (before 1605?) a "life of Tamberlaine in verse," the best of her early writings according to her daughter's memoir (190).

46 The paradox of wilderness in search of domesticity can be partially deciphered by Fowler's alignment of wildness with chastity and tameness with submission to a lover's will, in regard to Wyatt's "Whoso list to hunt." (See his review, "Power to the Self.") Webster's adventuress is wildly venturesome in the social terms of marital choice, and determinedly wild in her marital chastity. (Such double chiastic wildness also seems in play in the Wyatt poem Fowler argues about with Stephen Greenblatt in this review of *Renaissance Self-Fashioning*.) For the duchess the real wild is the uncharted social waste she seeks to colonize and cultivate in marriage, though she must enter it by means anything but domestic from the culture's normative viewpoint.

47 See Luckyj, *A Winter's Snake* 76–91 for a related sympathetic treatment of Julia.

48 Cf. Rose, *Expense* 168.

49 The couple's direct sexual step here was frequently taken onstage without negative comment. Compare similar episodes in the following plays: *Sir Giles Goosecap*; Middleton, *The Family of Love*; Haughton, *Englishmen for my Money*; Tourneur, *The Atheist's Tragedy*; Dekker, *I The Honest Whore*; Heywood, *The English Traveller*. (I owe this list to Meader, *Courtship in Shakespeare* 186–93.)

50 Myrrha's speech funds defenses of incest or dark sexuality in Marston's *Dutch Courtesan* (2.1), Tourneur's *Atheist's Tragedy* (4.3), and Massinger's *Unnatural Combat* (5.2). Dorothy Stephens suggests further to me that Britomart's brief envy of Myrrha for at least possessing her outrageous love (after seeing Arthegall in the magic mirror) may mediate between Ovid and Webster here. See *The Faerie Queene* 3.2.41–43.

51 Leech comments that "this longing for the first chaos links her with many characters in Elizabethan and Jacobean drama whose ambitions are thwarted and who would in anger overturn the hierarchies of 'degree.'" He quotes Northumberland's "Let order die!" speech from *Henry IV, Part Two*, and suggests that "just as Shakespeare wished to make clear the nature and ultimate goal of rebellion, so here Webster shows us a woman at odds with life itself ... There is a grandeur in the egoism, but its implications are essentially anarchic" (*John Webster* 76–77). But Leech has omitted the definitive case of *King Lear*, and in any event, the moral weight of rebellion depends on what is being rejected.

52 In this I thus disagree with the dystopic reading of Jardine, in "A Case

Study," which seems to me to approach congruence with some older anti-duchess readings, from a quite different direction.

53 MacCaffrey, "Place and Patronage" 104.

54 For discussions which presume Antonio to be ambitious in the wooing scene see Berry, *The Art of John Webster* 108–9, and Best, "A Precarious Balance" 169.

55 For galley life see Alberto Tenenti, *Piracy* 112–16.

56 Stone, *Crisis of the Aristocracy* 65–128 and *passim*.

57 See Marx, *The German Ideology, Part One* 42.

58 Marx, *The Communist Manifesto* 9.

59 Ornstein adumbrated this idea in less detail, suggesting that Bosola "seeks to give meaning to his life by loyal service" (*The Moral Vision of Jacobean Tragedy* 143).

60 Marx, *Economic and Philosophical Manuscripts of 1844* 110–11.

61 See Sorel, *Reflections on Violence* 39, 287.

62 It can also operate by *recontextualizing*, seizing membership in some transhistorical community: something like Machiavelli's own escapist evening resort to the ancients, or even the communal interlocution of such as Virgil, Sidney, and Spenser. For Machiavelli see Rebhorn, *Foxes and Lions* 244–46; for the poetic-community parallel I thank Dorothy Stephens.

63 See Lukacs, "Reification" 139–40; Jauss, "The Idealist Embarrassment." Hunter speaks to the same issues: "[Flamineo and Bosola], like Malevole, are the individualists who know all the rules for individualists, know the meaninglessness of success, yet carry on, as if hypnotized by their own expertise. They indeed of all characters in the plays are least able to achieve any of their desired ends. As tool-villains they have to obey the rules of those who have hired them, and lack even the satisfaction of a Lodovico in 'limning' the night-piece of *The White Devil* (1612) – a satisfaction that seems to survive even when the artist himself is about to be 'dis-limbed' " ("English Folly and Italian Vice"104).

64 For more on this emphasis on style and manner see Whigham, *Ambition and Privilege* 34–39, 88–95.

65 Bosola's rejection of this strategy connects with his ridicule of the Old Lady (2.1.21–44) for what may be termed the conspicuous ontological repair of cosmetics, and with the equally bitter mock-instruction he gives Castruchio in how to "be taken for an eminent courtier" (2.1.1ff.). The energy of these otherwise disconnected speeches may easily be read as self-castigation deflected onto an easy target; see Whigham, *Ambition and Privilege* 116–18, 223 n.40.

66 The nostalgic edge of Bosola's praise ("yet" – 285) can be explained by the resentful claim of Castiglione's Vincent Calmeta that "now adaies very few are in favor with princes, but such as be malapert" (*Book of the Courtier* 110). Perhaps the ambitious always fear they have been left behind without realizing it; in any case, in that world rivals are always – contradictorily – presumptuous, versions of the self, deserving.

67 Among those who have made this connection are Best ("Precarious Balance" 173), Bradbrook (*John Webster* 159), and Selzer ("Merit and

Degree" 75). See also Rose's discussion of the contrast between (a) emergent bourgeois notions of merit and marriage and (b) residual elite notions of dualized female identity (idealizing and degrading) and political tyranny (*Expense* 165–66).

68 Warren, "*The Duchess of Malfi* on the Stage" 66.
69 Burke, *The Philosophy of Literary Form* 3–8.

Works cited

EARLY TEXTS

An Admonition to the Parliament (1571). *Puritan Manifestoes: A Study of the Origin of the Puritan Revolt, with a reprint of the Admonition to the Parliament and kindred documents, 1572*. Ed. W. H. Frere and C. E. Douglas. 1907; rpt. New York: Burt Franklin, 1972: 1–55.

The Anchor Bible, Leviticus 1–16. Trans. Jacob Milgrom. New York: Doubleday, 1991.

Arden of Faversham (1592). Ed. M. L. Wine. Manchester University Press, 1973.

Arden of Faversham (1592). Ed. Martin White. New York: Norton, 1982.

Ascham, Roger. *English Works*. Ed. William Aldis Wright. 1904; rpt. Cambridge University Press, 1970.

Bacon, Francis. *Essays* (1625). New York: Everyman, 1906.

Bale, John. *The Pageant of the Popes, now Englished with Additions by J. Studley* (1574).

Beaumont, Francis, and John Fletcher. *The Dramatic Works in the Beaumont and Fletcher Canon*. Ed. Fredson Bowers. Cambridge University Press, 1966.

Camden, William. *Poems*. Ed. George Burke Johnston. *SP* 72 (1975).

Cary, Elizabeth. *The Tragedy of Mariam* ... with *The Lady Falkland her Life*. Ed. Barry Weller and Margaret W. Ferguson. Berkeley: University of California Press, 1994.

Castiglione, Baldassare. *The Book of the Courtier* (1528). Trans. Thomas Hoby. 1561; rpt. New York: Everyman, 1966.

Cavendish, Margaret, Duchess of Newcastle. *The Life of William Cavendish, Duke of Newcastle* ... *[with] The True Relation of my Birth Breeding and Life* (1667). Ed. C. H. Firth. 2nd edn., revised. London: Routledge, 1906.

Chapman, George. *The Widow's Tears*. Ed. Ethel M. Smeak. Lincoln: University of Nebraska Press, 1966.

Daborne, Robert. *A Christian Turned Turk* (1610). Ed. A. E. H. Swaen. *Anglia* 20 (1897–98): 153–256.

Dekker, Thomas, John Ford, and William Rowley. *The Witch of Edmonton* (1621). Commentary by Simon Trussler, notes by Jacqui Russell. London: Methuen, 1983.

Donne, John, *John Donne*. Ed. John Carey. The Oxford Authors. Oxford University Press, 1990.

Drayton, Michael. *Works*. Ed. J. William Hebel. Corr. edn. Oxford: Shakespeare Head Press, 1961.

E., T. *The Lawes Resolution of Womens Rights* (1602?). 1632; rpt. Norwood NJ: Walter J. Johnson, 1979.

Filmer, Robert. *Patriarcha and Other Writings*. Ed. Johann P. Somerville. Cambridge University Press, 1991.

Ford, John. *The Broken Heart* (1633). Ed. T. J. B. Spencer. Manchester University Press, 1980.

Fraser, Russell A. and Norman Rabkin, eds. *Drama of the English Renaissance*. 2 vols. New York: Macmillan, 1976.

The Geneva Bible: A Facsimile of the 1560 Edition. Madison: University of Wisconsin Press, 1969.

Hall, Joseph. *Virgidemiarum* (1598). In *Poems*. Ed. Arnold Davenport. Liverpool University Press, 1969: 5–99.

Herbert, George. *The Works of George Herbert*. Ed. F. E. Hutchinson. Oxford: Clarendon, 1941.

Heywood, Thomas. *Dramatic Works*. 6 vols. 1874; rpt. New York: Russell, 1964.

Jonson, Ben. *Ben Jonson*. Ed. C. H. Herford, Percy Simpson, and Evelyn Simpson. 11 vols. Oxford: Clarendon, 1925–52.

Kyd, Thomas. *The First Part of Hieronymo* and *The Spanish Tragedy* (1605). Ed. Andrew S. Cairncross. Lincoln: University of Nebraska Press, 1967.

　The Spanish Tragedy (1592). Ed. J. R. Mulryne. 1970; 2nd edn. New York: Norton, 1989.

　The Spanish Tragedy (1592). Ed. Philip Edwards. 1959; rpt. Manchester University Press, 1977.

　The Works of Thomas Kyd. Ed. Frederick S. Boas. 1901; rpt. Oxford: Clarendon, 1955.

Leicester's Commonwealth (1584). (*History of Queen Elizabeth, Amy Robsart, and the Earl of Leicester, being a reprint of Leycesters Commonwealth* [1641].) Ed. Frank J. Burgoyne. London: Longmans, 1904.

Locrine (1595). *The Shakespeare Apocrypha*. Ed. C. F. Tucker Brooke. London: Oxford University Press, 1908.

The London Prodigal (1605). *The Shakespeare Apocrypha*. Ed. C. F. Tucker Brooke. Oxford: Clarendon, 1908.

Marlowe, Christopher. *Dido Queen of Carthage* and *The Massacre at Paris*. Ed. H. J. Oliver. London: Methuen, 1968.

Marston, John. *Parasitaster, or The Fawn* (1604). Ed. David A. Blostein. Manchester University Press, 1978.

　The Dutch Courtesan (1605). *The Selected Plays of John Marston*. Ed. MacDonald P. Jackson and Michael Neill. Cambridge University Press, 1986.

　The Malcontent (1604). Ed. Bernard Harris. 1967; rpt. New York: Norton, 1987.

Massinger, Philip. *The Plays and Poems of Philip Massinger*. Eds. Philip Edwards and Colin Gibson. Oxford: Clarendon, 1976.

Middleton, Thomas. *A Trick to Catch the Old One* (1605). Ed. G. J. Watson. London: Benn, 1968.

　The Phoenix [1604], by Thomas Middleton: A Critical, Modernized Edition. Ed. John Bradbury Brooks. 1965; rpt. New York: Garland, 1980.

Michaelmas Term (1607). Ed. Richard Levin. Lincoln: University of Nebraska Press, 1966.

Women Beware Women (1622). Ed. J. R. Mulryne. London: Methuen, 1975.

Nashe, Thomas. *Works.* Ed. R. B. McKerrow. Oxford: Blackwell, 1966.

Ovid. *Metamorphoses.* Trans. Frank Justus Miller. Loeb Classical Library. Cambridge: Harvard University Press, 1916.

Pausanias. *Description of Greece.* Trans. W. H. S. Jones. Loeb Classical Library. London: Heinemann, 1954.

Puttenham, George. *The Arte of English Poesie* (1589). Ed. Gladys Doidge Willcock and Alice Walker. Cambridge University Press, 1936.

Rogers, Thomas. *Leicester's Ghost* (1602–04). Ed. Franklin B. Williams, Jr. Chicago: University of Chicago Press, 1972.

Scot, Reginald. *The Discoverie of Witchcraft* (1584). 1930; rpt. New York: Dover, 1972.

Shakespeare, William. *Hamlet* (1600). Ed. Harold Jenkins. London: Methuen, 1982.

Henry V (1599). Ed. Gary Taylor. Oxford University Press, 1984.

The Complete Works of Shakespeare. Ed. David Bevington. 4th edn. New York: Harper, 1992.

Spenser, Edmund. *The Faerie Queene* (1596). Ed. A. C. Hamilton. London: Longman, 1977.

The Shorter Poems of Edmund Spenser. Ed. William A. Oram *et al.* New Haven: Yale University Press, 1989.

Statutes of the Realm, from Magna Carta to the End of the Reign of Queen Anne ... from original records and authentic manuscripts. London, 1810–28.

Stubbes, Philip. *The Anatomie of Abuses* (1583). Amsterdam: Theatrum Orbis Terrarum, 1972.

Swinburne, Henry. *A Treatise of Spousals* (ca. 1590). 1686; New York: Garland, 1978.

Taylor, John (the "Water Poet"). "The Unnatural Father." In *Works* (1630). Part II. 1869; rpt. New York: Burt Franklin, 1967: 135–42.

Tourneur, Cyril. *The Atheist's Tragedy* (1611). Ed. Brian Morris and Roma Gill. London: Benn, 1976.

A True Discourse Historicall of the succeeding Governors in the Netherlands, and the Civil Warres there begun in the yeere 1565 (1602). Cited in *The Works of Beaumont and Fletcher.* Ed. Alexander Dyce (1844): 7.133 (note to *The Woman's Prize, or The Tamer Tamed* 2.2).

Two Most Unnaturall and Bloodie Murthers (1605). Rpt. in *A Yorkshire Tragedy* (94–110).

A Warning for Fair Women: A Critical Edition (1599). Ed. Charles Dale Cannon. The Hague: Mouton, 1975.

Watson, Thomas. *The Hecatompathia or Passionate Century of Love* (1582). In *Poems.* Ed. Edward Arber. Arber's English Reprints. London, 1870.

Webster, John. *The Complete Works of John Webster.* Ed. F. L. Lucas. 4 vols. London: Chatto, 1927.

The Duchess of Malfi. Ed. John Russell Brown. London: Methuen, 1964.

Whythorne, Thomas. *Autobiography.* Modern Spelling Edition. Ed. James M. Osborn. London: Oxford University Press, 1962.

Wilkins, George. *The Miseries of Enforced Marriage* (1607). Ed. Glenn H. Blayney. Malone Society Reprints, 1963.

Wyatt, Thomas. *The Complete Poems*. Ed. R. A. Rebholz. New Haven: Yale University Press, 1978.

Yarrington, Robert. *Two Lamentable Tragedies* (1601). Tudor Facsimile Texts. 1913; rpt. New York: AMS, 1970.

A Yorkshire Tragedy (1608). Ed. A. C. Cawley and Barry Gaines. Manchester University Press, 1986.

LATER TEXTS

Aberle, David F. *et al.* "The Incest Taboo and the Mating Pattern of Animals." In *Marriage, Family, and Residence*. Ed. Paul Bohannon and John Middleton. Garden City NY: Natural History, 1968: 3–19.

Abrams, M. H., ed. *The Norton Anthology of English Literature: Major Authors*. 5th edn. New York: Norton, 1987.

Adelman, Janet. *Suffocating Mothers: Fantasies of Maternal Origin in Shakespeare's Plays, 'Hamlet' to 'The Tempest'*. New York: Routledge, 1992.

Aggeler, Geoffrey. "The Eschatological Crux in *The Spanish Tragedy*." *JEGP* 86 (1987): 319–31.

Allen, D. C. "On *Venus and Adonis*." In *Elizabethan and Jacobean Studies presented to Frank Percy Wilson in honour of his seventieth birthday*. Oxford: Clarendon, 1959: 100–11.

Allison, Alexander W. "Ethical Themes in *The Duchess of Malfi*." *SEL* 4 (1964): 263–73.

Althusser, Louis. "Ideology and Ideological State Apparatuses." In *Lenin and Philosophy*. Trans. Ben Brewster. New York: Monthly Review Press, 1971: 127–86.

Amussen, Susan. *An Ordered Society: Gender and Class in Early Modern England*. Oxford: Basil Blackwell, 1988.

Ardener, Shirley. "The Nature of Women in Society." In *Defining Females: The Nature of Women in Society*. Ed. Shirley Ardener. New York: Wiley, 1978: 9–48.

Attwell, David. "Property, Status, and the Subject in a Middle-Class Tragedy: *Arden of Faversham*." *ELR* 21 (1991): 328–48.

Auden, W. H. "The Joker in the Pack." In *The Dyer's Hand and Other Essays*. 1948; rpt. New York: Vintage, 1968: 246–72.

Baker, Susan C. "The Static Protagonist in *The Duchess of Malfi*." *TSLL* 22 (1980) 343–57.

Barber, C. L. " 'The forme of Faustus fortunes good or bad.' " Reprinted and revised by Richard P. Wheeler from *Tulane Drama Review* 8 (1964): 92–119, in *Creating Elizabethan Tragedy: The Theater of Marlowe and Kyd*. Ed. Richard P. Wheeler. Chicago: University of Chicago Press, 1988: 87–130.

Barish, Jonas. "*The Spanish Tragedy*, or The Pleasures and Perils of Rhetoric." In *Elizabethan Theater*. Ed. J. R. Brown and Bernard Harris. Stratford-upon-Avon Studies 9. New York: St. Martin's, 1967: 59–85.

Bellamy, John. *The Tudor Law of Treason: An Introduction*. London: Routledge, 1979.

Belsey, Catherine. *The Subject of Tragedy: Identity and Difference in Renaissance Drama*. London: Methuen, 1985.

Berger, Harry Jr. "What Did the King Know and When Did He Know It? Shakespearean Discourses and Psychoanalysis." *SAQ* 88 (1989): 832–41.

Berggren, Paula S. "Womanish Mankind: Four Jacobean Heroines." *International Journal of Women's Studies* 1 (1978): 349–62.

Berry, Ralph. *The Art of John Webster*. Oxford: Clarendon, 1972.

Best, Michael R. "A Precarious Balance: Structure in *The Duchess of Malfi*." In *Shakespeare and Some Others*. Ed. Alan Brissenden. Adelaide: University of Adelaide Press, 1976: 159–77.

Blayney, Glenn H. "G. Wilkins and the Identity of W. Calverley's Guardian." *N&Q* 298 (1953): 329–30.

"Variants in the First Quarto of *The Miseries of Inforst Mariage*." *The Library*, series 5, 9 (1954): 178–79.

"Field's Parody of a Murder Play." *N&Q* 200 (1955): 19–20.

"Wardship in English Drama 1600–1650." *SP* 53 (1956): 470–84.

"Wilkins's Revisions in *The Miseries of Inforst Mariage*." *JEGP* 56 [1957]: 23–41.

Boehrer, Bruce Thomas. *Monarchy and Incest in Renaissance England: Literature, Culture, Kinship, and Kingship*. Philadelphia: University of Pennsylvania Press, 1992.

Boklund, Gunnar. *'The Duchess of Malfi': Sources, Themes, Characters*. Cambridge: Harvard University Press, 1962.

Boose, Lynda E. "The Father and the Bride in Shakespeare." *PMLA* 97 (1982): 325–47.

"Othello's Handkerchief: 'The Recognizance and Pledge of Love.'" *ELR* 5 (1975): 360–70.

"Scolding Brides and Bridling Scolds: Taming the Woman's Unruly Member." *SQ* 42 (1991): 179–213.

Bourdieu, Pierre. *Outline of a Theory of Practice*. Trans. Richard Nice. 1972; Cambridge University Press, 1977.

Bowers, Fredson. "Kyd's Pedringano: Sources and Parallels." *Harvard Studies and Notes in Philology and Literature* 13 (1931): 241–49.

Elizabethan Revenge Tragedy, 1587–1642. Princeton University Press, 1940.

Bradbrook, Muriel C. *John Webster, Citizen and Dramatist*. New York: Columbia University Press, 1980.

Braden, Gordon. "Senecan Tragedy and the Renaissance." *Illinois Classical Studies* 9 (1984): 277–92.

Renaissance Tragedy and the Senecan Tradition. New Haven: Yale University Press, 1985.

Braunmuller, A. R. "'Second Means': Agent and Accessory in Elizabethan Drama." In *The Elizabethan Theatre* XI. Eds. A. L. Magnusson and C. E. McGee. Port Credit, Ontario: P. D. Meany, 1990: 177–203.

Bray, Alan. *Homosexuality in Renaissance England*. London: Gay Men's Press, 1982.

Brennan, Elizabeth M. "The Relationship between Brother and Sister in the Plays of John Webster." *MLR* 58 (1963): 488–94.

Brodsky, Vivien. "Widows in Late Elizabethan London: Remarriage, Economic

Opportunity and Family Orientations." In *The World We Have Gained: Histories of Population and Social Structure (Essays presented to Peter Laslett on his Seventieth Birthday)*. Eds. Lloyd Bonfield, Richard M. Smith, and Keith Wrightson. Oxford: Basil Blackwell, 1986: 122–54.

Brown, Paul. " 'This thing of darkness I acknowledge mine': *The Tempest* and the Discourse of Colonialism." *Political Shakespeare: New Essays in Cultural Materialism*. Ed. Jonathan Dollimore and Alan Sinfield. Ithaca: Cornell University Press, 1985: 48–71.

Burke, Kenneth. "Literature as Equipment for Living." *The Philosophy of Literary Form: Studies in Symbolic Action*. 3rd rev. edn. Berkeley: University of California Press, 1973: 293–304.

The Philosophy of Literary Form: Studies in Symbolic Action. 3rd ed. Berkeley: University of California Press, 1973.

A Grammar of Motives. 1945; rpt. Berkeley: University of California Press, 1969.

A Rhetoric of Motives. 1950; rpt. Berkeley: University of California Press, 1969.

Bushby, Frances. *Three Men of the Tudor Time*. London: Nutt, 1911.

Cain, William E. "Notes Toward a History of Anti-Criticism." *NLH* 20 (1988): 33–48.

Calderwood, James L. "*The Duchess of Malfi*: Styles of Ceremony." *EIC* 12 (1962): 133–47.

Chesnais, J. *Histoire Générale des Marionettes*. Paris, 1947.

Christian, Barbara. "The Race for Theory." *Feminist Studies* 14 (1988): 67–79.

Churchill, Caryl. *Vinegar Tom* (1978). In *Plays: One*. New York: Routledge, 1985.

Clark, A. M. *Thomas Heywood: Playwright and Miscellanist*. Oxford: Basil Blackwell, 1931.

Clark, Sandra. "*Hic Mulier, Haec Vir*, and the Controversy over Masculine Women." *SP* 82 (1985): 157–83.

Coursen, Herbert. "The Unity of *The Spanish Tragedy*." *SP* 65 (1968): 768–82.

Crawford, Patricia. "Attitudes to Menstruation in Seventeenth-Century England." *P&P* 91 (1981): 47–73.

Cressy, David. "Describing the Social Order in Elizabethan and Stuart England." *L&H* 3 (1976): 29–44.

"Kinship and Kin Interaction in Early Modern England." *P&P* 113 (1986): 38–69.

"Purification, Thanksgiving, and the Churching of Women in Post-Reformation England." *P&P* 141 (1993): 106–46.

Cust, Lionel. "Arden of Feversham [*sic*]." *Archaeologia Cantiana: Being Transactions of the Kent Archaeological Society* 34 (London, 1920).

Daniel, P. A. "Shakspeare's[?] 'Yorkshire Tragedy,' 1608." *The Athenaeum* 2710 (Oct. 4, 1879): 432.

Davis, Natalie Zemon. "Women on Top." *Society and Culture in Early Modern France*. Stanford University Press, 1975: 124–51.

Derrett, J. Duncan M. [sic] *Henry Swinburne (?1551–1624): Civil Lawyer of York*. Borthwick Papers 44. York, 1973.

Dolan, Frances E. "Gender, Moral Agency, and Dramatic Form in *A Warning for Fair Women*," *SEL* 29 (1989): 201–18.

"Home-Rebels and House-Traitors: Murderous Wives in Early Modern England." *Yale Journal of Law and the Humanities* 4 (1992): 1–31.

"The Subordinate('s) Plot: Petty Treason and the Forms of Domestic Rebellion." *SQ* 43 (1992): 317–40.

Dollimore, Jonathan. "Shakespeare, Cultural Materialism, Feminism and Marxist Humanism." *NLH* 21 (1990): 471–93.

"Subjectivity, Sexuality, and Transgression: The Jacobean Connection." *RenD* 27 (1986): 53–81.

Sexual Dissidence: Augustine to Wilde, Freud to Foucault. New York: Oxford University Press, 1991.

Douglas, Mary. "A Distinctive Anthropological Perspective." In *Constructive Drinking: Perspectives on Drink from Anthropology.* Ed. Mary Douglas. Cambridge University Press, 1987: 3–15.

"Standard Social Uses of Food: Introduction." In *Food in the Social Order: Studies of Food and Festivities in Three American Communities.* Ed. Mary Douglas. New York: Russell Sage Foundation, 1984: 1–39.

Edwards, Philip. "Shakespeare and Kyd." In *Shakespeare, Man of the Theater.* Ed. Kenneth Muir, Jay L. Halio, and D. J. Palmer. Newark: University of Delaware Press, 1983: 148–54.

Thomas Kyd and Early Elizabethan Tragedy, Writers and their Work No. 192. London: Longmans, 1966.

Ekeblad, Inga-Stina. "The 'Impure Art' of John Webster." *RES* 9 (1958): 253–67.

Elliott, G. R. "The Initial Contrast in *Lear*." *JEGP* 58 (1959): 251–63.

Empson, William. "Mine Eyes Dazzle." *EIC* 14 (1964): 80–86.

"The Spanish Tragedy." In *Elizabethan Drama: Modern Essays in Criticism.* Ed. R. J. Kaufmann. Oxford University Press, 1961: 60–80; rpt. from *Nimbus* 3 (1956): 16–29.

Erlanger, Rachel. *Lucrezia Borgia: A Biography.* New York: Hawthorn, 1978.

Firth, Raymond. *We the Tikopia: A Sociological Study of Kinship in Primitive Polynesia.* New York: American, 1936.

Fish, Stanley. *Surprised by Sin: The Reader in Paradise Lost.* Berkeley: University of California Press, 1967.

Fleay, F. G. *A Biographical Chronicle of the English Drama, 1559–1642.* 1891.

Forsyth, Robert S. "Notes on *The Spanish Tragedy*." *PQ* 5 (1926): 78–84.

Foucault, Michel. *The Archaeology of Knowledge.* Trans. A.M. Sheridan Smith. 1969; New York: Harper, 1972.

Fowler, Alastair. "Power to the Self." *TLS*, September 4, 1981: 1011–12.

Fraser, Antonia. *The Weaker Vessel.* New York: Knopf, 1984.

Freud, Sigmund. *Civilization and its Discontents.* Rpt. in *The Freud Reader.* Ed. Peter Gay. New York: Norton, 1989: 722–72.

Friedlander, Marc. "Some Problems of *A Yorkshire Tragedy*." *SP* 35 (1938): 238–53.

Friedman, A. B., and Richard H. Osberg. "Gawain's Girdle as Traditional Symbol." *Journal of American Folklore* 90 (1977): 301–15.

Furnivall, F. J., ed. *Child Marriages, Divorces, and Ratifications. Etc., in the Diocese of Chester, 1561–6*. EETS 108. London, 1897.

Fusero, Clemente. *The Borgias*. Trans. Peter Green. New York: Praeger, 1972.

Garber, Marjorie. *Vested Interests: Cross-Dressing and Cultural Anxiety*. New York: Routledge, 1991.

Gardiner, S. R. *What Gunpowder Plot Was*. 1897.

Geertz, Clifford. "Anti Anti-Relativism." *American Anthropologist* 86 (1984): 263–78.

Giddens, Anthony. *The Consequences of Modernity*. Stanford University Press, 1990.

Modernity and Self-Identity: Self and Society in the Late Modern Age. Stanford University Press, 1991.

The Constitution of Society: Outline of the Theory of Structuration. Berkeley: University of California Press, 1984.

Godelier, Maurice. "The Origins of Male Domination." *New Left Review* 27 (1981): 3–17.

Goffman, Erving. "Where the Action Is." *Interaction Ritual: Essays on Face-to-Face Behavior*. Garden City: Anchor, 1967: 149–270.

Relations in Public: Microstudies of the Public Order. New York: Harper, 1971.

Goody, Jack. "A Comparative Approach to Incest and Adultery." In *Marriage, Family, and Residence*. Ed. Paul Bohannon and John Middleton. Garden City: Natural History, 1968: 21–46.

The Development of the Family and Marriage in Europe. Cambridge University Press, 1983.

Gorrell, Robert M. "John Payne Collier and *The Murder of John Brewen*." *MLN* 57 (1942): 441–44.

Greenblatt, Stephen. *Renaissance Self-Fashioning from More to Shakespeare*. Chicago: University of Chicago Press, 1980.

Gusfield, Joseph. "Passage to Play: Rituals of Drinking Time in American Society." In *Constructive Drinking: Perspectives on Drink from Anthropology*. Ed. Mary Douglas. Cambridge University Press, 1987: 73–90.

Haller, William, and Malleville Haller. "The Puritan Art of Love." *HLQ* 5 (1942): 235–72.

Harding, Davis P. "Elizabethan Betrothals and *Measure for Measure*." *JEGP* 49 (1950): 139–58.

Harris, Barbara J. "Power, Profit, and Passion: Mary Tudor, Charles Brandon, and the Arranged Marriage in Early Tudor England." *Feminist Studies* 15 (1989): 59–88.

Harte, N. B. "State Control of Dress and Social Change in Pre-Industrial England." In *Trade, Government and Economy in Pre-Industrial England: Essays presented to F. J. Fisher*. Ed. D. C. Coleman and A. H. John. London: Weidenfeld, 1976: 132–65.

Heal, Felicity. *Hospitality in Early Modern England*. Oxford: Clarendon, 1990.

Hegel, G. F. W. *Phenomenology of Spirit*. Trans. A. V. Miller. Oxford: Clarendon, 1977.

Helgerson, Richard. *The Elizabethan Prodigals*. Berkeley: University of California Press, 1976.

Henderson, Katherine Usher and Barbara F. McManus. *Half Humankind:*

Contexts and Texts of the Controversy about Women in England, 1540–1640. Urbana: University of Illinois Press, 1985.

Hodge, Bob. "Mine Eyes Dazzle: False Consciousness in Webster's Plays." In David Aers, Bob Hodge, and Gunther Kress, *Literature, Language, and Society in England, 1580–1680.* Totowa: Barnes, 1981: 100–21.

Houlbrooke, Ralph A. *The English Family 1450–1700.* London: Longman, 1984.

Howard, G. E. *A History of Matrimonial Institutions.* Chicago: University of Chicago Press, 1904.

Howard, Jean E. "Crossdressing, The Theatre, and Gender Struggle in Early Modern England." *SQ* 39 (1988): 418–40.

Hunter, G. K. "English Folly and Italian Vice: The Moral Landscape of John Marston." In *Jacobean Theater.* Ed. John Russell Brown and Bernard Harris. New York: Capricorn, 1960: 85–111.

"Ironies of Justice in *The Spanish Tragedy*." *RenD* 8 (1965): 89–104.

Hurstfield, Joel. *The Queen's Wards: Wardship and Marriage under Elizabeth I.* Cambridge: Harvard University Press, 1958.

Ingram, Martin. "Ridings, Rough Music and the 'Reform of Popular Culture' in Early Modern England." *P&P* 105 (1984): 79–113.

Church Courts, Sex, and Marriage in England, 1570–1640. Cambridge University Press, 1987.

Jaffa, Harry V. "The Limits of Politics: King Lear, Act 1, Scene 1." In *Shakespeare's Politics.* Ed. Allan Bloom and Harry V. Jaffa. 1964; rpt. Chicago: University of Chicago Press, 1981: 113–45.

Jardine, Lisa. "*The Duchess of Malfi*: A Case Study in the Literary Representation of Women." In *Teaching the Text.* Ed. Susanne Kappeler and Norman Bryson. London: Routledge, 1983: 203–17.

Still Harping on Daughters: Women and Drama in the Age of Shakespeare. 1983; rpt. New York: Columbia University Press, 1989.

Jauss, Hans-Robert. "The Idealist Embarrassment: Observations on Marxist Aesthetics." *NLH* 7 (1975): 195–200.

Jensen, Ejner. "Kyd's *Spanish Tragedy*: The Play Explains Itself." *JEGP* 64 (1965): 7–16.

Jones, Ann Rosalind, and Peter Stallybrass. "The Politics of *Astrophil and Stella*." *SEL* 24 (1984): 53–68.

Jones, Ernest. *Hamlet and Oedipus.* 1949; rpt. Garden City: Anchor, 1954.

Kahn, Coppélia. "The Cuckoo's Note: Male Friendship and Cuckoldry in *The Merchant of Venice*." In *Shakespeare's Rough Magic: Renaissance Essays in Honor of C. L. Barber.* Ed. Peter Erickson and Coppélia Kahn. Newark NJ: University of Delaware Press, 1985: 104–12.

Kaufmann, R. J. "Ford's Tragic Perspective." *TSLL* 1 (1960): 522–37.

Kelly, Henry A. *The Matrimonial Trials of Henry VIII.* Stanford University Press, 1976.

Kristeva, Julia. *Powers of Horror: An Essay on Abjection.* Trans. Leon S. Roudiez. New York: Columbia University Press, 1982.

Kussmaul, Ann. *Servants in Husbandry in Early Modern England.* Cambridge University Press, 1981.

Laqueur, Thomas. *Making Sex: Body and Gender from the Greeks to Freud.* Cambridge: Harvard University Press, 1990.

Leech, Clifford. *John Webster: A Critical Study.* London: Hogarth, 1951.

Webster: *The Duchess of Malfi.* Studies in English Literature 8. London: Edward Arnold, 1963.

Leinwand, Theodore B. "Negotiation and New Historicism." *PMLA* 105 (1990): 477–90.

Lévi-Strauss, Claude. *The Elementary Structures of Kinship.* Boston: Beacon, 1969.

Levin, Michael. "'*Vindicta mihi!*': Meaning, Morality, and Motivation in *The Spanish Tragedy.*" *SEL* 4 (1964): 307–24.

Levin, Richard. "A Marston-Wilkins Borrowing." *N&Q* 217 (1972): 453.

Levine, Laura. *Men in Women's Clothing: Anti-theatricality and Effeminization 1579 to 1642.* Cambridge University Press, 1994.

Lewalski, Barbara K. "Biblical Allusion and Allegory in *The Merchant of Venice.*" In *Twentieth Century Interpretations of 'The Merchant of Venice'.* Ed. Sylvan Barnet. Englewood Cliffs, NJ: Prentice-Hall, 1970: 35–40.

Lewis, C. S. *The Allegory of Love.* Oxford University Press, 1936.

Lieblein, Leanore. "The Context of Murder in English Domestic Plays, 1590–1610." *SEL* 23 (1983): 181–96.

Luckyj, Christina. *A Winter's Snake: Dramatic Form in the Tragedies of John Webster.* Athens: University of Georgia Press, 1989.

Lukacs, George. "Reification and the Consciousness of the Proletariat." In *History and Class Consciousness.* Trans. Rodney Livingstone. Cambridge: MIT Press, 1971: 83–223.

McAlindon, Thomas. "The Ironic Vision: Diction and Theme in Marlowe's *Doctor Faustus.*" *RES* N.S. 32 (1981): 129–41.

McCabe, Richard A. *Incest, Drama, and Nature's Law 1550–1700.* Cambridge University Press, 1993.

MacCaffrey, Wallace T. "Place and Patronage in Elizabethan Politics." In *Elizabethan Government and Society.* Ed. S. T. Bindoff, Joel Hurstfield, and C. H. Williams. London: Athlone, 1961: 95–126.

Macfarlane, Alan. *The Family Life of Ralph Josselin.* Cambridge University Press, 1970.

Witchcraft in Tudor and Stuart England. New York: Harper, 1970.

Maclean, Ian. *The Renaissance Notion of Women: A Study in the Fortunes of Scholasticism and Medical Science in European Intellectual Life.* Cambridge University Press, 1980.

Magnin, Charles. *Histoire des Marionettes en Europe.* Paris, 1862.

Malcolmson, Cristina. "'What You Will': Social Mobility and Gender in *Twelfth Night.*" In *The Matter of Difference: Materialist Feminist Criticism of Shakespeare.* Ed. Valerie Wayne. Ithaca: Cornell University Press, 1991: 29–57.

Mallett, Michael. *The Borgias: The Rise and Fall of a Renaissance Dynasty.* London: Bodley Head, 1969.

Mallin, Eric S. "Emulous Factions and the Collapse of Chivalry: *Troilus and Cressida.*" *Representations* 29 (1990): 145–79.

Marcus, Leah. "Shakespeare's Comic Heroines, Elizabeth I, and the Political Uses of Androgyny." In *Women in the Middle Ages and the Renaissance: Literary and Historical Perspectives.* Ed. Mary Beth Rose. Syracuse: Syracuse University Press, 1986: 135–53.

Marotti, Arthur F. "Countertransference, the Communication Process, and the Dimensions of Psychoanalytic Criticism." *Critical Inquiry* 4 (1978): 471–89.

Marx, Karl *The German Ideology, Part One*. Ed. C. J. Arthur. New York: International, 1947.

The Communist Manifesto. In *Basic Writings on Politics and Philosophy*. Ed. Lewis S. Feuer. Garden City: Anchor, 1959: 1–41.

Economic and Philosophical Manuscripts of 1844. Ed. Dirk H. Struik. New York: International, 1964.

Maxwell, Baldwin. "*A Yorkshire Tragedy*." In *Studies in the Shakespeare Apocrypha*. New York: 1956: 138–96.

Meader, William G. *Courtship in Shakespeare*. New York: Columbia University Press, 1954.

Mehl, Dieter. *The Elizabethan Dumb Show: The History of a Dramatic Convention*. London: Methuen, 1965.

Middleton, Russell. "A Deviant Case: Brother–Sister and Father–Daughter Marriage in Ancient Egypt." *American Sociological Review* 27 (1962): 603–11.

Mikesell, Margaret. "Catholic and Protestant Widows in *The Duchess of Malfi*." *Renaissance and Reformation* 7 (1983): 265–79.

Montrose, Louis. " 'Shaping Fantasies': Figurations of Gender and Power in Elizabethan Culture." *Representations* 1 (1983): 61–94.

" 'Eliza, Queen of Shepheardes' and the Pastoral of Power." *ELR* 10 (1980): 153–82.

" 'The Place of a Brother' in *As You Like It*: Social Process and Comic Form." *SQ* 32 (1981): 28–54.

"Gifts and Reasons: The Contexts of Peele's *Araygnement of Paris*." *ELH* 47 (1980): 433–61.

"The Purposes of Playing: Reflections on a Shakespearean Anthropology." *Helios* N.S. 7 (1980): 51–74.

"The Work of Gender in the Discourse of Discovery." *Representations* 33 (1991): 1–41.

The Purpose of Playing: Shakespeare and the Cultural Politics of the Elizabethan Theater. In press, University of Chicago Press.

Mulryne, J. R. "*The White Devil* and *The Duchess of Malfi*." In *Jacobean Theater*. Ed. John Russell Brown and Bernard Harris. New York: Capricorn, 1960: 201–25.

Nohrnberg, James. *The Analogy of 'The Faerie Queene'*. Princeton University Press, 1976.

Orgel, Stephen. *Impersonations: The Performance of Gender in Renaissance England*. In press. Cambridge University Press.

Orlin, Lena Cowen. "Man's House as his Castle in *Arden of Faversham*." *Medieval and Renaissance Drama in England* 2 (1985): 57–89.

Ornstein, Robert. *The Moral Vision of Jacobean Tragedy*. Madison: University of Wisconsin Press, 1960.

Ortner, Sherry B. "Is Female to Male as Nature Is to Culture?" In *Woman, Culture, and Society*. Ed. Michelle Zimbalist Rosaldo and Louise Lamphere. Stanford University Press, 1974: 67–87.

Parker, Patricia. *Literary Fat Ladies: Rhetoric, Gender, Property*. London: Methuen, 1987.

Parsons, Talcott. "The Incest Taboo in Relation to Social Structure." *British Journal of Sociology* 5 (1954): 101–17; rpt. in *The Family: Its Structures and Functions*. Ed. Rose Laub Coser. New York: St. Martin's, 1974: 13–30.

Paster, Gail Kern. *The Body Embarrassed: Drama and the Disciplines of Shame in Early Modern England*. Ithaca: Cornell University Press, 1993.

Person, Ethel Spector. "Sexuality as the Mainstay of Identity: Psychoanalytic Perspectives." *Signs* 5 (1980): 605–30.

Peterson, Joyce E. *Curs'd Example: 'The Duchess of Malfi' and Commonweal Tragedy*. Columbia: University of Missouri Press, 1978.

Pitt-Rivers, Julian. "Honor and Social Status." In *Honour and Shame: The Values of Mediterranean Society*. Ed. J. G. Peristiany. Chicago: University of Chicago Press, 1966: 19–77.

Pollock, Frederick and F. W. Maitland. *The History of English Law*. Cambridge University Press, 1911.

Poster, Mark *Existential Marxism in Postwar France: from Sartre to Althusser*. Princeton University Press, 1975.

Price, Hereward T. "Like Himself." *RES* 16 (1940): 178–81.

Quaife, G. R. *Wanton Wenches and Wayward Wives: Peasants and Illicit Sex in Early Seventeenth Century England*. New Brunswick: Rutgers University Press, 1969.

Rackin, Phyllis. "Androgyny, Mimesis, and the Marriage of the Boy Heroine on the English Renaissance Stage." *PMLA* 102 (1987): 29–41.

Randall, Dale B. J. "The Rank and Earthy Background of Certain Physical Symbols in *The Duchess of Malfi*." *RenD* 18 (1987): 171–203.

Rebhorn, Wayne A. *Foxes and Lions: Machiavelli's Confidence Men*. Ithaca: Cornell University Press, 1988.

Ridley, Jasper. *Statesman and Saint: Cardinal Wolsey, Sir Thomas More, and the Politics of Henry VIII*. New York: Viking, 1982.

Rose, Mary Beth. *The Expense of Spirit: Love and Sexuality in Renaissance Drama*. Ithaca: Cornell University Press, 1988.

   "Where Are the Mothers in Shakespeare? Options for Gender Representation in the English Renaissance." *SQ* 42 (1991): 291–314.

Rubin, Gayle. "The Traffic in Women: Notes on the 'Political Economy' of Sex." In *Toward an Anthropology of Women*, Ed. Rayna R. Reiter. New York: Monthly Review Press, 1975: 157–210.

Sacks, Peter. "When Words Prevail Not: Grief, Revenge, and Language in Kyd and Shakespeare." *ELH* 49 (1982): 576–601.

Sartre, Jean-Paul. *Being and Nothingness: An Essay on Phenomenological On- tology*. Trans. Hazel E. Barnes. 1943; New York: Pocket, 1956.

Scarisbrick, J. J. *Henry VIII*. Berkeley: University of California Press, 1968.

Schaar, Claes. " 'They hang him in the arbor.' " *ES* 47 (1966): 27–28.

Schanzer, Ernst. "The Marriage-Contracts in *Measure for Measure*." *Shake- speare Survey* 13 (1960): 81–9.

Scott, Joan W. "Deconstructing Equality-Versus-Difference: or, The Uses of Poststructuralist Theory for Feminism." *Feminist Studies* 14 (1988): 33–50.

Sedgwick, Eve Kosovsky. *Between Men: English Literature and Male Homosocial Desire*. New York: Columbia University Press, 1985.

Epistemology of the Closet. Berkeley: University of California Press, 1990.

Selzer, John L. "Merit and Degree in Webster's *The Duchess of Malfi*." *ELR* 11 (1981): 70–80.

Shapiro. James. "'Tragedies Naturally Performed': Kyd's Representation of Violence." In *Staging the Renaissance: Reinterpretations of Elizabethan and Jacobean Drama*. Ed. David Scott Kastan and Peter Stallybrass. New York: Routledge, 1991: 99–113.

Sklar, Elizabeth S. "Bassanio's Golden Fleece." *TSLL* 18 (1976): 500–07.

Slater, Miriam. *Family Life in the Seventeenth Century: The Verneys of Claydon House*. London: Routledge, 1984.

Slater, Philip. "Social Limitations on Libidinal Withdrawal." In *The Family: Its Structures and Functions*. Ed. Rose Laub Coser. New York: St. Martin's, 1974: 111–33.

Smith, Alan Gordon. *The Babington Plot*. London: Macmillan, 1936.

Smith, Bruce R. *Homosexual Desire in Shakespeare's England: A Cultural Poetics*. Chicago: University of Chicago Press, 1991.

Smith, James L. "'They hang him in the arbor': A Defence of the Accepted Text." *ES* 47 (1966): 372–73.

Somerville, J. P. *Politics and Ideology in England, 1603–1640*. London: Longman, 1986.

Sorel, Georges. *Reflections on Violence*. Trans. T. E. Hulme. London: Allen, 1916.

Spargo, J. W. *Juridical Folklore in England, Illustrated by the Cucking-Stool*. Durham NC: Duke University Press, 1944.

Spierenberg, Pieter. *The Spectacle of Suffering: Executions and the Evolution of Repression: from a Preindustrial Metropolis to the European Experience*. Cambridge University Press, 1984.

Spriet, Pierre. "Antisocial Behavior and the Code of Love in Kyd's *Spanish Tragedy*." *Cahiers Elisabéthains* 17 (1980): 1–9.

Stallybrass, Peter. "Patriarchal Territories: The Body Enclosed." In *Rewriting the Renaissance: The Discourses of Sexual Difference in Early Modern Europe*. Ed. Margaret W. Ferguson, Maureen Quilligan, and Nancy J. Vickers. Chicago: University of Chicago Press, 1986: 123–42.

Steen, Sara Jayne. "The Crime of Marriage: Arbella Stuart and *The Duchess of Malfi*." *Sixteenth-Century Journal* 22 (1991): 61–76.

Stone, Lawrence. "Social Mobility in England, 1500–1700." *P&P* 33 (1966): 17–55.

The Crisis of the Aristocracy, 1558–1641. Oxford: Clarendon, 1965.

The Family, Sex and Marriage in England 1500–1800. London: Weidenfeld, 1977.

Strier, Richard. "Faithful Servants: Shakespeare's Praise of Disobedience." In *The Historical Renaissance: New Essays on Tudor and Stuart Literature and Culture*. Ed. Heather Dubrow and Richard Strier. Chicago: University of Chicago Press, 1988: 104–33.

"Sanctifying the Aristocracy: 'Devout Humanism' in François de Sales, John Donne, and George Herbert." *Journal of Religion* 69 (1989): 36–59.

Resistant Structures: Particularity, Radicalism, and Renaissance Texts. Berkeley: University of California Press, 1995.

Sullivan, Garrett A. Jr., "'Arden lay murdered in that plot of ground': Surveying, Land, and *Arden of Faversham.*" *ELH* 61 (1994): 231–52.

Sykes, H. Dugdale. *Sidelights on Shakespeare.* Stratford-upon-Avon: Shakespeare Head Press, 1919.

Tenenti, Alberto. *Piracy and the Decline of Venice, 1580–1615.* Trans. Janet and Brian Pullam. 1961; Berkeley: University of California Press, 1967.

Therbörn, Göran. *The Ideology of Power and the Power of Ideology.* London: Verso, 1980.

Thirsk, Joan. "Younger Sons in the Seventeenth Century." *History* (London) 54 (1969): 358–77.

Thomas, Keith. "The Place of Laughter in Tudor and Stuart England." *TLS*, 21 January 1977: 77.

Tilley, Morris P. *A Dictionary of the Proverbs in England in the Sixteenth and Seventeenth Centuries.* Ann Arbor: University of Michigan Press, 1950.

Todd, Barbara J. "The Remarrying Widow: A Stereotype Reconsidered." In *Women in English Society 1500–1800.* Ed. Mary Prior. London: Methuen, 1985: 54–92.

Traub, Valerie. *Desire and Anxiety: Circulations of Sexuality in Shakespearean Drama.* London: Routledge, 1992.

Underdown, David. "The Taming of the Scold: The Enforcement of Patriarchal Authority in Early Modern England." In *Order and Disorder in Early Modern England.* Ed. Anthony Fletcher and John Stevenson. Cambridge University Press, 1985: 116–36.

Unterman, Alan. *Dictionary of Jewish Lore and Legend.* London: Thames, 1991.

Valverde, Mariana. "Beyond Gender Dangers and Private Pleasures: Theory and Ethics in the Sex Debates." *Feminist Studies* 15 (1989): 237–54.

Wadlington, Warwick. *Reading Faulknerian Tragedy.* Ithaca: Cornell University Press, 1987.

Wadsworth, Frank W. "'Rough Music' in *The Duchess of Malfi*: Webster's Dance of Madmen and the Charivari Tradition." In *Rite, Drama, Festival, Spectacle: Rehearsals toward a Theory of Cultural Performance.* Ed. John J. MacAloon. Philadelphia: ISHI, 1984: 58–75.

Wagner, A. R. *English Genealogy.* 2nd edn. Oxford: Clarendon, 1972.

Walter, John, and Keith Wrightson. "Dearth and the Social Order in Early Modern England." *P&P* 71 (1976): 22–42.

Warnicke, Retha M. *The Rise and Fall of Anne Boleyn: Family Politics at the Court of Henry VIII.* Cambridge University Press, 1989.

Warren, Michael. "*The Duchess of Malfi* on the Stage." In *John Webster.* Ed. Brian Morris. Mermaid Critical Commentaries. Proceedings of the York Symposium, 1969. London: Benn, 1970: 47–68.

Wayne, Valerie. "Refashioning the Shrew." *ShakS* 17 (1984): 159–87.

Wentersdorf, Karl B. "The Marriage Contracts in 'Measure for Measure.'" *ShS* 32 (1979): 129–44.

Whigham, Frank. "Ideology and Class Conduct in *The Merchant of Venice.*" *RenD* N.S. 10 (1979): 93–115.

"Elizabethan Aristocratic Insignia." *TSLL* 27 (1985): 325–53.

Ambition and Privilege: The Social Tropes of Elizabethan Courtesy Theory. Berkeley: University of California Press, 1984.

"Sexual and Social Mobility in *The Duchess of Malfi.*" *PMLA* 100 (1985): 167–86.

Wiggins, Martin. *Journeymen In Murder: The Assassin in English Renaissance Drama.* Oxford: Clarendon, 1992.

Willbern, David. "Shakespeare's Nothing." In *Representing Shakespeare: New Psychoanalytic Essays.* Ed. Murray Schwartz and Coppelia Kahn. Baltimore: Johns Hopkins University Press, 1980: 244–63.

"Thomas Kyd's *The Spanish Tragedy*: Inverted Vengeance." *American Imago* 28 (1971): 247–67.

Williams, Raymond. *Marxism and Literature.* Oxford University Press, 1977.

Williamson, Marilyn. "The Ring Episode in *The Merchant of Venice.*" *SAQ* 71 (1972): 587–94.

The Patriarchy of Shakespeare's Comedies. Detroit: Wayne State University Press, 1986.

Wojciehowski, Dolora. "For the Love of the Father: Repetition and Ambivalence in *King Lear* Criticism." *MOSAIC* 25 (1992): 15–31.

Wolfram, Sybil. *In-Laws and Outlaws: Kinship and Marriage in England.* New York: St. Martin's, 1987.

Woodbridge, Linda. *Women and the English Renaissance: Literature and the Nature of Womankind, 1540–1620.* Urbana: University of Illinois Press, 1986.

Wrightson, Keith. "The Social Order of Early Modern England: Three Approaches." In *The World We Have Gained: Histories of Population and Social Structure (Essays presented to Peter Laslett on his Seventieth Birthday).* Ed. Lloyd Bonfield, Richard M. Smith, and Keith Wrightson. Oxford: Basil Blackwell, 1986: 177–202.

English Society 1580–1680. New Brunswick NJ: Rutgers University Press, 1982.

"Yorick" (pseudonym of P. C. Ferrigni). *La Storia dei Burattini.* 1884.

Index

Aberle, David F. 271n1
Abrams, M. H. 231n55
Adelman, Janet 228n25, 262n26
Admonition to the Parliament, An 251n45
Aggeler, Geoffrey 244n110
Allen, D. C. 240n71
Allison, Alexander W. 275n35
Althusser, Louis 263n36
Amussen, Susan 229n33
Anchor Bible, The 274n28
Arden of Faversham 8, 9, 10, 30, 63–120,
    125, 146, 165, 215, 225, 233n13,
    262n25, 264n39, 269n81, 271n98
Ardener, Shirley 233n20
Ascham, Roger 124
Attwell, David 248n31
Auden, W. H. 5–6, 50, 58, 155, 236n41,
    274n22

Babington, Anthony 252n49
Bacon, Francis 5
Baker, Susan C. 275n34
Bale, John, *The Pageant of the Popes*
    273n18
Barber, C. L. 228n13, 248n29
Barish, Jonas 231n4, 235n33, 239n68,
    244n107
Beaumont, Francis, and John Fletcher 194
Bellamy, John 238n55
Belsey, Catherine 78–79, 244n109, 248n30,
    254n57
Berger, Harry Jr. 227n10
Berggren, Paula S. 276n45
Berry, Ralph 277n54
Best, Michael R. 277n54, 277n67
Blayney, Glenn H. 229n36, 263n35, 264n44,
    264n46, 264n50, 266n62, 270n90
Boas, Frederick S. 258n84
Bodin, Jean 17
Boehrer, Bruce 229n31
Boklund, Gunnar 275n37
Boleyn, Anne 12, 82

Boose, Lynda E. 236n44, 238n53, 265n54,
    268n79
Borgia, Lucrezia 273n18
Bourdieu, Pierre 2, 11, 16, 17, 18, 27, 77,
    269n86, 269n88, 272n6
Bowers, Fredson 231n2, 243n101
Bradbrook, Muriel 191, 277n67
Braden, Gordon 242n98, 250n39
Bradley, A. C. 167
Braunmuller, A. R. 229n38
Bray, Alan 264n50
Brennan, Elizabeth M. 274n26
Brodsky, Vivien 202, 247n21
Brooke, C. F. Tucker 186
Brown, Paul 98
Bull Durham 238n53
Burke, Kenneth 3, 5, 15, 36, 49, 188, 189,
    191–92, 204, 224, 228n16, 230n46,
    235n30
Bushby, Frances 246n11

Cain, William E. 227n4
Calderwood, James L. 272n12, 275n37
Calverley, Walter 121, 122, 127, 178, 180–
    87, 225
Calvin, John 17
Cambyses 57
Camden, William 274n23
Cardano, Girolamo 241n83
Carton, Evan 20
Cary, Elizabeth 260n5, 276n45
Cary, Henry (first Viscount Falkland) 123,
    124
Cary, Lucius (second Viscount Falkland)
    123, 124
Castiglione, Baldassare 214, 277n66
Cavendish, Margaret (Duchess of
    Newcastle) 163, 210–11
Cawley, A. C. 186, 270n91, 270n92
Cecil, Sir Robert 31, 270n91
Cecil, William (Lord Burghley) 31, 144,
    247n21

Chapman, George, *The Widow's Tears* 203
charivari 199
Chaucer, Geoffrey 236n42, 237n48, 264n47
Chesnais, J. 241n83
Christian, Barbara 227n4
Churchill, Caryl 15, 16
Clark, A. M. 270n90
Clark, Sandra 228n26
Cobham, Anne, Lady 270n91
Cope, Jackson I. 241n83
Coursen, Herbert 238n55
Crawford, Patricia 274n28
Cressy, David 11, 193, 197–98, 252n47
Cunningham, Karen 250n40, 252n49
Cust, Lionel 246n10, 246n12, 253n56

Daborne, Robert 243n101
Daniel, P. A. 263n35
Davis, Natalie Zemon 228n24, 275n29
Dekker, Thomas
    The Honest Whore, Part One 276n49
    Satiromastix 231n1
Dekker, Thomas, John Ford, and William
    Rowley, *The Witch of Edmonton* 30,
    145, 225, 266n64
Derrett, J. Duncan M. [*sic*] 249n34
Dolan, Frances E. 98, 233n13, 233n14,
    245n2, 245n4, 249n36, 249n37, 255n68,
    255n69
Dollimore, Jonathan 228n25, 229n26
Donne, John 258n82, 259n88
Douglas, Mary 133
Drayton, Michael 252n49

E., T., *The Lawes Resolution of Womens
    Rights* 202
Edwards, Philip 22, 61, 231n1, 237n49,
    240n72
Ekeblad, Inga-Stina 274n29
Elizabeth I 11, 20, 125, 212, 215, 229n27
Elliott, G. R. 232n8
elopement 263n37
Elyot, Thomas 17
Empson, William 237n50, 238n55, 273n18,
    275n37
enforced marriage 71–74, 85, 110, 117–18,
    121–26
Erasmus, Desiderius 244n105
Erlanger, Rachel 273n18

Filmer, Robert 253n55
First Part of Hieronymo, The 38, 39,
    236n47, 247n23
Firth, Raymond 189–90, 196–97
Fish, Stanley 240n75
Fleay, F. G. 270n90

Fleming, Abraham 124
Fletcher, John 103–04, 236n39, 247n24
Florio, John 188
Ford, John 193, 233n12, 234n26
Forsyth, Robert S. 235n35
Foucault, Michel 230n45, 230n50
Fowler, Alastair 236n40, 276n46
Fraser, Antonia 236n44
Freud, Sigmund 5, 20, 228n13
Friedlander, Marc 270n90
Friedman, A. B. 237n53
Fuller, Thomas 12
Furnivall, F. J. 130
Fusero, Clemente 273n18

Gaines, Barry 186, 270n91, 270n92
Gammer Gurton's Needle 256n72
Garber, Marjorie 228n26
Gardiner, S. R. 253n49
Geertz, Clifford 227n4
Geneva Bible, The 255n71
Gerard, Balthazar 247n24
Giddens, Anthony 2–4, 17, 18, 263n36,
    267n72
Godelier, Maurice 15
Goffman, Erving 242n91, 270n96
Goody, Jack 189, 229n32, 229n33, 229n34,
    229n35, 252n48, 265n56, 271n2, 271n4
Gorrell, Robert M. 258n84
Greenblatt, Stephen 236n40, 276n46
Gusfield, Joseph 133–34

Hall, Joseph 35
Haller, William, and Malleville Haller
    249n33
hangman, the 103, 256n75
Harding, Davis P. 249n34, 260n14
Harris, Barbara J. 27–28, 30, 234n25,
    245n8
Harte, N. B. 228n23
Haughton, William, *Englishmen for my
    Money* 276n49
Heal, Felicity 254n64
Hegel, G. W. F. 8, 195
Helgerson, Richard 261n17
Henderson, Katherine Usher 228n24
Henry IV (of France) 273n20
Henry VIII 12–13, 41, 43, 63, 66–67, 82,
    211
Herbert, George 242n94, 259n89
Heywood, Thomas 193
    The English Traveller 276n49
    If You Know Not Me, You Know Nobody
    274n21
Highley, Christopher 240n80
Holinshed, Raphael 67–71, 83, 84, 86, 117

Homer *The Odyssey* 136
Houlbrooke, Ralph 124, 157, 233n17
Howard, Catherine 12, 25–26
Howard, G. E. 260n14
Howard, Jean E. 228n26
Howard, Thomas 25
Hunter, G. K. 61, 274n22, 277n63
Hurstfield, Joel 125, 229n36, 235n29, 264n45

incest 189–95
Ingram, Martin 193, 199, 203, 229n33, 249n34, 252n48, 275n29

Jaffa, Harry 232n8
James I 11, 215, 273n17
Jardine, Lisa 15, 228n23, 228n25, 228n26, 276n44, 276n52
Jauss, Hans-Robert 277n63
Jenkins, Harold 247n22
Jensen, Ejner 38
Jones, Ann Rosalind 235n34
Jones, Ernest 272n10
Jonson, Ben 193, 231n1
    Sejanus 217
Josselin, Ralph 124

Kahn, Coppélia 251n44
Kaufmann, R. J. 227n1
Kelly, Henry A. 229n31
Kojeve, Alexandre 228n18
Kristeva, Julia 228n20
Kussmaul, Ann 88, 252n54
Kyd, Thomas 8–10, 14, 15, 22–62, 64, 65, 74, 84, 85, 89, 92, 96, 100, 102, 108, 109, 117, 120, 188, 190, 202, 204, 205, 211, 214, 222, 247n23, 248n26, 254n61, 258n84, 273n14

Laqueur, Thomas 228n25
Leech, Clifford 190–91, 272n12, 275n37, 276n51
Leicester, Earl of (Robert Dudley) 243n101
Leinwand, Theodore 15
Lévi-Strauss, Claude 28, 137
Levin, Michael 242n94
Levin, Richard 269n84
Levine, Laura 228n26
Lewalski, Barbara K. 254n57
Lewis, C. S. 235n36
Lieblein, Leanore 245n9
Locrine 258n83
London Prodigal, The 270n95
Lucas, Sir John 163
Lucas, F. L. 190
Luckyj, Christina 276n47

Lukacs, George 218, 219–20, 277n63
Lyly, John 218–19

MacCaffrey, Wallace 212
Macfarlane, Alan 124, 245n4, 247n21, 249n38
Machiavelli, Niccolo 277n62
Maclean, Hugh 228n24
Magnin, Charles 241n83
Maitland, F. W. 267n65
Malcolmson, Cristina 229n44, 272n12
Mallett, Michael 273n18
Mallin, Eric S. 239n66, 240n76, 265n53
Maltese Falcon, The 263n34
Marcus, Leah 229n27
Marlowe, Christopher 115, 201, 237n49
    Doctor Faustus 5, 10, 32, 83, 88, 111, 149, 248n29, 265n51
    The Jew of Malta 220, 254n65
    The Massacre at Paris 249n32
    Tamburlaine 32, 45, 55, 60, 92, 99, 201, 204
Marotti, Arthur F. 271n3
Marston, John 193
    The Dutch Courtesan 261n19, 276n50
    The Fawn 262n28, 269n82, 269n84
    The Malcontent 189, 241n85, 277n63
Marx, Karl 13, 19, 216
Mary I (of England) 12, 274n21
Massinger, Philip 193
    A New Way to Pay Old Debts 129, 130, 260n12, 261n16
    The Unnatural Combat 276n50
Maxwell, Baldwin 186–87, 260n2, 270n90, 271n100, 271n101
McAlindon, Thomas 250n40
McCabe, Richard A. 272n12, 273n14
Meader, William G. 276n49
Mehl, Dieter 239n67, 244n103
Middleton, Russell 272n6
Middleton, Thomas 148, 193
    The Family of Love 276n49
    Michaelmas Term 268n75
    The Phoenix 267n70
    The Revenger's Tragedy 188
    A Trick to Catch the Old One 169, 261n19, 265n55
    Women Beware Women 28, 207
Middleton, Thomas, and Thomas Dekker, *The Roaring Girl* 265n58
Middleton, Thomas, and William Rowley, *The Changeling* 5, 8, 31, 129, 204–05, 220, 227n12, 238n53, 254n65, 264n41
Mikesell, Margaret 275n40
Montrose, Louis Adrian 229n27, 252n51, 257n78, 268n77

More, Thomas 38, 67
Mulryne, J. R. 39, 43, 190–91, 196, 235n28
Murder of John Brewen, The 258n84

Narcissus 200
Nashe, Thomas 81
Nohrnberg, James 196, 275n32
North, Christian 68
North, Edward (first Lord North) 67
North, Mary 68
North, Roger (second Lord North) 68
North, Thomas 68

oaths 81–82, 92–95, 98–99, 100–07
orality 102, 104, 105–06, 120, 132–77,
    250n43, 255n67
Orgel, Stephen 228n26, 264n50
Orlin, Lena Cowen 246n9, 246n17, 246n18,
    247n19
Ornstein, Robert 277n59
Ortner, Sherry B. 262n24
Osberg, Richard H. 238n53
Ovid 124, 209, 273n18

Parker, Matthew 12
Parker, Patricia 233n19, 236n44
Parsons, Talcott 189–90, 272n4
Paster, Gail Kern 255n71, 256n72, 259n87,
    268n75, 269n80
Pausanias 200
per verba de praesenti, spousals 126, 129,
    141, 206–08, 249n34
Person, Ethel Spector 229n26
Peterson, Joyce E. 272n12, 275n37
Petrarca, Francesco 235n34
Philip II (of Spain) 12
pissing against the wall 255n71
Pitt-Rivers, Julian 1, 192, 203–04, 275n29
Poincaré, Henri 17
Pollock, Frederick 267n65
Poster, Mark 228n18
Price, Hereward T. 258n81, 273n18
prostitution 69, 165–66, 170
puppets 241n83
Puttenham, George 201, 215, 275n36

Quaife, G. R. 268n76

Rackin, Phyllis 228n26
Randail, Dale B. J. 275n31
Rebhorn, Wayne 231n6, 277n62
Rich, Sir Richard 67
Ridley, Jasper 237n52
Riggs, David 231n6
rings 84–87, 251n44, 251n45
Rogers, Thomas 243n101

Rose, Mary Beth 211, 260n3, 272n12,
    276n48, 278n67
Rowse, John 271n98
Rubin, Gayle 28, 30, 130
Rumrich, John 237n48, 239n63

Sacks, Peter 238n58
Sartre, Jean-Paul 7, 138, 151, 182, 200–01
Scarisbrick, J. J. 239n64
Schaar, Claes 240n78
Schanzer, Ernst 249n34
Scot, Reginald 124
Scott, Joan W. 227n4
Sedgwick, Eve Kosovsky 41–42, 130, 152,
    229n26, 233n18
Selzer, John L. 273n18, 277n67
Shakespeare, William 210, 231n56, 270n90
    All's Well that Ends Well 129
    Antony and Cleopatra 202
    As You Like It 148, 166, 257n78, 262n25,
        265n58, 269n81
    The Comedy of Errors 240n77, 254n65
    Coriolanus 259n88
    Cymbeline 262n25, 267n68
    Hamlet 7–9, 24, 31, 39, 49, 59, 60, 61, 99,
        134, 137, 188, 198, 222, 231n5, 247n21,
        250n40, 252n46, 262n25, 263n30,
        274n26
    Henry IV, Part One 4, 35, 97, 100, 108,
        109, 114, 120, 135, 139, 261n23,
        262n24, 263n30, 268n75
    Henry IV, Part Two 149, 151, 153, 165,
        264n48, 268n76, 276n51
    Henry V 15, 96, 101, 107, 216, 241n82,
        256n73, 258n81, 259n88
    Julius Caesar 254n65
    King Lear 5, 7–8, 9, 20, 25, 31, 52, 60, 70,
        88, 137, 152, 158, 177, 188, 205, 207,
        216–17, 221, 222, 223, 247n21, 263n31,
        268n74, 276n51
    Macbeth 56, 83, 108, 149, 201, 204,
        242n95, 242n96, 256n71, 266n51,
        272n99
    Measure for Measure 103, 129, 256n75,
        266n65
    The Merchant of Venice 14, 34, 91, 115,
        141, 151, 204, 205, 253n57, 254n62,
        265n58, 269n83
    The Merry Wives of Windsor 262n28
    A Midsummer Night's Dream 248n29
    Much Ado about Nothing 201, 236n37
    Othello 4, 8, 9, 14, 31, 49, 54, 116, 131,
        169, 184, 187, 198, 204, 205, 219,
        242n93
    Richard II 44, 147, 252n49
    Richard III 7

Romeo and Juliet 205
Sonnets 182
The Taming of the Shrew 207, 269n83
The Tempest 98
Timon of Athens 266n63
Troilus and Cressida 134, 155, 263n30
Twelfth Night 70, 71, 213
Shapiro, James 232n8, 243n102
Sidney, Philip 235n34
Sir Gawain and the Green Knight 237n53
Sir Giles Goosecap 276n49
Sklar, Elizabeth S. 254n60
Slater, Miriam 27, 28–29, 72, 136, 202–03,
    234n24, 245n4, 247n20, 265n55,
    275n39
Slater, Philip 193–94, 274n27
Smith, Alan Gordon 252n49
Smith, Bruce R. 264n50
Smith, James L. 240n78
Somerset, Duke of (Edward Seymour) 65–
    66
Somerville, J. P. 265n59
Sorel, Georges 218
"Spanish Tragedy, The" (ballad) 234n27
Spargo, J. W. 275n30
Spenser, Edmund 34, 48, 136, 170, 236n28,
    241n86, 276n50
Spierenberg, Pieter 103, 256n75, 256n77
Spriet, Pierre 235n32
Sprigge, William 253n56
Stallybrass, Peter 137, 235n34, 268n80
Statutes of the Realm 25–26, 232n11,
    233n13, 248n27, 249n36, 257n79
Steen, Sara Jayne 275n37
Stephens, Dorothy 267n71, 269n87,
    276n50, 277n62
Stettin, Duke of 199
Stone, Lawrence 6, 31, 45, 190, 215,
    234n22, 239n60, 242n90, 244n4, 245n7,
    246n15, 246n16, 260n6, 263n33
Stow, John 67–71
Strier, Richard 227n2, 229n38, 232n8,
    235n34, 242n89, 242n94, 247n19,
    249n36, 251n45, 252n53, 254n61,
    257n80
Strype, John 12
Stuart, Arbella 275n37
Stubbes, Philip 252n51
Sullivan, Garrett A. Jr. 246n17
Sunset Boulevard 274n24
Swinburne, Henry 249n34
Sykes, H. Dugdale 270n90

Taylor, Gary 256n73
Taylor, John (the "Water Poet") 242n92,
    271n98

Tenenti, Alberto 277n55
Therbörn, Göran 4, 28, 154, 263n36
Thirsk, Joan 253n56, 267n73
Thomas, Keith 275n29
Thompson, E. P. 245n4
Tilley, Morris P. 32, 216, 236n40, 254n62
Todd, Barbara J. 202–03, 276n43
Tourneur, Cyril, *The Atheist's Tragedy* 193,
    273n14, 276n49, 276n50
Traub, Valerie 228n25, 264n50
treason, high 25–26
treason, petty 26, 81–82, 88–89, 118, 125,
    233n13
True Tragedy of Richard III, The 254n66
Tudor, Mary (sister to Henry VIII) 30, 40–
    41, 239n62, 241n88
Two Most Unnatural and Bloodie Murthers
    121, 129, 144, 179, 180–88, 264n44,
    270n93

Underdown, David 236n44
Unterman, Alan 239n63

Valverde, Mariana 228n25
Verney, Elizabeth 72
Verney, Ralph 72, 136

Wadlington, Warwick 230n49
Wadsworth, Frank W. 274n29
Wagner, A. R. 11–12
Wallenda, Karl 182
Walter, John 255n67
wardship 13, 125, 142–47
Warnicke, Retha 229n31, 245n8, 249n38,
    257n79
Warning for Fair Women, A 233n14,
    247n25, 264n51
Warren, Michael 220
Watson, Thomas 32–36, 47, 226
Wayne, Valerie 236n44
Webster, John
    The White Devil 7, 14, 75, 183, 205, 207,
    211, 218, 252n49, 277n63
    The Duchess of Malfi 7, 8, 9–10, 30,
    31, 41, 42, 46, 70, 71, 81, 83, 85,
    100, 129, 155, 188–224, 225, 232n7,
    243n100
Wentersdorf, Karl B. 249n34
Whigham, Frank 3, 228n23, 229n44,
    238n53, 242n90, 246n16, 248n27,
    252n52, 254n60, 277n64, 277n65
White, Martin 69, 83, 117, 258n85
Whytford, Richard 130
Whythorne, Thomas 204
Wiggins, Martin 240n73, 243n101, 244n1,
    254n63, 254n65, 255n66, 274n20

Wilkins, George, *The Miseries of Enforced Marriage* 9–10, 13, 30, 121–79, 226, 255n71
Willbern, David 241n87, 244n104, 251n44
Williams, Raymond 2
Williamson, Marilyn 251n44
Wine, M. L. 67, 69, 71, 73, 120, 246n19, 250n43, 254n59, 254n66, 258n83, 259n91
Wojciehowski, Dolora 269n89
Wolfram, Sybil 239n64, 251n46, 254n58, 266n65

Woodbridge, Linda 228n24
Wrightson, Keith 10, 17–18, 123, 190, 215, 230n53, 255n67, 260n4
Wyatt, Thomas 274n21, 276n46

Yarrington, Robert, *Two Lamentable Tragedies* 242n91, 250n41, 254n65, 271n99
"Yorick" (P. C. Ferrigni) 241n83
Yorkshire Tragedy, A 9–10, 30, 31–32, 121, 127, 144, 147, 149, 179, 180–87

Cambridge Studies in Renaissance Literature and Culture

1. *Drama and the market in the age of Shakespeare*
   DOUGLAS BRUSTER, University of Chicago

2. *The Renaissance dialogue: literary dialogue in its social and political contexts, Castiglione to Galileo*
   VIRGINIA COX, University College London

3. *Spenser's secret career*
   RICHARD RAMBUSS, Tulane University

4. *Shakespeare and the geography of difference*
   JOHN GILLIES, La Trobe University

5. *Men in women's clothing: anti-theatricality and effeminization, 1579–1642*
   LAURA LEVINE, Wellesley College

6. *The reformation of the subject: Spenser, Milton, and the English Protestant epic*
   LINDA GREGERSON, University of Michigan

7. *Voyages in print: English travel to America, 1576–1624*
   MARY C. FULLER, Massachusetts Institute of Technology

8. *Subject and object in Renaissance culture*
   edited by MARGRETA DE GRAZIA, MAUREEN QUILLIGAN, PETER STALLYBRASS, University of Pennsylvania

9. *Shakespeare and the theatre of wonder*
   T. G. BISHOP, Case Western Reserve University

10. *Anxious masculinity in early modern England*
    MARK BREITENBERG

11. *Seizures of the will in early modern English drama*
    FRANK WHIGHAM, University of Texas at Austin